SOMALIA

MINERAL, MINING SECTOR
INVESTMENT AND BUSINESS GUIDE
VOLUME 1
STRATEGIC INFORMATION AND REGULATIONS

International Business Publications, USA
Washington DC, USA - Somalia

SOMALIA
MINERAL, MINING SECTOR INVESTMENT AND BUSINESS GUIDE
VOLUME 1 STRATEGIC INFORMATION AND REGULATIONS

UPDATED ANNUALLY

We express our sincere appreciation to all government agencies and international organizations which provided information and other materials for this guide

Cover Design: International Business Publications, USA

International Business Publications, USA. *has used its best efforts in collecting, analyzing and preparing data, information and materials for this unique guide. Due to the dynamic nature and fast development of the economy and business environment, we cannot warrant that all information herein is complete and accurate. IBP does not assume and hereby disclaim any liability to any person for any loss or damage caused by possible errors or omissions in the guide.*
This guide is for noncommercial use only. Use this guide for any other purpose, included but not limited to reproducing and storing in a retrieval system by any means, electronic, photocopying or using the addresses or other information contained in this guide for any commercial purposes requires a special written permission from the publisher.

2012 Updated Reprint International Business Publications, USA
ISBN 1-4330-4534-6

For customer service and information, please contact:

in the USA: **International Business Publications, USA**
                  P.O.Box 15343, Washington, DC 20003
                  Phone: (202) 546-2103, Fax: (202) 546-3275.
                  E-mail: rusric@erols.com

Printed in the USA

SOMALIA

MINERAL, MINING SECTOR INVESTMENT AND BUSINESS GUIDE

VOLUME 1
STRATEGIC INFORMATION AND REGULATIONS

TABLE OF CONTENTS

**For additional analytical, business and investment opportunities information,
please contact Global Investment & Business Center, USA
at (202) 546-2103. Fax: (202) 546-3275. E-mail: rusric@erols.com**

**For additional analytical, business and investment opportunities information,
please contact Global Investment & Business Center, USA
at (202) 546-2103. Fax: (202) 546-3275. E-mail: rusric@erols.com**

**For additional analytical, business and investment opportunities information,
please contact Global Investment & Business Center, USA
at (202) 546-2103. Fax: (202) 546-3275. E-mail: rusric@erols.com**

For additional analytical, business and investment opportunities information,
please contact Global Investment & Business Center, USA
at (202) 546-2103. Fax: (202) 546-3275. E-mail: rusric@erols.com

For additional analytical, business and investment opportunities information,
please contact Global Investment & Business Center, USA
at (202) 546-2103. Fax: (202) 546-3275. E-mail: rusric@erols.com

**For additional analytical, business and investment opportunities information,
please contact Global Investment & Business Center, USA
at (202) 546-2103. Fax: (202) 546-3275. E-mail: rusric@erols.com**

STRATEGIC AND DEVELOPMENT PROFILES

STRATEGIC PROFILE

Capital (and largest city)	Mogadishu 2°02′N 45°21′E2.033°N 45.35°E
Official language(s)	Somali, Arabic
Ethnic groups	Somalis (85%), Benadiris, Bantus and other non-Somalis (15%)
Demonym	Somali; Somalian
Government	Coalition government
- President	Sharif Sheikh Ahmed
- Prime Minister	Abdiweli Mohamed Ali
Formation	
- British Somaliland	1884
- Italian Somaliland	1889
- Union and independence	1 July 1960
Area	
- Total	637,657 km^2 (43rd) 246,200 sq mi
Population	
- 2010 estimate	9,359,000 (89th)
- Density	14/km^2 (209) 36/sq mi
GDP (PPP)	2009 estimate
- Total	$5.731 billion (155th)
- Per capita	$600 (224th)
HDI (2009)	N/A (Not ranked)
Currency	Somali shilling (SOS)
Time zone	EAT (UTC+3)
- Summer (DST)	not observed (UTC+3)
Drives on the	right
ISO 3166 code	SO
Internet TLD	.so
Calling code	252

Somalia and formerly known as the Somali Democratic Republic under communist rule, is a country located in the Horn of Africa. Since the outbreak of the Somali Civil War in 1991 there has been no central government control over most of the country's territory. The internationally recognized Transitional Federal Government controls only a small part of the country. Somalia has been characterized as a failed state[6][7][8][9] and is one of the poorest[10] and most violent states in the world.[11][12]

Somalia lies in the eastern-most part of Africa. It is bordered by Djibouti to the northwest, Kenya to the southwest, the Gulf of Aden with Yemen to the north, the Indian Ocean to the east, and Ethiopia to the west. It has the longest coastline on the continent,[13] and its terrain consists mainly of plateaus, plains and highlands. Hot conditions prevail year-round, along with periodic monsoon winds and irregular rainfall.[14]

For additional analytical, business and investment opportunities information, please contact Global Investment & Business Center, USA at (202) 546-2103. Fax: (202) 546-3275. E-mail: rusric@erols.com

In antiquity, Somalia was an important centre for commerce with the rest of the ancient world,[15][16] and according to most scholars, Somalia is where the ancient Land of Punt was situated.[17][18] During the Middle Ages, several powerful Somali empires dominated the regional trade, including the Ajuuraan State, the Sultanate of Adal, the Warsangali Sultanate and the Gobroon Dynasty. In the late nineteenth century, the British and Italians gained control of parts of the coast, and established British Somaliland and Italian Somaliland[19] In the interior, Muhammad Abdullah Hassan's Dervish State successfully repulsed the British Empire four times and forced it to retreat to the coastal region,[20] but the Dervishes were finally defeated in 1920 by British airpower. Italy acquired full control of their parts of the region in 1927. This occupation lasted until 1941, when it was replaced by a British military administration. Northern Somalia would remain a protectorate, while southern Somalia became a trusteeship. 1960 saw the union of the two regions into the independent Somali Republic under a civilian government. Mohamed Siad Barre seized power in 1969 and established the Somali Democratic Republic. In 1991, Barre's government collapsed as the Somali Civil War broke out.

Since 1991, no central government has controlled the entirety of the country, despite several attempts to establish a unified central government.[23] The northwestern part of the country has been relatively stable under the self-declared, but unrecognized, sovereign state of Somaliland.[24] The self-governing region of Puntland covers the northeast of the country. It declares itself to be autonomous, but not independent from Somalia. The Islamist Al-Shabaab controls a large part of the south of the country. Without a central government, Somalia's inhabitants subsequently reverted to local forms of conflict resolution, either civil, Islamic, or customary law. The internationally recognized Transitional Federal Government controls only parts of the capital and some territory in the centre of the nation, but has reestablished national institutions such as the Military of Somalia, and is working towards eventual national elections in 2011, when the interim government's mandate expires.[25][26] During the two decades of war and lack of government, Somalia has maintained an informal economy, based mainly on livestock, remittance/money transfer companies, and telecommunications

Official name: Jamhuriyadda Dimugradiga ee Soomaaliya (The Somali Democratic Republic)
Area: 738,000 square km
Population: 9.28 million
Capital: Mogadishu
Official language: Somali, Arabic
Currency: Somali shilling (SoSh) = 100 centesimi
GDP per capita: US$270
GDP real growth: -3.20%
Inflation: 100.00% 100.00%
Foreign debt: US$2.64 billion

Background: Intermittent civil war has been a fact of life in Somalia since 1977. In 1991, the northern portion of the country declared its independence as Somaliland; although de facto independent and relatively stable compared to the tumultuous south, it has not been recognized by any foreign government. Beginning in 1993, a two-year UN humanitarian effort (primarily in the south) was able to alleviate famine conditions, but when the UN withdrew in 1995, having suffered significant casualties, order still had not been restored.

GEOGRAPHY

Location: Eastern Africa, bordering the Gulf of Aden and the Indian Ocean, east of Ethiopia
Geographic coordinates: 10 00 N, 49 00 E

For additional analytical, business and investment opportunities information, please contact Global Investment & Business Center, USA at (202) 546-2103. Fax: (202) 546-3275. E-mail: rusric@erols.com

Map references: Africa

Area:
total: 637,657 sq km
land: 627,337 sq km
water: 10,320 sq km

Area - comparative: slightly smaller than Texas

Land boundaries:
total: 2,366 km
border countries: Djibouti 58 km, Ethiopia 1,626 km, Kenya 682 km

Coastline: 3,025 km
Maritime claims:
territorial sea: 200 nm
Climate: principally desert; December to February - northeast monsoon, moderate temperatures in north and very hot in south; May to October - southwest monsoon, torrid in the north and hot in the south, irregular rainfall, hot and humid periods (tangambili) between monsoons
Terrain: mostly flat to undulating plateau rising to hills in north

Elevation extremes:
lowest point: Indian Ocean 0 m
highest point: Shimbiris 2,416 m

Natural resources: uranium and largely unexploited reserves of iron ore, tin, gypsum, bauxite, copper, salt
Land use:
arable land: 2%
permanent crops: 0%
permanent pastures: 69%
forests and woodland: 26%
other: 3%
Irrigated land: 1,800 sq km
Natural hazards: recurring droughts; frequent dust storms over eastern plains in summer; floods during rainy season
Environment - current issues: famine; use of contaminated water contributes to human health problems; deforestation; overgrazing; soil erosion; desertification
Environment - international agreements:
party to: Endangered Species, Law of the Sea
signed, but not ratified: Marine Dumping, Nuclear Test Ban

Geography - note: strategic location on Horn of Africa along southern approaches to Bab el Mandeb and route through Red Sea and Suez Canal.

PEOPLE

Population: 7,253,137
note: this estimate was derived from an official census taken in 1975 by the Somali Government; population counting in Somalia is complicated by the large number of nomads and by refugee movements in response to famine and clan warfare (July 2000 est.)

For additional analytical, business and investment opportunities information,
please contact Global Investment & Business Center, USA
at (202) 546-2103. Fax: (202) 546-3275. E-mail: rusric@erols.com

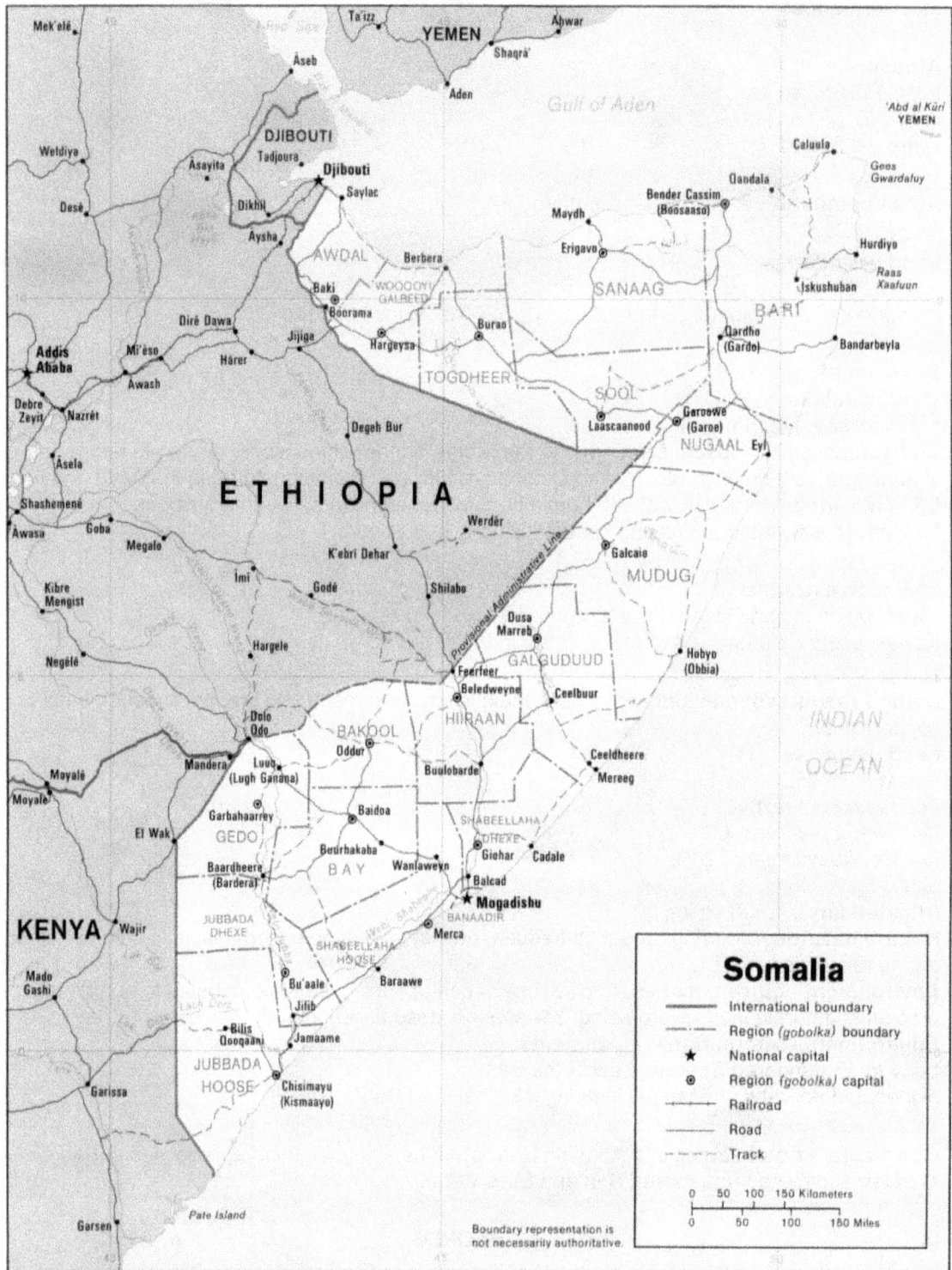

Age structure:
0-14 years: 44% (male 1,610,945; female 1,608,209)

For additional analytical, business and investment opportunities information,
please contact Global Investment & Business Center, USA
at (202) 546-2103. Fax: (202) 546-3275. E-mail: rusric@erols.com

15-64 years: 53% (male 1,938,263; female 1,892,752)
65 years and over: 3% (male 90,717; female 112,251)

Population growth rate: 2.9%
Birth rate: 47.7 births/1,000 population
Death rate: 18.69 deaths/1,000 population
Net migration rate: 0 migrant(s)/1,000 population

Sex ratio:
at birth: 1.03 male(s)/female
under 15 years: 1 male(s)/female
15-64 years: 1.02 male(s)/female
65 years and over: 0.81 male(s)/female
total population: 1.01 male(s)/female

Infant mortality rate: 125.77 deaths/1,000 live births

Life expectancy at birth:
total population: 46.23 years
male: 44.66 years
female: 47.85 years

Total fertility rate: 7.18 children born/woman

Nationality:
noun: Somali(s)
adjective: Somali

Ethnic groups: Somali 85%, Bantu, Arabs 30,000
Religions: Sunni Muslim
Languages: Somali (official), Arabic, Italian, English

Literacy:
definition: age 15 and over can read and write
total population: 24%
male: 36%
female: 14%

GOVERNMENT

Country name:
conventional long form: none
conventional short form: Somalia
former: Somali Republic, Somali Democratic Republic

Data code: SO
Government type: none
Capital: Mogadishu

For additional analytical, business and investment opportunities information,
please contact Global Investment & Business Center, USA
at (202) 546-2103. Fax: (202) 546-3275. E-mail: rusric@erols.com

Administrative divisions: 18 regions (plural - NA, singular - gobolka); Awdal, Bakool, Banaadir, Bari, Bay, Galguduud, Gedo, Hiiraan, Jubbada Dhexe, Jubbada Hoose, Mudug, Nugaal, Sanaag, Shabeellaha Dhexe, Shabeellaha Hoose, Sool, Togdheer, Woqooyi Galbeed

Independence: 1 July 1960 (from a merger of British Somaliland, which became independent from the UK on 26 June 1960, and Italian Somaliland, which became independent from the Italian-administered UN trusteeship on 1 July 1960, to form the Somali Republic)

National holiday: NA
Constitution: 25 August 1979, presidential approval 23 September 1979
Legal system: NA
Suffrage: 18 years of age; universal

Executive branch:

chief of state: Transitional Federal President Sheikh SHARIF Sheikh Ahmed (since 31 January 2009); note - a transitional governing entity with a five-year mandate, known as the Transitional Federal Institutions (TFIs), was established in October 2004; the TFIs relocated to Somalia in June 2004
head of government: Prime Minister Omar Abdirashid Ali SHARMARKE (since 13 February 2009)
cabinet: Cabinet appointed by the prime minister and approved by the Transitional Federal Assembly
election results: Sheikh SHARIF Sheikh Ahmed was elected president by the expanded Transitional Federal Assembly in Djibouti

Legislative branch: unicameral National Assembly
note: fledgling parliament; a 275-member Transitional Federal Assembly; the new parliament consists of 61 seats assigned to each of four large clan groups (Darod, Digil-Mirifle, Dir, and Hawiye) with the remaining 31 seats divided between minority clans

Judicial branch: following the breakdown of the central government, most regions have reverted to local forms of conflict resolution, either secular, traditional Somali customary law, or Shari'a (Islamic) law with a provision for appeal of all sentences

Political parties and leaders: none

Political pressure groups and leaders: numerous clan and subclan factions are currently vying for power

International organization participation: ACP, AfDB, AFESD, AL, AMF, CAEU, ECA, FAO, G-77, IBRD, ICAO, ICRM, IDA, IDB, IFAD, IFC, IFRCS, IGAD, ILO, IMF, IMO, Intelsat, Interpol, IOC, IOM (observer), ITU, NAM, OAU, OIC, UN, UNCTAD, UNESCO, UNHCR, UNIDO, UPU, WFTU, WHO, WIPO, WMO, WTrO (observer)

Diplomatic representation in the US: Somalia does not have an embassy in the US (ceased operations on 8 May 1991)

Diplomatic representation from the US: the US does not have an embassy in Somalia; US interests are represented by the US Embassy in Nairobi at Moi Avenue and Haile Selassie Avenue; mail address: P. O. Box 30137, Unit 64100, Nairobi; APO AE 09831; telephone: [254] (2) 334141; FAX [254] (2) 340838

Flag description: light blue with a large white five-pointed star in the center; design based on the flag of the UN (Italian Somaliland was a UN trust territory)

Government - note: While chaos and clan fighting continue in most of Somalia, some orderly government has been established in the northern part. In May 1991, the elders of clans in former British Somaliland established the independent Republic of Somaliland, which, although not recognized by any government, maintains a stable existence, aided by the overwhelming dominance of the ruling clan and the economic infrastructure left behind by British, Russian, and American military assistance programs. Neighboring Puntland has also made strides towards reconstructing legitimate, representative government. In February 1996, the EU agreed to finance the reconstruction of the port of Berbera; since then, other aid projects have been assumed by the EU and by a non-governmental Italian organization.

ECONOMY

Economy - overview: Despite the lack of effective national governance, Somalia has maintained a healthy informal economy, largely based on livestock, remittance/money transfer companies, and telecommunications. Agriculture is the most important sector, with livestock normally accounting for about 40% of GDP and more than 50% of export earnings. Nomads and semi-pastoralists, who are dependent upon livestock for their livelihood, make up a large portion of the population. Livestock, hides, fish, charcoal, and bananas are Somalia's principal exports, while sugar, sorghum, corn, qat, and machined goods are the principal imports. Somalia's small industrial sector, based on the processing of agricultural products, has largely been looted and sold as scrap metal. Somalia's service sector also has grown. Telecommunication firms provide wireless services in most major cities and offer the lowest international call rates on the continent. In the absence of a formal banking sector, money transfer/remittance services have sprouted throughout the country, handling up to $1.6 billion in remittances annually. Mogadishu's main market offers a variety of goods from food to the newest electronic gadgets. Hotels continue to operate and are supported with private-security militias. Somalia's arrears to the IMF continued to grow in 2008.

GDP (purchasing power parity): $5.733 billion (2009 est.)
country comparison to the world: 155
$5.59 billion (2008 est.)
$5.451 billion (2007 est.)
note: data are in 2009 US dollars

GDP (official exchange rate): $2.483 billion

GDP - real growth rate: 2.6% (2009 est.)
country comparison to the world: 73
2.6% (2008 est.)
2.6% (2007 est.)

GDP - per capita (PPP):	$600 (2009 est.) country comparison to the world: 224 $600 (2008 est.) $600 (2007 est.) *note:* data are in 2009 US dollars
GDP - composition by sector:	*agriculture:* 65% *industry:* 10% *services:* 25%
Labor force:	3.7 million (few skilled laborers)
Labor force - by occupation:	*agriculture:* 71% *industry and services:* 29%
Unemployment rate:	NA%
Population below poverty line:	NA%
Household income or consumption by percentage share:	*lowest 10%:* NA% *highest 10%:* NA%
Inflation rate (consumer prices):	NA%; note - businesses print their own money, so inflation rates cannot be easily determined
Budget:	*revenues:* $NA *expenditures:* $NA
Agriculture - products:	bananas, sorghum, corn, coconuts, rice, sugarcane, mangoes, sesame seeds, beans; cattle, sheep, goats; fish
Industries:	a few light industries, including sugar refining, textiles, wireless communication
Industrial production growth rate:	NA%
Electricity - production:	269 million kWh
Electricity - consumption:	250.2 million kWh
Electricity - exports:	0 kWh
Electricity - imports:	0 kWh
Oil - production:	0 bbl/day
Oil - consumption:	5,000 bbl/day
Oil - exports:	NA bbl/day
Oil - imports:	NA bbl/day
Oil - proved reserves:	0 bbl
Natural gas - production:	0 cu m

Natural gas - consumption:	0 cu m
Natural gas - proved reserves:	5.663 billion cu m
Exports:	$241 million f.o.b.
Exports - commodities:	livestock, bananas, hides, fish, charcoal, scrap metal
Exports - partners:	UAE 49.8%, Yemen 21.5%, Oman 6% (2006)
Imports:	$576 million f.o.b.
Imports - commodities:	manufactures, petroleum products, foodstuffs, construction materials, qat
Imports - partners:	Djibouti 31%, India 8.2%, Kenya 8.1%, Brazil 7.7%, Oman 5.5%, UAE 5.2%, Yemen 5%
Debt - external:	$3 billion
Economic aid - recipient:	$60 million
Currency (code):	Somali shilling (SOS)
Exchange rates:	Somali shillings per US dollar - 1,438.3 (2006) official rate; the unofficial black market rate was about 23,000 shillings per dollar as of February 2007 *note:* the Republic of Somaliland, a self-declared independent country not recognized by any foreign government, issues its own currency, the Somaliland shilling
Fiscal year:	NA

COMMUNICATIONS

Telephones - main lines in use:	100,000
Telephones - mobile cellular:	500,000
Telephone system:	*general assessment:* the public telecommunications system was almost completely destroyed or dismantled by the civil war factions; private wireless companies offer service in most major cities and charge the lowest international rates on the continent *domestic:* local cellular telephone systems have been established in Mogadishu and in several other population centers *international:* country code - 252; international connections are available from Mogadishu by satellite (2001)
Radio broadcast stations:	AM 0, FM 11 (also 1 station each in Puntland and Somaliland), shortwave 1 (in Mogadishu)
Television broadcast stations:	4 (2 in Mogadishu and 2 in Hargeisa)
Internet country	.so

For additional analytical, business and investment opportunities information, please contact Global Investment & Business Center, USA at (202) 546-2103. Fax: (202) 546-3275. E-mail: rusric@erols.com

code:

Internet hosts: 3

Internet users: 94,000

TRANSPORTATION

Railways: 0 km
Highways:
total: 22,100 km
paved: 2,608 km
unpaved: 19,492 km
Pipelines: crude oil 15 km
Ports and harbors: Bender Cassim (Boosaaso), Berbera, Chisimayu (Kismaayo), Merca, Mogadishu
Merchant marine: none
Airports: 61
Airports - with paved runways:
total: 7
over 3,047 m: 4
2,438 to 3,047 m: 1
1,524 to 2,437 m: 1
914 to 1,523 m: 1
Airports - with unpaved runways:
total: 54
2,438 to 3,047 m: 3
1,524 to 2,437 m: 12
914 to 1,523 m: 29
under 914 m: 10

MILITARY

Military branches: no functioning central government military forces; clan militias continue to battle for control of key economic or political prizes
Military manpower - availability:
males age 15-49: 1,772,631
Military manpower - fit for military service:
males age 15-49: 984,103
Military expenditures - dollar figure: $NA
Military expenditures - percent of GDP: NA%

TRANSNATIONAL ISSUES

Disputes - international: most of the southern half of the boundary with Ethiopia is a Provisional Administrative Line; territorial dispute with Ethiopia over the Ogaden.

IMPORTANT INFORMATION FOR UNDERSTANDING SOMALIA

OFFICIAL NAME (Former): Somali Democratic Republic

WAR IN SOMALIA (2006–2009)

The **War in Somalia** was an armed conflict involving largely Ethiopian and Somali Transitional Federal Government (TFG) forces and Somali troops from Puntland versus the Somali Islamist umbrella group, the Islamic Court Union (ICU), and other affiliated militias for control of the country. There is a clear connection between War in Somalia (2009–) and the War of 2006. The war officially began shortly before July 20, 2006 when U.S. backed Ethiopian troops invaded Somalia to prop up the TFG in Baidoa The TFG in Somalia invited Ethiopians to intervene, which became an "unpopular decision" that failed to strengthen the government. Subsequently the leader of the ICU, Sheik Hassan Dahir Aweys, declared "Somalia is in a state of war, and all Somalis should take part in this struggle against Ethiopia". On December 24, Ethiopia stated it would actively combat the ICU.

Ethiopia's prime minister, Meles Zenawi, said Ethiopia entered hostilities because it faced a direct threat to its own borders. "Ethiopian defense forces were forced to enter into war to protect the sovereignty of the nation," he said. "We are not trying to set up a government for Somalia, nor do we have an intention to meddle in Somalia's internal affairs. We have only been forced by the circumstances."

The ICU, which controlled the coastal areas of southern Somalia, engaged in fighting with the forces of the Somali TFG, and the autonomous regional governments of Puntland and Galmudug, all of whom were backed by Ethiopian troops. The outbreak of heavy fighting began on December 20 with the Battle of Baidoa, after the lapse of a one-week deadline the ICU imposed on Ethiopia (on December 12) to withdraw from the nation. Ethiopia, however, refused to abandon its positions around the TFG interim capital at Baidoa. On December 29, after several successful battles, TFG and Ethiopian troops entered Mogadishu relatively unopposed. The UN also stated that many Arab nations including Egypt were also supporting the ICU through Eritrea. Although not announced until later, a small number of U.S. special forces troops accompanied Ethiopian and TFG troops after the collapse and withdrawal of the ICU to give military advice and to track suspected al-Qaida fighters. Both American support for the TFG and various Arab Nations' support for the ICU were isolated cases from the central motive of the war between the allied Ethiopian & Somali government forces and the allied ICU & Eritrean forces.

As of January 2007, Ethiopia said it would withdraw "within a few weeks"but the TFG, US and UN officials oppose Ethiopian withdrawal because it would create a "security vacuum," while the ICU has demanded immediate Ethiopian withdrawal.

The two sides had traded war declarations and gun fire on several occasions before. Eastern African countries and international observers fear the Ethiopian offensive may lead to a regional war, involving Eritrea, a long-time enemy of Ethiopia, who Ethiopia claims to be a supporter of the ICU.

As of January 2009, Ethiopian troops withdrew from Somalia following a two year insurgency which lead to loss of territory and effectiveness of the TFG and a power sharing deal between Islamists splinter group led by Sheikh Sharif Sheikh Ahmed's Alliance for the Re-liberation of Somalia (ARS) and TFG Prime Minister Nur Hassan in Djibouti. The al Shabaab who has separated from the ICU rejects the peace deal and continued to take territories including Baidoa. Another Islamist group, Ahlu Sunnah Waljama'ah, which is allied to the transitional government and supported by Ethiopia, continues to attack al Shabab and take over towns as well.

After the parliament took in 200 officials from the moderate Islamist opposition, ARS leader Sheikh Ahmed was elected TFG President on January 31, 2009. Since then, the al shabab

For additional analytical, business and investment opportunities information,
please contact Global Investment & Business Center, USA
at (202) 546-2103. Fax: (202) 546-3275. E-mail: rusric@erols.com

radical islamists have accused the new TFG President of accepting the secular transitional government and have continued the civil war since he arrived in Mogadishu at the presidential palace

FORCES INVOLVED

The scope of forces involved are difficult to calculate because of many factors, including lack of formal organization or record-keeping, and claims which remained masked by disinformation. Ethiopia for months leading up to the war maintained it had only a few hundred advisors in the country. Yet independent reports indicated far more troops. According to the BBC, "The United Nations estimated that at least 8,000 Ethiopian troops may be in the country while the AP suggests the number closer to 12-15,000 while regional rival Eritrea has deployed some 2,000 troops in support of the Islamic group." Ethiopia only admitted to 3,000–4,000 being involved,[16] though the ICU claimed the Ethiopians had 30,000 troops while Eritrea denies having any troops in Somalia In addition, the TFG alleged there were up to 8,000 foreign mujahideen fighting on behalf of the ICU, based on the ICU's worldwide appeal for Muslim mujahideen to come fight for their cause. Somali government troops and allied militias estimated roughly 10,000.

HISTORICAL BACKGROUND

A broader perspective shows many incidents of Ethiopian-Somali conflict. Boundary disputes over the Ogaden region date to the 1948 settlement when the land was granted to Ethiopia. Somali disgruntlement with this decision has led to repeated attempts to invade Ethiopia with the hopes of taking control of the Ogaden to create a Greater Somalia. This plan would have reunited the Somali people of the Ethiopian-controlled Ogaden with those living in the Republic of Somalia. Shy of that, ethnic and political tensions have caused cross-border clashes over the years.

> 1960–1964 Border Dispute
> 1977–1978 Ogaden War
> 1982 August Border Clash
> 1998–2000 Cross-border warfare during the chaotic warlord-led era.

Conflicts between Ethiopia and Somalia are not limited to the 20th–21st Centuries. Wars between Somalia, or its precursor Islamic states, and Ethiopia, stretch back to 16th century. For example, Ahmad ibn Ibrihim al-Ghazi was a 16th Century Islamic leader popular in Somali culture for his jihad against the Ethiopians during the rise of the Adal Sultanate.
Therefore, painful living history, oral and cultural traditions, long-standing ethnic divisions and sectarian differences lay between the two nations and fuel the conflict.

DIPLOMATIC AND HUMANITARIAN EFFORTS

The war is being responded to by high-level diplomatic engagements, including the UN Security Council, the EU, Arab League, and African Union. Many humanitarian organizations are making appeals to stem the conflict before it causes catastrophic civilian suffering.

INFORMATION WARFARE, DISINFORMATION AND PROPAGANDA

Even before the beginning of the war there have been significant assertions and accusations of the use of disinformation and propaganda tactics by various parties to shape the causes and course of the conflict. This includes assertions of falsification of the presence or number of forces involved, exaggeration or minimization of the casualties inflicted or taken, influence or control of media outlets (or shutting them down), and other informational means and media to sway popular support and international opinion.

For additional analytical, business and investment opportunities information,
please contact Global Investment & Business Center, USA
at (202) 546-2103. Fax: (202) 546-3275. E-mail: rusric@erols.com

JULY–OCTOBER 2006

Ethiopian troops moved into Somalian territory on July 20, 2006.
On August 1, 2006, the ICU sent technicals out towards the Ethiopian border north of Beledweyne. Ethiopian troops were reportedly sent across the border to stop the ICU's advance.
On October 9, it was reported Ethiopian troops seized Burhakaba. Another article seemed to indicate the Ethiopian control was a troop convoy passing through. Islamists claim the town reverted to their control after the Ethiopians departed. SomaliNet reports the elders asked the government to leave to avoid bloodshed in their town. The article said it was government troops, and not Ethiopians who had come to the town.

NOVEMBER - DECEMBER 2006

An Ethiopian column of 80 vehicles was hit by landmines then attacked with gunfire by a group of about 50 troops loyal to the ICU on November 19, 2006 near Berdaale, 30 miles (50 km) west of Baidoa. Six Ethiopians were reported killed in the attack. Two Ethiopian trucks burned and two were overturned.

An exchange of mortar shells between Islamic Courts Union and Ethiopian forces occurred in Galkayo on November 28, 2006 with both Islamists and Ethiopian forces facing off. Ethiopian and Islamist forces in Galkayo, central Somalia, were less than 5 kilometers away from one another.

On November 30, an Ethiopian military convoy in Somalia was ambushed by fighters loyal to the Islamic Courts Union. Eyewitnesses said a truck was blown up and there was an exchange of fire. The ICU claim 20 soldiers died. Ethiopia's parliament voted the same day to authorize the government take "all necessary" steps to rebuff any potential invasion by Somalia's Islamists.
On December 8, 2006, fighters from Somalia's Islamic Courts Union clashed with Somalian pro-government forces, allegedly in cooperation with Ethiopian troops. Sheikh Sharif Sheikh Ahmed, head of the Islamic Courts, told a crowd in Mogadishu that fighting had started in Dinsor in the south, and called on all Somalis to "stand up and defeat the enemies". Another official said Ethiopian troops had shelled the town of Bandiradley. The Deputy Defence Minister of the Somali government, Salat Ali Jelle, confirmed the fighting but denied any Ethiopian troops were involved. The Ethiopian government has denied repeated claims that its troops are fighting alongside Somali government militia.

Witnesses in Dagaari village near Bandiradley said that they saw hundreds of Ethiopian troops and tanks take up positions near the town with militiamen from the northeastern semi-autonomous region of Puntland.

On December 9, fighters from Somalia's Islamic Courts and pro-government soldiers clashed in a second day of fighting. The fighting occurred 40 kilometers from the interim government's headquarters in Baidoa. Mohamed Ibrahim Bilal, an Islamic Courts official, said that the government had launched a counterattack at Rama'addey village, while Ali Mohamed Gedi, the prime minister, claimed that Islamic Courts fighters had attacked government positions.
On December 13, a Reuters report said that the ICU claimed 30,000 Ethiopian troops were involved in Somalia, while 4,000 foreign fighters were involved on the side of the ICU. Ethiopia denied having troops other than "military advisors" present.

On December 20, major fighting broke out around the TFG capital of Baidoa. Thirteen trucks filled with Ethiopian reinforcements were reported en route to the fighting. Leaders of both groups briefly kept an option open for peace talks brokered by the EU.

On December 22, nearly 20 Ethiopian tanks headed toward the front line. According to government sources Ethiopia had 20 T-55 tanks and four attack helicopters in Baidoa.

On December 23, Ethiopian tanks and further reinforcements arrived in Daynuunay, 30 kilometres east of Baidoa; prompting ICU forces to vow all-out war despite a commitment to a EU-brokered peace. Heavy fighting continued in Iidale and Dinsoor.

On December 24, Ethiopia admitted its troops were fighting the Islamists, after stating earlier in the week it had only sent several hundred military advisors to Baidoa. Heavy fighting erupted in border areas, with reports of air strikes and shelling, including targets near the ICU-held town of Beledweyne. According to Ethiopian Information Minister Berhan Hailu: "The Ethiopian government has taken self-defensive measures and started counter-attacking the aggressive extremist forces of the Islamic Courts and foreign terrorist groups."

On December 25, Ethiopian and Somali forces captured Beledweyne. Defending ICU forces fled Beledweyne concurrent to Ethiopian airstrikes against the Mogadishu and Bali-Dogle airports. Heavy fighting was also reported in Burhakaba.

On December 26, the ICU was in retreat on all fronts, losing much of the territory they gained in the months preceding the Ethiopian intervention. They reportedly fell back to Daynuunay and Mogadishu.

On December 27, Ethiopian and Somali government forces were en route to Somalia's capital, Mogadishu after capturing the strategic town of Jowhar, 90km north from the capital. The ICU were in control of little more than the coast, abandoning many towns without putting up a fight. Also, the UIC top two commanders, defense chief Yusuf Mohammed Siad Inda'ade and his deputy Abu Mansur were away on the Hajj pilgrimage in Mecca.

After the Fall of Mogadishu to the Ethiopian and government forces on December 28, fighting continued in the Juba River valley, where the ICU retreated, establishing a new headquarters in the city of Kismayo. Intense fighting was reported on December 31 in the Battle of Jilib and the ICU frontlines collapsed during the night to artillery fire, causing the ICU to once again go into retreat, abandoning Kismayo, without a fight and retreating towards the Kenyan border.

2007

Military events in 2007 focused on the southern section of Somalia, primarily the withdrawal of ICU forces from Kismayo, and their pursuit using Ethiopian air strikes in Afmadow district concurrent to the Battle of Ras Kamboni. During this battle, the U.S. launched an airstrike conducted by an AC-130 gunship against suspected Al-Qaeda operatives. In addition, there were various insurgent attacks in Mogadishu and around the country against Ethiopian and government forces, as well as inter-clan militia violence. The government meanwhile called for a disarmament of the militias, and declared martial law.

SOMALILAND

Having secured the southern and central area of Somalia, the Transitional Federal Government is faced with the controversial issue of whether, and how, to unify the entirety of Somalia as it existed in 1991. Since that year, Somaliland has been operating as a *de facto* independent nation, though unrecognized internationally. According to the Transitional Federal Charter, the Somali Republic includes the area of Somaliland in the definition of its sovereign territory. There are various political forces involved. Ethiopia depends on Somaliland to provide port facilities since the loss of the coast with Eritrea, and generally supports the idea of Somaliland independence, while Eritrea supports Somaliland being reabsorbed into Somalia to make a larger nation to counter Ethiopia's dominance on the region. As well, eastern Somaliland is disputed with Puntland because of clan ties.

On January 11, Somaliland and Ethiopia held talks regarding further economic ties.

On January 14, 2007, leaders of Somaliland's three main political parties, the UDUB, Kulmiye, and UCID, held a press conference warning of regional war if Somalia tried to reabsorb Somaliland. On January 16, tens of thousands protested in Hargeisa against the prospect of reunification, burning Somalian flags. The next day, January 17, thousands of demonstrations in favor of joining the TFG took place in the Sool and Sanag regions of Somaliland.

ETHIOPIAN WITHDRAWAL

On January 16, the newly-appointed mayor of Mogadishu, Mayor Mohamud Hassan "Adde Gabow," along with the new administration of Banadir district, asked for the removal of Ethiopian troops from the capital.

On January 17, reports came from central Somalia that Ethiopian troops were withdrawing from the towns of Idadou and Baldawin. Meanwhile African Union nations continued to plan a peacekeeping mission to Somalia. However, the government said that the process of withdrawal had not yet occurred, and that an announcement would precede such a move.

WEAPONS

The Ethiopian Army is equipped with predominantly Soviet-made weapons while TFG and Islamic weapons vary, having mostly small arms. The following table should not be considered exhaustive.

Type	Ethiopian Army	TFG	Islamists
Tanks	T-55, T-62, T-72	none	none
APC's/IFV's	BTR-40, M113	technicals	technicals
Artillery	2A18, M1937 Howitzer, BM-21, 120mm mortars	120mm mortars	120mm mortars
Aircraft	MiG-21, MiG-23, Su-27	none	none
Helicopters	Mi-6, Mi-8, Mi-24	none	none
Small Arms, Light Weapons	AK-47, Heckler & Koch G3, PKM, DShK, ZU-23, RPG-2, RPG-7	AK-47, Heckler & Koch G3, PKM, DShK, ZU-23, RPG-2, RPG-7	AK-47, DShK, Browning M2, ZU-23, M79, RPG-7

KEY PEOPLE

TFG

An August 24, 2006 article in the Sudan Tribune identified several warlords involved with TFG military units:

Abdullahi Yusuf Ahmed – TFG president, former leader of the SSDF.
Mohamed Omar Habeeb (Mohamed Dheere) – controlled Jowhar region with the help of Ethiopia; after losing in Mogadishu as part of the ARPCT, regrouped his militia in Ethiopia & since returned (see Battle of Jowhar).
Muuse Suudi Yalahow – Controlled Medina District in Mogadishu but was forced to flee by the ICU. Has since returned to the city.
Hussein Mohamed Farrah – son of late General Mohamed Farrah Aidid. Although his father was a key anti-U.N. force in the mid-1990s, Farrah is a naturalized U.S. citizen and former U.S. Marine who controlled Villa Somalia. Former leader of the SRRC militia. The

Sudan Tribune says Farrah is in the patronage of Ethiopia, and Western interests see him as their best hope to improve Somali-Western relations.

Abdi Hasan Awale Qeybdiid – former finance minister under Gen. Aidid; arrested in Sweden for warcrimes, but later released due to lack of evidence.

Colonel Hasan Muhammad Nur Shatigadud – affiliated with the Rahanweyn Resistance Army (RRA). Came to power after his militia (with the help of Ethiopian paramilitary forces) drived out Aidid's militia from Baidoa, which became the seat of the transitional government. Presently TFG Minister of Finance.

Mohamed Qanyare Afrah – former Security Minister and member of ARPCT

Barre Aadan Shire "Hiiraale" – leader of the Juba Valley Alliance (JVA); controls Kismayo (and until its loss to the ICU, Marka region).

Hassan Abdullah Qalaad

ICU

Sharif Ahmed, head of the ICU executive committee

Hassan Dahir Aweys, head of the ICU shura council, former Somali colonel, listed by the U.S. as a terrorist for heading Osama bin Laden-supported Al-Itihaad al-Islamiya in the 1990s.

Hassan Abdullah Hersi al-Turki, led forces which captured Juba Valley, on U.S. terrorist list for taking over the leadership of Aweys' group

Abu Taha al-Sudan, reported to have led the ICU troops in the Battle of Baidoa, former Al-Itihaad al-Islamiya, wanted by the U.S. as the financier of the 1998 United States embassy bombings and involvement in the 2002 Mombasa hotel bombing

Saleh Ali Saleh Nabhan, listed as a terrorist by the U.S. for reported involvement in the 2002 Mombasa hotel bombing, said to have been a target of the U.S. AC-130 raid in January 2007

Fazul Abdullah Mohammed, listed as a terrorist by the U.S. for reported involvement in the 1998 U.S. embassy bombings. Some sources claim that he was a target of the U.S. AC-130 raid. His death by the AC-130 raid was later reported by Somali authorities, but denied by US officials.

Aden Hashi Farah, led commandos of the ICU's Hizbul Shabaab movement against Ethiopian-backed forces in the Battle of Baidoa, before fleeing and being targetted by the U.S. AC-130 raid that took the lives of eight people on January 8, 2007.

GEOGRAPHY

Somalia is located on the east coast of Africa on and north of the Equator and, with Ethiopia and Djibouti, is often referred to as the Horn of Africa. It comprises Italy's former Trust Territory of Somalia and the former British Protectorate of Somaliland (now seeking recognition as an independent state). The coastline extends 2,720 kilometers (1,700 mi.).

The northern part of the country is hilly, and in many places the altitude ranges between 900 and 2,100 meters (3,000 ft.-7,000 ft.) above sea level. The central and southern areas are flat, with an average altitude of less than 180 meters (600 ft.). The Juba and the Shebelle Rivers rise in Ethiopia and flow south across the country toward the Indian Ocean. The Shebelle, however, does not reach the sea.

**For additional analytical, business and investment opportunities information,
please contact Global Investment & Business Center, USA
at (202) 546-2103. Fax: (202) 546-3275. E-mail: rusric@erols.com**

Major climatic factors are a year-round hot climate, seasonal monsoon winds, and irregular rainfall with recurring droughts. Mean daily maximum temperatures range from 30°C to 40°C (85° F-105°F), except at higher elevations and along the east coast. Mean daily minimums usually vary from about 15°C to 30°C (60°F-85°F). The southwest monsoon, a sea breeze, makes the period from about May to October the mildest season at Mogadishu. The December-February period of the northeast monsoon also is relatively mild, although prevailing climatic conditions in Mogadishu are rarely pleasant. The "tangambili" periods that intervene between the two monsoons (October-November and March-May) are hot and humid.

PEOPLE

As early as the seventh century A.D., indigenous Cushitic peoples began to mingle with Arab and Persian traders who had settled along the coast. Interaction over the centuries led to the emergence of a Somali culture bound by common traditions, a single language, and the Islamic faith.

Today, about 60% of all Somalis are nomadic or semi-nomadic pastoralists who raise cattle, camels, sheep, and goats. About 25% of the population are settled farmers who live mainly in the fertile agricultural zone between the Juba and Shebelle Rivers in southern Somalia. The remainder of the population (15%-20%) is urban.

Sizable ethnic groups in the country include Bantu agricultural workers, several thousand Arabs and some hundreds of Indians and Pakistanis. Nearly all inhabitants speak the Somali language, which remained unwritten until October 1973, when the Supreme Revolutionary Council (SRC) proclaimed it the nation's official language and decreed an orthography using Latin letters. Somali is now the language of instruction in schools, to the extent that these exist. Arabic, English, and Italian also are used extensively.

HISTORY

Early history traces the development of the Somali people to an Arab sultanate, which was founded in the seventh century A.D. by Koreishite immigrants from Yemen. During the 15th and 16th centuries, Portuguese traders landed in present Somali territory and ruled several coastal towns. The sultan of Oman and Zanzibar subsequently took control of these towns and their surrounding territory.

Somalia's modern history began in the late l9th century, when various European powers began to trade and establish themselves in the area. The British East India Company's desire for unrestricted harbor facilities led to the conclusion of treaties with the sultan of Tajura as early as 1840. It was not until 1886, however, that the British gained control over northern Somalia through treaties with various Somali chiefs who were guaranteed British protection. British objectives centered on safeguarding trade links to the east and securing local sources of food and provisions for its coaling station in Aden. The boundary between Ethiopia and British Somaliland was established in 1897 through treaty negotiations between British negotiators and King Menelik.

For additional analytical, business and investment opportunities information, please contact Global Investment & Business Center, USA at (202) 546-2103. Fax: (202) 546-3275. E-mail: rusric@erols.com

During the first two decades of this century, British rule was challenged through persistent attacks led by Mohamed Abdullah. A long series of intermittent engagements and truces ended in 1920 when British warplanes bombed Abdullah's stronghold at Taleex. Although Abdullah was defeated as much by rival Somali factions as by British forces, he was lauded as a popular hero and stands as a major figure of national identity to some Somalis.

In 1885, Italy obtained commercial advantages in the area from the sultan of Zanzibar and in 1889 concluded agreements with the sultans of Obbia and Aluula, who placed their territories under Italy's protection. Between 1897 and 1908, Italy made agreements with the Ethiopians and the British that marked out the boundaries of Italian Somaliland. The Italian Government assumed direct administration, giving the territory colonial status.

Italian occupation gradually extended inland. In 1924, the Jubaland Province of Kenya, including the town and port of Kismayo, was ceded to Italy by the United Kingdom. The subjugation and occupation of the independent sultanates of Obbia and Mijertein, begun in 1925, were completed in 1927. In the late 1920s, Italian and Somali influence expanded into the Ogaden region of eastern Ethiopia. Continuing incursions climaxed in 1935 when Italian forces launched an offensive that led to the capture of Addis Ababa and the Italian annexation of Ethiopia in 1936.

Following Italy's declaration of war on the United Kingdom in June 1940, Italian troops overran British Somaliland and drove out the British garrison. In 1941, British forces began operations against the Italian East African Empire and quickly brought the greater part of Italian Somaliland under British control. From 1941 to 1950, while Somalia was under British military administration, transition toward self-government was begun through the establishment of local courts, planning committees, and the Protectorate Advisory Council. In 1948 Britain turned the Ogaden and neighboring Somali territories over to Ethiopia.

In Article 23 of the 1947 peace treaty, Italy renounced all rights and titles to Italian Somaliland. In accordance with treaty stipulations, on September 15, 1948, the Four Powers referred the question of disposal of former Italian colonies to the UN General Assembly. On November 21, 1949, the General Assembly adopted a resolution recommending that Italian Somaliland be placed under an international trusteeship system for 10 years, with Italy as the administering authority, followed by independence for Italian Somaliland. In 1959, at the request of the Somali Government, the UN General Assembly advanced the date of independence from December 2 to July 1, 1960.

Meanwhile, rapid progress toward self-government was being made in British Somaliland. Elections for the Legislative Assembly were held in February 1960, and one of the first acts of the new legislature was to request that the United Kingdom grant the area independence so that it could be united with Italian Somaliland when the latter became independent. The protectorate became independent on June 26, 1960; five days later, on July 1, it joined Italian Somaliland to form the Somali Republic.

In June 1961, Somalia adopted its first national constitution in a countrywide referendum, which provided for a democratic state with a parliamentary form of government based on European models. During the early post-independence period, political parties reflected clan loyalties, which contributed to a basic split between the regional interests of the former British-controlled north and the Italian-controlled south. There also was substantial conflict between pro-Arab, pan-Somali militants intent on national unification with the Somali-inhabited territories in Ethiopia and Kenya and the "modernists," who wished to give priority to economic and social development and improving relations with other African countries. Gradually, the Somali Youth League, formed under British auspices in 1943, assumed a dominant position and succeeded in cutting across regional and clan loyalties. Under the leadership of Mohamed Ibrahim Egal, prime minister from

1967 to 1969, Somalia greatly improved its relations with Kenya and Ethiopia. The process of party-based constitutional democracy came to an abrupt end, however, on October 21, 1969, when the army and police, led by Maj. Gen. Mohamed Siad Barre, seized power in a bloodless coup.

Following the coup, executive and legislative power was vested in the 20-member Supreme Revolutionary Council (SRC), headed by Maj. Gen. Siad Barre as president. The SRC pursued a course of "scientific socialism" that reflected both ideological and economic dependence on the Soviet Union. The government instituted a national security service, centralized control over information, and initiated a number of grassroots development projects. Perhaps the most impressive success was a crash program that introduced an orthography for the Somali language and brought literacy to a substantial percentage of the population.

The SRC became increasingly radical in foreign affairs, and in 1974, Somalia and the Soviet Union concluded a treaty of friendship and cooperation. As early as 1972, tensions began increasing along the Somali-Ethiopian border; these tensions heightened after the accession to power in Ethiopia in 1973 of the Mengistu Hailemariam regime, which turned increasingly toward the Soviet Union. In the mid-1970s, the Western Somali Liberation Front (WSLF) began guerrilla operations in the Ogaden region of Ethiopia. Fighting increased, and in July 1977, the Somali National Army (SNA) crossed into the Ogaden to support the insurgents. The SNA moved quickly toward Harer, Jijiga, and Dire Dawa, the principal cities of the region. Subsequently, the Soviet Union, Somalia's most important source of arms, embargoed weapons shipments to Somalia. The Soviets switched their full support to Ethiopia, with massive infusions of Soviet arms and 10,000-15,000 Cuban troops. In November 1977, President Siad Barre expelled all Soviet advisers and abrogated the friendship agreement with the U.S.S.R. In March 1978, Somali forces retreated into Somalia; however, the WSLF continues to carry out sporadic but greatly reduced guerrilla activity in the Ogaden. Such activities also were subsequently undertaken by another dissident group, the Ogaden National Liberation Front (ONLF).

Following the 1977 Ogaden war, President Barre looked to the West for international support, military equipment, and economic aid. The United States and other Western countries traditionally were reluctant to provide arms because of the Somali Government's support for insurgency in Ethiopia. In 1978, the United States reopened the U.S. Agency for International Development mission in Somalia. Two years later, an agreement was concluded that gave U.S. forces access to military facilities in Somalia. In the summer of 1982, Ethiopian forces invaded Somalia along the central border, and the United States provided two emergency airlifts to help Somalia defend its territorial integrity.

From 1982 to 1990 the United States viewed Somalia as a partner in defense. Somali officers of the National Armed Forces were trained in U.S. military schools in civilian as well as military subjects. Within Somalia, Siad Barre's regime confronted insurgencies in the northeast and northwest, whose aim was to overthrow his government. By 1988, Siad Barre was openly at war with sectors of his nation. At the President's order, aircraft from the Somali National Air Force bombed the cities in the northwest province, attacking civilian as well as insurgent targets. The warfare in the northwest sped up the decay already evident elsewhere in the republic. Economic crisis, brought on by the cost of anti-insurgency activities, caused further hardship as Siad Barre and his cronies looted the national treasury.

By 1990, the insurgency in the northwest was largely successful. The army dissolved into competing armed groups loyal to former commanders or to clan-tribal leaders. The economy was in shambles, and hundreds of thousands of Somalis fled their homes. In 1991, Siad Barre and forces loyal to him fled the capital; he later died in exile in Nigeria. In the same year, Somaliland declared itself independent of the rest of Somalia, with its capital in Hargeisa. In 1992, responding

For additional analytical, business and investment opportunities information, please contact Global Investment & Business Center, USA at (202) 546-2103. Fax: (202) 546-3275. E-mail: rusric@erols.com

to political chaos and widespread deaths from civil strife and starvation in Somalia, the United States and other nations launched Operation Restore Hope. Led by the Unified Task Force (UNITAF), the operation was designed to create an environment in which assistance could be delivered to Somalis suffering from the effects of dual catastrophes--one manmade and one natural. UNITAF was followed by the United Nations Operation in Somalia (UNOSOM). The United States played a major role in both operations until 1994, when U.S. forces withdrew.

The prevailing chaos in much of Somalia after 1991 contributed to growing influence by various Islamic groups, including al-Tabliq, al-Islah (supported by Saudi Arabia), and Al-Ittihad Al-Islami (Islamic Unity). These groups, which are among the main non-clan-based forces in Somalia, share the goal of establishing an Islamic state. They differ in their approach; in particular, Al-Ittihad supports the use of violence to achieve that goal and has claimed responsibility for terrorist acts. In the mid-1990s, Al-Ittihad came to dominate territory in Puntland as well as central Somalia near Gedo. It was forcibly expelled from these localities by Puntland forces as well as Ethiopian attacks in the Gedo region. Since that time, Al-Ittihad has adopted a longer term strategy based on integration into local communities and establishment of Islamic schools, courts, and relief centers.

After the attack on the United States of September 11, 2001, Somalia gained greater international attention as a possible base for terrorism--a concern that became the primary element in U.S. policy toward Somalia. The United States and other members of the anti-terrorism coalition examined a variety of short- and long-term measures designed to cope with the threat of terrorism in and emanating from Somalia. Economic sanctions were applied to Al-Ittihad and to the Al-Barakaat group of companies, based in Dubai, which conducted currency exchanges and remittances transfers in Somalia. The United Nations also took an increased interest in Somalia, including proposals for an increased UN presence and for strengthening a 1992 arms embargo.

POLITICAL CONDITIONS

In the wake of the collapse of the Somali Government, factions organized around military leaders took control of Somalia. The resulting chaos and loss of life promoted the international intervention led by the United States, UNITAF. That operation was followed by the United Nations Operation in Somalia (UNOSOM), which ended in 1994. Since 1991, there have been more than a dozen efforts at national reconciliation; to date, none has been successful. Various groupings of Somali factions have sought to control the national territory (or portions thereof) and have fought small wars with one another. Mohamed Ibrahim Egal was selected by elders in 1991 as President of the "Republic of Somaliland," which is made up of the former northwest provinces of the republic. In 1998, the area of Puntland in the northeast declared itself autonomous (although not independent) as the "State of Puntland," with its capital at Garowe. Puntland declared it would remain autonomous until a federated Somalia state was established. Abdullahi Yusuf, Puntland's original president, ruled until mid-2001. In November 2001, a convention of elders, in a process disputed by Abdullayi, selected Col. Jama Ali Jama to succeed him. Forces loyal to Abdullayi, who had retreated to Galkayo, attacked Garowe in November, resulting in a de facto division of Puntland. As many as 30 other factions vie for some degree of authority in the country.

Efforts at mediation of the Somali internal dispute have been undertaken by many regional states. In the mid-1990s, Ethiopia played host to several Somali peace conferences and initiated talks at the Ethiopian city of Sodere, which led to some degree of agreement between competing factions. The Governments of Egypt, Yemen, Kenya, and Italy also have attempted to bring the Somali factions together. In 1997, the Organization of African Unity and the Intergovernmental Authority on Development (IGAD) gave Ethiopia the mandate to pursue Somali reconciliation. In 2000, Djibouti hosted a major reconciliation conference (the 13th such effort), which in August resulted in creation of the Transitional National Government, with a 3-year mandate to pursue national reconciliation. In early 2002, Kenya organized a further reconciliation effort under IGAD auspices.

The absence of a central government in Somalia since 1991 has allowed outside forces to become more influential by supporting various groups and persons in Somalia. Djibouti, Eritrea, and Arab states have supported the TNG. Ethiopia has provided political support to Somaliland and assisted a group of southern warlords organized as

DEFENSE

The Somali National Army was made up of the army, navy, air force, and air defense command. The Somali Government's demise led to the de facto dissolution of the national armed forces. Efforts by the Transitional National Government to reestablish a regular armed force have made little progress. Various groups and factions control militias ranging in strength from hundreds to thousands. These militias are in general poorly trained and lightly armed, although some groups possess limited inventories of older armored vehicles and other heavy weapons and small arms are prevalent throughout Somalia.

FOREIGN RELATIONS

After independence, Somalia followed a foreign policy of nonalignment. It received major economic assistance from the United States, Italy, and the Federal Republic of Germany, as well as from the Soviet Union and China. The government also sought ties with many Arab countries, and the current Transitional National Government has been accepted by the Arab League and the Islamic Conference.

The status of expatriate Somalis has been an important foreign and domestic issue. A goal of Somali nationalism is to unite the other Somali-inhabited territories with the republic consistent with the objectives of pan-Somali tradition. This issue has been a major cause of past crises between Somalia and its neighbors--Ethiopia, Kenya, and Djibouti.

In 1963, Somalia severed diplomatic relations with the United Kingdom for a period following a dispute over Kenya's northeastern region (Northern Frontier District), an area inhabited mainly by

For additional analytical, business and investment opportunities information,
please contact Global Investment & Business Center, USA
at (202) 546-2103. Fax: (202) 546-3275. E-mail: rusric@erols.com

Somalis. Somalia urged self-determination for the people of the area, while Kenya refused to consider any steps that might threaten its territorial integrity. Related problems have arisen from the boundary with Ethiopia and the large-scale migrations of Somali nomads between Ethiopia and Somalia.

In the aftermath of the 1977-78 Somali-Ethiopian war, the Government of Somalia continued to call for self-determination for ethnic Somalis living in the Ogaden region of eastern Ethiopia. At the March 1983 Nonaligned Movement summit in New Delhi, President Siad stated that Somalia harbored no expansionist aims and was willing to negotiate with Ethiopia.

Since the fall of the Barre regime, the foreign policy of the various entities in Somalia has centered on gaining international recognition, winning international support for national reconciliation, and obtaining international economic assistance.

U.S.-SOMALI RELATIONS

U.S. diplomatic relations with Somali were interrupted by the fall of the government and have not yet been re-established. The United States maintains informal contacts with a number of entities in Somalia.

The U.S. Embassy has been closed since 1991. U.S. contacts with Somalia, including consular coverage, are maintained by U.S. Embassy Nairobi, Kenya.

TRAVEL WARNING!

There is no recognized government in Somalia. Travel into and within Somalia is extremely dangerous. The Department of State recommends that travelers not go to Somalia.

Daallo, Djibouti, and Yemeni Airlines operate scheduled international flights between Hargeisa and Addis Ababa, Sanaa, and Aden. Somalia is 8 hours ahead of Eastern Standard Time and does not observe daylight saving time.

TRAVEL AND BUSINESS INFORMATION

The U.S. Department of State's Consular Information Program provides Consular Information Sheets, Travel Warnings, and Public Announcements.

Consular Information Sheets exist for all countries and include information on entry requirements, currency regulations, health conditions, areas of instability, crime and security, political disturbances, and the addresses of the U.S. posts in the country.

Travel Warnings are issued when the State Department recommends that Americans avoid travel to a certain country.

Public Announcements are issued as a means to disseminate information quickly about terrorist threats and other relatively short-term conditions overseas which pose significant risks to the security of American travelers. Free copies of this information are available by calling the Bureau of Consular Affairs at 202-647-5225 or via the fax-on-demand system: 202-647-3000. Consular

For additional analytical, business and investment opportunities information,
please contact Global Investment & Business Center, USA
at (202) 546-2103. Fax: (202) 546-3275. E-mail: rusric@erols.com

Information Sheets and Travel Warnings also are available on the Consular Affairs Internet home page: http://travel.state.gov. Consular Affairs Tips for Travelers publication series, which contain information on obtaining passports and planning a safe trip abroad are on the internet and hard copies can be purchased from the Superintendent of Documents, U.S. Government Printing Office, telephone: 202-512-1800; fax 202-512-2250.

Emergency information concerning Americans traveling abroad may be obtained from the Office of Overseas Citizens Services at (202) 647-5225. For after-hours emergencies, Sundays and holidays, call 202-647-4000.

Passport information can be obtained by calling the National Passport Information Center's automated system ($.35 per minute) or live operators 8 a.m. to 8 p.m. (EST) Monday-Friday ($1.05 per minute). The number is 1-900-225-5674 (TDD: 1-900-225-7778). Major credit card users (for a flat rate of $4.95) may call 1-888-362-8668 (TDD: 1-888-498-3648). It also is available on the internet.

Travelers can check the latest health information with the U.S. Centers for Disease Control and Prevention in Atlanta, Georgia. A hotline at 877-FYI-TRIP (877-394-8747) and a web site at http://www.cdc.gov/travel/index.htm give the most recent health advisories, immunization recommendations or requirements, and advice on food and drinking water safety for regions and countries. A booklet entitled Health Information for International Travel (HHS publication number CDC-95-8280) is available from the U.S. Government Printing Office, Washington, DC 20402, tel. (202) 512-1800.

Information on travel conditions, visa requirements, currency and customs regulations, legal holidays, and other items of interest to travelers also may be obtained before your departure from a country's embassy and/or consulates in the U.S. (for this country, see "Principal Government Officials" listing in this publication).

U.S. citizens who are long-term visitors or traveling in dangerous areas are encouraged to register at the U.S. embassy upon arrival in a country (see "Principal U.S. Embassy Officials" listing in this publication). This may help family members contact you in case of an emergency.

STRATEGIC INFORMATION ON THE COUNTRY

GEOGRAPHY

Area: 637,657 sq. km.; slightly smaller than Texas.
Cities: *Capital*--Mogadishu. *Other cities*--Hargeisa, Kismayo, Bosasso, Baidoa.
Terrain: Mostly flat to undulating plateau rising to hills in the north.
Climate: Principally desert; December to February--northeast monsoon, moderate temperatures in north, and very hot in the south; May to October--southwest monsoon, torrid in the north, and hot in the south; irregular rainfall; hot and humid periods (tangambili) between monsoons.

Somalia is situated on the horn of East Africa and is bordered by the Gulf of Aden and Djibouti to the north, the Indian Ocean to the east and south, to the north and northwest by Ethiopia and Kenya to the southwest.

The northern region is mountainous with plateaus ranging 3,000 and 7,000 ft. To the northeast there is an extremely dry dissected plateau that reaches a maximum height of 8,250 ft. South and west of this region, extending to the Shebeli River, lies a plateau whose maximum elevation is 2,250 ft. The region between the Juba and Shebeli rivers is low agricultural land, and the area that extends southwest of the Juba River to the Kenyan border is low pasture land.

The Juba and Shebeli rivers originate in Ethiopia and flow toward the Indian Ocean. They provide water for irrigation but are not navigable by commercial vessels. The Shebeli dries up before reaching the ocean. Despite its lengthy shore line, Somalia has no natural harbours because of inshore coral reefs.

Africa's easternmost country, Somalia has a land area of 637,540 square kilometers, slightly less than that of the state of Texas. Somalia occupies the tip of a region commonly referred to as the Horn of Africa--because of its resemblance on the map to a rhinoceros's horn--that also includes Ethiopia and Djibouti.

Somalia's terrain consists mainly of plateaus, plains, and highlands. In the far north, however, the rugged east-west ranges of the Karkaar Mountains lie at varying distances from the Gulf of Aden coast. The weather is hot throughout the year, except at the higher elevations in the north. Rainfall is sparse, and most of Somalia has a semiarid-to- arid environment suitable only for the nomadic pastoralism practiced by well over half the population. Only in limited areas of moderate rainfall in the northwest, and particularly in the southwest, where the country's two perennial rivers are found, is agriculture practiced to any extent.

The local geology suggests the presence of valuable mineral deposits. As of 1992, however, only a few significant sites had been located, and mineral extraction played a very minor role in the economy.

Somalia's long coastline (3,025 kilometers) has been of importance chiefly in permitting trade with the Middle East and the rest of East Africa. The exploitation of the shore and the continental shelf for fishing and other purposes had barely begun by the early 1990s. Sovereignty was claimed over territorial waters up to 200 nautical miles.

CLIMATE

Climate is the primary factor in much of Somali life. For the large nomadic population, the timing and amount of rainfall are crucial determinants of the adequacy of grazing and the prospects of relative prosperity. During droughts such as occurred during 1974-75 and 1984-85, starvation can occur. There are some indications that the climate has become drier in the last century and that the increase in the number of people and animals has put a growing burden on water and vegetation.

Somalis recognize four seasons, two rainy (*gu* and *day*) and two dry (*jiilaal* and *hagaa*). The *gu* rains begin in April and last until June, producing a fresh supply of pasture and for a brief period turning the desert into a flowering garden. Lush vegetation covers most of the land, especially the central grazing plateau where grass grows tall. Milk and meat abound, water is plentiful, and animals do not require much care. The clans, reprieved from four months' drought, assemble to engage alternately in banter and poetic exchange or in a new cycle of hereditary feuds. They also offer sacrifices to Allah and to the founding clan ancestors, whose blessings they seek. Numerous social functions occur: marriages are contracted, outstanding disputes are settled or exacerbated, and a person's age is calculated in terms of the number of *gus* he or she has lived. The *gu* season is followed by the *hagaa* drought (July-September) and the *hagaa* by the *day* rains (October-November). Next is *jiilaal* (December-March), the harshest season for pastoralists and their herds.

Most of the country receives less than 500 millimeters of rain annually, and a large area encompassing the northeast and much of northern Somalia receives as little as 50 to 150 millimeters. Certain higher areas in the north, however, record more than 500 millimeters a year, as do some coastal sites. The southwest receives 330 to 500 millimeters. Generally, rainfall takes the form of showers or localized torrential rains and is extremely variable.

Mean daily maximum temperatures throughout the country range from 30° C to 40° C, except at higher elevations and along the Indian Ocean coast. Mean daily minimum temperatures vary from 20° C to more than 30° C. Northern Somalia experiences the greatest temperature extremes, with readings ranging from below freezing in the highlands in December to more than 45° C in July in the coastal plain skirting the Gulf of Aden. The north's relative humidity ranges from about 40 percent in midafternoon to 85 percent at night, varying somewhat with the season. During the colder months, December to February, visibility at higher elevations is often restricted by fog.

Temperatures in the south are less extreme, ranging from about 20° C to 40° C. The hottest months are February through April. Coastal readings are usually five to ten degrees cooler than those inland. The coastal zone's relative humidity usually remains about 70 percent even during the dry seasons.

TERRAIN, VEGETATION, AND DRAINAGE

Physiographically, Somalia is a land of limited contrast. In the north, a maritime plain parallels the Gulf of Aden coast, varying in width from roughly twelve kilometers in the west to as little as two kilometers in the east. Scrub-covered, semiarid, and generally drab, this plain, known as the *guban* (scrub land), is crossed by broad, shallow watercourses that are beds of dry sand except in the rainy seasons. When the rains arrive, the vegetation, which is a combination of low bushes and grass clumps, is quickly renewed, and for a time the *guban* provides some grazing for nomad livestock.

Inland from the gulf coast, the plain rises to the precipitous northward-facing cliffs of the dissected highlands. These form the rugged Karkaar mountain ranges that extend from the northwestern border with Ethiopia eastward to the tip of the Horn of Africa, where they end in sheer cliffs at Caseyr. The general elevation along the crest of these mountains averages about 1,800 meters above sea level south of the port town of Berbera, and eastward from that area it continues at 1,800 to 2,100 meters almost to Caseyr. The country's highest point, Shimber Berris, which rises to 2,407 meters, is located near the town of Erigavo.

Southward the mountains descend, often in scarped ledges, to an elevated plateau devoid of perennial rivers. This region of broken mountain terrain, shallow plateau valleys, and usually dry watercourses is known to the Somalis as the Ogo.

In the Ogo's especially arid eastern part, the plateau-- broken by several isolated mountain ranges--gradually slopes toward the Indian Ocean and in central Somalia constitutes the Mudug Plain. A major feature of this eastern section is the long and broad Nugaal Valley, with its extensive network of intermittent seasonal watercourses. The eastern area's population consists mainly of pastoral nomads. In a zone of low and erratic rainfall, this region was a major disaster area during the great drought of 1974 and early 1975.

The western part of the Ogo plateau region is crossed by numerous shallow valleys and dry watercourses. Annual rainfall is greater than in the east, and there are flat areas of arable land that provide a home for dryland cultivators. Most important, the western area has permanent wells to which the predominantly nomadic population returns during the dry seasons. The western plateau slopes gently southward and merges imperceptibly into an area known as the Haud, a broad, undulating terrain that constitutes some of the best grazing lands for Somali nomads, despite the lack of appreciable rainfall more than half the year. Enhancing the value of the Haud are the natural depressions that during periods of rain become temporary lakes and ponds.

The Haud zone continues for more than sixty kilometers into Ethiopia, and the vast Somali Plateau, which lies between the northern Somali mountains and the highlands of southeast Ethiopia, extends south and eastward through Ethiopia into central and southwest Somalia. The portion of the Haud lying within Ethiopia was the subject of an agreement made during the colonial era permitting nomads from British Somaliland to pasture their herds there. After Somali independence in 1960, it became the subject of Somali claims and a source of considerable regional strife.

Southwestern Somalia is dominated by the country's only two permanent rivers, the Jubba and the Shabeelle. With their sources in the Ethiopian highlands, these rivers flow in a generally southerly direction, cutting wide valleys in the Somali Plateau as it descends toward the sea; the plateau's elevation falls off rapidly in this area. The adjacent coastal zone, which includes the lower reaches of the rivers and extends from the Mudug Plain to the Kenyan border, averages 180 meters above sea level.

The Jubba River enters the Indian Ocean at Chisimayu. Although the Shabeelle River at one time apparently also reached the sea near Merca, its course is thought to have changed in prehistoric times. The Shabeelle now turns southwestward near Balcad (about thirty kilometers north of Mogadishu) and parallels the coast for more than eighty-five kilometers. The river is perennial only to a point southwest of Mogadishu; thereafter it consists of swampy areas and dry reaches and is finally lost in the sand east of Jilib, not far from the Jubba River. During the flood seasons, the Shabeelle River may fill its bed to a point near Jilib and occasionally may even break through to the Jubba River farther south. Favorable rainfall and soil conditions make the entire riverine region a fertile agricultural area and the center of the country's largest sedentary population.

In most of northern, northeastern, and north-central Somalia, where rainfall is low, the vegetation consists of scattered low trees, including various acacias, and widely scattered patches of grass.

For additional analytical, business and investment opportunities information, please contact Global Investment & Business Center, USA at (202) 546-2103. Fax: (202) 546-3275. E-mail: rusric@erols.com

This vegetation gives way to a combination of low bushes and grass clumps in the highly arid areas of the northeast and along the Gulf of Aden.

As elevations and rainfall increase in the maritime ranges of the north, the vegetation becomes denser. Aloes are common, and on the higher plateau areas of the Ogo are woodlands. At a few places above 1,500 meters, the remnants of juniper forests (protected by the state) and areas of *candelabra euphorbia* (a chandelier-type cactus) occur. In the more arid highlands of the northeast, boswellia and commiphora trees are sources, respectively, of the frankincense and myrrh for which Somalia has been known since ancient times.

A broad plateau encompassing the northern city of Hargeysa, which receives comparatively heavy rainfall, is covered naturally by woodland (much of which has been degraded by overgrazing) and in places by extensive grasslands. Parts of this area have been under cultivation since the 1930s, producing sorghum and corn; in the 1990s it constituted the only significant region of sedentary cultivation outside southwestern Somalia.

The Haud south of Hargeysa is covered mostly by a semiarid woodland of scattered trees, mainly acacias, underlain by grasses that include species especially favored by livestock as forage. As the Haud merges into the Mudug Plain in central Somalia, the aridity increases and the vegetation takes on a subdesert character. Farther southward the terrain gradually changes to semiarid woodlands and grasslands as the annual precipitation increases.

The region encompassing the Shabeelle and Jubba rivers is relatively well watered and constitutes the country's most arable zone. The lowland between the rivers supports rich pasturage. It features arid to subarid savanna, open woodland, and thickets that include frequently abundant underlying grasses. There are areas of grassland, and in the far southwest, near the Kenyan border, some dry evergreen forests are found.

Along the Indian Ocean from Mereeg, about 150 kilometers northeast of Mogadishu, southwestward to near Chisimayu lies a stretch of coastal sand dunes. This area is covered with scattered scrub and grass clumps where rainfall is sufficient. Overgrazing, particularly in the area between Mogadishu and Chisimayu, has resulted in the destruction of the protective vegetation cover and the gradual movement of the once-stationary dunes inland. Beginning in the early 1970s, efforts were made to stabilize these dunes by replanting.

Other vegetation includes plants and grasses found in the swamps into which the Shabeelle River empties most of the year and in other large swamps in the course of the lower Jubba River. Mangrove forests are found at points along the coast, particularly from Chisimayu to near the Kenyan border. Uncontrolled exploitation appears to have caused some damage to forests in that area. Other mangrove forests are located near Mogadishu and at a number of places along the northeastern and northern coasts.

ADMINISTRATIVE STRUCTURE

PRINCIPAL COMMERCIAL CENTRES AND TOWNS

Mogadishu city (1990 est. pop. 1,200,000), capital of Somalia, a port on the Indian Ocean. It is the country's largest city and chief commercial center.

Hargeysa, (1990 est. 43,627) also Harghessa, town, northern Somalia, capital of Hargeysa Province, in the Galgodon (Ogo) Highlands. The town is located in a stock-raising area, and trade in wool, hides, and skins is conducted here.

For additional analytical, business and investment opportunities information,
please contact Global Investment & Business Center, USA
at (202) 546-2103. Fax: (202) 546-3275. E-mail: rusric@erols.com

Kismaayo, also Kismayu or Chisimaio, town, southern Somalia, in Lower Jubba region. A deepwater port on the Indian Ocean, it is one of the nation's principal commercial and manufacturing centers. Industries include meat, fish, turtle, and leather processing.

Marka, also Merka or Merca, town, southeastern Somalia, in Banaadir Region, on the Indian Ocean, near Mogadishu. The town has oilseed-processing and fishing industries, and textiles, boats, and paper products are manufactured here. Bananas are exported, shipped to the coast from the rich irrigated area around nearby Janhale on the Shabeelle (Shebele) River, 13 km (8 mi) to the northwest.

For additional analytical, business and investment opportunities information, please contact Global Investment & Business Center, USA at (202) 546-2103. Fax: (202) 546-3275. E-mail: rusric@erols.com

GOVERNMENT & POLITICAL SYSTEM

PRESIDENT ABDULLAHI YUSUF AHMED

Abdullahi Yusuf Ahmed

Colonel **Abdullahi Yusuf Ahmed** (Somali: **Cabdullaahi Yuusuf Axmed**) was born December 15, 1934 in the town of Galkacyo, Mudug Region. He is now the transitional President of Somalia. He was elected by a session of the transitional Parliament held in neighbouring Kenya's capital, Nairobi, on October 10, 2004, and sworn in on October 14, 2004. He has been living in the Kenyan capital since his election. The election took place in Kenya because the Somali capital was regarded as being too dangerous.

The President pledged to promote reconciliation and to set about rebuilding the country. However, his government has been plagued by internal disagreements.

In particular, Mr Ahmed is at loggerheads with some warlords and government members over where the administration should be based. The president and prime minister oppose a move to Mogadishu, citing security reasons.

The make up of a possible foreign peacekeeping force - in particular the inclusion of Ethiopian troops - is another bone of contention. Ethiopia has been accused of backing rival Somali warlords in order to keep the country weak.

A former army officer and leader of the SSDF, Mr Yusuf led a guerrilla movement in the 1970s aimed at ousting the Somali dictator Siad Barre.

In the 1990s Mr Ahmed emerged as the pre-eminent leader of his native Puntland region; he declared the territory autonomous in 2002. On July 23, 2002 he became the President of Puntland and served in this position until his term expired on July 1, 2001. However, after this he continued to declare himself to be the President of Puntland and started against the new leadership. In May 2002 he gained control of Puntland's capital and was recognized as President of Puntland again, though rebellions continued until 2003. Ahmed then continued serving as

For additional analytical, business and investment opportunities information, please contact Global Investment & Business Center, USA at (202) 546-2103. Fax: (202) 546-3275. E-mail: rusric@erols.com

President of Puntland until October 2004 when he resigned to become President of Somalia. He is said to have an authoritarian approach to leadership.

However, he helped relocate the Transitional Federal Institutions along with his Prime Minister Ali Mohammed Ghedi and the Speaker of the Parliament Sharif Adan from Nairobi to the cities of Mogadishu and Jowhar.

In May 2006, the Second Battle of Mogadishu started and CNN reported that there were Transitional government forces in action, but Abdullahi Yusuf told the BBC the alliance of warlords are not fighting on behalf of the government. How CNN concluded otherwise is not yet known.

At present, Yusuf Ahmed resides in Baidoa with parts of his government. Several people have left his government after the victories of the Islamic Court Union. An arangement has been made with the Islamic Court Union in Khartoum on 5 september 2006. The interim-government of Yusuf Ahmed and the Islamic Court Union will merge into a new transistory government of Somalia. The Islamic Court Union had the precondition that the Ethiopian army should leave the country. The rise of the Islamists has damaged Yusuf's dream of establishing central rule in Somalia for the first time in 15 years.

CABINET

	MINISTRY	Tel. +253 22
1	Foreign Affairs	4007
2	Presidency (Post Vacant)	3901
3	Interior	3675
4	Defence	5043
5	Planning	3686
6	Public Works	3431
7	Finance	3605
8	Health	3429
9	Education	3904
10	Commerce	3017
11	Livestock	3920
12	Agriculture	3662
13	Range and Rural Development	3692
14	Fisheries Costal Development	3632
15	Mineral and Water Resources	3615
16	Civil Aviation	3223

For additional analytical, business and investment opportunities information, please contact Global Investment & Business Center, USA at (202) 546-2103. Fax: (202) 546-3275. E-mail: rusric@erols.com

17	Information and National Guidance	5109
18	Rehabilitation and Reconstruction	3026
19	Justice	3453
20	Religious Affairs	-
21	Tourism	-

POLITICAL CONDITIONS

In the wake of the collapse of the Somali Government, factions organized around military leaders took control of Somalia. The resulting chaos and loss of life promoted the international intervention led by the United States, UNITAF. That operation was followed by the United Nations Operations in Somalia, UNOSOM, which ended in 1994. Since that time, various groupings of Somali factions have sought to control the national territory and have fought small wars with one another. Hussein "Aideed", and Ali Mahdi Mohamed, leaders of such factions, both claimed executive power in a new "government" based in Mogadishu. Mohamed Ibrahim Egal, first President of Somalia, was selected by elders as President of "Somaliland" which is made up of the former northwest provinces of the republic. As many as 30 other factions vie for some degree of authority in the country.

Efforts at mediation of the Somali internal dispute have been undertaken by many regional states. Ethiopia has played host to several Somali peace conferences and initiated talks at the Ethiopian city of Sodere, which led to some degree of agreement between competing factions. The Governments of Egypt, Yemen, Kenya, and Italy also have attempted to bring the Somali factions together. In 1997, the Organization of African Unity and the Inter-Governmental Agency on Development gave Ethiopia the mandate to pursue Somali reconciliation.

FOREIGN RELATIONS

Since independence, Somalia has followed a foreign policy of nonalignment. It has received major economic assistance from the United States, Italy, and the Federal Republic of Germany, as well as from the Soviet Union and China. The government has sought close ties with many Arab countries.

The status of expatriate Somalis is an important foreign and domestic issue. A goal of Somali nationalism is to unite the other Somali-inhabited territories with the republic consistent with the objectives of pan-Somali tradition. This issue has been a major cause of past crises between Somalia and its neighbors--Ethiopia, Kenya, and Djibouti.

In 1963, Somalia severed diplomatic relations with the United Kingdom for a period following a dispute over Kenya's northeastern region (Northern Frontier District), an area inhabited mainly by Somalis. Somalia urged self-determination for the people of the area, while Kenya refused to consider any steps that might threaten its territorial integrity. Related problems have arisen from the boundary with Ethiopia and the large-scale migrations of Somali nomads between Ethiopia and Somalia. Since 1981, the Somali Government and Kenya have embarked on a rapprochement that brought an exchange of senior Kenyan and Somali officials in May 1983, and a visit to Mogadishu by Kenyan President Daniel Arap Moi in July 1984.

In the aftermath of the 1977-78 Somali-Ethiopian war, the Government of Somalia continued to call for self-determination for ethnic Somalis living in the Ogaden region of eastern Ethiopia. At

For additional analytical, business and investment opportunities information, please contact Global Investment & Business Center, USA at (202) 546-2103. Fax: (202) 546-3275. E-mail: rusric@erols.com

the March 1983 Nonaligned Movement summit in New Delhi, President Siad stated that Somalia harbors no expansionist aims and is willing to negotiate with Ethiopia.

Since the fall of the Barre regime, Somali foreign policy has centered on winning international support for various plans for national reconciliation.

DEFENSE

The Somali National Army was made up of the army, navy, air force, and air defense command. High-ranking army officials play a major role in Somalia's political affairs. The total strength of the army was about 50,000 personnel. Most Somali military equipment and weaponry are Soviet hardware delivered between 1972 and 1977. About 50% of that equipment was lost during the 1977 Ogaden war, and much of the remainder is rapidly deteriorating. In recent years the government has turned to Western countries in seeking new and modern weaponry for its military. Western military aid has centered on modest deliveries of defensive arms, training, and improved maintenance. The People's Republic of China, Egypt, Italy, Saudi Arabia, and the United States have provided most of Somalia's recent foreign military assistance. The Somali Government's demise led to the de facto dissolution of the national armed forces.

U.S.-SOMALI RELATIONS

U.S. diplomatic relations with Somali were interrupted by the fall of the government and have not yet been re-established.

GOVERNMENT PRIOR TO THE CIVIL WAR

In January 1991, a bloody rebellion that had begun in 1988 finally succeeded in ending the twenty-one-year authoritarian regime of President Mahammad Siad Barre. The civil war had taken more than 50,000 civilian lives and had left the capital, Mogadishu, in shambles. Many other cities and towns also were in ruins, and hundreds of thousands of Somalis had fled to neighboring countries as refugees.

Although the major clans had been united in their opposition to Siad Barre, their leaders had no common political vision of Somalia's future. Consequently, civil strife continued at a reduced level after Siad Barre was deposed. The dominant faction in the north, the Somali National Movement (SNM), refused to accept the legitimacy of the provisional government established by the United Somali Congress (USC). Responding to widespread popular resentment of the central government, in June 1991 the SNM declared an independent Republic of Somaliland in the region that had constituted the British Somaliland before independence and unification with the former colony of Italian Somaliland in 1960.

The legacy Siad Barre left of a country devastated by civil war and riven by intense clan rivalries contrasted starkly with the future he had envisaged for Somalia when he took power in a military coup d'état in October 1969. Siad Barre, at the time a major general and commander of the army, and his fellow officers overthrew an elected civilian government that had become widely perceived as corrupt and incompetent. Siad Barre was determined to implement policies to benefit the country economically and socially and to diminish the political influence of the clans. During his regime's early years, Somalia experienced considerable economic development and efforts were made to replace clan loyalty with national pride.

However, Siad Barre proved susceptible to a cult of personality and over the years grew increasingly intolerant of criticism. Following his army's disastrous 1978 defeat in Ethiopia, Siad

**For additional analytical, business and investment opportunities information,
please contact Global Investment & Business Center, USA
at (202) 546-2103. Fax: (202) 546-3275. E-mail: rusric@erols.com**

Barre's rule became more authoritarian and arbitrary, which only caused opposition to his regime to increase. Forsaking appeals to nationalism, Siad Barre tried to maintain control by exploiting historical clan animosities and by relying more and more on the loyalty of his own family and clan. By the mid-1980s, the opposition to Siad Barre had developed into several organized movements determined to overthrow his regime by force. Angered by what he perceived as local support of the opposition, particularly in the north, Siad Barre ordered the machine-gunning of livestock herds and the poisoning of wells in disaffected rural areas, as well as the indiscriminate bombing of cities. In the most notorious of these air attacks, the north's administrative center and largest city, Hargeysa, was virtually leveled in 1988.

Siad Barre's tactics inflamed popular anger and greatly strengthened the appeal of the various guerrilla groups. Nevertheless, the opposition's ultimate triumph caught the rebels themselves by surprise. Their only common goal, to be rid of Siad Barre, was achieved by USC forces essentially without assistance from the other rebel groups. USC fighters had entered Mogadishu clandestinely at the end of December 1990 to assist clan members who had formed popular committees of self-defense to protect themselves from attacks by a rival clan that supported Siad Barre. The presence of the USC guerrillas prompted the intervention of the Red Berets (Duub Cas), an elite military unit whose members acted as bodyguards for Siad Barre, and which was commanded by Siad Barre's eldest son. The fighting quickly escalated, forcing the USC to send more of its forces into the city. The USC guerrillas and the Red Berets battled in the streets of the capital for four weeks. After the USC defeated Siad Barre's forces, the other rebel movements declined to cooperate with it. Each of the several opposition groups drew its primary support from a particular clan-family , and Siad Barre's sudden removal from the political scene opened the way for traditional clan suspicions to reassert themselves. The reemergence of clan politics cast doubt on the prospects for Somalia's stability and unity.

By September 1991, intense rivalry among leaders of the USCdominated interim government had degenerated into street fighting within the Mogadishu area. Because the different clans resorted to the use of armed force to buttress their claims for political power, government and civil society disintegrated, and essential services such as food distribution collapsed. Nature compounded the political disaster with a prolonged drought. In 1992 severe famine affected much of southern Somalia. International relief agencies mounted a food and medical aid campaign, but an estimated 80 percent of food shipments were looted by armed groups affiliated with various clans. The worsening situation prompted the United Nations (UN) to intervene. On April 22, 1992, the UN proposed to send a 550-man mission to Somalia; and on April 24, in UN Resolution 751, the Security Council voted to send fifty UN observers to monitor the cease-fire in Mogadishu.

GOVERNMENT STRUCTURE

Following its defeat of Siad Barre, the Executive Committee of the USC announced the formation of an interim provisional government, even though it did not exercise effective authority over the entire country. The USC chose one of its own members, Ali Mahdi Mahammad (b. 1939), as provisional president. The president served as head of state, but the duties and responsibilities of the office were not defined. For the most part, the provisional president retained the same powers that had been stipulated in the constitution of 1979. This included the authority to appoint a prime minister, and subsequently Mahammad named Umar Arteh Ghalib to that position on interim basis. Ghalib's cabinet, called the Provisional Government of National Unity, initially consisted of twenty-seven full ministers and eight deputy ministers. The ministerial portfolios included agriculture, commerce, culture and higher education, defense, exports, finance, fisheries, health, industry, information, interior, justice, labor and social affairs, livestock and forestry, petroleum and minerals, post and telecommunications, public works and housing, reconstruction and settlement, transportation, tourism, and youth.

For additional analytical, business and investment opportunities information,
please contact Global Investment & Business Center, USA
at (202) 546-2103. Fax: (202) 546-3275. E-mail: rusric@erols.com

Although the president announced that elections for a permanent government would be held as soon as security had been reestablished, rivalries within the USC, as well as opposition to the interim government in other parts of the country, made the questions of elections a moot point. Mahammad's most serious challenger was General Mahammad Faarah Aidid, leader of a USC faction that supported cooperation with the SNM. Initially, Aidid contested the authority of the Mogadishu-based USC Executive Committee to form an interim government without consultation with other political groups that had opposed the Siad Barre regime. Relations between the Mahammad and Aidid wings of the USC continued to deteriorate throughout the spring and summer of 1991. By September, Aidid had established his own rival government in the southern part of the capital. A series of clashes between forces loyal to Aidid and those loyal to Mahammad compelled the latter to retreat to northern Mogadishu.

Mahammad was a member of the Abgaal clan of the Hawiye clanfamily , whereas Aidid was a member of that same clan-family's Habar Gidir clan. The Abgaal clan comprised nine subclans, several of which traditionally have been dominant in the Mogadishu area. Because Abgaal leaders had not become involved in the struggle against Siad Barre until 1989, other clans tended to view them as upstarts trying to usurp control of the opposition movement. This perception was especially strong among the Habar Gidir clan, whose five subclans lived predominantly in central Somalia. Some Habar Gidir leaders had joined the SNM as early as 1984, and they had resisted efforts to create a separate Hawiye force--the USC--between 1987 and 1989. Once the USC was established, Aidid emerged as leader of the mainly Habar Gidir faction that maintained an affiliation with the SNM. The Abgaal and Habar Gidir wings of the USC were clearly distinct by November 1990 when Aidid, on behalf of this group, signed an agreement with the SNM and the Somali Patriotic Movement (SPM) to unify military operations.

Despite their political differences, both Mahammad and Aidid had long histories of opposition to Siad Barre. A former teacher and civil servant, Mahdi Mahammad had been elected to the 123-member National Assembly of the Republic in the March 1969 parliamentary elections. Following the military coup in October 1969, Mahdi Mahammad was arrested along with several other civilian politicians. He was released after several years in prison and subsequently became a successful Mogadishu entrepreneur. During the 1980s, he served as director of a local UN office. Eventually Mahammad used his wealth to provide crucial financial support to the USC guerrillas. In May 1990, he was one of 114 prominent citizens who signed a public manifesto calling on the government to resign and requesting that Siad Barre introduce democratic reforms. When Siad Barre began arresting signatories to the manifesto, Mahammad fled to exile in Italy, where he worked in the USC's Rome office.

The appointment of Ghalib as provisional prime minister demonstrated the sensitivity of Mahammad and other USC leaders to the role of clans in the country's politics. Ghalib belonged to the important Isaaq clan-family of northern Somalia. Although the main opposition group in the north, the SNM, was closely identified with the Isaaqs, Ghalib was not an SNM member. Rather, his political career had associated him with national government. From 1969 to 1976, Ghalib had served as Siad Barre's first foreign minister. He was dismissed after disagreeing with Siad Barre's increasingly overt policy of supporting the ethnic Somali insurrection in Ethiopia's Ogaden (Ogaadeen) region. Ghalib was subsequently arrested, and in 1989, after spending seven years in prison without charges, he was tried for treason and sentenced to death. Following protests from various foreign governments, Siad Barre commuted Ghalib's sentence but kept him under house arrest. In late January 1991, as his regime was collapsing, Siad Barre asked Ghalib to form a new government that would negotiate with the rebels, but the USC military successes forced Siad Barre's flight from the capital before any transfer of power could be completed.

CONSTITUTION

For additional analytical, business and investment opportunities information, please contact Global Investment & Business Center, USA at (202) 546-2103. Fax: (202) 546-3275. E-mail: rusric@erols.com

The provisional government called for a new constitution to replace the 1979 document that had been the law of the land at the time of Siad Barre's overthrow. The provisional government created a Ministry of Constitutional Affairs, which was charged with planning for a constitutional convention and revising an October 1990 draft constitution that Siad Barre had proposed in an unsuccessful effort to stem opposition to his rule. As of May 1992, however, the lack of consensus among the USC-dominated government and the various guerrilla groups that controlled more than half of the nation had prevented completion of a final version of the new constitution. Consequently, those provisions of the constitution of 1979 that had not been specifically voided by the interim government remained in force.

Like its 1984 amendments, the constitution of 1979 had been approved in a popular referendum. Somalia had universal suffrage for persons over eighteen years of age, but women did not play a significant role in politics. The constitution of 1979 resembled the constitution of 1961, also approved in a nationwide referendum after the former Italian and British colonies had been unified as independent Somalia. The main difference between the two documents concerned executive power. The constitution of 1961 had provided for a parliamentary democracy, with the prime minister and Council of Ministers (cabinet) being drawn from the membership of the legislature. The legislature also elected the head of state, or president of the republic. The constitution of 1979 provided for a presidential system under which the president served as both head of state and head of government. As head of government, the president selected the members of the Council of Ministers, which he chaired. The constitution of 1979 initially called for the president to be elected to a six-year, renewable term of office by a two-thirds majority vote of the legislature. Constitutional amendments enacted in 1984 provided for direct popular election of the president to a seven-year term. The first presidential election was held in 1986. Siad Barre, the sole candidate, received 99.9 percent of the votes.

Both the 1961 and 1979 constitutions granted broad powers to the president. The constitution of 1979 authorized the president to conduct foreign affairs, declare war, invoke emergency powers, serve as commander in chief of the armed forces, and appoint one or more vice presidents, the president of the Supreme Court, up to six members of the national legislature, and the members of the Council of Ministers. Both constitutions also provided for a unicameral legislature subject to stand for election at least once every five years; the president could dissolve the legislature earlier.

LEGISLATURE

Although the Siad Barre government suspended the National Assembly following the 1969 coup, a decade later it created a new single-chamber legislature, the People's Assembly. The constitution of 1979 stipulated that the People's Assembly have 177 members, including 6 members appointed by the president and 171 chosen by popular election. By contrast, the precoup National Assembly had only 123 members. Members of the People's Assembly served a five-year term. Two such assemblies were elected, one in 1979 and another in 1984. The elections scheduled for 1989 were postponed as a result of the civil strife that by then had engulfed most of the country.

Critics and opponents of the regime were not permitted to run in either the 1979 or the 1984 election. Instead, the government drew up lists of candidates, all of whom were members of the only legally permitted party (the Somali Revolutionary Socialist Party--SRSP), and submitted the entire lists for voter approval. In both instances, the government announced that more than 99 percent of the electorate had approved the official lists. The People's Assembly also did not truly debate any legislation. It met for several days each year and ratified whatever laws the executive had decided to submit for its "approval."

For additional analytical, business and investment opportunities information,
please contact Global Investment & Business Center, USA
at (202) 546-2103. Fax: (202) 546-3275. E-mail: rusric@erols.com

The People's Assembly was not in session when the Siad Barre government was toppled. The provisional government announced its intention to hold elections for a new legislature, but as of the spring of 1992 the continuing political disturbances in the country had prevented the formulation of definite plans for such elections.

LOCAL GOVERNMENT

One of the consequences of the civil strife that began in 1988 was the alienation of many local governments from the effective authority of Mogadishu. Whereas the domestic situation as of May 1992 remained unstable, the trend appeared to be toward a decentralized system of local government similar to that existing prior to the 1969 coup. The constitution of 1961 had provided for the decentralization of administrative functions wherever feasible, and throughout the country elected councils had been responsible for municipal and district government. However, direct supervision of local government affairs by central authorities also was part of Somalia's recent history, and a return to a centralized system could not be ruled out. Indeed, the local government structures that existed in 1992 were the same ones that had been established during Siad Barre's dictatorship.

One of Siad Barre's first decrees following the 1969 military coup dissolved all the elected municipal and district councils. This edict was followed by acts that eventually reorganized local government into sixteen regions, each containing three to six districts, with the exception of the capital region (Banaadir), which was segmented into fifteen districts. Of the total eightyfour districts, some were totally urban, while others included both urban and rural communities. Local government authority was vested in regional and district councils, the members of which were appointed by the central government. A 1979 law authorized district council elections, but reserved to the government the right to approve candidates before their names were submitted to voters. Permanent settlements in rural areas had elected village councils, although all candidates had to be approved by government officials at the district level.

The Ministry of Local Government and Rural Development exercised authority over the structure of local government. Throughout Siad Barre's twenty-one-year rule, a high-ranking military officer usually headed this ministry. Military officers also were appointed as chairmen of the regional councils. Most members of the regional and district councils were drawn from the army, the police, and security personnel. Such practices ensured that those in charge of carrying out administrative functions at the local level were directly responsible to Mogadishu.

All levels of local government were staffed by personnel of the national civil service who had been assigned to their posts by the central authorities. Local councils were permitted to plan local projects, impose local taxes, and borrow funds (with prior ministerial approval), for demonstrably productive development projects.

LEGAL SYSTEM

At independence, Somalia had four distinct legal traditions: English common law, Italian law, Islamic sharia or religious law, and Somali customary law (traditional rulers and sanctions). The challenge after 1960 was to meld this diverse legal inheritance into one system. During the 1960s, a uniform penal code, a code of criminal court procedures, and a standardized judicial organization were introduced. The Italian system of basing judicial decisions on the application and interpretation of the legal code was retained. The courts were enjoined, however, to apply English common law and doctrines of equity in matters not governed by legislation.

In Italian Somaliland, observance of the sharia had been more common than in British Somaliland, where the application of Islamic law had been limited to cases pertaining to marriage, divorce, family disputes, and inheritance. Qadis (Muslim judges) in British Somaliland also adjudicated customary law in cases such as land tenure disputes and disagreements over the payment of *diya* or blood compensation. In Italian Somaliland, however, the sharia courts had also settled civil and minor penal matters, and Muslim plaintiffs had a choice of appearing before a secular judge or a qadi. After independence the differences between the two regions were resolved by making the sharia applicable in all civil matters if the dispute arose under that law. Somali customary law was retained for optional application in such matters as land tenure, water and grazing rights, and the payment of *diya*.

The military junta suspended the constitution of 1961 when it took power in 1969, but it initially respected other sources of law. In 1973 the Siad Barre regime introduced a unified civil code. Its provisions pertaining to inheritance, personal contracts, and water and grazing rights sharply curtailed both the sharia and Somali customary law. Siad Barre's determination to limit the influence of the country's clans was reflected in sections of the code that abolished traditional clan and lineage rights over land, water resources, and grazing. In addition, the new civil code restricted the payment of *diya* as compensation for death or injury to the victim or close relatives rather than to an entire *diya*-paying group. A subsequent amendment prohibited the payment of *diya* entirely.

The attorney general, who was appointed by the minister of justice, was responsible for the observance of the law and prosecution of criminal matters. The attorney general had ten deputies in the capital and several other deputies in the rest of the country. Outside of Mogadishu, the deputies of the attorney general had their offices at the regional and district courts.

COURTS

The constitution of 1961 had provided for a unified judiciary independent of the executive and the legislature. A 1962 law integrated the courts of northern and southern Somalia into a four-tiered system: the Supreme Court, courts of appeal, regional courts, and district courts. Sharia courts were discontinued although judges were expected to take the sharia into consideration when making decisions. The Siad Barre government did not fundamentally alter this structure; nor had the provisional government made any significant changes as of May 1992.

At the lowest level of the Somali judicial system were the eighty-four district courts, each of which consisted of civil and criminal divisions. The civil division of the district court had jurisdiction over matters requiring the application of the sharia, or customary law, and suits involving claims of up to 3,000 Somali shillings. The criminal division of the district court had jurisdiction over offenses punishable by fines or prison sentences of less than three years.

There were eight regional courts, each consisting of three divisions. The ordinary division had jurisdiction over penal and civil cases considered too serious to be heard by the district courts. The assize division considered only major criminal cases, that is, those concerning crimes punishable by more than ten years' imprisonment. A third division handled cases pertaining to labor legislation. In both the district and regional courts, a single magistrate, assisted by two laymen, heard cases, decided questions of fact, and voted on the guilt or innocence of the accused.

Somalia's next-highest tier of courts consisted of the two courts of appeal. The court of appeals for the southern region sat at Mogadishu, and the northern region's court of appeals sat at Hargeysa. Each court of appeal had two divisions. The ordinary division heard appeals of district court decisions and of decisions of the ordinary division of the regional courts, whereas the assize division was only for appeals from the regional assize courts. A single judge presided over cases in both divisions. Two laymen assisted the judge in the ordinary division, and four laymen assisted the judge in the assize division. The senior judges of the courts of appeal, who were called presidents, administered all the courts in their respective regions.

The Supreme Court, which sat at Mogadishu, had ultimate authority for the uniform interpretation of the law. It heard appeals of decisions and judgments of the lower courts and of actions taken by public attorneys, and settled questions of court jurisdiction. The Supreme Court was composed of a chief justice, who was referred to as the president, a vice president, nine surrogate justices, and four laymen. The president, two other judges, and four laymen constituted a full panel for plenary sessions of the Supreme Court. In ordinary sessions, one judge presided with the assistance of two other judges and two laymen. The president of the Supreme Court decided whether a case was to be handled in plenary or ordinary session, on the basis of the importance of the matter being considered.

Although the military government did not change the basic structure of the court system, it did introduce a major new institution, the National Security Courts (NSCs), which operated outside the ordinary legal system and under the direct control of the executive. These courts, which sat at Mogadishu and the regional capitals, had jurisdiction over serious offenses defined by the government as affecting the security of the state, including offenses against public order and crimes by government officials. The NSC heard a broad range of cases, passing sentences for embezzlement by public officials, murder, political activities against the state, and thefts of government food stocks. A senior military officer was president of each NSC. He was assisted by two other judges, usually also military officers. A special military attorney general prosecuted cases brought before the NSC. No other court, not even the Supreme Court, could review NSC sentences. Appeals of NSC verdicts could be taken only to the president of the republic. Opponents of the Siad Barre regime accused the NSC of sentencing hundreds of people to death for political reasons. In October 1990, Siad Barre announced the abolition of the widely feared and detested courts; as of May 1992, the NSCs had not been reinstituted by the provisional government.

Before the 1969 coup, the Higher Judicial Council had responsibility for the selection, promotion, and discipline of members of the judiciary. The council was chaired by the president of the Supreme Court and included justices of the court, the attorney general, and three members elected by the National Assembly. In 1970 military officers assumed all positions on the Higher Judicial Council. The effect of this change was to make the judiciary accountable to the executive. One of the announced aims of the provisional government after the defeat of Siad Barre was the restoration of judicial independence.

FOREIGN RELATIONS

The provisional government established in February 1991 inherited a legacy of problematic relations with neighboring states and economic dependence on aid from Arab and Western nations. Relations between Somalia and its three neighbors-- Djibouti, Ethiopia, and Kenya--had been poisoned for more than two decades by Somalia's irredentist claims to areas inhabited by ethnic Somalis in each of these three states. The 1977-78 Ogaden War with Ethiopia, although a humiliating defeat for Somalia, had created deep suspicions in the Horn of Africa concerning the intentions of the Siad Barre regime. The continuing strain in Somali-Ethiopian relations tended to reinforce these suspicions.

Civil strife in Ethiopia and repressive measures in the Ogaden caused more than 650,000 ethnic Somalis and Oromo residing in Ethiopia to flee to Somalia by early 1978. The integration of so many refugees into an essentially agrarian society afflicted by persistent drought was beyond Somalia's economic capacity. In the absence of a peace agreement, prospects for repatriation continued to be virtually nonexistent. The Siad Barre government's solution to this major political,

For additional analytical, business and investment opportunities information,
please contact Global Investment & Business Center, USA
at (202) 546-2103. Fax: (202) 546-3275. E-mail: rusric@erols.com

social, and economic problem was to make the search for generous financial assistance a focal point of its foreign policy.

RELATIONS WITH OTHER AFRICAN STATES

For ten years after the Ogaden War, the Siad Barre government refused to renounce its public support of the Ethiopian guerrilla organization, the Western Somali Liberation Front, and provided it with clandestine military assistance to carry out raids inside Ethiopia. The Mengistu government responded in kind by providing bases, sanctuary, and military assistance to the SSDF and the SNM. Siad Barre's fear of Ethiopian military power induced him in the early 1980s to begin a process of rapprochement with Somalia's other neighbors, Kenya and the former French territory of Djibouti. Kenya had long suspected Somalia of encouraging separatist activities among the predominantly ethnic Somali population in its Northern Frontier District. Following a 1981 summit meeting with Kenyan president Daniel arap Moi in Nairobi, Siad Barre's public renunciation of any Somali territorial claims on Kenya helped dissipate mistrust.

Beginning in 1982, both Kenya and Djibouti, apparently encouraged by Siad Barre's stated willingness to hold direct talks with Mengistu, made diplomatic efforts to mediate between Somalia and Ethiopia. It was not until 1986, however, that Siad Barre and Mengistu finally agreed to meet. This first meeting since before the Ogaden War took place in the city of Djibouti and marked the beginning of a gradual rapprochement. Siad Barre's willingness to defuse the situation along the Somali-Ethiopian border stemmed from the combined pressures of escalating guerrilla activity, overt Ethiopian military threats, drought, and the destabilizing presence of hundreds of thousands of Ethiopian refugees. Siad Barre and Mengistu held a second meeting in April 1988, at which they signed a peace agreement and formally reestablished diplomatic relations. Both leaders agreed to withdraw their troops from their mutual borders and to cease support for armed dissident groups trying to overthrow the respective governments in Addis Ababa and Mogadishu.

The peace accord failed to provide Siad Barre respite from guerrilla activity and probably contributed to his eventual demise. Anticipating the possibility of being expelled from Ethiopia, the SNM decided to relocate within Somalia itself, a decision that drastically changed the nature of the conflict in the north. Despite the termination of Ethiopian assistance, SNM guerrillas continued to defeat Siad Barre's forces with relative ease; by August 1988 they had captured Hargeysa and other northern towns. Siad Barre responded by ordering massive aerial bombing, carried out by foreign mercenary pilots, that damaged or destroyed virtually every building in Hargeysa. The brutal attack, which resulted in thousands of civilian casualties and brought both domestic and international opprobrium upon the Siad Barre regime, failed to crush the SNM. Fighting not only intensified in the north over the next eighteen months, but also spread throughout the country, forcing an estimated 800,000 Somalis to seek refuge in Ethiopia.

In March 1990, Siad Barre accused Ethiopia of having violated the 1988 peace agreement by providing continued military support to the SNM. However, by this time the Mengistu government was as beleaguered as the Siad Barre regime by armed opposition movements and was not in a position to assist any Somali rebels. Soon after Siad Barre fled Mogadishu in January 1991, Mengistu followed his example by fleeing Addis Ababa as guerrilla armies closed upon the Ethiopian capital. Throughout 1991 the new provisional governments in Somalia and Ethiopia regarded each other cautiously. Both were threatened by separatist movements and both had an interest in maintaining the integrity of internationally recognized borders. As conditions in Somalia worsened on account of civil strife, the collapse of central authority, and the disruption of food production and distribution, tens of thousands of Somalis fled to Ethiopia, creating a massive refugee situation in that country by early 1992.

For additional analytical, business and investment opportunities information, please contact Global Investment & Business Center, USA at (202) 546-2103. Fax: (202) 546-3275. E-mail: rusric@erols.com

Sharing land borders with both Somalia and Ethiopia, Djibouti believed it was in the long-term interests of the Horn of Africa region if both countries remained intact. Djibouti's president, Hassan Gouled Aptidon, attempted to mediate between the provisional government and the SNM and offered his capital as a neutral meeting place. In June 1991, Djibouti served as the venue for a national reconciliation conference between the USC and several other groups.

With most of Djibouti's diverse population consisting of ethnic Somalis, Aptidon's concern about Somalia's future was not entirely altruistic. The Somalis of Djibouti belonged overwhelmingly to the Iise clan, traditional rival of the Isaaqs who dominated the SNM. The Djibouti Iise tended to be suspicious of the Isaaq, believing that they discriminated against their Iise kinsmen in northern Somalia. This concern had prompted Djibouti in 1990 to assist in the formation and training of a separate Iise movement that challenged the SNM before and after the overthrow of Siad Barre. From Djibouti's perspective, a united Somalia composed of many clans afforded more protection to the Iise than a northern republic controlled by Isaaq.

Kenya was concerned about the situation in southern Somalia, which continued to be unstable throughout 1991. Somali refugees, both civilian and military, had crossed the border into northern Kenya to escape the fighting. The refugees included more than fifty close associates of Siad Barre who were granted political asylum. Since the provisional government had announced its intention to try these officials, this action had the potential to provoke political problems between Kenya and Somalia. By early 1992, tens of thousands of Somalis were being sheltered in makeshift refugee camps in northern Kenya.

RELATIONS WITH ARAB COUNTRIES

Somalia has a long history of cultural, religious, and trade ties with the Arabs of the Arabian Peninsula, which lies across the Gulf of Aden. Although Somalis ethnically are not Arabs, they identify more with Arabs than with their fellow Africans. Thus it was not surprising when Somalia joined the League of Arab States (Arab League) in 1974, becoming the first non-Arab member of that organization. Initially, Somalia tended to support those Arab countries such as Algeria, Iraq, and Libya that opposed United States policies in the Middle East. After its defeat in the Ogaden War, the Siad Barre regime aligned its policies more closely with those of Egypt and Saudi Arabia. Subsequently, both of these countries began to provide military aid to Somalia. Other Arab states, in particular Libya, angered Siad Barre by supporting Ethiopia. In 1981 Somalia broke diplomatic relations with Libya, claiming that Libyan leader Muammar al Qadhafi was supporting the SSDF and the nascent SNM. Relations were not restored until 1985.

Throughout the 1980s, Somalia became increasingly dependent upon economic aid from the conservative, wealthy oil-exporting states of Kuwait, Qatar, Saudi Arabia, and the United Arab Emirates. This dependence was a crucial factor in the Siad Barre regime's decision to side with the United States-led coalition of Arab states that opposed Iraq following that country's invasion of Kuwait in 1990. Support for the coalition brought economic dividends: Qatar canceled further repayment of all principal and interest on outstanding loans, and Saudi Arabia offered Somalia a US$70 million grant and promised to sell it oil at below prevailing international market prices.

RELATIONS WITH THE UNITED STATES

Prior to the Ogaden War, Somalia had been allied with the Soviet Union, and its relations with the United States were strained. Largely because the Soviet Union sided with Ethiopia in the Ogaden War, a United States-Somali rapprochement began in 1977 and culminated in a military access agreement in 1980 that permitted the United States to use naval ports and airfields at Berbera, Chisimayu, and Mogadishu, in exchange for military and economic aid. The United States subsequently refurbished facilities originally developed by the Soviet Union at the Gulf of Aden port of Berbera. The United States Rapid Deployment Force used Berbera as a base for its Operation Bright Star exercises in 1981, and American military advisers were permanently stationed there one year later. Somali military units participated in Operation Bright Star joint maneuvers in 1985. The base at Berbera was used in the fall of 1990 during the deployment of personnel and supplies to Saudi Arabia in preparation for the Persian Gulf War.

Controversy over the Siad Barre government's human rights policies clouded the future of United States military cooperation with Somalia. Siad Barre's policy of repression in the north aroused criticism of his regime in the United States Congress, where the Foreign Affairs Committee of the House of Representatives held extensive hearings during July 1988 on human rights abuses in Somalia. In 1989, under congressional pressure, the administration of President George Bush terminated military aid to Somalia, although it continued to provide food assistance and to operate a small International Military Education and Training program. In 1990 Washington revealed that Mogadishu had been in default on loan repayments for more than a year. Therefore, under the terms of the Brooke Amendment, this meant that Somalia was ineligible to receive any further United States aid. During the height of the fighting in Mogadishu in January 1991, the United States closed its embassy and evacuated all its personnel from the country. The embassy was ransacked by mobs in the final days of the Siad Barre regime. The United States recognized the provisional government shortly after its establishment. Since the outbreak of the civil war, the United States has consistently urged all parties to come together to resolve their dispute by peaceful means. The United States government has supported the territorial unity of Somalia and as of May 1992 has refused to recognize the independence of northern Somalia proclaimed by the SNM.

SOMALILAND

It has been nearly nine years since the people of northwest Somalia gathered in Burao to declare themselves separate from the chaos of the rest of their country. They created a government. They rebuilt their villages and businesses. The self-proclaimed Republic of Somaliland has become one of Africa's fledgling success stories -- but a success the outside world has been reluctant to help because no one is quite sure what to do with it. Somaliland presents a quandary because it wants to be recognized as an independent nation. Its people argue that this would acknowledge their land as an island of peace separate from Somalia, a country so lawless that Kofi Annan, the U.N. secretary-general, recently referred to it as a "black hole."

African leaders hold few notions as sacred as the usually arbitrary borders drawn by and inherited from their European colonial rulers, because those frontiers define their power. But in this case, if Somaliland -- whose desired borders exactly mirror those of an old British protectorate -- becomes independent, what might happen to the borders of Nigeria, whose vast territory is riven by ethnic and religious differences? Or to Congo, Sudan and Angola, where competing factions and countries have exploited civil wars to carve fiefs that are essentially self-contained states?

The rest of the world, and the United States in particular, has done its best to forget Somalia since 1993. That year, 24 peacekeepers were killed in an ambush in June and, four months later, 18 U.S. servicemen died in a battle in Mogadishu during the U.N. effort to bring food and stability to a starving Somalia.

The United States, which had entered Somalia with great fanfare in 1992, proclaiming this the sort of intervention that would define the new world order that was supposed to follow the Cold War, pulled out soon after those killings. So did the United Nations. Outside help dried up to nearly nothing. And Somalia became a symbol for anarchy, the disaster of misplaced foreign aid -- and an example of how costly it can be for the West to intervene in conflicts it does not understand.

For additional analytical, business and investment opportunities information, please contact Global Investment & Business Center, USA at (202) 546-2103. Fax: (202) 546-3275. E-mail: rusric@erols.com

Now, a new consensus has begun to emerge among many outside nations and certainly among Somalis themselves: Something needs to be done.

For the outside world, there is another motive to attempt to restore something resembling order to Somalia, which has been without a central government since 1991, when the dictatorship of Siad Barre was overthrown after 22 years of misrule and an interminable civil war. The warlords and militias -- though substantially weakened -- continue to block peace.

In this power vacuum, diplomats and other experts say, Somalia is becoming a center for Islamic fundamentalism, for the smuggling of arms and drugs and the export of terrorism. Parts of the bombs that exploded in August 2002 at the U.S. Embassies in Kenya and Tanzania reportedly passed through Somalia, as did the bombings' suspected mastermind, Osama bin Laden, supposedly sometime later.

"We share the concerns that this place is in a state of chaos and is definitely a breeding ground for all kinds of trouble," said one U.S. official.

That is exactly how the rest of Somalia is viewed by the people of Somaliland, who consider themselves different from the south. Since the days of colonialism -- when the Somali people were divided into five different states -- Somaliland has had its own history: Until 1960, it was a British protectorate. Although it united with the Italian Somali colony four days after independence, creating modern Somalia, Somaliland was never happy with the arrangement.

So in 1991, after Barre fell, a group of elders, intellectuals and other leaders came to Burao to create the independent Somaliland republic. Progress was slow -- two civil wars were fought since then -- but over time the clan militias disarmed. The people created an unusual parliament, mixing democracy with the traditional leadership of elders and clans. And Somaliland has largely been blessed with peace.

But the success of Somaliland rests on a shaky foundation. Its greatest accomplishment is undoubtedly peace, though the price is high: Over 70 percent of the national budget (itself only $20 million) goes to maintaining a huge army and police force -- composed of former militia members who have agreed not to fight each other in return for their jobs.

That leaves nothing for education, health or roads. Many Somalis are thus becoming impatient with Egal and his government. Moreover, many in Somaliland distrust Egal, fearing that he may compromise on Somaliland's independence -- and may, as many foreign powers have urged him to do, find a way to reunite with the south.

Egal argues that the answer to Somaliland's problems lies in recognition from other nations, which would open the floodgates for foreign aid and borrowing. As it stands, the United Nations and European Union are the biggest investors in Somaliland's recovery, but the money is "peanuts," as one European aid worker put it.

On a recent trip abroad, Egal and his ministers argued their case with senior officials in Italy, Libya and the United States. They received lots of sympathy but little success. The international community, Somaliland leaders say, has promised a peace dividend for parts of Somalia that find stability. But without recognition, Somaliland has been unable to get money from institutions like the World Bank or the International Monetary Fund.

Both Annan and American officials have discussed a kind of compromise -- a special status, similar to the West Bank or Kosovo, that would allow Somaliland to gain loans and more aid from

For additional analytical, business and investment opportunities information,
please contact Global Investment & Business Center, USA
at (202) 546-2103. Fax: (202) 546-3275. E-mail: rusric@erols.com

outside nations without full recognition. But that seems unlikely to happen as long as a new peace initiative, led by the neighboring nation of Djibouti, still holds promise.

This initiative is different from previous efforts because it is looking for leadership in the south, not among the warlords, but from elders, intellectuals and women's groups as well as businessmen and religious leaders. Still, few experts hold much hope that even after nearly a decade of anarchy Somalia is ready to find peace - or that Somaliland will go along.

And if these talks do not find answers, many experts say, it may finally be time to think seriously about the question of recognizing Somaliland.

FROM COLONIES TO DICTATORSHIP

The Republic of Somaliland is a product of the basic statelessness of Somali culture, a light form of colonialism during British rule, and the absolutely dysfunctional nature of the state-building process in the south in the former Somalia Italiana (Italian- Somaliland). The rest needs no elaboration for anyone familiar with the Somali people and their way of life. The best characterization of the style of Somali politics is given by the title of I. M. Lewis's classic work on Somalia: A Pastoral Democracy. " Pastoral Anarchy" might have been even closer to the mark. The second is less obvious. The British governed their various colonies in every possible way, ranging from heavy-handed direct administration to indirect rule. British Somaliland, like southern Sudan, belongs to the no-government category. Interested only in getting cheap meat to feed its Aden garrison and in keeping the French out, England treated its Somali colony with benign neglect. As a result, at independence in 1960 the territory was economically underdeveloped but blessedly untempered with at the level of native political institutions. The Somali system of peacemaking, vital in a conflictual nomadic society, remained largely intact.

The third factor is even less well known. When the UN was given the task in 1946 of administering Italy's former colonies, no ready solution presented itself. After the Soviet Union volunteered to act as trustee, Washington panicked and quickly brokered what amounted to a series of stopgap arrangements. This resulted in the weak Idris monarchy in Libya, the catastrophic Ethiopian trusteeship over Eritrea, and a renewed UN-sponsored Italian presence in Somalia Italiana.

Given the lack of personnel, most of the Italian administrators who went back to Mogadishu in 1947 and 1948 were the old fascist cadres of the 1920s and 1930s. They had learned little and forgotten nothing. During the 1950s their younger colleagues followed in their footsteps. Thus at independence in 1960 a basically stateless society was saddled with an authoritarian bureaucracy and a centralized state that had done its best to erase the traditional native institutions that it Considered backward. And it is that state the northern Somali people, victims of the "Greater Somalia" dream, decided to join at independence. The state for all of Somalia was not the state of all the Somali people; it was the state of the Italian-trained Southerners.

General Mohamed Siad Barre's military takeover in October 1969 served only to reinforce this trend, especially after he was warmly embraced by the Soviet Union. The Russians gave the regime the best administrative tools for totalitarianism known at the time: a single party, a controlled press, an omnipresent security apparatus, and an impressive military arsenal. After its defeat in the war against Ethiopia in 1978, the Siad Barre regime became even more repressive. In 1981 a small group of exiles from the former British Somaliland created in London the Somali National Movement (SNM), whose official aim was to overthrow the dictatorship. Among them, however, were a number who already thought that divorcing from the southerners might be a less politically correct but more interesting war aim.

For additional analytical, business and investment opportunities information, please contact Global Investment & Business Center, USA at (202) 546-2103. Fax: (202) 546-3275. E-mail: rusric@erols.com

The SNM fought, alone at first but with the financial backing of the Issaq clan diaspora in the Persian Gulf countries. After 1984, President Mengistu Haile Mariam of Ethiopia began to aid the guerrilla movement for geopolitical reasons; the worsening of the war in Eritrea led him to make peace with Somalia in 1988.

The SNM, abandoned by its protector, gambled on an all-out invasion and took over the major cities of northern Somalia immediately after the Ethiopian-Somali peace treaty in May 1988. A terrible repression followed, especially in the city of Hargeisa, which Siad Barre ordered destroyed by a deluge of artillery fire and air raids; 50,000 people died in one month and 350,000 fled to Ethiopia on foot. The war became merciless. Other insurgent fronts appeared in the south, and in January 1991 the regime collapsed, with Siad Barre fleeing the capital in a tank. The result was not peace, but anarchy.

SOMALILAND REBORN

In October 1990, as the war was drawing to an end, the two main southern guerrilla groups, the Somali Patriotic Movement (SNM) and the United Somali Congress (USC), Joined with the SNM. The three agreed to fight the dictatorship lo the end without any negotiation or compromise; they also agreed not to create a new government entity without consulting each other. When Mogadishu fell to the rebels, this compact was betrayed. Mohammed Ali Mahdi, the leader of one of the USC factions, created a government on his own. The USC, a Hawiye-based movement, began ruthlessly killing all non-Hawiye living in Mogadishu in an attempt at "clan-cleansing." The victims were not only civilians belonging to the Darod group of clans that had supported Siad Barre, but also the northern Issaq who had fought him.

For the northerners, who already disliked their southern brethren's behavior during the war, this was the last straw. In February and March 1991, a shir (assembly) was held in Berbera in which the Issaq, the major northern clan family, decided that union with the south was a bad idea; they also decided not to take revenge on the prisoners of war they held but instead to release them to go home.

The Issaq, however, made up only about 70 per-cent of the northern population; the remainder was composed of the four other clan groups in Somaliland, the Issa, Gadabursi, Dolbahante, and Warsangeli.(The Issaaq clan family is made up of the Habr Awal, the Habr Garhadjis and the Habr Ja'alo clans.) These clan groups had mainly sided with Siad Barre, fearing that an SNM victory and eventual Somaliland secession would leave them uncomfortable minorities in an Issaq-dominated country. Prisoners of war from these northern clans were also pardoned and returned to their clan areas. Their worst fears were soon confirmed when a second shin held this time in Burao, proclaimed in May the independence of the former British colony of Somaliland. Abd-er-Rahman Tur, the head of the SNM, automatically became President of the reborn country [(3) We say "reborn" because Somaliland had briefly existed as a separate state between June 27, 1960, when it was granted independence by Great Britain, and June 30, 1960, when it decided to merge with the former Italian Somaliland.

Thus, as civil war raged in the south, both between the guerrillas and the remnants of the former regime and between the various components of the guerrilla movement itself, the north seemed to be making a start in the right direction. This did not last long: in October 1991 it faced its first armed rebellion. The rebellion occurred because the SNM leadership (which had become the leadership of Somaliland) was mainly controlled by the Habr Garhadjis group of clans, a situation that was bound to be challenged by other members of the Issaq family. At the same time, the Habr Awal of the Issa Mussa sub-clan, a majority in the area of Berbera harbor, refused to share port revenues with other clans. In a cash-strapped country they wanted to keep for themselves the only source of cash around: the mono) from customs.

For additional analytical, business and investment opportunities information, please contact Global Investment & Business Center, USA at (202) 546-2103. Fax: (202) 546-3275. E-mail: rusric@erols.com

The dominant Habr Garhadjis, claiming to be acting "in the interest of the state," attacked Berbera. This could have been the start of total clan anarchy like that seen in the south. It was not, for two key reasons. First, unlike the southern guerrilla groups, the SNM was a well-organized, 'old' movement with strong grassroots support. Issaq civilians from all clans roundly condemned the violence by their armed sons. Second, the peace mechanisms that had existed before the war were still available.

In September 1992, after nine months of sporadic fighting, popular pressure finally led to the convening of a large shir in the town of Sheikh. Peace was made between the two main clan actors in the conflict, the Habr Garhadjis and the Issa Mussa subclan. A few months later, rebounding from this success, the country's leaders arranged for what they called a "second national conference" (the first having been the Burao shir that had proclaimed independence). This new gathering lasted almost five months, from January until May 1993. We should perhaps say a few words about the nature of a Somali shir. A shir is, as was noted, an assembly, but it does not have much in common with the Western concept. A shir is a traditional conflict resolution structure of that brings together all the mature men of the clans involved in a conflict. Women, children, and young hot-blooded warriors are excluded. Men lounge under thorn trees during the hot, dry day. They chat and drink tea. They also spend long hours chewing qat, the mildly euphoric drug grown in the Horn of Africa, smoking, greeting each other, delighting in the pleasure of meeting old friends or old foes.

Slowly, everything will come into focus. People will come and go. Small groups will sit apart and hotly debate issues. Poems will be composed and sung. There will be praise and laughter, even insults at times. Small fights may break out, quickly stopped by other shir participants. Old quarrels will resurface, murders of 20 or 30 years ago. Impassioned speeches will be made, some completely irrelevant but highly gratifying to the orators in this beautifully oral culture.

Finally, judgments will be rendered and maag (blood price compensation in cash or camels) will have to be paid, which some will not be able to afford. Friends and relatives will band together to help make recompense.

At the same time, like so many sideshows but in fact essential to the success of the main event, matrimonial arrangements will be decided, camels will be bought a d sold, business deals struck news exchanged, future political alliances brokered. The entire assembly will look like a giant social gathering rather than a political conference.

At some point, things will jell. The various pieces that make up the main issue for which the shir was called will fall into place because a social climate conducive to a solution will have slowly emerged. The result will be a proper peace, a real peace felt from inside a peace that will have nothing in common with the quick-fix conferences in air-conditioned hotels in Addis Ababa organized by the UN in 1993 and 1994. Somalis attended then to get the per diem, go shopping, and return home, scheming on how to get more cash from the stupid GAL (Christians); peace was the last thing on their minds. In such a traditionally violent society as Somalia's, peace is not something to be treated lightly -- and conferences in international hotels are a very light treatment in Somali terms because they do not address the real issues, because they do not fit into an all-inclusive social process, and because they do not involve the necessary people.

In the south, the UN organized conferences with the warlords, which was akin to asking a fox for his opinion on poultry raising. In Somaliland, people still close to the traditional fibers of their culture knew better than to make this mistake. The shir was designed to politely marginalize the warlords by diluting their rapacious energy in the soothing wisdom of older men. This was, however, difficult to achieve. The second national conference in Borama between January and May 1993 had elected a new President, Mohammed Ibrahim Egal. Egal is a Habr Awal of the Issa

Mussa subclan. The Habr Garhadjis did not fully accept their electoral defeat, and after a long interlude of uneasy peace from May 1993 to October 1994 fighting broke out again, this time with the Habr Garhadjis as challengers.

The war lasted about a year. During a major shir in October 1995, an "almost general" peace was made, the Habr Yunis subclan reconciling with the Habr Awal and their Habr Ja'alo allies. Why call it an "almost general" peace? Because the Eidagalley subclan stayed out; many people think that the lack of a proper reconciliation process with this group is the Achilles' heel of the regime. But peace had finally broken out amp there was now room for a half-modern, half-traditional process of institution-making.

PUTTING A GOVERNMENT IN PLACE

The institutionalization of the Somaliland state began in October 1996 with the third national conference. The conference was held in Hargeisa and lasted until March 1997. This time the eastern non-Issaq clans (the Warsangeli and especially the Dolbahante) were deeply involved. The two clan wars of 1992 and 1994-1995 had been fought among the various Issaq clans while their non-Issaq former enemies had remained a minority of bystanders. It was only in late 1996 that the non-Issaq thought it worthwhile to become seriously involved. They realized that the Issaq were serious in their attempts at peacemaking among themselves and wanted to create viable institutions for the self-proclaimed republic.

During its six-month tenure the third national conference wrote a Constitution; created a two-chamber assembly with a parliament and a "Senate of the Clans" based not on individual but on clan representation; organized a supreme court; and formalized the presidential and cabinet roles. Most important, the conference's creations were actually put to work. An assembly was elected. The supreme court also convened and - test of all tests- decided to free Mahmood Abdi Shidde, the irksome chief editor of the main opposition paper, Jumhuriyya, who had been arrested on orders from President Egal.

This largely successful effort immediately paid dividends in the eastern part of the country, where the Dolbahante had previously remained aloof. They now had one of their own, Mohammed Salah Nur "Fagadeh," in the important Ministry of Foreign Affairs, and decided to throw in their lot with "Somaliland" despite some reservations.

FINANCIAL WOES

The country's economy is generally not bad, with cattle exports to Saudi Arabia and the Persian Gulf states steadily expanding. A ban on Cattle exports that was initiated by Saudi Arabia at the prompting of Egypt and the Arab League (both wanting to destroy Somaliland which they consider secessionist) has recently crippled the trade. Since cattle exports are the government's only tax base, a continuation of the ban could cause the infant state to collapse (it is already unable to pay for its large and somewhat unruly clanic army)]. The major problem is the lack of a banking system, serious public accounting, and, consequently, a reliable tax base. Somaliland expects some form of foreign help in correcting these deficiencies. As President Egal said recently in a tongue-in-cheek remark during a press conference in Paris: "At first, we were very bitter about not being recognized by the international community. But when we saw the UNOSOM mess in the south, we thought maybe this was a blessing in disguise. Still, we should not stretch this too far."

Yet the situation has been stretched far. While $4 billion was spent in the southern United States-United Nations adventure without furthering the cause of peace, not a penny went to Somaliland, which has had to pull itself up by its own bootstraps. There is no school system, no reliable health care, only a threadbare road maintenance service, and a small and underpaid civil service. There is also a legacy of the past: an oversize army , nobody knows how to trim that consumes 70 percent of the government's budget.

The army is a financial drain, but without cash to demobilize it, it is also a time bomb. While Somaliland's militiamen are more disciplined than their southern brethren, they are not basically different from them. They are young, restless, and have a history of violence, and they are unable to marry and integrate socially because they do not have the money it would take. With money, or even better, cattle, they could settle down. The cattle are available at a price. But there is no financing. And as long as these young men are kept under arms, there can be no budget surplus.

This is of course a vicious circle the international community could break at a very low cost. President Egal's recent tour of Ethiopia, Eritrea, Italy, and France was a step in the right direction. Ethiopia and Eritrea have exchanged quasi-ambassadorial envoys with Hargeisa. Djibouti has done the same. Paris is prudent, but Rome has offered some budget support and promised to sponsor a motion at the European Parliament in Strasbourg to give Somaliland a "national authority" status somewhat similar to that held by the Palestinian Authority.

On a continent where success stories are rare, Somaliland's modest progress deserves a better response than the international cold shoulder it has received so far. This is especially true because its brand of peacemaking is real, grounded in the cultural traditions of its people and not in the benevolent but ill-informed efforts of foreigners.

**For additional analytical, business and investment opportunities information,
please contact Global Investment & Business Center, USA
at (202) 546-2103. Fax: (202) 546-3275. E-mail: rusric@erols.com**

SOMALIA: CURRENT CONDITIONS AND PROSPECTS FOR A LASTING PEACE[1]

---

[1] Ted Dagne Specialist in African Affairs August 6, 2010 Congressional Research Service
tdagne@crs.loc.gov, 7-7646

In October 2002, the Inter-Governmental Authority for Development (IGAD) launched a peace process designed to end factional fighting in Somalia, led by the government of Kenya. In September 2003, the parties agreed on a Transitional National Charter (TNC). In August 2004, a 275-member Transitional Parliament was inaugurated in Kenya. In October 2004, parliament elected Abdullahi Yusuf Ahmed as the new president of Somalia. In June 2006, the forces of the Islamic Courts Union (ICU) took control of the capital, Mogadishu. During the six-month rule by the ICU, Mogadishu became relatively peaceful, but efforts to bring peace did not lead to a major breakthrough. On December 28, 2006, Ethiopian troops captured Mogadishu with little resistance from the ICU. The Ethiopian intervention led to more chaos and instability in Somalia. In January 2007, the Transitional Federal Government (TFG) came to the capital, Mogadishu, from Baidoa after the ouster of the ICU.

Humanitarian, political, and security conditions continue to deteriorate across south-central Somalia. In the past two years, more than 22,000 civilians have been killed, an estimated 1.1 million people displaced, and 476,000 Somalis have fled to neighboring countries. In 2008, fighting between insurgent groups and Ethiopian-TFG forces intensified, and by late 2008, the TFG had lost control of most of south-central Somalia to insurgent groups. In January 2009, Ethiopian forces completed their withdrawal from Somalia. In late December 2008, President Yusuf resigned from office and left for Yemen.

In June 2008, the TFG and the Alliance for the Re-Liberation of Somalia (ARS), a group dominated by members of the ICU, signed an agreement in Djibouti mediated by then-United Nations Special Envoy Ahmedou Ould-Abdullah. The parties agreed to a cease-fire, the withdrawal of Ethiopian forces, and the deployment of a United Nations peacekeeping force. A number of towns, including the third-largest town, Kismaayo, are now under the control of Al-Shabaab, a group opposed to the TFG. In February 2008, then-Secretary of State Condoleezza Rice designated Al-Shabaab as a Foreign Terrorist Organization. In January 2009, the Somali Parliament elected the leader of the ARS, Sheikh Sharif Sheikh Ahmad, as president. In February 2009, President Ahmad appointed Omar Abdirashid Ali Sharmarke as prime minister.

The Obama Administration is actively engaged in support of the TFG and in an effort to contain terrorist groups in Somalia and the region. The U.S. Congress has passed a number of resolutions and has conducted multiple hearings on Somalia. The United States provided an estimated $403.8 million in assistance to Somalia in FY2009. In FY2010, Somalia is expected to receive an estimated $133.8 million. The Obama Administration has requested $84.9 million for FY2011. The United States also provides material support to TFG forces.

On July 11, 2010, Al-Shabaab carried out multiple suicide bombings in Kampala, Uganda. An estimated 76 people, including one American, were killed and more than 80 injured.

RECENT DEVELOPMENTS

Al-Shabaab's Attacks in Kampala

On July 11, 2010, the Somali terrorist group Al-Shabaab carried out multiple suicide bombings in Kampala, Uganda. An estimated 76 people, including one American, were killed and more than 80 injured. The United Nations, the African Union, and the United States condemned the terrorist attacks. More than 20 suspects are currently in prison in Uganda.

The attacks took place at a rugby club and Ethiopian restaurant while people were watching the final match of the World Cup. The following day, an Al-Shabaab official, Ali Mohamud Rage, stated that "we are sending a message to Uganda and Burundi, if they do not take out their

For additional analytical, business and investment opportunities information,
please contact Global Investment & Business Center, USA
at (202) 546-2103. Fax: (202) 546-3275. E-mail: rusric@erols.com

AMISOM troops from Somalia, blasts will continue and it will happen in Bujumbura (Burundi's capital) too."[1]

The international community condemned the attacks. In an interview with the South African Broadcasting Corporation, President Obama stated that he had called President Museveni to express "the condolences of the American people for this horrific crime that had been committed." The United Nations Security Council in a statement said "members of the Security Council condemn in the strongest terms the terrorist attacks that occurred in Kampala, Uganda, on 11 July 2010, causing numerous deaths and injuries." The African Union also condemned the attacks.

In late July 2010, at the 15th Assembly of the Heads of State and Government of the African Union in Kampala, Uganda, the African Union agreed to send an estimated 4,000 more troops to strengthen AMISOM. Guinea and Djibouti pledged a battalion each. Members of the Inter-Governmental Authority for Development (IGAD) also agreed in early July to send an estimated 2,000 troops.

TFG RESHUFFLE

In mid-May 2010, the Somali Speaker of Parliament resigned after several months of dispute with the Prime Minister and Deputy Prime Minister. A day later, President Sheikh Sharif Sheikh Ahmad fired the Prime Minister. In late May, President Ahmad reinstated the Prime Minister. The reversal of the decision may be temporary or pre-planned to oust the Speaker from office. In late May 2010, the Finance and Deputy Prime Minister, Sheik Sharif Hassan, ran for Speaker and won the support of 217 members of parliament (MPs) out of 550. During the vote, an estimated 388 MPs were present. Four ministers resigned in protest, arguing that this was pre-planned and that Hassan used government resources to bribe members of parliament to support his candidacy. The former Speaker was targeted by the current Speaker and the President because he was pushing for parliament to resume its session in order to question government officials about government activities and responsibilities. The Prime Minister and the Deputy Prime Minster pushed for parliament to remain in recess. In June 2010, the Somali government appointed a new cabinet. The new cabinet includes members of Ahlu Sunna Wal Jamaa, who signed an agreement with the TFG a few months earlier.

THE UNITED STATES AND SOMALIA

The Obama Administration is actively engaged in support of the TFG and in an effort to contain terrorist groups in Somalia and the region. The U.S. Congress has passed a number of resolutions and conducted multiple hearings on Somalia. In early August 2009, Secretary of State Hilary Clinton met with President Sheik Sharif Ahmad of Somalia in Kenya. The Secretary expressed

U.S. support for the TFG. President Sheikh Sharif briefed the Secretary and her delegation about the challenges facing his government and asked for U.S. support. In late September 2009, President Ahmad came to the United States to address the U.N. General Assembly, and visited in Washington to meet with U.S. officials and Somali community members. In late September 2009, he expressed concern that pledges made by some governments to the TFG have not been delivered. He made the point that every time a pledge is made to the TFG, the insurgents also get support from their allies. He asserted that the insurgents get the support faster and the TFG has to wait for months.[2]

U.S. ASSISTANCE TO SOMALIA

For additional analytical, business and investment opportunities information, please contact Global Investment & Business Center, USA at (202) 546-2103. Fax: (202) 546-3275. E-mail: rusric@erols.com

The United States provided an estimated $403.8 million in assistance to Somalia in FY2009. In FY2010, Somalia is expected to receive an estimated $133.8 million. The Obama Administration has requested $84.9 million for FY2011. The United States also provides material support to TFG forces.

Table 1. U.S.Assistance to Somalia

($ in thousands)

FY2009		FY2010	FY2011
Actual		Estimate	Request
Total	403,838	133,820	84,958
Development Assistance			
Economic Support Fund	32,250	28,270	25,818
Global Health and Child Survival-USAID	1,550	1,550	1,550
International Military Education and Training		40	40
International Narcotics Control and Law Enforcement			2,000
Nonproliferation, Antiterrorism, Demining and Related Programs		2,000	2,000
Peacekeeping Operations	246,600	102,000	53,550
Public Law 480 (Food Aid)	123,438		

U.S. CONCERNS

On August 5, 2010, more than a dozen Somali Americans/permanent residents were arrested. Attorney General Eric Holder announced that 14 people are being charged with providing support to Al-Shabaab. Two indictments unsealed in Minnesota states that Amina Farah Ali and Hawo Mohamed Hassan raised funds for Al-Shabaab. The indictment states that 12 money transfers were made in 2008 and 2009. Holder stated at a press conference that "the indictments unsealed today shed further light on a deadly pipeline that has routed funding and fighters to the Al Shabab terror organization from cities across the United States. These arrests and charges should serve as an unmistakable warning to others considering joining terrorist groups like Al Shabab—if you choose this route, you can expect to find yourself in a U.S. jail cell or a casualty on the battlefield in Somalia."

HUMAN RIGHTS AND HUMANITARIAN CONDITIONS

The humanitarian situation in Somalia remains dire, according to United Nations officials and Somali humanitarian workers. The fighting in Mogadishu has added more challenges to already poor conditions on the ground. Targeted attacks on humanitarian groups have made delivery of assistance difficult. The Obama Administration has also suspended assistance in areas controlled by Al Shabaab. An estimated 1.1 million people have been displaced and more than 475,000 have fled to neighboring countries in the past two years. Human rights groups and Somali observers estimate more than 22,000 people have been killed over the past two years. Civilians,

[3] Director of National Intelligence Dennis C. Blair, Annual Threat Assessment of the U.S. Intelligence Community for the Senate Select Committee on Intelligence, February 2, 2010.

humanitarian workers, journalists, and human rights advocates have been the primary targets of the insurgents, TFG, and Ethiopian security forces. According to Amnesty International, "rape, killings and looting have become widespread. Entire neighborhoods have been destroyed." A number of Somali journalists covering the crisis in Somalia have been assassinated by insurgents and security forces over the past 18 months. Dozens of humanitarian and human rights advocates have been killed, injured, or imprisoned. Because of these targeted attacks, many human rights advocates and journalists have fled Somalia to neighboring countries for safety. Somalis working for international NGOs and foreign media have also been attacked by insurgents and TFG/Ethiopian security forces.

AL-SHABAAB AND THE ISLAMIC MOVEMENTS IN SOMALIA

BACKGROUND

The United States, Somalia's neighbors, and some Somali groups have expressed concern over the years about the spread of Islamic fundamentalism in Somalia. In the mid-1990s, Islamic courts began to emerge in parts of the country, especially in the capital of Mogadishu. These courts functioned as local governments and often enforced decisions by using their own militia. Members of the Al Ittihad Al Islami[4] militia reportedly provided the bulk of the security forces for these courts in the 1990s. The absence of central authority in Somalia created an environment conducive to the proliferation of armed factions throughout the country. Somali factions, including the so-called Islamic groups, often go through realignments or simply disappear from the scene. Very little is known about the leadership or organizational structure of these groups.

There have been a number of radical Islamic groups in Somalia whose prominence alternately waxed and waned: Al Ittihad Al Islami (Islamic Union), Al Islah (Reform), Al Tabligh (Conveyers of God's Work). In 1995, a group called Jihad Al Islam, led by Sheikh Abbas bin Omar, emerged in Mogadishu and gave the two main warlords, General Mohammed Farah Aideed and Ali Mahdi, an ultimatum to end their factional fighting. The group claimed at that time that it maintained offices in several countries, including Yemen, Pakistan, Kenya, and Sudan. Some members of this group later formed the Sharia (Islamic law) Implementation Club (SIC) in 1996. SIC's principal objective was to establish Sharia courts throughout the country. Some members of the Mogadishu-based former Transitional National Government (TNG) reportedly were key players in the establishment of these courts. Very little is known about al-Islah, although it is perceived as a group dominated by Hawiye clan businessmen. According to the State Department's 2006 *Country Reports on Terrorism*, "while numerous Islamist groups engaged in a broad range of activities operate inside Somalia, few of these organizations have any known links to terrorist activities. Movements such as Harakat al-Islah (al-Islah), Ahlu Sunna wal Jamaa (ASWJ), and Majma Ulimadda Islaamka ee Soomaaliya (Majma') sought power by political rather than violent means and pursued political action via missionary or charity work."

[4] The 2005 U.S. State Department Country Report on Terrorism described Al Ittihad Al Islami as "a Somali extremist group that was formed in the 1980s and reached its peak in the early 1990s, failed to obtain its objective of establishing a Salafist emirate in Somalia and steadily declined following the downfall of the Siad Barre regime in 1991 and Somalia's subsequent collapse into anarchy. AIAI was not internally cohesive, lacked central leadership, and suffered divisions between factions."

In late September 2001, the Bush Administration added Al Ittihad to a list of terrorism-related entities whose assets were frozen by an Executive Order 13224. Bush Administration officials accused Al Ittihad Al Islami of links with Al Qaeda. None of the groups mentioned above remain active, although some of their leaders are now leaders of groups engaged in terrorist activities in

Somalia. The leader of Hizbul Islam, Sheikh Hassan Aweys, who is on the U.S. terrorist list, was a leader in Al Ittihad Al Islami. In the late 1990s, after a Ethiopia and its Somali allies attacked and crushed Al-Ittihad, a number of its fighters, the current leadership of Al-Shabaab, went to Afghanistan and others went underground.

THE EVOLUTION OF AL-SHABAAB

In 2003, the leadership of Al-Ittihad, including Sheik Ali Warsame, brother in law of Sheik Hassan Aweys and a number of other top leaders, met and later decided to form a new political front. The young members of Al-Ittihad disagreed with the decision of the older leadership in 2003 and decided to form their own movement. These young leaders, some of whom had fought in Afghanistan, met in Laasa aanood, a town in northern Somalia, and later formed a group known then as Harakat Al-Shabaab Al-Mujahedeen, currently known as Al-Shabaab. The current leader of Al-Shabaab, Ahmed Abdi Godane, the late Aden Hashi Ayrow, Ibrahim Haji Jama, Mukhtar Robow, helped form the new movement. The primary objective of this group was irredentism and to establish a "Greater Somalia" under Sharia. But Al-Shabaab was not active and did not control any territory in Somalia until 2007-2008.

The Ethiopian invasion and the ouster of the Courts from power in December 2006 contributed to the emergence of a strong resistance movement. The leadership of the Islamic Courts moved to Eritrea, while the Al-Shabaab secretive leadership slowly took control over the resistance movement. Many Somalis joined the fight against the Ethiopian forces. Some of these volunteers did not know or had only limited knowledge of the intent and objectives of Al-Shabaab. By mid2007, the true leaders of Al-Shabaab emerged and the ties with Al-Qaeda became clear. In February 2008, then Secretary of State Condoleezza Rice designated Al-Shabaab as a Foreign Terrorist Organization and as a Specially Designated Global Terrorist. The TFG was able to win over some Al-Shabaab fighters to join the government side.

THE LEADERSHIP OF AL-SHABAAB

The leaders of Al-Shabaab are not well known, with few exceptions. Some of the key commanders and leaders of Al-Shabaab come from Somaliland. Ahmed Abdi Godane (also known as Abu Zubayr), who is designated by the U.S. as a terrorist and who trained and fought in Afghanistan, is a key commander from Somaliland. Mukhtar Robow (Abu Mansur), who is also designated as a terrorist, is considered one of the key leaders of the Shabaab and a former spokesman, although in recent months he has been marginalized and has been at odds with the other commanders, especially Godane. Robow is now the commander of the Bay and Bakool regions. Another key leader is Ibrahim Haji Jama (al-Afghani), who is on the U.S. terrorism list and also from Somaliland, and reportedly trained and fought in Afghanistan. Other key leaders of Al-Shabaab include Bashir Mohamed Mohamud, Sudi Arable, Fuad Ahmed Khalaf "Shangole," Ali Mohamed Hussein Rage (current Al-Shabaab Spokesman), Ahmed Korgab, and Mohamed Fidow.

FOREIGN FIGHTERS AND AL-SHABAAB

Some observers and security officials estimate there are several hundred foreign fighters in Somalia. U.S. officials have long expressed concern about the presence of known terrorist individuals in Somalia. Some observers contend that Somalia is being used as a transit and hiding place by some of these individuals, including Harun Fazul, the leader of the 1998 and 2002 bombings, Saleh Nabhan, and Talha al-Sudani. Nabhan was killed by U.S. forces in September 2009, and al-Sudani was reportedly killed in Somalia in 2007.

For additional analytical, business and investment opportunities information, please contact Global Investment & Business Center, USA at (202) 546-2103. Fax: (202) 546-3275. E-mail: rusric@erols.com

In May 2009, the U.S. State Department issued a press release confirming the presence of foreign fighters in Mogadishu, while France, the United Nations, and the African Union made similar statements. According to senior security sources in Mogadishu and regional officials, some of the foreign fighters are now commanding both Somali and foreign fighters in Mogadishu and other parts of Somalia. In May 2009, a spokesman of Al-Shabaab admitted that foreign fighters have joined the fighting. According to Sheik Husayn Fidow, "the Muslim people of Somalia have asked for assistance from other Muslim nations worldwide." In response to these well-coordinated attacks, TFG President Sheik Sharif Ahmad stated that his government will respond forcefully.

Some of the top foreign commanders in Al-Shabaab include:

> Fazul Abdullah (also known as Harun Fazul) from Comoros and the mastermind of the 1998 U.S. embassy bombings in Kenya and Tanzania.
> Sheik Mohamed Abu Faid, Saudi national.
> Abu Mansur Al Ameriki, American national.
> Abu Musa Mombasa, Pakistani national.
> Mohamoud Mujajir, Sudanese national.
> Abu Suleiman Al-Banadiri, Somali of Yemeni decent.

AL-SHABAAB AND OTHER SOMALI TERRORIST GROUPS IN SOMALIA

On February 1, 2010, Al-Shabaab and the Ras Kamboni group, led by Hassan Al Turki, reportedly agreed to merge under one name: Al-Shabaab Mujahidin Movement. Both Al-Shabaab and the Ras Kamboni group have been coordinating their attacks against the TFG and working closely with foreign fighters over the past two years. Senior TFG officials consider the merger a reaffirmation of a pre-existing informal alliance between the two groups.[5] The merger is also triggered in part due to defections and the reported illness of Hassan Al-Turki, the leader of Ras Kamboni. Al Turki, an Ethiopian from the Ogaden clan, was designated as a terrorist by the United States in 2004. Another possible reason for the merger is due to the expected major military offensive by TFG forces against Al-Shabaab and its allies. A number of negotiations on merger with Hizbul Islam have failed.

[5] Ted Dagne interviewed President Sheik Sharif Ahmad of Somalia and other senior officials, January 29 and February 1, 2010.

AL-SHABAAB LOSING SUPPORT?

Internal divisions and defections seem to be weakening Al-Shabaab. Two senior Al-Shabaab leaders, Mohamed Faruq and Ali Hassan Gheddi, defected with an estimated 550 fighters to join the TFG. Ahlu Sunna Wal Jamaa, a militia group that was previously opposed to the TFG, has been working closely with the TFG against Al-Shabaab and other anti-government militia groups. Al-Shabaab brutal measures against the civilian population has contributed to a widespread anti-Shabaab sentiments. The December 2009 suicide bombing during a graduation ceremony for medical students at a hotel in Mogadishu further eroded Al-Shabaab's popularity. Al-Shabaab unpopular. The attack reportedly killed 23 people, including three TFG ministers. The suicide bombing was carried out by a Danish citizen of Somali descent. Among the dead and wounded were students, family members, journalists, members of parliament, and faculty members. One of the ministers killed, Ibrahim Addou, was an American citizen and a former faculty member at American University in Washington, DC. Al-Shabaab recruitment among the Somali Diaspora seems to be declining due to increased law enforcement monitoring and also growing anti-Shabaab sentiment, although some foreigners are going to Somalia to join the movement.

HIZBUL ISLAM LEADER SHEIK SHARIF HASSAN AWEYS

In late April 2009, Sheik Sharif Hassan Aweys returned to Mogadishu from Eritrea. Sheik Aweys had remained in Eritrea and formed his own faction after the top leadership of the ARS signed an agreement in Djibouti with other Somali parties, which led to the formation of the current government. ARS-Asmara, under the leadership of Aweys, did not garner significant support, although Aweys intensified his support for the extremist groups inside Somalia. ARS-Asmara leaders were not in full agreement with Aweys and his support for the extremist groups inside Somalia. They provided written documentation to this effect to a visitor in April 2009. These leaders stated that they formed their own organization and would disassociate themselves from Aweys. Sheik Aweys came under intense pressure from some of his supporters to return to Mogadishu, and he also came to the conclusion that he was isolated and losing support in Eritrea. Sheik Aweys seemed confused at times and routinely contradicted himself in an interview in Asmara, Eritrea. When asked if he was prepared to state publicly his support for a peaceful participation in the current political process, Aweys responded positively.

However, when he was asked whether he would denounce terrorism and call for an end to violence against civilians, Aweys stated that since he considers the American interpretation of terrorism as anti-Islam, he "cannot condemn terrorism." Doing so, he asserted, is "denouncing his own religion." Aweys believes that he was placed on the U.S. terrorism list because of his religion and beliefs. When asked if he wished to be removed from the list, Aweys stated that he would not seek to be removed because that would be going against his religion. Sheik Aweys asserted that since there are no major differences among Somalis, if left alone, Somalis will find their own solution. When confronted about his role in support of terrorism and violence in Somalia, he characterized these acts as a struggle against the enemies of Somalia. Upon his return to Mogadishu in late April 2009, Sheik Aweys discovered that the clan elders and militia who supported him in the past now wanted him to work with the government and end the violence. The militia group he helped create, Hizbul Islam, also was split and some have joined Al-Shabaab. Some of the top leaders of the Al-Shabaab also want him to declare an alliance with Osama Bin Laden and cut his ties with Eritrea, measures he has resisted thus far.

PEACEKEEPING MISSION: BACKGROUND

On December 6, 2006, the United Nations Security Council passed Resolution 1725, "reiterating its commitment to a comprehensive and lasting settlement of the situation in Somalia through the Transitional Federal Charter, and stressing the importance of broad-based and representative institutions and of an inclusive political process, as envisaged in the Transitional Federal Charter." U. N. Security Council Resolution 1725 further called for "all Member States, in particular those in the region, to refrain from any action in contravention of the arms embargo and related measures, and should take all actions necessary to prevent such contravention." Moreover, the Security Council expressed its "willingness to engage with all parties in Somalia who are committed to achieving a political settlement through peaceful and inclusive dialogue, including the Union of Islamic Courts." The Security Council, acting under Chapter VII of the Charter of the United Nations, authorized the Inter-Governmental Authority for Development (IGAD) and the African Union to establish "a protection and training mission in Somalia." U. N. Security Council Resolution 1725 specifically stated that countries bordering Somalia "would not deploy troops to Somalia."

On February 20, 2007, the U.N. Security Council passed resolution 1744 reiterating its support for the Transitional Federal Institutions and authorizing the African Union to establish a mission in Somalia. Resolution 1744 calls for "a national reconciliation congress involving all stakeholders, including political leaders, clan leaders, religious leaders, and representatives of civil society."

For additional analytical, business and investment opportunities information, please contact Global Investment & Business Center, USA at (202) 546-2103. Fax: (202) 546-3275. E-mail: rusric@erols.com

The resolution, while it welcomed the withdrawal of Ethiopian troops from Somalia, did not include a provision that restricts the participation of Somalia's immediate neighbors in the peacekeeping operation as resolution 1725 did.

The Security Council unanimously adopted Resolution 1772 on August 20, 2007, authorizing the African Union to maintain its operation in Somalia for an additional six months. The resolution also authorized peacekeeping forces on the ground to take all necessary measures to support and protect those involved in the Reconciliation Congress. Finally, Resolution 1772 called on all Member States, especially those in close proximity to Somalia, to comply with the arms embargo that was established in 1992 by Resolution 733.

THE AFRICAN UNION MISSION IN SOMALIA (AMISOM)

At the African Union Summit in late January 2007, several African countries pledged to contribute troops for a peacekeeping mission in Somalia. Ghana, Nigeria, Burundi, Uganda, and Malawi have pledged troops. The African Union is facing difficulties in convincing governments to make serious troop contributions to the mission. Observers contend that without a negotiated settlement with groups still outside the TFG, it will be difficult to maintain peace and stability in Somalia. In late July 2010, at the 15th Assembly of the Heads of State and Government of the African Union in Kampala, Uganda, the African Union agreed to send an estimated 4,000 more troops to strengthen AMISOM. Guinea and Djibouti pledged a battalion each. Members of the Inter-Governmental Authority for Development (IGAD) also agreed in early July to send an estimated 2,000 troops. As of July 2010, there were an estimated 6,000 AMISOM peacekeeping personnel in Somalia. As of July 2010, an estimated 26 Ugandan peacekeepers and 29 peacekeepers from Burundi have been killed.

The African Union peacekeeping mission is mandated to:

> support dialogue and reconciliation in Somalia, working with all stakeholders;
> provide, as appropriate, protection to the TFIs and their key infrastructure, to enable them carry out their functions;
> assist in the implementation of the National Security and Stabilization Plan of Somalia, particularly the effective reestablishment and training of all inclusive Somali security forces, bearing in mind the programs already being implemented by some of Somalia's bilateral and multilateral partners;
> provide, within capabilities and as appropriate, technical and other support to the disarmament and stabilization efforts;
> monitor, in areas of deployment of its forces, the security situation;
> facilitate, as may be required and within capabilities, humanitarian operations, including the repatriation and reintegration of refugees and the resettlement of IDPs; and
> protect its personnel, installations and equipment, including the right of selfdefense.[6]

POLITICAL DEVELOPMENTS: BACKGROUND

In February 2009, President Ahmad appointed Omar Abdirashid Ali Sharmarke as prime minister. Sharmarke is the son of the former President of Somalia, who was killed during the 1969 military coup. Sharmarke received overwhelming support in the Transitional Parliament. The appointment of Sharmarke provided important representation in the new government for the Darod clan. Sharmarke belongs to the same sub-clan, the Majertain, as former president Yusuf. Moreover, the Transitional Parliament was expanded in 2008 and now includes an additional 149 members from the main opposition group, the ARS. Parliament also extended the mandate of the Transitional Federal Government by another two years until 2011. Some observers expressed

For additional analytical, business and investment opportunities information, please contact Global Investment & Business Center, USA at (202) 546-2103. Fax: (202) 546-3275. E-mail: rusric@erols.com

concern about the size of the new parliament, while others argued that it was a necessary measure to make the parliament more inclusive.

In late December 2008, President Yusuf resigned from office and left for Yemen. President Yusuf was opposed to the Djibouti peace process and repeatedly clashed with his prime minister. In January 2009, the Somali Transitional Parliament elected the leader of the ARS, Sheikh Sharif Sheikh Ahmad as president. President Ahmad is seen by many Somalis as a leader with the best chance of bringing peace and stability to Somalia and as someone who can bring those elements outside the peace process to join the new government. In January 2009, President Ahmad went to Ethiopia and took part in the African Union (AU) summit, where he was welcomed by member states. In 2006, Ethiopian forces attacked and forced out Ahmad's Islamic Courts Union from power. However, President Ahmad was warmly welcomed by Ethiopian authorities during the AU summit in Ethiopia.

Humanitarian and security conditions continue to deteriorate in south-central Somalia, despite some political progress and a recent peace agreement between the Somali Transitional Federal Government (TFG) and the Alliance for the Re-Liberation of Somalia (ARS), a group formed by former members of the Islamic Courts Union (ICU) and Somalis from different backgrounds. The ouster from power of the ICU by Ethiopian forces in December 2006 created a security vacuum that was soon occupied by the more radical elements of the ICU's military factions. The moderate leadership of the ICU became marginalized, splintered, and weakened over the past year. U.S., TFG, and Ethiopian officials labeled the entire leadership of the ICU as extremist and terrorist in 2006. Eighteen months later, however, the same governments supported the inclusion of some former ICU members in a U.N.-led peace process.

In May-June, 2008, TFG and ARS officials met in Djibouti under the auspices of the United Nations. Officials from the United States, Europe, the African Union, the Arab League, the Organization of Islamic Conference, and regional governments took part as observers during the talks in Djibouti. The parties agreed on a wide range of issues, including cessation of hostilities and a commitment to find a durable peace agreement.[7] The parties agreed to support the deployment of a United Nations peacekeeping force and the phased withdrawal of Ethiopian forces from Somalia. The agreement, however, links the withdrawal of Ethiopian forces with the deployment of a U.N. peacekeeping force, although Ethiopian forces have already withdrawn from some areas. In addition, in November 2008, the Ethiopian government announced that its forces would pull out of Somalia by the end of 2008. In January 2009, Ethiopian forces completed their withdrawal from Somalia. The parties also agreed to provide unhindered humanitarian access to civilians in need and to establish a Joint Security Committee to ensure implementation of security arrangements and create an interim joint security force.[8] The parties established a High Level Committee, chaired by the United Nations, to deal with political, justice, and governance issues.

The Djibouti agreement is complicated and has repeatedly been undermined by infighting within the TFG, insecurity, the growing influence of insurgent groups, and limited support by the international community. The TFG forces, under the leadership of President Yusuf, were weak, ineffective, and seriously debilitated by defections. In 2008-2009, an estimated 40% of the police force, trained by the United Nations, left the force due to lack of payment. Some donor governments have withheld funds pledged to the TFG due to lack of transparency and human rights abuses. Infighting within the TFG, especially between then-Prime Minister Nur Adde and then-President Yusuf, weakened the TFG. In November 2007, Prime Minister Nur Adde replaced Ali M. Ghedi, a man seen by many Somalis as ineffective and highly partisan.

Prime Minister Nur Adde, who was seen by many Somalis and Somali observers as a key actor to bridge the gap between the TFG and the opposition, often clashed with President Yusuf. In

For additional analytical, business and investment opportunities information, please contact Global Investment & Business Center, USA at (202) 546-2103. Fax: (202) 546-3275. E-mail: rusric@erols.com

July 2008, the prime minister dismissed the mayor of Mogadishu and governor of Benadir region, Mohamed Dheere, because of mismanagement of funds. In protest, 10 pro-Yusuf ministers resigned, triggering a crisis within the TFG. In August 2008, the prime minister and the president met in Ethiopia, and later reached an agreement on a number of issues. In Mid-December 2008, President Yusuf fired Prime Minister Nur and named Mohamed Mohamud Guled as the new prime minister. The prime minister rejected his dismissal, arguing that President Yusuf lacked the legal authority to dismiss him and that only Parliament has the power to dismiss the prime minister. On December 15, 2008, a majority of the Somali Parliament voted in support of Prime Minister Nur Adde. The government of Kenya imposed a travel ban and asset freeze against President Yusuf.

[7] CRS interview with senior TFG officials and members of the Somali opposition in Kenya, May and August 2008. [8] United Nations Political Office for Somalia (UNPOS), August 2008.

SECURITY CONDITIONS: BACKGROUND

In late September 2009, government forces seized control of Beledweyne from Hizbul Islam. Beledweyne, a town near the Ethiopian border, has changed hands several times in the past six months. Meanwhile, attacks against government forces and African Union peacekeeping troops in Mogadishu intensified in September. An estimated 21 people, including 17 African Union peacekeepers, were killed in a suicide attack in late September 2009. The Deputy Force Commander was one of the victims in the attack. Al-Shabaab used two stolen United Nations trucks to carry out the attack against the AMISOM headquarters in Mogadishu. Two of the suicide bombers are believed to be Somali-Americans.

In mid-September 2009, U.S. forces killed Saleh Ali Saleh Nabhan, a senior al-Qaeda member suspected of attacks against the U.S. embassies in Kenya and Tanzania and the leader of the terrorist attack against the Paradise Hotel in Mombasa, Kenya, in 2002. Several other foreign fighters were killed along with Nabhan. The killing of Nabhan has reportedly shaken the leadership of Al-Shabaab, according to regional and Somali security sources. Of the three most wanted al-Qaeda leaders in East Africa, the only one left is the leader of the group and the mastermind of the U.S. embassy bombings: Haroon Fazul. The killing of Nabhan is likely to weaken the link between the Shabaab and al-Qaeda, and it may take some time for al-Qaeda to replace Nabhan with someone familiar with that region. Earlier that year, Al-Shabaab and Hizbul Islam made important gains in Mogadishu and other parts of Somalia, in large part due to defections to the insurgency and lack of resources by the TFG. The TFG forces later regrouped, and by mid-June managed to regain some lost ground in Mogadishu.

In early May 2009, Somali extremist groups backed by foreign fighters launched a major offensive against the TFG and AMISOM. More than 300 people were killed during that period and many more wounded. The primary objective of this offensive is to oust the TFG from power and force AMISOM to leave Somalia. Several Al-Shabaab factions, Hizbul al-Islam, and foreign fighters have been engaged in a series of battles against government forces. Al-Shabaab also reportedly assassinated a number of senior TFG officials, including the police chief and the Minister of Interior. Senior Somali officials, African Union sources, and other regional officials estimate that more than 400 foreign fighters from Afghanistan, Yemen, Pakistan, the United States, Canada, United Kingdom, Kenya, and Saudi Arabia have been engaged in support of the Al-Shabaab forces. More than 290 fighters reportedly entered Mogadishu in early May, and an estimated 50 fighters were in Mogadishu for much longer. Some of these fighters have been killed in battles in Mogadishu, according to senior officials in Mogadishu. The insurgents receive support from outside and from some Somali businessmen, who are unhappy with the TFG leadership. Over the years, some Somali businessmen backed one faction or another to protect business or clan interests.

As of January 2010, insurgent groups were in control of most of south-central Somalia, including the third-largest town, Kismaayo. TFG forces, as well as the African Union Mission to Somalia (AMISOM), do not have control or presence outside Baidoa and Mogadishu. Even in the case of Mogadishu, the insurgents control some parts of Mogadishu and some of their forces are active outside the capital. The Al-Shabaab forces also have expanded their military operations to other parts of Somalia and routinely assassinate opponents and government officials.

In late October 2008, simultaneous and well-coordinated suicide attacks in Puntland and Somaliland reportedly killed an estimated 20 people and injured many more. The targets of the attacks were the Ethiopian Consulate, the office of the United Nations Development Program (UNDP), and a security office close to the Presidential Palace. The suicide mission was reportedly carried out by members of the Al-Shabaab, although no organization claimed credit for the attacks. One of the suicide bombers was an American-Somali from Minneapolis who, according to press reports, left the U.S. to take part in the suicide attacks. Reportedly, over a dozen Somali youth from Minneapolis have left the United States, and some community leaders believe they went to Somalia to join the insurgency. There is no clear evidence of how many and for what purpose these Somalis left Minneapolis.[9] Over the past decade, many Somalis have returned to Somalia to work as journalists, humanitarian workers, and teachers. A number of these Somalis have been killed in the past two years by insurgents and security forces.

The TFG remains vulnerable and its ability to defeat the insurgents depends on resources, including Armored Personnel Carriers (APCs), mobility, and a well-organized and sustainable military operation. The presence of the African Union force has helped prevent the takeover of Mogadishu by the insurgents. But the African Union force does not have a Chapter 7 mandate, requiring the force to be on the defensive rather than take offensive measures against the insurgents. The African Union force has used its long-range artilleries against the insurgents. These measures have weakened and forced the insurgents to remain outside the range of these weapons. But the most serious challenge facing the TFG forces and those of the AU is that the insurgents are highly decentralized and move in small units, and operate independently of one another.

SOMALI PIRACY IN THE HORN OF AFRICA[10]

OVERVIEW

Somali pirates have intensified their attacks in the Gulf of Aden, carrying out attacks on over 111 commercial ships, and successfully hijacked an estimated 40 ships in 2008. In 2009, there were 217 incidents, with 47 vessels hijacked. In 2009, the Ukrainian-owned ship, *MV Faina*, which was carrying 33 T-72 tanks and other weapons and a Japanese-owned ship, *MV Chemstar*, were released. In February 2010, a Libyan-owned cargo ship, reportedly flying a North Korean flag, was hijacked by Somali pirates. The *MV Rim* was hijacked outside the internationally recommended transit corridor in the Gulf of Aden. The pirates have reportedly earned more than $120 million in ransom payments, and have released a number of ships and crew members. The United States, Russia, India, and several other countries have deployed warships to tackle piracy in the Horn of Africa region. In February 2009, the U.S. Navy arrested 16 suspected Somali pirates. In December 2008, the Indian Navy reportedly arrested 23 Somali and Yemeni pirates. Moreover, the Russian Navy also arrested a number of suspected Somali pirates. According to the International Maritime Bureau (IMB), piracy in 2009 surpassed that of 2008. In 2010, there were more than 32 attacks, seven successful, by Somali pirates.

In January 2009, the United States and Britain signed legal agreements with the Government of Kenya to extradite suspected pirates to be prosecuted in Kenya. An estimated 90 pirates have been detained. Some insurgent leaders have warned the pirates to end the piracy and to release crew members and ships currently controlled by the pirates. On December 16, 2008, the United Nations Security Council passed a resolution authorizing the use of "all necessary measures" by foreign military forces to stop piracy in Somalia. The resolution authorizes military operations inside Somalia and in its airspace for one year, with the consent of the TFG.

WHO ARE THE PIRATES?

The number of Somali pirates is unknown. While there are more pirates now than in previous years, the pirates do not seem to have a unified organization with a clear command structure. Many of these pirates are reportedly fishermen and former militia members of the Somali warlords. The pirates primarily come from the Puntland region of Somalia and are members of different clans. Some press reports have suggested that the pirates are being controlled and directed by the Islamic insurgents in south-central Somalia. There is no evidence, however, to support this assertion, and during the six months the ICU was in power, the leaders took measures to end piracy and other criminal activities. In November 2008, Sheik Hassan Aweys called on the pirates to end their criminal activities, and other insurgent leaders threatened to take military action against the pirates. The pirates, however, are not operating alone, according to a number of Somali and regional sources. Some Somali businessmen and officials in Puntland are reportedly behind the piracy. The pirates are reportedly receiving valuable information about the types of ships, cargo, and timing from Somalis in the Persian Gulf.[11] They also possess sophisticated technology, including Global Position Systems (GPS), Automatic Identification System (AIS), and satellite phones.

THE VIEWS FROM SOMALIA

Some Somalis view the piracy crisis as a foreign problem with little impact on their daily life. Some argue that the piracy problem will continue as long as the ship owners are willing to pay the pirates ransom. In the face of difficult economic conditions and a growing humanitarian crisis, many Somalis resent the fact that the piracy problem has received a great deal of international attention. Some Somali community leaders contend that some Somalis get involved in criminal activities in order to survive, while many others have made these kinds of criminal activities a lifetime profession. Since the collapse of the Siad Barre government in 1991, Somalis have been principal victims of criminals. Somalis had to pay "taxes" to warlords in order to pass from one neighborhood to another. Humanitarian assistance convoys are routinely targeted by criminal elements, forcing humanitarian agencies to hire gunmen for protection. Many Somalis contend that in the absence of a better alternative, they have come to accept life with all the difficulties they face daily.[12]

Some Somalis argue that the fishermen have become pirates because their way of life was destroyed by illegal fishing and toxic waste dumping that has been ignored by foreign governments. In 2005, the United Nations Environment Program (UNEP) released a report documenting the damages resulting from toxic waste dumping on Somalia's shores. According to a UNEP spokesman, "there's uranium radioactive waste, there's lead, there's heavy metals like cadmium and mercury, there's industrial waste, and there's hospital wastes, chemical wastes, you name it." According to the report, the primary reason for toxic dumping in Somalia is cost. The report states that it costs $2.5 per ton to dump toxic waste in Africa compared to $250 per ton to dump waste in Europe.[13] In July 2008, then-United Nations Special Envoy Ould-Abdallah stated that "because there is no (effective) government, there is so much irregular fishing from European and Asian countries." The Special Envoy argued that it is important to tackle these illegal activities by some countries, and not to solely focus on the problem of piracy.[14]

For additional analytical, business and investment opportunities information, please contact Global Investment & Business Center, USA at (202) 546-2103. Fax: (202) 546-3275. E-mail: rusric@erols.com

POLICY OPTIONS TO ADDRESS PIRACY

The United Nations Security Council has passed resolutions on piracy in the Horn of Africa. Another way that the international community has responded to the threat of piracy is by deploying warships to the Gulf of Aden. Since the deployment of these warships to the region, however, the number of hijacked ships has increased. Somali community leaders and regional analysts argue that the groups most capable and best positioned to handle the piracy problem are the Islamic insurgents and the clan elders. The Islamic Courts dealt with this problem effectively when they were in power, according to senior leaders of the Islamic Courts and independent observers. The Islamic insurgents claim that they are opposed to these kinds of criminal activities for religious reasons. The Islamic leadership sees the piracy problem as a source of concern because they fear that they could be erroneously or deliberately linked to the piracy phenomenon and become targets of punitive action by the international community. Another option is to provide quick and robust economic incentives to lure the unemployed away from piracy and other criminal activities.

POLICY OPTIONS IN DEALING WITH POLITICAL AND SECURITY PROBLEMS

Some suggest that the international community may consider engagement with the Islamic insurgents and clan elders as a means to resolve the political and security problems facing Somalia. According to some observers, it is pivotal to strengthen the moderate elements of the Islamic movements discretely. Most observers believe that the Al-Shabaab can only be contained by another Islamic movement supported by clan elders. Some of the most influential leaders in the Al-Shabaab are on the U.N. and U.S. Terrorism Lists. Some observers argue that removing some of these individuals from these lists in exchange for some concessions, including an end to the insurgency and acceptance of a negotiated settlement, should be considered as an option. One of the facilitators of the Djibouti talks was a Somali man on a U.N. Terrorism List. According to

U.N. officials, that man is no longer on that List.

Some of the leaders in the Al-Shabaab seem determined to continue their military campaign and are not inclined to participate in negotiations. According to some experts, targeted measures, including sanctions and assassination of the most extreme elements of the Al-Shabaab, could pave the way for other moderate leaders to emerge. However, others believe that this option is likely to backfire in the short term and increase anti-Western violence. Another option is to refer some of these individuals to the International Criminal Court (ICC) for war crimes.

The most effective way of containing the extremists, most observers contend, is to look for a Somali-led solution, both political and military. The TFG, Islamic Courts, Somaliland, Puntland, and other moderate Somali forces could form a coalition to contain the advances of the most extreme elements of the Al-Shabaab politically and militarily. Such a coalition is likely to get more support of the Somali population rather than a peacekeeping force. The coalition can be assisted by neighboring countries. A Somali-led initiative would take away one of the most powerful justifications used by the Al-Shabaab to wage war, the presence of foreign forces. A unified regional approach is pivotal, however. Most believe that Eritrea has leverage over some of the influential Islamic leaders, some of whom are in Eritrea.

BACKGROUND: 2006-2008

On December 24, 2006, Ethiopian and TFG forces launched a military campaign against the forces of the ICU, a group that took over power in Mogadishu in June 2006. On December 28, 2006 Ethiopian troops captured Mogadishu with little resistance from the ICU. The ICU leadership decided a day before the Mogadishu attack to leave the city in order to avoid bloodshed and the destruction of Mogadishu, according to a senior official of the ICU.[15] On January 1, 2007, the ICU lost its last stronghold, Kismaayo, after its forces withdrew to an area near the Kenyan border, although most of its fighters and leaders either simply melted into society throughout Somalia or fled to neighboring countries. Some of the top leaders of the ICU are in Yemen, Djibouti, Kenya, and Somalia.[16] In late January, the Chairman of the Executive Committee of the Somali Council of Islamic Courts (SCIC), formerly known as ICU, Sharif Sheik Ahmed, traveled to Kenya. On January 24, 2007, the U.S. Ambassador to Kenya, Michael Ranneberger, reportedly met with Sheik Ahmed. Other leaders of the Courts have also been approached by U.S. officials as part of a new strategy to reach out to Court officials and others to participate in proposed negotiations among Somali groups and the TFG.

The Ethiopian military intervention, while it has accomplished its military objective of ousting the Courts from Mogadishu and other areas the Courts controlled, was criticized by governments and regional organizations. The African Union, the European Commission, the Arab League, and others have called for the deployment of a United Nations peacekeeping force. Ethiopian officials argued that their military action was justified because the Islamic Courts posed a serious threat to Ethiopia and regional stability, and because the Islamic Courts is an extremist, Jihadist group. Ethiopian and U.S. officials also have accused the Courts of being influenced or tied to well-known terrorist individuals and Al Qaeda. Islamic Courts officials have repeatedly rejected these allegations and on a number of occasions have offered to work with U.S. officials, according to one senior Courts official. Allegations about the presence of the three suspects involved in the bombings of the U.S. embassies in Tanzania and Kenya in 1998 were made on many occasions over the years. However, the Islamic Courts did not exist as an organized group when these allegations were made. Those in charge of Mogadishu and other areas in southern Somalia were the warlords who were and in some cases still are ministers in the current Transitional Federal Government.

On January 8, 2007, the U.S. Air Force, using AC-130 gun ships, attacked several locations in southern Somalia, reportedly to kill the three terror suspects in the 1998 U.S. embassy bombings

[15] Author interview with senior ICU official in late December 2006. [16] Author interview with senior ICU official and regional sources in the Horn of Africa.

in Kenya and Tanzania. Reportedly, the United States launched another attack the following day, although U.S. officials deny any further attacks. The British humanitarian group, Oxfam, stated in a press release that an estimated 70 people were killed in the bombings and vital water resources were destroyed in Afmadow district. A number of governments criticized the U.S. attacks, including officials in Europe and the government of Djibouti, where U.S. forces are currently stationed. Djiboutian Foreign Minister Mahmoud Ali Yusuf told the BBC that the raid was counterproductive to achieving peace. He also stated that his government had not been informed about the air strikes. According to a *New York Times* article, the United States actively coordinated with Ethiopian forces in targeting suspected terrorists and Islamic Union forces.[17]

U.S. Special Operations troops from Task Force 88 were reportedly deployed to Ethiopia and entered Somalia. Moreover, the United States reportedly shared intelligence with the Ethiopian

For additional analytical, business and investment opportunities information, please contact Global Investment & Business Center, USA at (202) 546-2103. Fax: (202) 546-3275. E-mail: rusric@erols.com

military and used an airstrip in Eastern Ethiopia to launch attacks inside Somalia. A senior Ethiopian government official denied that there was any coordination with U.S. forces.

During the occupation, Ethiopian troops came under attack, and a number of Ethiopian soldiers were killed by snipers or in ambushes. Some Somalis and human rights advocates are concerned over what some people refer to as a witch hunt by TFG and Ethiopian security forces. Ethiopian and TFG security forces reportedly went house to house to arrest Oromos (an Ethiopian ethnic group), supporters of the Islamic Courts, and members of the TFG considered not supportive of the new Somali government and the Ethiopian intervention. The government of Kenya deported dozens of Somalis and other nationals to TFG officials and Ethiopian security forces, according to Kenyan sources. In one particular case, Kenyan officials reportedly blindfolded and handcuffed 30 individuals and returned them to Mogadishu, where these detainees were taken by Ethiopian and TFG security personnel to unknown locations, according to Somali sources and government officials in the region. A number of Kenyan Muslims who were in Ethiopian detention were released in 2008.

On January 17, 2007, the Transitional Federal Parliament ousted the Speaker of Parliament, Sharif Hassan Sheik Adan, from his position. The former Speaker, who has been a vocal critic of the Ethiopian intervention and the U.S. air strike, has a strong following in Mogadishu and was active in reaching out and engaging the Islamic Courts officials when they had control over Mogadishu. Then U.S. Assistant Secretary of State for Africa Jendayi Fraser stated in mid-January 2007 that "the no-confidence motion brought against the Parliament Speaker is likely to have a negative impact on this process of dialogue."[18] In late January, the TFG elected Sheikh Adan Mohamed Nur Madobe, a former warlord and an ally of President Abdullahi Yusuf, as Speaker of Parliament.

THE ISLAMIC COURTS UNION: BACKGROUND

In early 2006, factional violence in Mogadishu once again erupted, killing hundreds of civilians and displacing many more people. The surge in violence was between militia loyal to the Islamic Courts and a self-proclaimed anti-terrorism coalition backed by powerful local warlords. The fighting in Mogadishu erupted when the forces loyal to a well-known warlord and then Minister of National Security of the TFG, Mohamed Qanyare, attacked one of the Courts. The fighting received unusual attention in Somalia and in the region due, in large part, to reports that the warlords were backed by the United States government. The Bush Administration acknowledged that Washington was assisting "responsible individuals" to help bring stability and fight terrorism in Somalia. Then-Assistant Secretary of State for Africa, Jendayi Fraser reportedly stated that the United States "will work with those elements that will help us to root out Al Qaeda and prevent Somalia becoming a safe haven for terrorists."[19] In late June 2006, Fraser stated that the United States has three major policy goals in Somalia: counter-terrorism efforts, creation of an effective government, and responding to the humanitarian needs of the Somali people.

On February 18, 2006, the Alliance for the Restoration of Peace and Counter-Terrorism (ARPCT) was created, allegedly to fight terrorism. Very little is known about ARPCT, although the founders of the Alliance are known warlords who contributed to numerous armed clashes and instability in Somalia over the past decade. Members of the Alliance reportedly include Bashir Rage, Mohammed Qanyare Afrah, Muse Sudi Yalahow, Omar Finnish, and Abdirashid Shire Ilqyete. These actors were seen by many Somali groups as major obstacles to the creation of central authority in Mogadishu, as agreed to by all major Somali groups under the IGAD peace agreement in 2004. In early June 2006, Prime Minister Ali Mohamed Gedi dismissed four ministers from the Transitional Federal Government belonging to ARPCT.

These ministers include Mohamed Qanyare (National Security Minister), Musa Sudi Yalahow (Commerce Minister), Issa Botan Alin (Rehabilitation Minister), and Omar Finnish (Minister for Religious Affairs). The warlords were dismissed because they reportedly ignored calls by Prime Minister Ghedi's government to stop the fighting in Mogadishu. The Islamic Courts leaders argued then that the TFG did nothing to challenge these warlords and kept them in senior positions in the TFG until the Islamic Courts defeated the warlords in Mogadishu. In late July 2006, members of the TFG parliament complained that the U.S. government bypassed the TFG and provided support to the warlords, the same warlords who obstructed peace in Somalia. A member of the TFG parliament told a U.S. Congressional delegation in August 2006 that "you cannot fight terrorism by supporting warlords."[20]

In early June 2006, the forces of the Islamic Courts captured Mogadishu, forcing ARPCT militia to flee the capital. The chairman of the Islamic Courts, Sharif Shaykh Ahmed, stated that his group would negotiate with the TFG. In response to accusations that the Islamic Courts Union was associated with or had harbored international terrorist elements, Shaykh Ahmed stated that "we are not terrorists and we will not allow anyone to hijack the capital. We have said hundreds of times that America's talk of terrorism in Somalia is fabricated and serves suspicious political purposes."[21]

The forces of the Islamic Courts Union strengthened and expanded areas under their control after the defeat of the warlords in Mogadishu. The Islamic Courts forces captured the towns of Jowhar and Beledweyne in mid-June 2006. For the first time in years, Mogadishu became relatively peaceful, and the Islamic Courts received support from the population in areas it controlled. The level of support enjoyed by the Islamic Courts, however, is difficult to measure, although the group had constituencies from multiple sub-clans and had broad support among Somali women. According to Somali sources in Mogadishu and Islamic Courts officials, the people provided crucial support by feeding their forces and working with Islamic Courts officials in bringing peace and stability. During the Mogadishu fighting, women supporters of ICU played important roles. Since the Islamic Courts largely functioned as providers of social services, the Courts did not maintain a large fighting force. The warlords maintained a robust force in different parts of Mogadishu, with heavy weapons and "technicals" (machine-guns mounted on pickup trucks). The Islamic Courts group had only four technicals when the fighting erupted with Qanyare and other warlords, according to a senior Courts official. The ICU success in Mogadishu effectively led to the collapse of the ARPCT and forced the warlords to flee.

Negotiations between the Transitional Federal Government and the Islamic Courts in Sudan did not lead to a major breakthrough, although the talks ended speculation that the Islamic Courts rejected negotiations. The Islamic Courts leaders stated that they would work with the Baidoabased transitional government, although disagreement on key issues remained. In June 2006, the transitional parliament voted in favor of a foreign peacekeeping force. But this move was rejected by some Islamic Courts leaders as being unnecessary and counter-productive. Earlier, in 2005, the African Union had approved a proposal for Uganda and Sudan to deploy a peacekeeping force to Somalia under the auspices of the IGAD. The deployment did not take place in large part because of the refusal of the United Nations Security Council to remove a United Nations arms embargo on Somalia. The Bush Administration did not support the lifting of the arms embargo, although the United Nations Security Council did provide the necessary exemption in December 2006.

In mid-June 2007, an International Somalia Contact Group, consisting of the United States, Norway, United Kingdom, Sweden, Italy, Tanzania, and the European Union, was formed and met to discuss the unfolding Somalia crisis. The United Nations, the African Union, the Arab League, and IGAD were also invited as observers. The Contact Group did not invite Somalia's immediate neighbors, in part due to Somali opposition and international concern that these countries are engaged in activities in support of or against some groups in Somalia. In a press release after its first meeting, the Contact Group stated that "the goal of the International Contact Group will be to encourage positive political developments and engagement with actors inside Somali to support the implementation of the Transitional Federal Charter and Institutions. The Contact Group will seek to support efforts, within the framework of the Transitional Federal Institutions, to address the humanitarian needs of the Somali people, establish effective governance and stability, and address the international community's concern regarding terrorism." Meanwhile, in early January 2007, the International Contact Group on Somalia issued another communiqué strongly urging that it is "essential that an inclusive process of political dialogue and reconciliation embracing representative clan, religious, business, civil society, women's, and other political groups who reject violence and extremism be launched without delay."

The Islamic Courts, while well received by the people in the areas the Courts controlled, received negative press coverage, especially in the West. The Courts' activities were often characterized as extremist and jihadist. The ICU was accused of shutting down cinemas and prohibiting women from working. Some of these measures were taken by the Courts, although for reasons other than the Courts' alleged jihadist and extremist ideology. For example, movies were banned in the morning in response to requests from parents because Somali children were going to movies in the morning instead of school.[22] The ban on television did not take place, except for restrictions on watching soccer games late at night, according to Islamic Courts officials and Somali residents in Mogadishu. This measure was reportedly taken because of disturbances and fighting late at night. There is no evidence to support the allegation that women were prohibited from working. Islamic Courts officials point out that in the short time they were in power, they did more than restore law and order. Properties taken by warlords were reportedly returned to the rightful owners. For example, the family of President Yusuf reportedly returned to Mogadishu after almost 16 years when the Courts restored order in the capital, according to an Islamic Courts official. Most important, they argue, they gave hope to the people of Somalia that they can live in peace after more than a decade of violence.

THE TOP LEADERS OF THE COURTS: BACKGROUND

The Islamic Courts Union, which emerged to the scene in 2006, included some of the top leaders of Al-Ittihad. General knowledge of the top leadership of the Islamic Courts Union, later renamed the Somali Council of the Islamic Courts (SCIC), is sketchy. The leadership was often referred to as jihadist, extremist, and at times terrorist by some observers without much evidence to support the allegations. For example, the assessment of the Islamic Courts by U.S. officials was that less than 5% of the Islamic Courts leadership can be considered extremist, according to a senior State Department official. In late June 2006, the Courts established a consultative body to function as the legislative (Shura) arm of the Courts. Hassan Dahir Aweys was elected to head the Legislative Council. Aweys was one of the top leaders of the now-defunct Al-Ittihad Al-Islamiya (AIAI—for more, see below) and was designated by the Bush Administration as a terrorist. Sharif Sheik Ahmed, the leader of the Courts, was appointed chairman of the Council's Executive Committee to lead the day-to-day affairs of the Courts. Some observers and government officials have erroneously described Aweys as the leader of the Courts. However, the moderate leader of the Courts, Sharif Sheik Ahmed, was never replaced by Aweys. Some observers argued that referring to Aweys as the leader of the Courts was deliberately designed by some groups and governments to give the Courts a negative image.

The leadership of the Islamic Courts remained largely under the control of religious scholars and academics (see "The Top Leaders of the Courts" below). The focus by some observers and officials on three individuals in 2006-2007, Aweys, Hassan Al-Turki, and Aden Ayro, may have been to show the Islamic Courts as a group controlled and influenced by these individuals. Al-

For additional analytical, business and investment opportunities information,
please contact Global Investment & Business Center, USA
at (202) 546-2103. Fax: (202) 546-3275. E-mail: rusric@erols.com

Turki, a man born in the ethnically Somali Ogaden region of Ethiopia, was listed by the Bush administration as a terrorist because of his membership in Al-Ittihad. According to Courts officials, Al-Turki did not even hold a leadership position within the organization. Both Aweys and Al-Turki were placed on the list because of their membership in Al-Ittihad. Ayro's role within the Courts was highly exaggerated since he did not hold a leadership position in the organization. Ayro was often referred to as the leader of Al-Shabaab, the Youth, although there is no evidence to support that he was the leader of that group. Ayro was suspected of killing four aid workers in the breakaway region of Somaliland as well as a Somali scholar in Mogadishu named Abdulqadir Yahya. In May 2008, Ayro was killed in a U.S. air strike. Since the killing of Ayro, the insurgency has intensified its attacks and is now in control of many parts of south-central Somalia.

THE EXECUTIVE COUNCIL (BEFORE THE SPLIT)

Sheikh Sharif Ahmed. Received a Law Degree from a University in Libya; served as President of Somali Intellectuals Associations; President of the District Court in Jowhar; President of Somali Council of Islamic Courts (SCIC); never been active in politics; married with two children. Now, Chairman of the ARS.

Abdurahman Muhamoud Farah. Vice President of SCIC. Studied in Mogadishu; a longtime advocate of peace and clan unity; never active in politics.

Abdulqadir Ali Omar. Vice President of SCIC. Longtime advocate of clan unity; religious scholar, and advocated against abuses by the warlords.

Ibrahim Hassan Addou. Foreign Secretary and a member of the Shura (Legislative Council) of the SCIC; Ph.D., MA, BA from American University, Washington, D.C.; Worked at American University from 1981 to 1992; held several positions at Benadir University in Mogadishu, including Vice President for Academic Affairs and President; married with three children.

THE LEGISLATIVE COUNCIL OR SHURA (BEFORE THE SPLIT)

Hassan Dahir Aweys. Speaker of the Shura. Former army officer in the Somali Armed Forces; fought in the Ethiopia-Somalia wars in the 1970s; former senior member of Al-Ittihad; fought against Ethiopia and Abdullahi Yusuf in the mid-1990s.

Omar Imam Abubakar. Number two in the Shura and effectively the most influential and active member of the Shura; received his Ph.D. from a University in Saudi Arabia; lectured in Mauritania and Somalia for many years.

Abdulahi Ali Afrah. Senior leader in the Shura. Holds a BA in Agriculture, longtime civil servant in the Siad Barre government; received an MA from a University in the U.S. and lived in Canada for many years. Muhamoud Ibrahim Suleh. Senior member of the Shura, son of a well-known religious leader.

THE ALLIANCE FOR THE RE-LIBERATION OF SOMALIA

In September 2007, Somalis from the Diaspora, civil society, opposition groups, and former members of parliament met in Eritrea and formed the Alliance for the Re-Liberation of Somalia (ARS). More than 400 people participated at the founding conference. Al-Shabaab did not participate, and later condemned the leadership of the Alliance. The Alliance significantly reduced the dominance of the Council of the Islamic Courts and brought into the leadership people from civil society, women's groups, and former members of the TFG. The Alliance also brought into the coalition people from different regions and clans of Somalia. In addition, individuals, such as Hassan Aweys, considered by the West as extremists or terrorists were not given leadership positions. According to the Alliance, the main objectives of the coalition are as follows:

> The liberation of Somalia from Ethiopia.
> Somali solutions by Somali stakeholders through dialogue and peaceful means.
> To establish a National Government "completely devote its utmost care to the welfare of the people, protect its rights, properties and promote its spiritual and material development."[23]
> Fighting crimes and violence targeted against civilian population, such as killing, raping, pillaging, dislodging and displacing.
> Resettlement of displaced people.
> To organize general elections once peace and security are established.

In March 2008, the chairman of the ARS, in a letter to the President of the Security Council, wrote, "A peacekeeping mission would be possible only after the departure of the Ethiopian troops. Experience has shown that when peacekeepers are unilaterally imposed by the Security Council, they turn into peace enforcers. To avoid such a situation, the consent of the parties to the conflict is essential." In January 2008, the ARC leadership informed a congressional delegation that the ARS will accept a humanitarian cease-fire, zones of tranquility, and negotiations with the TFG and others once Ethiopian forces are replaced by a neutral force. This position led to a split of the ARS. Many of the top leaders of the ARC left Eritrea for Djibouti to participate in the U.N.-sponsored negotiations.

Table 2. The Leadership of the Executive Council of the ARS Before the Split

Name	Title	Affiliation
Sheikh Sharif Sheikh Ahmed	Chairman	Somali Council of the Islamic Courts (SCIC)
General Jama Mohmed Galib	Vice Chairman	Civil Society
Zakaria Hagi Mohamud Abdi	Vice Chairman	Parliament
Prof. Ibrahim Hassan Addou, Ph.D.	Foreign Affairs Advisor	SCIC
Dr. Mohamed Ali Dahir	Administration Consultant	Somali intellectual
Prof. Abdirahman Ibrahim Ibbi	Assistant to the Chairman	Parliament
Ambassador Yusuf H. Ibrahim	Foreign Affairs Secretary	Parliament
Ahmed Abdullahi Sheikh	Information Secretary	Civil Society
Col. Omar Hashi Aden	Interior Secretary	Parliament
Col. Omar Hashi Aden	Interior Secretary	Parliament
Abdifitah Mohamed Ali	Finance Secretary	SCIC
Yusuf Mohamed Siad	Defense Secretary	SCIC
Dr. Mohamed Ahmed Mohamed, MD	Health Secretary	Civil Society
Dr. Mohamed Ali Ibrahim, Ph.D.	Justice Secretary	SCIC

For additional analytical, business and investment opportunities information, please contact Global Investment & Business Center, USA at (202) 546-2103. Fax: (202) 546-3275. E-mail: rusric@erols.com

[23] Political program of the Alliance for the Re-Liberation of Somalia.

Name	Title	Affiliation
Dr. Mohamud Abdi Ibrahim	Relief and Rehabilitation	
Mrs. Fowsia Mohmed Sheikh	SecretaryHuman Rights Secretary	
Mohamud Ahmed Tarzan	Planning & Training Secretary	
Abdulkadir Mohmed Dhakane	Education Secretary Social Affairs	
Mohmed Ibrahim Garyare	Secretary Reconciliation Secretary	ParliamentDiaspora
Ahmed Abdulle Hussain	Auditing Secretary	Parliament Diaspora SCIC
Abdullahi Sheikh		SCIC

AL-ITTIHAD

Al-Ittihad was perhaps the most active and at one point most successful of all the Islamic groups. Al-Ittihad is an Islamic group whose principal ideology was to establish an Islamic state and to bring law and order by utilizing the Islamic court system. Founded in the late 1980s, Al-Ittihad unsuccessfully sought to replace clan and warlord politics with an Islamic state. In the early 1990s, Al-Ittihad had modest successes; for example, it administered territories under its control in the south. But Al-Ittihad never emerged as a major military or political force in Somalia. The clan-based groups and factions led by warlords in Mogadishu are secular and have been at odds with Al-Ittihad, even though some of these groups maintained tactical alliances from time to time with Al-Ittihad. Al-Ittihad's failure to maintain control over territories and spread its ideology led to a shift in strategy in the mid-1990s. Al-Ittihad abandoned its ambition to spread its ideology through military means and began to concentrate on providing social services to communities through Islamic schools and health care centers.

Al-Ittihad's social activities and religious objectives in Somalia seemed inconsistent with its activities in support of armed groups in the Somali-inhabited region of Ethiopia. In Ethiopia, Al-Ittihad was reportedly engaged in military activities in support of ethnic Somalis. Several anti-Ethiopian groups are active in the Somali region and Al-Ittihad cooperated with these groups in carrying out attacks against Ethiopian targets. In 1999, the Ogaden Islamic Union, under the leadership of Muhammad Muallem Omar Abdi, the Somali People's Liberation Front under the leadership of Ahmed Ali Ismail, and the Western Somali Liberation Front under the leadership of Muhammad Haji Ibrahim Hussein formed a coalition called the United Front for the Liberation of Western Somalia, their term for the Somali-inhabited region of Ethiopia.[24] The Ogaden National Liberation Front was engaged in military activities in the region, and in the past formed alliances with other Ethiopian opposition groups.

Many Somali watchers believe that Al-Ittihad's strength was highly exaggerated and that information about its alleged links with international terrorist organizations is unreliable. The State Department's *Country Reports on Terrorism* stated in 2006 that "in recent years the existence of a coherent entity operating as AIAI (Al-Ittihad) has become difficult to prove." There is no reliable information or pattern of behavior to suggest that Al-Ittihad had an international agenda, as was the case with the National Islamic Front (NIF) government of Sudan. Some observers note that if Al-Ittihad had a clear internationally oriented agenda, its obvious ally in the region would be the NIF regime in Sudan or the Sudanese-backed Eritrean Islamic Jihad. The Sudanese regime did back regional extremist groups and international terrorist organizations, but there was no apparent relationship between the NIF and Al-Ittihad. Many Somalis often refer to Al-Ittihad's social services and the peace and stability that prevailed in the areas it controlled.

In late September 2001, the Bush Administration added Al-Ittihad to a list of terrorism-related entities whose assets were frozen by an executive order. Bush Administration officials accused

**For additional analytical, business and investment opportunities information,
please contact Global Investment & Business Center, USA
at (202) 546-2103. Fax: (202) 546-3275. E-mail: rusric@erols.com**

Al-Ittihad of links with Al Qaeda. The Administration did not publicly offer evidence supporting its allegations, but some officials asserted that links between AIAI and Al Qaeda date back to the

U.S. presence in Somalia during Operation Restore Hope (1992-1994). This assertion, however, seems inconsistent with the reality on the ground at that time, according to some observers. Then, the dominant players in Mogadishu were the warlords and not Al-Ittihad. In early November 2001, federal authorities raided several Somali-owned money transfer businesses in the United States operated by Al-Barakaat Companies.

The Bush Administration ordered the assets of Al-Barakaat frozen because of its alleged links to Al Qaeda. U.S. officials, however, later seemed to back off from their earlier assertion that Al-Barakaat and individuals associated with the money transfer business sector are directly linked to Al Qaeda. In September 2002, U.S. officials cleared three Somalis and three Al-Barakaat branches accused of ties with Al Qaeda. The three individuals and businesses were removed from the U.S. Treasury Department list of terrorist supporters and their assets were also unfrozen. The United States has had no presence in Somalia since Washington pulled out of the peacekeeping operation in 1994. In September 2008, the European Court of Justice annulled the decision taken by the EU Council to freeze the assets of two Somalis and Al-Barakaat International Foundation of Sweden.

SOMALIA: BACKGROUND (1991-2006)

In 1991, General Mohamed Siad Barre, who came to power through a military coup in 1969, was ousted from power by several Somali armed groups. Following the collapse of central authority in Mogadishu, rival Somali groups engaged in armed struggle for personal political power and prevented food and medicine from reaching innocent civilians suffering from drought and famine. An estimated 500,000 people died from violence, starvation, and disease as Somalia was wracked by continued internal chaos. On November 9, 1992, then-President George H.W. Bush authorized Operation Restore Hope, using the U.S. military, to safeguard non-governmental organizations (NGOs) and their efforts to provide humanitarian assistance to the suffering Somali civilian population.

The U.S.-led United Task Force (UNITAF) successfully subdued the warlords and armed factions and enabled NGOs to safely provide humanitarian relief to Somalis. In May 1993, UNITAF handed over the operation to the United Nations. The U.N. effort was known as United Nations Operation in Somalia (UNOSOM) II. In May 1993, UNOSOM II coalition forces were attacked by one of the factions in Mogadishu. On October 3, 1993, after a 17-hour battle between U.S. troops and Somali factions in Mogadishu, in which 18 U.S. Rangers were killed, President Clinton ordered the withdrawal of U.S. troops from Somalia. In March 1994, the United States completely pulled out of Somalia and, one year later, the United Nations pulled out the remaining peacekeepers. Since the withdrawal of United Nations forces in March 1995, Somalia has been without a central government and has been splintered into several regions controlled by clan-based factions.

PEACE PROCESSES

There have been 14 Somali reconciliation or peace conferences to bring an end to the fighting in Somalia since the early 1990s. Some were held under the auspices of or were supported by the United Nations, or governments in the Horn of Africa. These efforts have largely failed to bring about lasting peace in Somalia. Moreover, competing efforts by international actors contributed to the failure of peace efforts in Somalia. In 1996, the government of Ethiopia convened a peace process in the resort town of Sodere, Ethiopia. Many political actors and armed factions participated, although a few boycotted the peace process. The Sodere process collapsed when the government of Egypt convened another meeting of the Somali groups in Cairo in 1997. Subsequently, the Cairo initiative failed when yet another peace conference was convened by Somali factions in Bosaso, Somalia in 1998. In February 2000, IGAD approved a peace plan proposed by the government of Djibouti. In May 2000, the Somali Reconciliation Conference opened in Arta, Djibouti in which 400 delegates took part for several months of deliberation. The Arta process was boycotted by several powerful warlords, as well as the governments of Somaliland and Puntland.

On August 13, 2000, participants agreed to the creation of a Transitional National Government (TNG) and a Transitional National Assembly (TNA). On August 26, 2000, participants nominated Abdulqassim Salad Hassan as president of the TNG. In October 2002, the Inter-Governmental Authority for Development launched another peace process, led by the government of Kenya. An estimated 350 delegates from different regions of Somalia participated in the opening session of the conference in the Kenyan town of Eldoret. The government of Somaliland boycotted the conference. In the first phase of the conference, the parties signed a temporary cease-fire, and agreed to respect and honor the outcome of the conference. The parties further agreed to establish a federal system of government and committed themselves to fight terrorism. In September 2003, the parties agreed on a Transitional National Charter, paving the way for a National Unity government.

In August 2004, a new Transitional Somali Parliament was inaugurated in Kenya. The 275member parliament consists of the major political factions and seems to represent all the major clans of Somalia. The Transitional Charter allocated 61 seats for the major four clans and 31 seats for the small clans. The Charter also allocated 12% of the seats to women. The Charter accepted Islam as the national religion and agreed that *Sharia* law would be the basis of national legislation. In fact, previous Somali constitutions had similar provisions. In October 2004, the Somali Transitional Parliament elected Abdullahi Yusuf Ahmed as the new president of Somalia. The swearing-in ceremony was attended by 11 heads of government from African countries and representatives from regional organizations and the United Nations.

In November 2004, President Abdullahi Yusuf Ahmed appointed Professor Ali Mohamed Gedi as prime minister. The transitional government, however, was not able to function effectively or move to Mogadishu in large part due to opposition from the warlords in Mogadishu, even though some of these warlords signed the agreement and were ministers in the government. The inability of the transitional government to establish effective control allowed warlords and clan factions to dominate many parts of Somalia until late December 2006. Some observers contend that the defeat of the warlords by the Islamic Courts paved the way for the establishment of central authority in Mogadishu.

NATIONAL RECONCILIATION CONFERENCE

Somalia's recent peace effort, the National Reconciliation Congress, convened in the Shagaani district of Mogadishu on July 15, 2007, after being postponed twice for logistical and security reasons. The first phase of the conference ended on August 30, 2007. Somali Ambassador to Kenya Mohammed Ali Nur spoke optimistically about the results of the first phase of the conference at a news conference in Nairobi, Kenya: "I am happy to announce the declaration of peace agreement between major clans who are participating in the congress has already been signed.... The transitional government has done and will continue doing its best to lead the process of reviving Somalia from the ashes of the vicious civil war." Whereas the first phase of the conference focused on the resolution of clan conflicts and disarmament, the second phase focused on issues such as power sharing, governance, sharing of natural resources, sea piracy, welfare, and internally displaced persons.

ETHIOPIA-SOMALIA RELATIONS

For over four decades, relations between successive Ethiopian governments and Somalia have been poor. Somalia invaded Ethiopia twice in the 1960s under Emperor Haile Selassie and in 1976 during the Mengistu Haile Mariam military rule. In the first war, the Ethiopian military commander General Aman Andom defeated Somali forces, but his request to go inside Somalia was rejected by the Emperor, and he was ordered to remain behind the border. The 1976 invasion of Ethiopia by Somali forces and the Western Somali Liberation Front (WSLF) initially succeeded, leading to the capture of many Ethiopian towns by Somali forces. Somali forces briefly captured the third-largest city, Dire Dawa, in Eastern Ethiopia. However, Ethiopian forces, with the support of Cuban and South Yemeni forces, were able to defeat the Somali forces, although elements of the Somali rebel forces remained in control of remote areas in the largely Somali inhabited areas of Ethiopia.

Both Ethiopian and Somali governments intervened in the internal affairs of the two countries, and successive governments on both sides supported each others' armed opposition groups. The current president of the Transitional Federal Government, President Abdullahi Yusuf, was one of the first to receive Ethiopia's assistance after he fled Somalia in the late 1970s. He was one of the first senior officials to challenge the Siad Barre government. Ethiopia was also the principal backer of the Somali National Movement (SNM), the group that liberated the northwest region of Somalia, currently known as Somaliland. The change of government in Ethiopia did not end Ethiopia's intervention in Somali affairs. The current government of Ethiopia became a key backer of a number of Somali factions and leaders, including the current president of the TFG, Abdullahi Yusuf, Hussein Aideed, and other Somali factions.

The Barre government was also a major sponsor of Ethiopian armed rebel groups. The current ruling party of Ethiopia, the Ethiopian People's Revolutionary Democratic Front (EPRDF), received assistance from Somali authorities and a number of the EPRDF leaders reportedly carried Somali-issued passports. Other rebel groups, including the Ogaden National Liberation Front (ONLF) and the Oromo Liberation Front (OLF), also received assistance from Somalia. The ouster of the Siad Barre government and the absence of a central government in Somalia ended support for Ethiopian armed groups, although some Somali factions continue to support the ONLF. For most of the 1990s, Ethiopia's primary concern was Al-Ittihad in Somalia and its activities in support of the ONLF.

Al-Ittihad and ONLF carried out a number of attacks against Ethiopian targets, and Ethiopian security forces have violently retaliated against these groups and their supporters. The fighting with Al-Ittihad was triggered in the early 1990s when Ethiopian security forces brutally cracked down on the Ogaden National Liberation Front, a member of the first transitional government of Ethiopia. The ONLF joined the transitional government of Ethiopia in part because the Ethiopian Transitional Charter provided nations and nationalities the right to self determination; however, the ONLF push for self determination created tension between the ruling EPRDF and the ONLF.

In the early 1990s, Ethiopian security forces assassinated a number of ONLF leaders, cracked down on the organization, and moved the Ethiopian Somali region capital from Gode to Jijiga, a central government stronghold. Members of the ONLF fled to Somalia and were embraced by Al-Ittihad, a fairly new group at that time. Hence, some observers view Al-Ittihad as a group largely concerned with domestic issues. Ethiopia's principal interest at that time was to ensure that a united Somalia did not pose a threat to Ethiopia and that the Somali-inhabited region of Ethiopia remained stable. Ethiopian forces attacked Somalia a number of times over the past decade and often maintained presence inside Somali territory. Ethiopia's relationship with the current president of the TFG was strengthened when Yusuf backed Ethiopia's efforts against Al-Ittihad in the 1990s. The Ethiopian government's animosity towards the ousted Shura leader of the Islamic Courts, Sheik Aweys, is linked to Aweys' role as one of the leaders of Al-Ittihad fighting against Ethiopia and that of Abdullahi Yusuf.

In 2004, the government of Ethiopia released a report, *the Federal Democratic Republic of Ethiopia's Foreign Policy, Security Policy and Strategy*. The 158-page report covers a wide range of issues, including Ethiopia's assessment of its relations with Somalia. The report states that Somalia attacked Ethiopia twice in pursuit of its Greater Somalia ambition. The report notes that "at this time the Greater Somalia agenda has failed." Moreover, the Greater Somalia agenda no longer poses a serious threat to Ethiopia. The report contends that the factionalization of Somalia has allowed anti-peace and extremists elements to become strong, posing a threat to Ethiopia. In order to reduce the threat from some parts of Somalia, the Ethiopian government must pursue a policy of engagement and support to Puntland and Somaliland, according to the report. The report also recommends a policy of targeting those armed elements that threaten Ethiopian security. This report was released two years before the Islamic Courts emerged, although the report gave the same labels of extremist, terrorist, and anti-peace to groups that were dominant at that time.

Legislation
H.Res. 339 Introduced 4/21, 2009; passed 4/22/2009.
H.Res. 859. Introduced 10/22/2009.
S.Res. 108 Introduced 4/22/2009; passed 4/22/2009.
H.Res. 1538 Introduced 7/20/2010; passed 7/27/2010.
H.RES. 1596 INTRODUCED 7/30/2010.
H.CON.RES. 303 INTRODUCED 7/22/2010.
S.RES. 573 INTRODUCED 6/29/2010.

Figure 1. Major Somali Clans and Subclans Figure 2. Map of Somalia

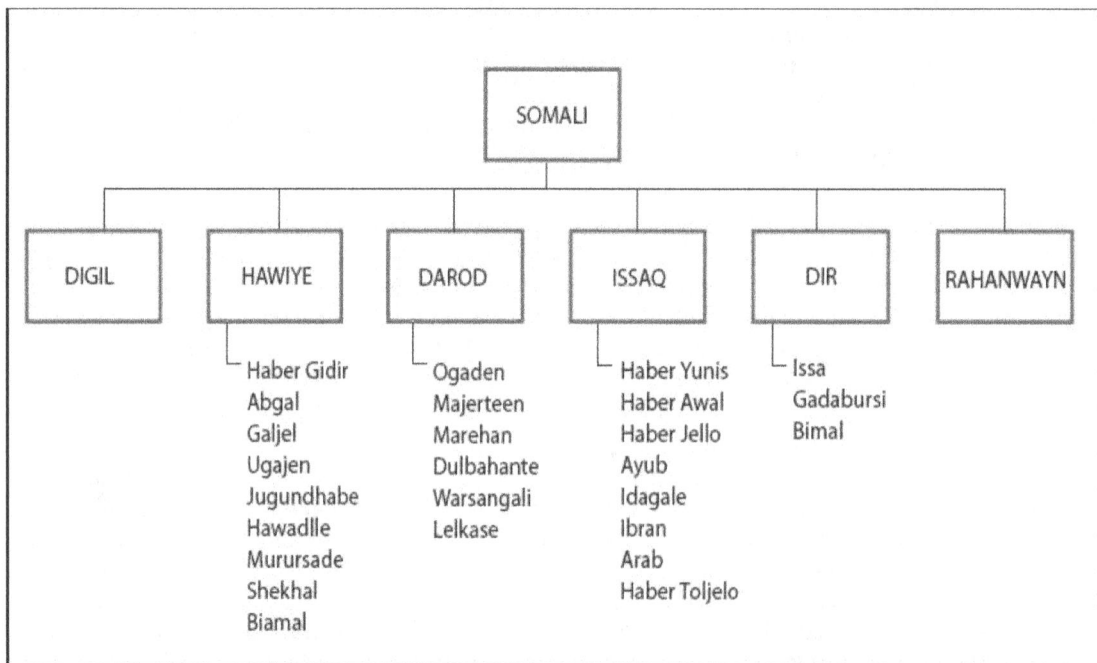

			SOMALI			
DIGIL	HAWIYE	DAROD	ISSAQ	DIR	RAHANWAYN

HAWIYE	DAROD	ISSAQ	DIR
Haber Gidir	Ogaden	Haber Yunis	Issa
Abgal	Majerteen	Haber Awal	Gadabursi
Galjel	Marehan	Haber Jello	Bimal
Ugajen	Dulbahante	Ayub	
Jugundhabe	Warsangali	Idagale	
Hawadlle	Lelkase	Ibran	
Murursade		Arab	
Shekhal		Haber Toljelo	
Biamal			

Source: Adapted by CRS. Cartographic Section, United Nations Department of Peacekeeping Operations, Map No. 3690 Rev. 7, January 2007.

Figure 3. Somali Refugees in the Region

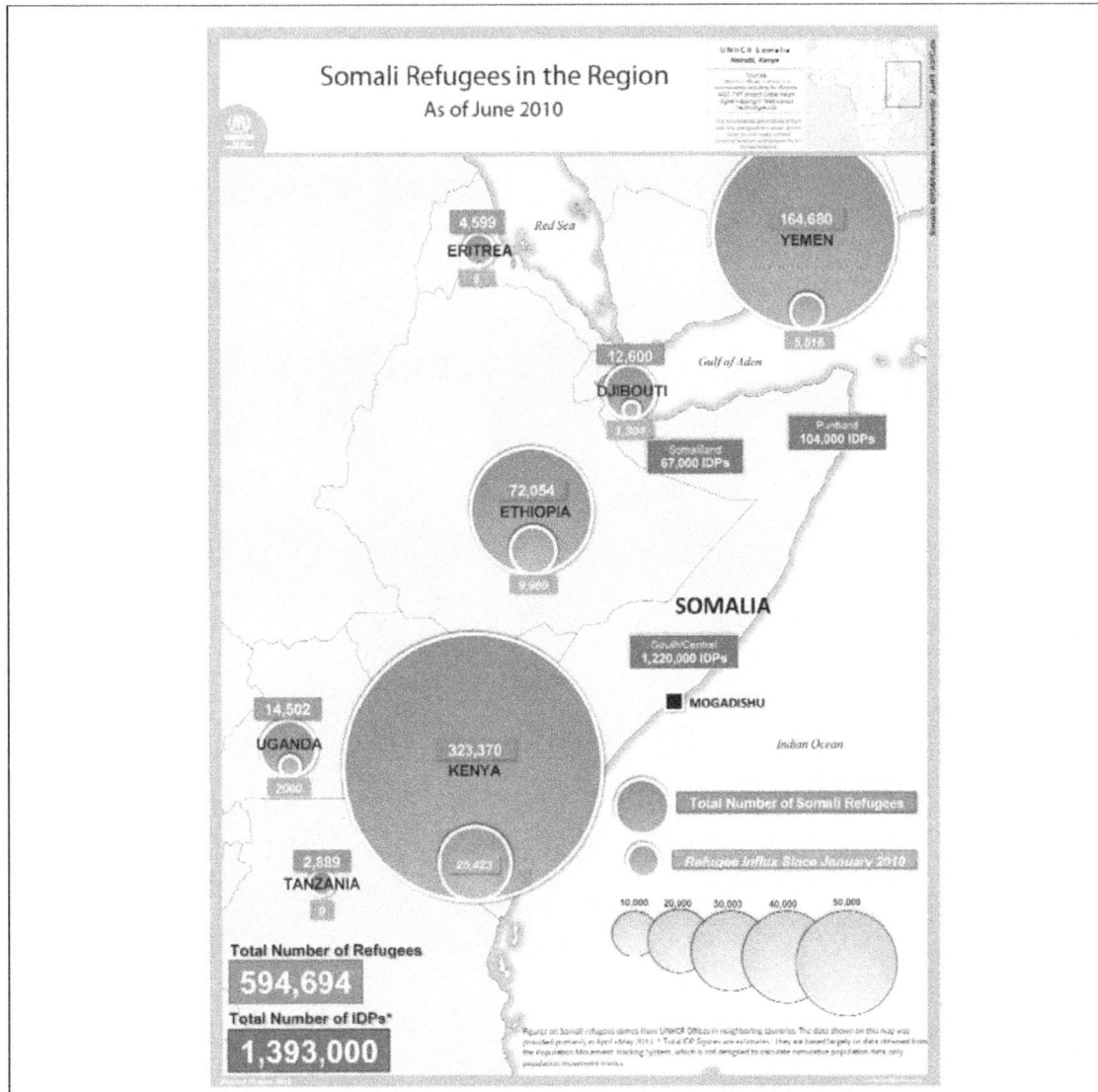

Source: United Nations.

Figure 4. Humanitarian Access vs. IDPs

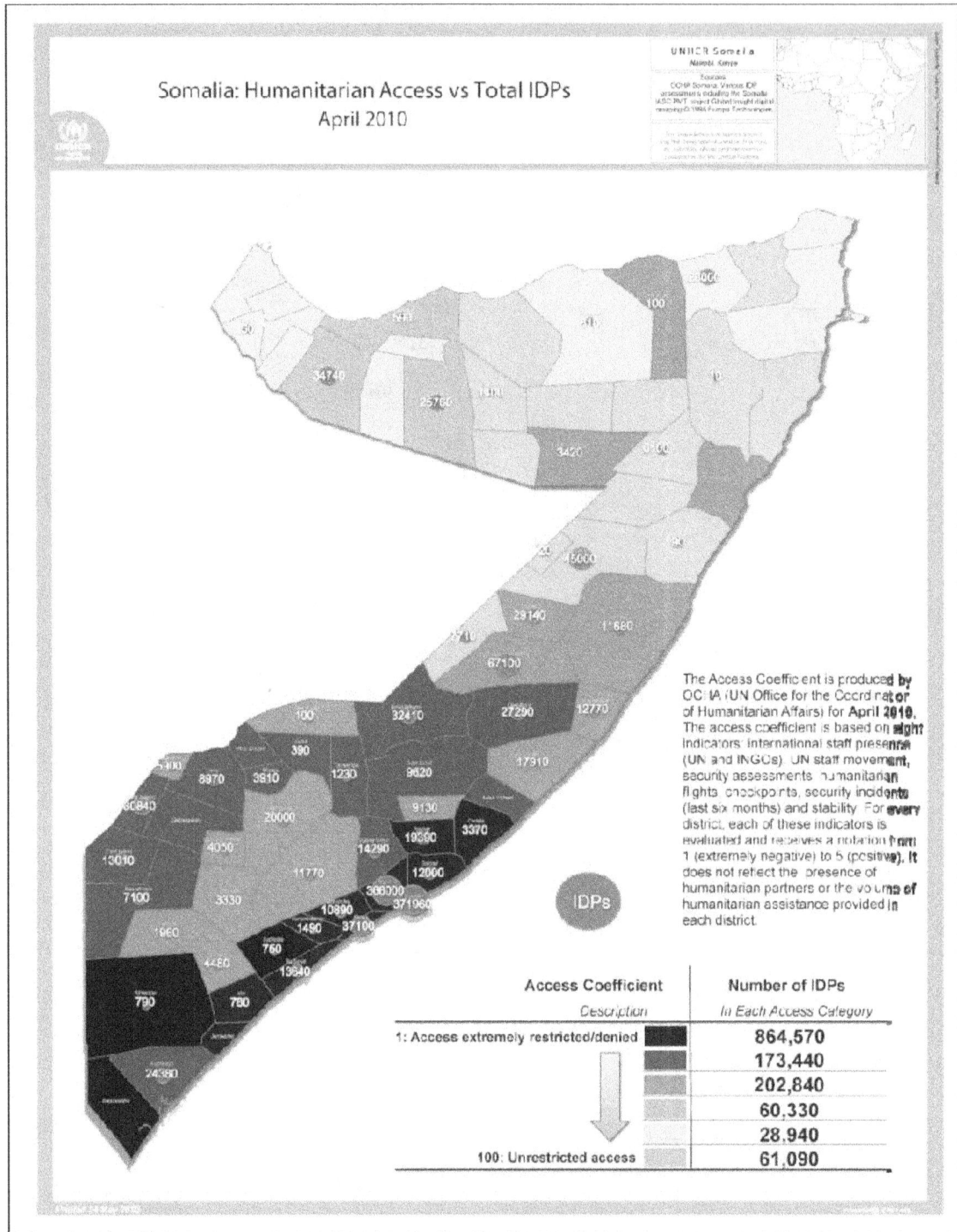

IMPORTANT INFORMATION FOR CONDUCTING BUSINESS

The agricultural sector is central to the Somali economy, with livestock rearing predominating in the North of the country, while crops like sugar cane, corn, and bananas are produced in the South. The major exports show a similar bias: livestock, bananas, meat, and wood, with periodic reduction in meat exports due to foreign restrictions following disease outbreaks, like Rift Valley fever. Flooding and drought are persistent problems, and there have been severe food shortages in recent years, foodstuffs being a major import. About 70% of Somalis are nomadic.

The country has been engaged in civil war since 1991, and there has been no internationally recognised government. The economy has suffered extensive damage, and some of the conventional aids to investment are not readily available, like information on investment procedures and statistical services. Steps are being made to establish a government, but the country remains divided, with two northern regions declaring autonomy, along former colonial boundaries. These zones have been relatively peaceful, and have seen more international assistance than the inaccessible warring regions.

The industrial sector is of limited size, in 1987 employing only 9% of the population. A large proportion of output depends on agricultural inputs, for example in textiles and food processing. A cement factory was recently opened, with capacity of 200,000 metric tons. Many manufactures are imported.

The mineral wealth of the country has not been fully determined, but includes uranium, gypsum, marble, and industrial metals. They have not yet been commercially exploited. There are also oil and natural gas deposits, although at present petroleum is one of the countrys largest imports. Most energy is generated by thermal sources.

The war has substantially affected Somalias infrastructure. There is no railway, so the underdevelopment of the road network is a serious constraint on land travel, although Mogadishu is said to be well connected, with improving facilities as a port. The telecommunications sector has also been damaged, although there is local Internet connection. The education system has been subject to severe pressure too.

There is considerable cross border migration between Somalia and her neighbours, due in part to the nomadic lifestyle, food shortages, and war in the region. The recent fighting in the country has encouraged a diaspora beyond the continent, and expatriates may eventually provide a source of funds for development. Tensions exist with the surrounding states. There is considerable potential for growth in tourism when peace returns.

The country started to liberalise in the early 1980s under IMF guidance, although the programme was not fully implemented. The World Bank is not currently active in the country. Inflation has been aggravated by forged banknotes entering the economy from a variety of sources.

BUSINESS CLIMATE AND OPPORTUNITIES IN SOMALIA

The anti-piracy patrol off the coast has had an impact. While last year, 40 percent of pirate attacks resulted in a captured ship, so far this year, only 25 percent of attacks have succeeded. Between the cost of the anti-piracy patrol, and the additional insurance, fuel and danger pay for the shipping companies, the Somali piracy is costing shippers, and their governments (who are paying for the anti-piracy patrol) over half a billion dollars a year. It is making it a little more expensive to use the Suez canal (but it is still cheaper than steaming around southern Africa.) The pirates are getting (in ransoms) less than ten percent of the money spent on dealing with the

For additional analytical, business and investment opportunities information, please contact Global Investment & Business Center, USA at (202) 546-2103. Fax: (202) 546-3275. E-mail: rusric@erols.com

piracy. Most of the money goes to insurance companies, security firms and suppliers of fuel and other items needed to maintain the foreign warships off the coast. The shipping industry is more confident that they can deal with the pirates, while the pirates are discouraged by the lower success rate and the increasing pressure they are getting from other Somalis.
Another factor in the declining pirate success has been the increased use of aerial patrols by the foreign task force. There are at least half a dozen maritime patrol aircraft stationed in Djibouti, and dozens of helicopters aboard the ships of the task force. All these aircraft make it difficult for the pirates to sneak up on ships (who are more wary, careful and prepared these days).

Puntland, a self-declared (since 1991) independent part northern Somalia, is offering to deal with the piracy problem by forming a real Coast Guard and stronger police force. All they need is recognition from the UN that Puntland is a real nation, and about $10 million to buy patrol boats and hire crews and cops. It's a tempting offer, which several other nations in the region have recommended, but the UN has not been eager to go this route (which means recognizing the fragmenting of Somalia into three states; Somaliland and Puntland in the north, and the other half, as Somalia, in the chaotic south). But the UN did give the Puntland government (which it talks to, even if it won't officially recognize) eleven vehicles (ten pickups and a larger truck) for their security forces. The U.S. could easily supply the money Puntland wants, but the corruption up north is a problem, as it is throughout the region. There's no assurance that the money for a Coast Guard would not largely disappear into someone's pocket.

The UN is trying to figure out how to deal with Eritrea, which is the major source of outside support for the Islamic radical groups inside Somalia. Cash poor Eritrea, in turn, is backed by oil rich Iran. The UN can't do much, unless they slap an naval and air blockade on Eritrea. This is unlikely, as the UN does not have the air and naval resources to implement this. A few press releases, calling Eritrea very naughty, are more likely.

Al Shabbab has imposed a curfew in the port town of Kiamayo, in the wake of attacks on their gunmen. The Islamic radicals have imposed strict Sharia (Islamic) law on the people of Kismayo (no booze, drugs, music, videos, dancing and so on), which is very unpopular. Now Kismayo also has problems with warships off the coast preventing cargo ships from docking there.

The activation of a new underwater fiber optic cable, being laid off the east coast of Africa, has been delayed by at least ten days (to early July) because of the pirates. The ships involved in the cable laying have had to take additional precautions to avoid being attacked. Once this cable is activated, the cost for Africans using the Internet will decline by over 40 percent. International phone calls will also be cheaper.

Russia has handed Iranians and Pakistanis, captured on a pirate mother ship, to Iran and Pakistan. Not all the pirates are Somali. A large minority are Yemeni and, as the Russian experience shows, some other nationalities as well.

Last month, the fighting in Mogadishu left over 200 dead, and caused 60,000 people to flee the city. So far this month, several thousand more civilians have fled, as government and al Shabaab militias fought over neighborhoods in the northern and southwest sections of the city. Al Shabaab is retreating this time, and there have been nearly fifty killed.

June 1, 2009: The fighting in Mogadishu resumed, after a lull of a few days. The government has brought in more men and drove al Shabaab (and related groups) out of a neighborhood on the outskirts of the city. The Islamic radicals continue to use suicide and roadside bombs, which continue to kill more civilians than armed men.

May 29, 2009: The Somali government declared a blockade of ports and airports controlled by Islamic radical groups like al Shabaab. This includes the port of Kismayo, where cargo ships are now being kept away by foreign warships. There are, however, no foreign warplanes available to keep aircraft from using airports in al Shabaab territory. This is how a lot of the weapons are getting to the radicals (often from Iran, via Eritrea.)

AGRI-BUSINESS

* Manufacture and distribution of appropriate agri-inputs.
* Supply and maintenance of agri-equipment, machinery and irrigation systems.
* Agro-forestry.
* Date palm cultivation.
* Cereal crop and horticultural production.
* Seed banking.
* Dairy and food products processing.
* Solar fruit drying.
* Packaging and labeling supply and services.
* Laboratory testing and animal health services.
* Related business support services.

BEEKEEPING & BEE

* Skilled master beekeeping trainers and service providers.
* Commercial-scale beekeeping.
* Manufacture and distribution of bee equipment (top bars, hive bodies, bee suits and bee veils, smokers, queen excluders and cages, muslin cloth and plastic buckets with covers).
* Production and distribution of beeswax, bee pollen, propolis and royal jelly.
* Supply and maintenance of refining equipment.
* Commercial honey refining; packaging and distribution.
* Packaging and labeling supply and services.
* Related business support services.

CONSTRUCTION & PROPERTY

* Property acquisition and management services.
* Architectural and civil engineering services.
* Residential, commercial and infrastructural civil/structural construction services and maintenance.
* Low-cost housing construction.
* Local construction materials production.
* Electrical and mechanical services.
* Heavy and light construction equipment and maintenance.
* Hard and soft residential and commercial furnishings and equipment manufacture and supply.
* Landscaping supplies and services.
* Security systems and services.
* Communications equipment and services.
* Related business support services.

As far as why Qaad is delivered from Kenya mostly, and from Ethopia as well, is that Somalis don't grow the drug. I am sure they have tried to grow it in their farms but probably it did not. Plus, I think somali farmers don't want to clash with crazy clerics that may not like having Qaad grown inside the country.

So the way the business is set up now is that Qaad is deliver from Kenya and it is a huge business in somalia. Back in our statist days our President Siyad Bare tried to make Qaad illegal for few years and his mission failed miserably. He could not stop the drug from coming into the country and he simply remove the restrictions on the drug when he reliaze their is nothing he could do to stop to stop people from chewing Qaad.

ECONOMY

Despite civil unrest, Somalia has maintained a healthy informal economy, based mainly on livestock, remittance/money transfer companies, and telecommunications. Livestock exports in recent years have been severely reduced by periodic bans, ostensibly for concerns of animal health, by Arabian Peninsula states. Drought has also impaired agricultural and livestock production. Because rainfall is scanty and irregular, farming generally is limited to certain coastal districts, areas near Hargeisa, and the Jubba and Shebelle River valleys. The modern sector of the agricultural economy consists mainly of banana plantations located in the south, which have used modern irrigation systems and up-to-date farm machinery. Somalia has meager natural resources such as oil, gemstones, and salt.

Economic progress in Somalia is decidedly mixed. As of January 2007, Somalia is still a fragile state with hundreds of thousands of refugees due to massive floods and the latest fighting of the civil war. However, when extreme poverty (percentage of individuals living on less than PPP$1 a day) was last measured by the World Bank in 1998, Somalia fared better than many other countries in Africa, over some of whom Somalia also had superior infrastructure. In the absence of a Somali state and its institutions, the private sector grew "impressively" according to the World Bank in 2003, particularly in the areas of trade, commerce, transport, remittance and infrastructure services and in the primary sectors, notably in livestock, agriculture and fisheries. In 2007, the United Nations reported that the country's service industry is also thriving. However with a GDP of $600 per capita the country is still relatively poor.

There are signs of growth in Somalia:

> Despite the seeming anarchy, Somalia's service sector has managed to survive and grow... Mogadishu's main market offers a variety of goods from food to the newest electronic gadgets. Hotels continue to operate, and militias provide security.
>
> —CIA Factbook

Anthropologist Spencer Heath MacCallum attributes this increased economic activity

960s. According to the United Nations, the average GDP per capita growth rate was negative at -0.9 percent during 1970-1990.

Due to the lack of government oversight or statistics, and the recent war, it is difficult to calculate the size or growth of the economy. For 1994, the CIA estimated GDP at $3.3 billion In 2001, it was estimated to be $4.1 billion. In 2005, the CIA estimated GDP to be $4.809 billion. Real growth in 2005 was projected at 2.4%, and 2.8% in 2008.

AGRICULTURE AND NATURAL RESOURCES

Agriculture is the most important sector, with livestock accounting for about 40% of GDP and about 65% of export earnings Nomads and semi-nomads, who are dependent upon livestock for their livelihood make up a large portion of the population. For them a major economic income source is the export of animal hides. After livestock, bananas are the principal export; sugar, sorghum, and maize are products for the domestic market.

At nearly 3 million head of goat and sheep in 1999, the northern ports of Bossaso and Berbera accounted for 95 percent of all goat and 52 percent of all sheep exports of East Africa. Somaliland exported more than 180 million metric tons of livestock and more than 480 million metric tons of agricultural products. Some countries such as Saudi Arabia have banned imports of Somali livestock because of inadequate inspection and certification, affecting negatively the economy.

A small fishing industry has begun in the north where tuna, shark, and other warm-water fish are caught, although fishing production is seriously affected by poaching, piracy, and the lack of ability to grant concessions because of the absence of a generally recognized government. Aromatic woods — frankincense and myrrh — from a small and diminishing forest area also contribute to the country's exports.

Minerals, including uranium, are found throughout the country, but they have not yet been exploited.

LIGHT INDUSTRY

With the help of Somalis living overseas, small industries such as textiles, handicrafts, meat processing, and printing are being established. Investors have returned in recent years; for example, a Coca-Cola bottling plant opened in Mogadishu in 2004.

TRANSPORTATION

Infrastructure such as roads are as numerous as those in neighbouring countries but of much lower quality. A World Bank report states the private sector has found it too hard to build roads due to high transaction costs and the fact that those who pay road fees are not the only ones using the road (see free rider problem), presenting a problem with recuperation of investment. The national road system nominally comprises 22,100 kilometers (13,702 mi.) of roads that include about 2,600 kilometers (1,612 mi.) of all-weather roads, although most roads have received little maintenance for years and have seriously deteriorated. There are no railways in Somalia, internal land based transportation is solely done by truck and bus.

Air transportation is provided by small air charter firms and craft used by drug importers/exporters. A number of airlines operate from Hargeisa. Some private airlines, including Air Somalia and Daallo Airlines, serve several domestic locations as well as Djibouti and the United Arab Emirates. In 1989, before the collapse of the government, the national airline had only one airplane. Now there are approximately fifteen airlines, over sixty aircraft, six international destinations, and more domestic routes. According to a World Bank report, the "private airline business in Somalia is now thriving with more than five carriers and price wars between the companies."

Bosaso currently has the busiest port in all of Somalia; other smaller ports are located at Merca and Brava. Absence of security and lack of maintenance and improvement are major issues at most Somali ports. The European Community and the World Bank jointly financed construction of a deepwater port at Mogadishu. The Soviet Union improved Somalia's deepwater port at Berbera in 1969. Facilities at Berbera were further improved by a U.S. military construction program completed in 1985, but they have become dilapidated. During the 1990s the United States renovated a deepwater port at Kismayo that serves the fertile Juba River basin and is vital to Somalia's banana export industry. On January 17, 2007, new port and airport directors were appointed by the TFG.

TELECOMMUNICATIONS

Somalia has some of the best telecommunications in Africa. Installation time for a land-line is just three days, while in the neighboring Kenya waiting lists are many years long. This may seem rather unexpected in a country engaged in civil war; the public telecommunications system was destroyed or dismantled at the outset of the civil war by different factions. Abdullahi Mohammed Hussein of Telecom Somalia explained this by that "the government post and telecoms company used to have a monopoly but after the regime was toppled, we were free to set up our own business", The Economist cited the telephone industry in anarchic Somalia as "a vivid illustration of the way in which governments...can often be more of a hindrance than a help."

Somalia is linked to the outside world via ship-to-shore communications (INMARSAT) as well as links to overseas satellite operators by private telecommunications operators in major towns. Wireless/mobile communications has also become an economic force in Somalia. Somalia has the cheapest cellular calling rates on the continent, with some companies charging less than a cent per minute.

Radio broadcasting stations operate at Mogadishu, Hargeisa, and Galkayo, with programs in Somali and some mother languages. There are two television broadcast stations in Mogadishu and one in Hargeisa.

Sanctions by the US in 2001 in the wake of the 9/11 attacks due to suspicions of terrorist funding set back Somali Internet development. Internet usage still continues to climb due to Internet cafés. From 200 users in all of Somalia in 1999 the number of users has grown to an estimated 90,000, or 11 persons per 1,000 in 2005, according to the ITU. The shared use of computers can be inferred by the lower estimate of 50,000 PCs in the country, for a ratio of about two users on average for every computer.

FINANCIAL SECTOR

Rival producers of Somali shillings emerged after 1991. These included the Na shilling, which failed to gain widespread acceptance, and the Balweyn I and II, which were forgeries of pre-1991 bank notes. A competition for seigniorage drove the value of the money down to about $0.04 per SoSh (1000) note, approximately the commodity cost. Consumers have refused to accept bills larger than the 1991 denominations, which has helped stopped the devaluation from spiraling further. The pre-1991 notes and the subsequent forgeries are treated as the same currency. It takes large bundles to make cash purchases. United States dollar is often used for larger transactions.

The relatively stable value of the currency in the 1990s compared to the 1980s is explained by Peter D. Little in *Somalia: Economy without a State* as resulting from the lack of a corrupt central government printing currency to pay for military expenditures and political cronies.

Traders avoid the need to carry large amounts of Somali shillings by converting them to U.S. dollars and then wiring them to money houses in Somalia. Because identification can be easily forged, those seeking to pick up wired money are required to answer questions about their clan and kinship relations. Private remittance companies known as hawala assist in the transfer of money.

Remittance services has become a large industry in Somalia. Successful people from the worldwide diaspora who fled because of the war contribute to the economy around $1 billion annually. In the absence of a formal banking sector, money exchange services have sprouted throughout the country, handling between $500 million and $1 billion in remittances annually. Due to the war, the actual size and growth rate of the economy is unknown.

For additional analytical, business and investment opportunities information, please contact Global Investment & Business Center, USA at (202) 546-2103. Fax: (202) 546-3275. E-mail: rusric@erols.com

CONSTRUCTION

Construction is sporadic, and at times heavily subsidized by aid agencies. Projects, such as the UN WFP program to repair the air strip in Bardheere, are resuscitating infrastructure, homes and commercial sites that have laid in ruins for years or decades. Some construction projects were begun under the Islamic Courts Union (ICU) in 2006, including re-opening the Mogadishu port and airport.

ENERGY AND UTILITIES

Electricity is furnished by entrepreneurs, who have purchased generators and divided cities into manageable sectors.

Petroleum exploration efforts, at one time under way, have ceased due to insecurity and instability. There are no proven oil reserves, but there are prospects to explore for oil in Puntland. Due to political instability and the protests of the Transitional Federal Government foreign investors are warned to not make deals until stability is restored. Production in the south of charcoal (as a biomass fuel) for export has led to widespread deforestation.

The private sector also supplies water. A report by WHO/UNICEF indicated that in 2004 only 29% of the population had access to safe drinking water.

CORRUPTION

The owner of Daallo Airlines says, "Sometimes it's difficult without a government and sometimes it's a plus," but "Corruption is not a problem, because there is no government." However, Transparency International's annual surveys indicate that Somalia is perceived as having extensive corruption, with Somalia rated at or near the highest level of corruption in the world in most years. Whether the situation has improved since Siyad Barre's governance, which allegedly featured some of the worst corruption in all of Africa, is open for interpretation. A more recent 2008 report rated Somalia as one hundred-eighty on a corruption scale

OIL IN SOMALILAND

Geologists have speculating about the possibility of oil in Somalia since the last century, but it took the US military Operation Restore Hope to bring this possibility to popular attention. The widespread notion that US troops are sent to Somalia to protect the interests of US oil companies, and their supposed huge oil finds, has been treated with amused derision in oil industry circles. But US military presence which aims to stabilize events in a region increasingly regarded as the backyard of its regional ally, Saudi Arabia, has not been discounted . Over the past l0 years most of the oil industry interest has focused on areas in the north, today the self-declared Republic of Somaliland, which troops have avoided. Any future oil exploration here will depend largely on the international community's recognition of the aspirations of the breakaway state.

Oil seeps were first identified by Italian and British geologists who surveyed the area during the colonial era. These predicted the presence of a sizable oil field just south of Berbera. But it took until the 1960s for the first wells to be drilled here. Three wells known as the Daga Shabell series, registered oil shows, but there was no real discovery . There were further small gas discoveries along the east coast and just offshore of Socotra, but nothing of commercial proportions.

Interest in this part of Somalia resumed in the mid-1970s to early 1980s when high oil prices gave oil companies a lot of cash to spend on exploration. A huge concession over northern Somalia, known as the Duban conscession , was awarded in 1980 to a consortium comprising two privately owned US oil companies , the Dallas-based Hunt Oil Company and the Houston-based

Quintana Oil Company. These tried unsuccessfully for two years to interest other industry partners to explore the region but eventually were obliged to relinquish the concession. Hunt continued exploring in Yemen and discovered the Alif field while Quintana, which is owned by the Cullen banking family, cut down all its international exploration and concentrated on operating the south Texas Tom O'Connor oil field which produces its principal cash flow.

The discovery of oil in Yemen inspired further industry interest in Somalia. There are geological similarities between south Yemen and north Somalia, but geologists warn that the analogy cannot be taken too far. Since south Arabia and the of Horn of Africa were once geologically connected, certain structural trends are traceable from one side of the Gulf of Aden to the other. There is no evidence yet to support speculation that a mirror image of Yemen's Alif fields will be found in Somalia, but this cannot be discounted either. However an idea which has spread among some Somali officials that their country holds oil fields similar to those in Saudi Arabia is nonsensical.

CONSPIRACY THEORIES

By the mid-1980s, one third of the country was under license and, in the north, all but one permit had been awarded. The old Hunt/ Quintana concession was divided into two with one part awarded to Chevron and the other to a partnership of Amoco and Canada's International Petroleum Corporation, which has its technical headquarters in Dubai. Philips and Agip also held concessions, but the greatest undertaking was Conoco's. Conoco has been exploring in Somalia since the 1970s and holds six permits in the north. Just before the civil war broke out in 1988 there were rumors that it had made a significant oil discovery close to the Ethiopian border.

Conoco officials acknowledge that they have always maintained contact with all the at warring sides in the Somali war. One inspired action fuelling the latest conspiracy theories was that the Conoco manager in Mogadishu allowed US troops to use the company office. The conspiracy theorists cited this as proof that the US is protecting its oil companies and promoting oil interests. Oil executives say it is common sense for any company in all unstable country to make friends with the prevailing 'good guys ". "When the US troops leave and another set of troops replaces them he will probably invite those in too, if he has any sense," was one company response.

When some degree of peace was restored in the north following its unilateral breakaway in 1991, Somaliland president Abduirahman Ahmed Ali said that Conoco had visited Somaliland several times and as planning to open an office in Hargeisa. The Hargeisa government invited the other oil companies with concessions in the north for talks at the same time, but these initiatives have almost ground to a halt. The breakaway republic is not recognized internationally and its grip of the Hargeisa government has weakened in the face of increasing unrest. However, the companies are not relinquishing their concessions, and their executives say that they remain ready to resume work in Sornaliland as soon as it is safe to do so. For its part, the Hargeisa government has said it will honour until their expiry the existing contracts which foreign companies signed with the former government of Siad Barre, while at the same time drafting its own , new petroleum legislation.

A PROJECT TO ESTABLISH A NATIONAL OIL COMPANY IS BEING COORDINATED FROM RIYADH

But in September 1992 a never development emerged which may influence the situation further. A project is under may to establish a Somali state oil company to be known as the Somali National Petroleum (SNPC). This is being coordinated by Omar Arteh Ghalib, who was prime minister in the provisional government of Ali Mahdi Mohamed. Ghalib is now based in Riyadh running a consultancy firm called the Nort Petroleum Development Corporation. Ghalib has told oil company executives that he is the only Somali politician to have kept up contacts with all opposing sides in the country and that he sees himself as a future president. This views is not shared by his compatriots in the Issak tribe, based in the north, who see him as a traitor. Nor is

For additional analytical, business and investment opportunities information,
please contact Global Investment & Business Center, USA
at (202) 546-2103. Fax: (202) 546-3275. E-mail: rusric@erols.com

the northern government interested in the formation of the proposed SNPC, and its officials insist that there will never be a united Somalia again.

The creation of SNPC is being assisted by a former Saudi Aramco exploration manager, Moudjahid al-Husseilli, now based in Bahrain, and the London -based International Engineering Consultants. The Saudi connection is viewed within the oil sector as continuation of the Kingdom's interest in targeting potential oil projects in the Horn of Africa. This started in the mid-1980's in the face of competition from Iran, but has so far been without any result. Private Saudi investors has at various times proposed refining projects in Somalia, Djibouti and Ethiopia. Somalia's only refinery, a 10,000 barrel-a-day plant outside Mogadishu, was a jointly developed with Iran and started operating in 1979. In the mid-1980s, there were plans for it to be upgraded by Romanian engineers using Saudi finances but these never materialised.

Nevertheless, Saudi Arabia's stance is seen as crucial to the future of Somalia's oil sector, , if and when peace comes. The signals from Riyadh have been mixed. Saudi Arabia did, not participate in the World Bank/UN Development Programme study of the petroleum potential of the Red Sea and Gulf of Aden area - a three-year international project between the regional governments. Canada, some European states and a number of Western oil companies. At the time, the Saudis said that they preferred to develop their own oil and gas resources in their part of the Red Sea. Since then , the involvement of private Saudi investors in oil projects in Yemen is seen a portent of what may eventually happen in Somalia. It is an obvious investment opportunity right in Saudi Arabia's backyard. The head offices of those oil companies holding concessions in Somalia have already been visited by numerous intermediaries and commission agents claiming to be acting for major Middle East financial interests.

TOO GREEDY

The companies see this as an ominous sign that future investors in Somalia may repeat the mistakes made in Yemen. Yemeni oil exploration is stalling because companies paid huge fees to intermediaries, followed by even larger signature bonuses to the government, in order to acquire concessions. The average size of oil finds in Yemen and local operating costs mean that such fees can never be recovered from profits. The Saudi-owned Nimir Petroleum Company , which won the bidding to take over oil production in the Shabwa field discovered by Soviet explorers, is the most prominent example. If the commission agents become too greedy in their quests find oil investment for Somalia - whenever this becomes possible - they could stifle an oil industry there before it is born.

PASTORALISM AND COMMERCE IN HISTORICAL PERSPECTIVE

The Somalis raise cattle, sheep, and goats, but the camel plays the central role as an indicator of wealth and success. Camels can survive in an environment where water and grazing areas are scarce and widely scattered. They provide meat, milk, and transportation for Somali pastoralists, and serve as their principal medium of exchange. Camels are provided as compensation for homicides and are a standard component of the dowry package.

For centuries, nomads have relied on their livestock for subsistence and luxuries. They have sold cows, goats, and older camels to international traders and butchers in the coastal cities, and in the urban markets have bought tea, coffee beans, and salt. In the nineteenth century, northern Somalis were quick to take advantage of the market for goats with middlemen representing the British, who needed meat for their enclave in Aden, a coaling station for ships traveling through the Suez Canal. By the turn of the century, about 1,000 cattle and 80,000 sheep and goats were being exported annually from Berbera to Aden.

For additional analytical, business and investment opportunities information, please contact Global Investment & Business Center, USA at (202) 546-2103. Fax: (202) 546-3275. E-mail: rusric@erols.com

Starting in the fifteenth century, the ports of Saylac and Berbera were well integrated into the international Arab economy, with weapons, slaves, hides, skins, gums, ghee (a type of butter), ostrich feathers, and ivory being traded. On the Banaadir coast, especially in Mogadishu but also in Merca and Baraawe, a lively trade with China, India, and Arabia existed as early as the fourteenth century. Finally, starting with the Somalis who for centuries have joined the crews of oceangoing ships, the exportation of labor has long been a crucial element in Somalia's ability to sustain itself.

THE COLONIAL ECONOMY

The colonial era did not spark foreign economic investment despite the competition of three major European powers in the area of present-day Somalia. Italy controlled southern Somalia; Britain northern Somalia, especially the coastal region; and France the area that became Djibouti. Italian parliamentary opposition restricted any government activity in Somalia for years after European treaties recognized Italian claims. In the early twentieth century, projects aimed at using Somalia as a settlement for Italian citizens from the crowded homeland failed miserably. Although in the early 1930s Benito Mussolini drew up ambitious plans for economic development, actual investment was modest.

There was still less investment in British Somaliland, which India had administered. During the prime mininstership of William Gladstone in the 1880s, it was decided that the Indian government should be responsible for administering the Somaliland protectorate because the Somali coast's strategic location on the Gulf of Aden was important to India. Customs taxes helped pay for India's patrol of Somalia's Red Sea Coast. The biggest investment by the British colonial government in its three-quarters of a century of rule was in putting down the rebellion of the dervishes. In 1947, long after the dervish war of the early 1900s, the entire budget for the administration of the British protectorate was only £213,139. If Italy's rhetoric concerning Somalia outpaced performance, Britain had no illusions about its protectorate in Somaliland. At best, the Somali protectorate had some strategic value to Britain's eastern trading empire in protecting the trade route to Aden and India and helping assure a steady supply of food for Aden.

The two major economic developments of the colonial era were the establishment of plantations in the interriverine area and the creation of a salaried official class. In the south, the Italians laid the basis for profitable export-oriented agriculture, primarily in bananas, through the creation of plantations and irrigation systems. In both the north and the south, a stable petty bourgeois class emerged. Somalis became civil servants, teachers, and soldiers, petty traders in coastal cities, and small-business proprietors.

The plantation system began in 1919, with the arrival in Somalia of Prince Luigi Amedeo of Savoy, duke of Abruzzi, and with the technical support of the fascist administration of Governor Cesare Maria de Vecchi de Val Cismon. The Shabeelle Valley was chosen as the site of these plantations because for most of the year the Shabeelle River had sufficient water for irrigation. The plantations produced cotton (the first Somali export crop), sugar, and bananas. Banana exports to Italy began in 1927, and gained primary importance in the colony after 1929, when the world cotton market collapsed. Somali bananas could not compete in price with those from the Canary Islands, but in 1927 and 1930 Italy passed laws imposing tariffs on all non-Somali bananas. These laws facilitated Somali agricultural development so that between 1929 and 1936 the area under banana cultivation increased seventeenfold to 3,975 hectares. By 1935 the Italian government had constituted a Royal Banana Plantation Monopoly (Regia Azienda Monopolio Banane--RAMB) to organize banana exports under state authority. Seven Italian ships were put at RAMB's disposal to encourage the Somali banana trade. After World War II, when the United

Nations (UN) granted republican Italy jurisdiction over Somalia as a trust territory, RAMB was reconstituted as the Banana Plantation Monopoly (Azienda Monopolio Banane--AMB) to encourage the revival of a sector that had been nearly demolished by the war.

Plantation agriculture under Italian tutelage had short-term success, but Somali products never became internationally competitive. In 1955 a total of 235 concessions embraced more than 45,300 hectares (with only 7,400 hectares devoted to bananas), and produced 94,000 tons of bananas. Under fixed contracts, the three banana trade associations sold their output to the AMB, which exacted an indirect tax on the Italian consumer by keeping out cheaper bananas from other sources. The protected Italian market was a mixed blessing for the Somali banana sector. Whereas it made possible the initial penetration by Somali bananas of the Italian marketplace, it also eliminated incentives for Somali producers to become internationally competitive or to seek markets beyond Italy.

The investment in cotton showed fewer long-term results than the investment in bananas. Cotton showed some promise in 1929, but its price fell following the collapse in the world market. Nearly 1,400 tons in 1929 exports shrank to about 400 tons by 1937. During the trust period, there were years of modest success; in 1952, for example, about 1,000 tons of cotton were exported. There was however, no consistent growth. In 1953 exports dropped by two-thirds. Two reasons are given for cotton's failure as an export crop: an unstable world market and the lack of Somali wage labor for cotton harvesting. Because of the labor scarcity, Italian concessionaires worked out coparticipation contracts with Somali farmers; the Italians received sole purchasing rights to the crop in return for providing seed, cash advances, and technical support.

Another plantation crop, sugarcane, was more successful. The sugar economy differed from the banana and cotton economies in two respects: sugar was raised for domestic consumption, and a single firm, the Italo-Somali Agricultural Society (Societa Agricola Italo-Somala--SAIS), headquartered in Genoa, controlled the sector. Organized in 1920, the SAIS estate near Giohar had, by the time of the trust period, a little less than 2,000 hectares under cultivation. In 1950 the sugar factory's output reached 4,000 tons, enough to meet about 80 percent of domestic demand; by 1957 production had reached 11,000 tons, and Italian Somaliland no longer imported sugar.

Labor shortages beset Italian concessionaires and administrators in all plantation industries. Most Somalis refused to work on farms for wage labor. The Italians at first conscripted the Bantu people who lived in the agricultural region. Later, Italian companies paid wages to agricultural families to plant and harvest export crops, and permitted them to keep private gardens on some of the irrigated land. This strategy met with some success, and a relatively permanent work force developed. Somali plantation agriculture was of only marginal significance to the world economy, however. Banana exports reached US$6.4 million in 1957; those of cotton, US$200,000. But in 1957 plantation exports constituted 59 percent of total exports, representing a major contribution to the Somali economy.

The colonial period also involved government employment of salaried officials and the concomitant growth of a small urban petty bourgeoisie. In the north, the British administration originally had concentrated on the coastal area for trading purposes but soon discovered that livestock to be traded came from the interior. Therefore, it was necessary to safeguard caravan routes and keep peace in port areas, requiring the development of police forces and other civil services. In British Somaliland, many of the nomads scorned European education and opposed the establishment of Christian missions. Consequently, only a small pool of literate Somalis was available to work for the British administration. Kenyans therefore were hired. In the south, however, Somalis sent children to colonial and mission schools, and the graduates found civil service positions in the police force and as customs agents, bookkeepers, medical personnel, and teachers. These civil servants became a natural market for new retail businesses, restaurants, and coffee shops. Hargeysa in the precolonial period had almost no permanent commercial establishments; by 1945, nearly 500 businesses were registered in the district. The new salaried class filled the ranks of the Somali nationalist movement after World War II. Literate in Italian or English, these urban Somalis challenged colonial rule.

ECONOMIC DEVELOPMENT, 1960-69

At independence the Somali economy was at a near subsistence level, and the new state lacked the administrative capacity to collect taxes from subsistence herders and farmers. The state could rely on the customs taxes from international trade, which were easier to collect, but tariffs failed to meet the needs of a government with ambitious development goals. Somalia therefore relied on Italian and British subsidies, which funded about 31 percent of the new nation's current budget in the first three years of independence.

Somalia also received grants and loans from countries in the East and the West, which made possible the articulation of an ambitious development plan by 1963. A five-year plan with a budget of more than US$100 million in grants and loans, it focused on investment in infrastructure. The plan's thesis was that plantation crops and livestock exports would increase if there were better roads, transportation facilities, ports, and irrigation works. Another large investment was made in the creation of model farms to attract farmers from around the country, who would learn improved techniques to apply on their own farms. Model farms in Baidoa in the Bay Region, Afgooye near Mogadishu, and Tog Wajaale, west of Hargeysa, were established during this period.

In the pastoral sector, the Livestock Development Agency, formed in 1965-66, emphasized veterinary services, the provision of water and of holding grounds for cattle while they were undergoing inoculation, and transportation. Somali pastoralists responded with enthusiasm to the prospects for wealth by entering the international market for livestock. In the early 1960s, the value and number of exported livestock approximately doubled, and livestock soon surpassed bananas as Somalia's leading export.

There were therefore some notable successes among Somalia's early development projects. The nation became nearly selfsufficient in sugar, and banana exports grew, albeit haltingly. Livestock exports increased, and investments in roads and irrigation facilities resulted in some genuine improvements.

But the 1960s also yielded great disillusionment. The country could not overcome its dependence on foreign assistance, even to meet its current budget. Moreover, imports of foreign grains increased rapidly, indicating that the agricultural sector was not meeting the needs of the growing urban population. The modern agricultural techniques of state farms had little influence on traditional farming practices. Because of a boom in livestock export from Hargeysa, cows, goats, and camels were becoming concentrated in northern Somalia, much to the detriment of rangelands. The UN Food and Agriculture Organization (FAO) foresaw the dire effects of the 1974 drought in a 1967 report that noted the severe range deterioration. Finally, and perhaps most important, many Somalis were enervated by the feeling that political incumbents, through electoral manipulations, were squandering the nation's economic resources for their private benefit.

SCIENTIFIC SOCIALISM, 1970-75

Relying on Soviet advisers and a committed group of Italian-educated Somali "leftist" intellectuals, Siad Barre announced the 1971-73 Three-Year Plan. The plan emphasized a higher standard of living for every Somali, jobs for all who sought work, and the eradication of capitalist exploitation. Agricultural "crash programs" and creation of new manufacturing plants were the immediate results.

Siad Barre quickly brought a substantial proportion of the modern economy under state control. The government nationalized banks, insurance companies, petroleum distribution firms, and the sugar-refining plant and created national agencies for construction materials and foodstuffs. Although the Somali neologism for socialism, *hantiwadaag*, could be translated as the "sharing of livestock," camel herds were not nationalized, and Siad Barre reassured pastoralists that *hantiwadaag* would not affect their animals. To mollify international business, in 1972 Siad Barre announced a liberal investment code. Because the modern economy was so small, nationalization was more showmanship than a radical change in the economy.

The creation of cooperatives soon became a cornerstone in building a socialist economy. In 1973 the government decreed the Law on Cooperative Development, with most funds going into the agricultural sector. In the pre-coup years, agricultural programs had received less than 10 percent of total spending. By 1974 the figure was 29.1 percent. The investment in cooperatives had limited long-term results, however. In Galole near Hargeysa, for example, a government team established a cooperative in 1973, and government funds helped purchase a tractor, a cooperative center, and a grain storage tank. Members received token salaries as well. But in July 1977, with the beginning of the Ogaden War, state involvement in Galole ended; by 1991 the cooperative was no longer in operation.

Cooperatives also aimed at the nomad, although on a smaller scale. The 1974-78 Development Plan allocated only 4.2 percent of the budgeted funds to livestock. Government officials argued that the scientific management of rangeland--the regeneration of grazing lands and the drilling of new water holes--would be possible only under socialist cooperation. In the fourteen government-established cooperatives, each family received an exclusive area of 200 to 300 hectares of grazing land; in times of drought, common land under reserve was to become available. The government committed itself to providing educational and health services as well as serving as a marketing outlet for excess stock. Neither agricultural nor fishing cooperatives, however, proved economically profitable.

Integrated agricultural development projects were somewhat more successful than the cooperatives. The Northwest Region Agricultural Development Project, for example, survived the 1980s. Building upon the bunding (creation of embankments to control the flow of water) done by the British in the 1950s and by the United States Agency for International Development (AID) in the 1960s, the World Bank picked up the program in the 1970s and 1980s. Yields from bunded farms increased between 2.40 and 13.74 quintals per hectare over the yields from unbunded farms. However, overall improvement in agricultural production was hardly noticeable at a macroeconomic level.

Somalia's rural-based socialist programs attracted international development agencies. The Kuwait Fund for Arab Economic Development (KFAED), AID, and the FAO participated first in the Northern Rangelands Development Project in 1977 and in the Central Rangelands Project in 1979. These projects called for rotating grazing areas, using reserves, and creating new boreholes, but the drought of 1974 and political events undid most efforts.

During 1974-75 a drought devastated the pastoral economy. Major General Husseen Kulmiye headed the National Drought Relief Committee, which sought relief aid from abroad, among other programs. By January 1975, China, the United States, the European Economic Community, the Soviet Union, Italy, Sweden, Switzerland, Sudan, Algeria, Yugoslavia, Yemen, and others had pledged 66,229 tons of grain, 1,155 tons of milk powder, and tons of other food products. Later

For additional analytical, business and investment opportunities information, please contact Global Investment & Business Center, USA at (202) 546-2103. Fax: (202) 546-3275. E-mail: rusric@erols.com

that year, with aid from the Soviet Union, the government transported about 90,000 nomads from their hamlets to agricultural and fishing cooperatives in the south. The regime established new agricultural cooperatives at Dujuuma on the Jubba River (about 18,000 hectares), Kurtun Waareycnear the Shabelle River (about 6,000 hectares), and Sablaale northwest of Chisimayu (about 6,000 hectares). The KFAED and the World Bank supported irrigation projects in these cooperatives, in which corn, beans, peanuts, and rice were planted. Because the government provided seeds, water, management, health facilities, and schools, as well as workers' salaries, the farms were really state-owned farms rather than cooperatives. Essentially, they became havens for women and children because after the drought the men went off inland with whatever money they had accumulated to buy livestock to replenish their stock of animals.

The government also established fishing cooperatives. Despite a long coastline and an estimated potential yield of 150,000 tons per year of all species of fish, in the early 1970s fishing accounted for less than 1 percent of Somalia's gross domestic product (GDP). In 1975 cooperatives were established at Eyl, a post in the Nugaal region; Cadale, a port 1200 kilometers northeast of Mogadishu; and Baraawe. The Soviet Union supplied modern trawlers; when Soviet personnel left Somalia in 1978, Australia and Italy supported these fishing projects. Despite their potential and broad-based international support, these cooperatives failed to become profitable.

Siad Barre emphasized the great economic successes of the socialist experiment, a claim that had some truth in the first five years of the revolution. In this period, the government reorganized the sole milk-processing plant to make it more productive; established tomato-canning, wheat flour, pasta, cigarette, and match factories; opened a plant that manufactured cardboard boxes and polyethylene bags; and established several grain mills and a petroleum refinery. In addition, the state put into operation a meat-processing plant in Chisimayu, as well as a fish-processing factory in Laas Qoray northeast of Erigavo. The state worked to expand sugar operations in Giohar and to build a new sugar-processing facility in Afgooye. In three of the four leading light industries--canned meats, milk, and textiles--there were increases in output between 1969 and 1975.

Progress in the early socialist period was not uniform, however. The government heralded various programs in the transport, packaging, irrigation, drainage, fertilization, and spraying of the banana crop. Yet, despite the boom year of 1972, banana exports declined.

THE SOCIALIST REVOLUTION AFTER 1975

Popular enthusiasm for the revolution began to dissipate by the mid-1970s. Many officials had become corrupt, using their positions for personal gain, and a number of ideologues had been purged from the administration as potential threats to their military superiors. Perhaps most important, Siad Barre's regime was focusing its attention on the political goal of "liberating" the Ogaden (Ogaadeen) rather than on the economic goal of socialist transformation. The Somali economy was hurt as much by these factors and by the economic cost of creating a large modern army as it was by the concurrent drought. Two economic trends from this period were noteworthy: increasing debt and the collapse of the small industrial sector.

During the 1970s, foreign debt increased faster than export earnings. By the end of the decade, Somalia's debt of 4 billion shillings equaled the earnings from seventy-five years' worth of banana exports (based on 1978 data). About one-third was owed to centrally planned economies (mainly the Soviet Union, US$110 million; China, US$87.2 million; with small sums to Bulgaria and the German Democratic Republic East Germany). Another one-third of the debt was owed to countries in the Organisation for Economic Cooperation and Development (OECD). Finally, one-third was owed to members of the Organization of the Petroleum Exporting Countries (OPEC) (principally Saudi Arabia, US$81.9 million; Abu Dhabi, US$67.0 million; the Arab Fund for

Economic and Social Development, US$34.7 million; Kuwait, US$27.1 million; and smaller amounts to Iraq, Qatar, the OPEC special account, Libya, and Algeria, in that order). Many loans, especially from the Soviet Union, were, in effect, written off. Later, many loan repayments to OECD states were rescheduled. But thanks to the accumulated debt burden, by the 1980s the economy could not attract foreign capital, and virtually all international funds made available to Somalia in rescheduling agreements came with the provision that international civil servants would monitor all expenditures. As a result of its international debt, therefore, Somalia lost control over its macroeconomic structure.

A second ominous trend in the 1975-81 period was the decline of the manufacturing sector. Exports of manufactured goods were negligible when the 1969 coup occurred; by the mid 1970s, manufactured goods constituted 20 percent of total exports. By 1978, as a consequence of the Ogaden War, such exports were almost nonexistent. Production likewise suffered. In 1969 Somalia refined 47,000 tons of sugar; by 1980 the figure was 29,100 tons. In 1975 the country produced 14.4 million cans of meat and 2,220 tons of canned fish. In 1979 it produced 1.5 million cans of meat and a negligible amount of canned fish. Textile output rose over the period. The only material produced, however, was a coarse fabric sold to rural people (and worn by the president) at less than cost. In milk, pasta, packaging materials, cigarettes, and matches, the trend was downward in the second half of the 1970s.

FROM SCIENTIFIC SOCIALISM TO "IMF-ISM," 1981-90

Its socialist program in disarray and its alliance with. Like most countries devastated by debt in the late 1970s, Somalia could rely only on the nostrums of the IMF and its program the Soviet Union lost in the wake of the 1977-78 Ogaden War, Somalia once again turned to the West of structural adjustment.

In February 1980, a standby macroeconomic policy agreement with the IMF was signed, but not implemented. The standby agreements of July 1981 and July 1982 were completed in July 1982 and January 1984, respectively. To meet IMF standards, the government terminated its policy of acting as the last-resort employer of all secondary school graduates and abolished its monopoly on grain marketing. The government then prepared a medium-term recovery program consisting of a public investment program for 1984-86 and a phased program of policy reforms. Because the International Development Association (IDA) considered this program too ambitious, the government scaled down its projects, most notably the construction of the Baardheere Dam, which AID had advised against. The government abandoned its first reform program in 1984. In March 1984, the government signed a letter of intent accepting the terms of a new US$183 million IMF extended credit facility to run for three years. In a Somali Council of Ministers meeting in April, however, this agreement was canceled by one vote, as the soldier-ministers chafed at the proposed 60 percent cut in the military budget. The agreement also called for a further devaluation of the shilling and reductions in government personnel.

A new crisis hit Somalia in June 1983. The Saudi Arabian government decided to stop importing Somali cattle, and this ban soon was expanded to include sheep and goats. Saudi officials claimed that rinderpest had been detected in Somali livestock, making them unsafe. Cynics pointed out that Saudi businessmen recently had invested in Australian ranches and were seeking to carve out an export market for their product. In any event, the ban created a large budget deficit, and arrears on debt service started to accumulate. A major obstacle to expanding livestock and other exports was Somalia's lack of communications infrastructure: good roads and shipping facilities as well as effective telecommunications and postal services. Lack of banking facilities also posed a problem. Somalia could not easily avoid the medicine of structural adjustment.

In March 1985, in negotiations with the Paris Club (the informal name for a consortium of eighteen Western creditor countries), Somalia's debt service schedule was restructured, and the government adopted a reform program that included a devaluation and the establishment of a free market for foreign exchange for most private transactions. In November 1985, in conjunction with the Consultative Group of Aid Donors, a technical body of the Paris Club, the government presented its National Development Strategy and Programme with a revised three-year investment program. Western aid officials criticized this program as too ambitious. In June 1986, the government negotiated an agricultural sector adjustment program with IDA. In September 1986, a foreign exchange auction system was initiated, but its operation encountered severe difficulties because to its complete dependence on external aid. Many exchange rates applicable to different types of transactions consequently came into existence.

AID prepared a second-stage project report in 1986 that renewed the call for privatization. It praised the government for permitting the free importation of petroleum products, but chided the Somalis for not yet allowing the free marketing of hides and skins. AID put great pressure on the government, especially by means of lobbyists, to take action on legislation to permit private banking. To encourage the private sector further, AID was prepared to fund the Somali Chamber of Commerce if the Somali government would allow it to become an independent body. The 1986 report went beyond privatization by calling for means of improving the government's revenue collection and budgetary control systems. Building a government capable of collecting taxes, making policy reforms, and addressing fiscal problems became the new focus. Along these lines, AID encouraged the elimination of civil service jobs. As of in 1985, although 5,000 civil servants had been dismissed AID felt that 80 percent of the civil service was still redundant. AID officials, however, urged pay raises for those in useful jobs.

Somalia's Five-Year Plan for 1987-91 largely reflected the international pressures and incentives of the IMF and AID. Privatization was written into the plan, as were development projects that were smaller in scale and more easily implemented. By 1988 the government had announced implementation of many IMFand AID-encouraged structural adjustment policies. In regard to foreign exchange, the government had taken many intermediate steps that would lead to the merger of the pegged and market rates. As for banking, legislation had been enacted allowing private banks to operate. In public finance, the government had reduced its deficit from 10 to 7 percent of GDP, as had been advised, but acknowledged that the increased taxes on fuel, rent, and sales had been only partially implemented. A value-added tax on fuel imports remained under consideration, but the tax on rental income had been increased and the sales tax raised from 5 to 10 percent. The government continued to procrastinate concerning public enterprises, holding only informal discussion of plans to liquidate unprofitable enterprises.

The IMF corrected some of the worst abuses of the socialist experiment. With the devaluation of the shilling, the real cost of foreign grain became apparent to consumers, and the relative price of domestic grain rose. Rectifying prices induced a 13.5 percent increase in agricultural output between 1983 and 1985. Inflation was tamed as well, falling from an annual rate of 59 percent in 1980 to 36 percent in 1986. World Bank officials used these data to publicize the Somali success in structural adjustment.

The overall picture was not that encouraging, however. Manufacturing output declined, registering a drop of 0.5 percent per annum from 1980 to 1987. Exports decreased by 16.3 percent per annum from 1979 to 1986. Moreover, the 0.8 percent rise in GDP per annum from 1979 to 1986 did not keep up with population growth. World Bank estimates put Somalia's 1989 (gross national product GNP at US$1,035 million, or US$170 per person, and further estimated that between 1980 and 1989 real GNP per person had declined at 1.7 percent per year.

For additional analytical, business and investment opportunities information, please contact Global Investment & Business Center, USA at (202) 546-2103. Fax: (202) 546-3275. E-mail: rusric@erols.com

In the period from 1987 to 1989, the economic results of agricultural production were mixed. Although corn, sorghum, and sugarcane were principal crops, livestock and bananas remained major exports. The value of livestock and banana exports in 1989 (the latest year for which data were available in May 1992) was US$26 million and US$25 million, respectively. Livestock, consisting primarily of camels, cattle, goats, and sheep, served several purposes. The animals provided milk and meat for domestic consumption, and livestock, hides, and skins for export.

As a result of the civil war in many areas, the economy deteriorated rapidly in 1989 and 1990. Previously, livestock exports from northern Somalia represented nearly 80 percent of foreign currency earned, but these exports came to a virtual halt in 1989. Shortages of most commodities, including food, fuel, medicines, and water, occurred virtually countrywide. Following the fall of the Siad Barre regime in late January 1991, the situation failed to improve because clan warfare intensified. Statistical data were minimal, however, for the period from 1990 onward.

For additional analytical, business and investment opportunities information, please contact Global Investment & Business Center, USA at (202) 546-2103. Fax: (202) 546-3275. E-mail: rusric@erols.com

MINERAL AND MINING SECTOR: STRATEGIC INFORMATION
SOMALIA

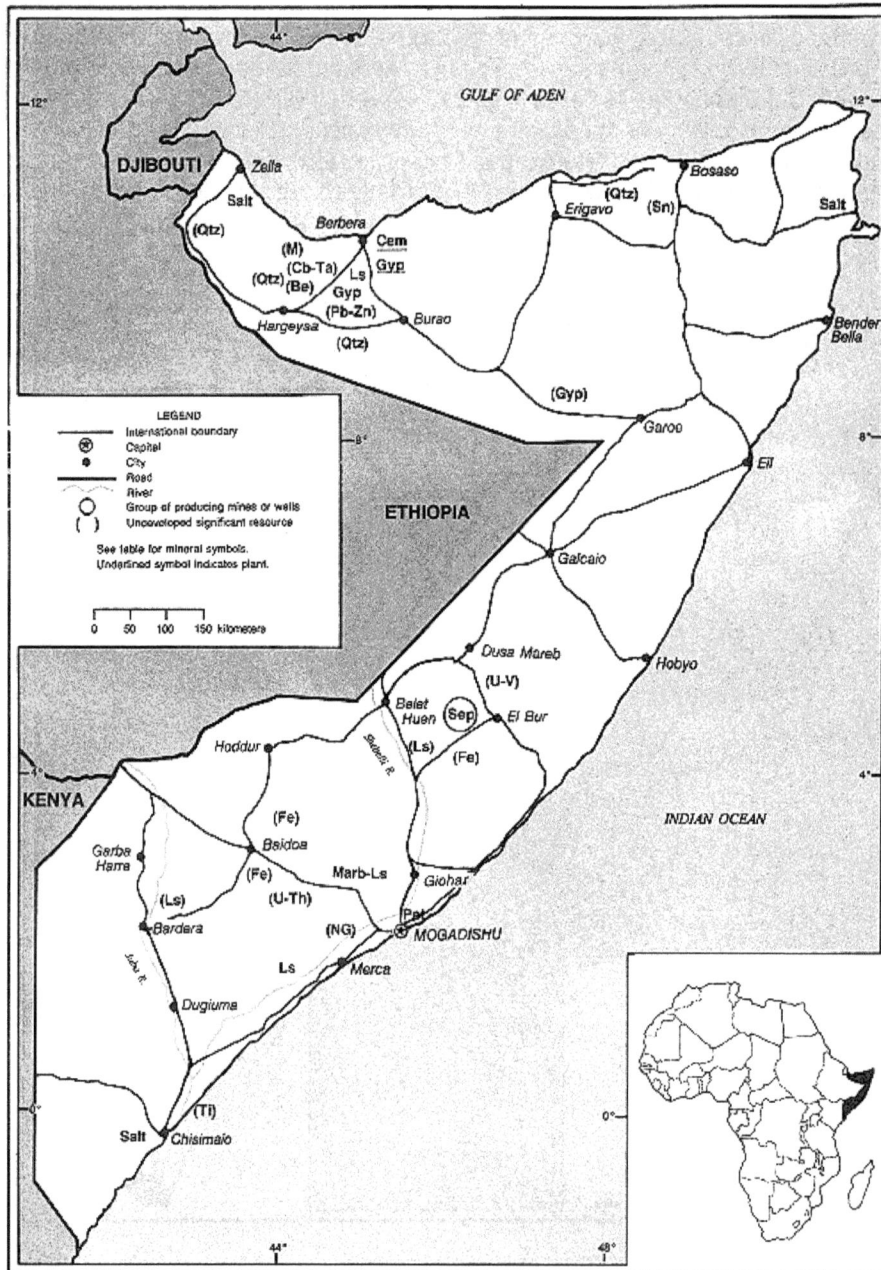

For additional analytical, business and investment opportunities information,
please contact Global Investment & Business Center, USA
at (202) 546-2103. Fax: (202) 546-3275. E-mail: rusric@erols.com

THE MINERAL INDUSTRY OF SOMALIA

Somalia, which is an East African country located on the Gulf of Aden and the Indian Ocean, produced small quantities of gemstones, granite, marble, niobium (columbium), salt, sandstone, and tantalum in recent years. The mineral industry made a small contribution to Somalia's exports and economy in general. The country also had deposits of feldspar, iron ore, kaolin, limestone, natural gas, quartz, silica sand, tin, and uranium.

Civil war continued in Somalia in 2010. African Union and Transitional Federal Government (TFG) military forces engaged in combat with the Al-Shabab militia in Mogadishu in August and early September. Al-Shabab, which was affiliated with Al-Qaeda, also engaged in combat with military forces of the semiautonomous region of Puntland in northern Somalia. In early December, Al-Shabab engaged in combat with the Hizbul Islam militia; the groups merged in late December. At yearend, Al-Shabab controlled most of southern and central Somalia (Gettleman, 2010; Gettleman and Ibrahim, 2010; Ibrahim, 2010a, b; Sheikh and Macharia, 2010).

Military forces from Ethiopia and the self-declared Republic of Somaliland (which maintains a separate regional governing authority) engaged in armed conflict with the Northern Somali Unionist Movement in July 2010. Somaliland's declaration of independence in 1991 and Puntland's declaration of autonomy in 1998 had not been internationally recognized.

PRODUCTION

Mineral production data continued to be unavailable because of the lack of a functioning central Government since 1991 and the conflict that pervaded most of the country. In 2006, a dimension stone operation that produced granite, marble, and sandstone started production in Somaliland. In 2008, niobium and tantalum mining operations started; it is unclear if production continued after a labor dispute in April 2009. The war forced the closure of Somalia's oil refinery and cement plant in 1991 and 1996, respectively.

STRUCTURE OF THE MINERAL INDUSTRY

Private companies produced granite, marble, and sandstone. Gemstone and salt mining operations appear to have been artisanal and small scale in nature. In 2006 (the latest year for which data were available), more than 1,600 workers were estimated to be employed in artisanal mining operations in Somaliland (Intermediate Technology Consultants Eastern Africa, 2006, p. 26). The country's cement plant and oil refinery were operated by parastatal companies before they were closed. The collapse of the central Government led to ambiguity over mineral rights.

MINERAL FUELS

Natural Gas and Petroleum.—Africa Oil Ltd. of Canada and Range Resources Ltd. of Australia explored for crude petroleum at the Dharoor Valley and the Nugaal Valley onshore blocks in Puntland. The companies planned to drill exploration wells at Dharoor Valley and Nugaal Valley in 2011 (Range Resources Ltd., 2011, p. 5).

OIL EXPLORATION IN PUNTLAND

Several key players are involved in **oil exploration in the Puntland** region of Somalia:

- Amsas Consulting an energy and resource consulting firm based in Melbourne, Australia was the first company to get involved in Puntland in the mid 90's after most major oil companies declared force-Majeure.The company has done some study recently in Puntland in December 2008. The only repository of data is with this company headed by Dr.Ali Abdullahi a former Presidential candidate in the Federal and State elections of 2004 and 2008.He was also instrumental in the setting up of the state of Puntland in 1996-1998.He was also a former Special Adviser on Energy and resources and has worked with many International Corporations and governments in Africa.
- Africa Oil Corporation, formerly Canmex Minerals, an oil company based in Vancouver, British ColumbiaCanada.
- Range Resources Limited-[1], a mineral exploration company based in Perth, Western Australia andMelbourne, Victoria, Australia
- Puntland State government of Somalia, where theNogal and Dharoor blocks are located.
- Transitional Government of Somalia

CONOCO AND PHILLIPS OPERATIONS

In the early 1990s, Conoco and Phillips Petroleum(before they merged) had concessions in the Nogal valley. They drilled two unsuccessful wells before abandoning their concessions and evacuated their personnel upon the collapse of the Siad Barregovernment.

CONSORT PRIVATE GETS RIGHTS IN PUNTLAND

Consort Private Limited, a holding company operated by two Australian deal-brokers Terry Donnelly and Anthony Black, traveled toPuntland in April 2005 to tour the country and meet with Puntland leaders.

On June 10, 2005, Puntland presidentMohamud Muse Hersi, planning and international cooperation minister Dr. Abdirahman Farole and Terry Donelly travel toDubai, UAE to begin negotiations on a deal. Later during the trip, the Puntland delegation lands in Nairobi, Kenya to take part of Somali transitional federal government's (TFG) relocation to Somalia. In Nairobi, it was reported that TFG President Abdullahi Yusuf (the previous and founding President of Puntland) and Puntland President Hersi became "angry" at each other because the TFG leadership refused to honor any agreement signed between a regional government (i.e. Puntland) and a foreign company.[2]

The Puntland delegation went ahead anyways, returned to Dubai and signed an agreement on August 30, 2005 at the Hilton Dubai with Consort Private for exclusive rights to explore and drill for oil in the Nogal and Dharoor blocks. Two days prior to this, the Somali Prime Ministersent a warning to non-Somali companies that any oil deals would have to go through the federal government, not any state government (this despite the fact that Puntland was and is independent of the federal government in all but name).[3]

While the details of the deal are known only to the four men who signed it, what is known is that following the deal, a number of Puntland ministers were added to the board of directors, and the government of Puntland by extension must have a sizeable (perhaps even controlling) share in Consort Private.

Not to be put off so easily, Somali TFG President Abdullahi Yusuf, in an interview with the BBC on September 9, 2005, says that legally "natural resources belonging to the nation is the responsibility of the federal government". A few weeks later on September 29, 2005 a delegation from Puntland composed of ministers and businessmen travelled to the TFG's interim capital at

For additional analytical, business and investment opportunities information,
please contact Global Investment & Business Center, USA
at (202) 546-2103. Fax: (202) 546-3275. E-mail: rusric@erols.com

Jowhar to led by finance minister Mohamed Yusuf "Gaagaab" to unsuccessfully negotiate again for Yusuf's signature on the deal.

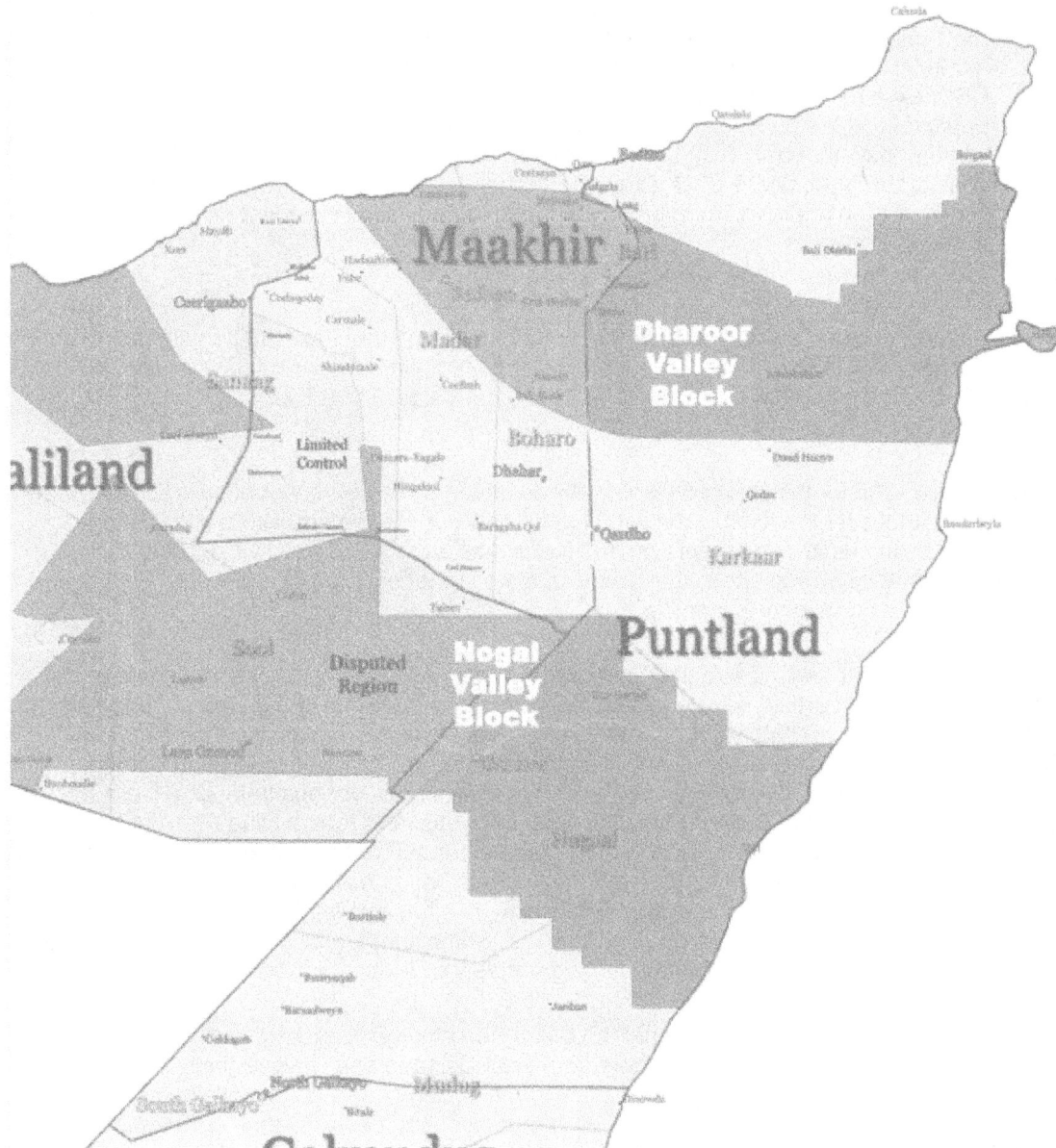

Dharoor and Nogal Blocks

RANGE RESOURCES PURCHASES EXPLORATION RIGHTS

Range Resources purchased 50.1% of Consort Private's exclusive rights to the Dharoor and Nogal blocks on October 5, 2005 in exchange for $2,500,000 USD in cash, 17 monthly payments of $200,000 USD, 85,000,000 shares of Range Resources stock and a further 85,000,000 stock options.[4] In June 2006 the remaining 49.9% was purchased from Consort Private with the key assistance of Sir Sam Jonah, who became the non-executive chairman of Range[5]

For additional analytical, business and investment opportunities information, please contact Global Investment & Business Center, USA at (202) 546-2103. Fax: (202) 546-3275. E-mail: rusric@erols.com

The deal had several terms, which hinged on certain conditions:

1. 6 month exclusive option to acquire Consort's interest on the terms set out below with an option fee of 100,000,000 listed Range shares (RRS) and 50,000,000 stock options (RRSO) payable subject to any necessary shareholder approvals;
2. 750,000,000 Range ordinary fully paid shares, 375,000,000 stock options (unlisted, $0.05 USD, expiring October 1, 2010) and $10,000,000 USD conditional on shareholder approval and the completion of a minimum $25,000,000 USD capital raising;
3. A further payment of 750,000,000 Range ordinary fully paid shares, 375,000,000 stock options (unlisted, $0.05 USD, expiring October 1, 2010) and $20,000,000 USD conditional on shareholder approval and upon completion of the first hydrocarbon well drilled in Puntland;
4. 2.5% net royalty on the Puntland Projects;

Range Resources issued a press release the same day stating that the TFG had signed off on the deal. The Prime Minister of the TFG, Ali Mohamed Gedi, fired back less than a week later on October 16, 2005, refuting this claim in a letter to the Australian Stock Exchange, where Range Resources is traded.

On November 2, 2005, Ali Mohamed Gedi finally accepted an "amendment of contract" between Puntland and Range, removing the last legal hurdle between Range and exploration. Range Resources does not have agreement from the traditional leaders and the civil society organizations of the SSC regions - where most of the oil prospecting is taking place. From a legal standpoint, it does not appear to need it.

The manner in which Puntland and their partners (Range Resources LTD, Canmex/African Oil Corp and other linked parties) have explored for minerals, oil and gas in the Dharoor and Nugaal valley has drawn criticism both within Puntland, Somalia and in the diaspora. Somalia is a patchwork of overlapping administrations, clans and traditional authorities, which in Puntland includes the Transitional Government, the Puntland Government, various traditional Harti clan leaders, and individual loyalties to a particular warlord or business leader. The President of Puntland has chosen to place himself above all these other authorities within Puntland, and critics claim the oil, mineral and gas exploration in Puntland has become an engine empowering conflict and war in northern Somalia. Since exploration began, this has spawned Puntland's war with Somaliland, Maakhir's purported break with Puntland, Somaliland's war with Maakhir, gun-battles outside of the Puntland State legislature, and a great deal of political uncertainty.[citation needed]

The Northern Somali Unionist Movement (NSUM), a Somali organization of unclear size or influence, claiming members and supporters from Sool, Sanaag and Cayn regions in the northern regions of Somalia, which are thought to contain some of Somalia's most promising geology oil wise, has issued a warning[6] to mineral and oil companies that they view their agreements with the Puntland and Transitional governments to be illegitimate and non-binding.

EXPLORATION PROBLEMS AND POLITICAL INSTABILITY

On February 26, 2006 the Puntland Parliament faced a confidence vote on President Hersi's Council of Ministers. Heated argument and disputes in the parliament turned ugly, and by the next day at least three armed men were reported dead near Garowe's Parliament House.

Puntland minister of planning and international cooperation, a key player in the negotiations with Consort Private and chief opponent of Range Resources/Africa Oil Corp. deal, Dr. Abdirahman Farole,

CANMEX/AFRICA OIL CORP. GETS INVOLVED

A Memorandum Of Understanding (MOU) signed on October 10 2006 between Canmex Minerals, Range and Puntland granted Canmex an 80% interest in the "licenses and operatorship" of the Dharoor and Nogal blocks, contingent upon:

1. Canmex to pay to Range a signing bonus in the aggregate amount of $5,000,000 USD within 10 days of signing the agreement[7]
2. The financial commitment over an initial four year period of $50,000,000 USD in exploration expenditures; and
3. The payment to Range of an additional $3,500,000 USD upon commencement of commercial production

With the signing bonus paid, and with approval of the Puntland parliament, Range, Puntland and Canmex hammered out a Production Sharing Agreement on January 23, 2007, that confirmed the terms of the MOU signed in October.[8]

In order to meet their financial obligations, Canmex sold 4,000,000 common shares in a non-brokered private placement in order to raise $20,000,000 USD. Canmex officially renamed itself Africa Oil Corp. (AOI.V) on August 20, 2007.

PM GEDI AND THE TFP BATTLE PRESIDENT YUSUF

In November 2006, while the TFG was besieged by Islamist armies in Baidoa and Ethiopia was preparing to invade the Union of Islamic Courts, President Yusuf traveled to the headquarters of the PRC's state-owned China National Offshore Oil Corporation (CNOOC) as well as the smaller China International Oil and Gas (CIOG) Group to ratify a deal with the oil group's chairman and chief executive officer, Fu Chengyu.

Seven months later, in Nairobi, TFG Energy Minister Abdullahi Yusuf Mohamad met withChen Zhuobiao, head of CNOOC operations in Africa, and Judah Jay, managing director of CIOG, to create the final agreement, which was signed by President Abdullahi Yusuf on July 18, 2007. The agreement gave CNOOC exclusive rights to the large offshore blocks off the coast of Mudug, for an undisclosed sum of money and unknown terms.[10]

Prime Minister Gedi decided to get in on all this action himself, and backtracked on his previous, lukewarm endorsement of Puntland's oil exploration agreement and instead proposed a draft law in the Transitional Federal Parliament in August 2007 that would nullify all agreements made after 1991 (when the last functional national government collapsed and the oil companies with existing concessions declared *Force Majeure*) thus giving the TFG free rein to resell all the exploration rights in the country. The exploration rights for all of Somalia would be sold to Indonesia's PT Medco Energi Internasional Tbk and the Kuwait Energy Company, and a National Oil Company of Somalia would be created, controlled by Gedi and parliament.

This directly confronted President Yusuf's deal with CNOOC, and so the two went to political war with each other, leading to Gedi's forced resignation after more than two months of backroom warfare, on October 29 2007.[citation needed]

UNCERTAINTY AS EXPLORATION BEGINS

For additional analytical, business and investment opportunities information, please contact Global Investment & Business Center, USA at (202) 546-2103. Fax: (202) 546-3275. E-mail: rusric@erols.com

Range and Africa Oil completed their initial survey of the Dharoor and Nogal basins in September 2007, as well as a full seismic survey of Nogal. Mobilization for drilling in Nogal and a seismic analysis of Dharoor began immediately during the winter of 2007.[11]

On December 12, 2007 the Puntland Minister of Fisheries and Ports Said Mohamed Rage resigned from parliament after a long dispute with President Hersi. Central to the feud was President Hersi's micromanagement of Bosaso port, which was supposed to be his domain, but also the resource agreement with Range and Africa Oil, which he opposed. A month earlier on November 22 2007, a Range team left the village of Buru after Said Mohamed Rage's clan asked for payment for it to remain there and the Hersi's government discouraged such payment.

President Hersi reshuffled his cabinet on December 16 2007 and created a new ministry of Oil and Resources, placing Hassan "Alore" Osman in charge of the ministry.[12]

TFG President Abdullahi Yusuf was hospitalized in London, England shortly thereafter, and there the issue rested until the president checked out of his London hospital room on February 3, 2008[13]. Before flying to Baidoa, President Yusuf landed in Addis Ababa on February 5, 2008 to meet with the Ethiopian government and also with Puntland President Hersi regarding the TFG's stance on the Puntland-Range-Africa Oil deal. President Hersi was also in Addis Ababa to meet with the Ethiopian government regarding the perceived relaxed attitude of Puntland towards Somali rebel groups using Bosaso port

DRILLING RIG CONSTRUCTION CONTRACTED TO SOUTHEAST ASIA, CHINA

Africa Oil Corp. signed a contract on February 19, 2008 with Energi Tata Persada Pte Ltd(ETP), a Singaporean registered company, for construction of the first drilling rig. ETP is a wholly owned subsidiary of Catur Khita Persada of Indonesia. Construction commenced on ETP rig No.3 at the Shengli fabrication plant in Dongying, China commenced shortly after the contract was signed.

According to the press release:

> The ETP rig is scheduled for delivery in mid May, 2008 and will immediately mobilize to Jebel Ali, Dubai. The mobilization into Somalia will be via chartered vessel and the current plan is to spud the first well during July.

> The ETP No 3 is a 1,500 HP unit, equipped with the latest drilling technology, including a top drive and three 1,600 HP pumps. The camp facility will house up to 150 persons and will also be brand new. ETP will also provide the trucking and hoisting equipment as part of their contractual obligations.[15]

SECURITY

Africa Oil and Range Resources employed a number of government troops to provide security for their ongoing seismic operation. A number of unarmed western security advisers were also employed on the ground in Puntland.

SOMALILAND INVASION OF SOOL

The region of Sool, which contains the majority of the Nugaal block, was invaded by Somaliland forces in late 2007, an invasion that captured virtually all of the region save for the enclave of Cayn by 2009. Puntland issued extremely confident-sounding declarations that they would recapture Sool any minute, "massive armies were mustering", etc, though by springtime 2008 it was clear that Somaliland was not going anywhere anytime soon. In April 2008, Africa Oil announced that as a result of the "deterioration of the security situation in parts of Somalia" the implementation of the Nugaal drill program would be delayed[16]. As they could not explore the actual area itself, the company instead purchased 2D survey data from the 1980s of the Nugaal Valley to analyze.

HYDROCARBON POTENTIAL OF SOMALILAND

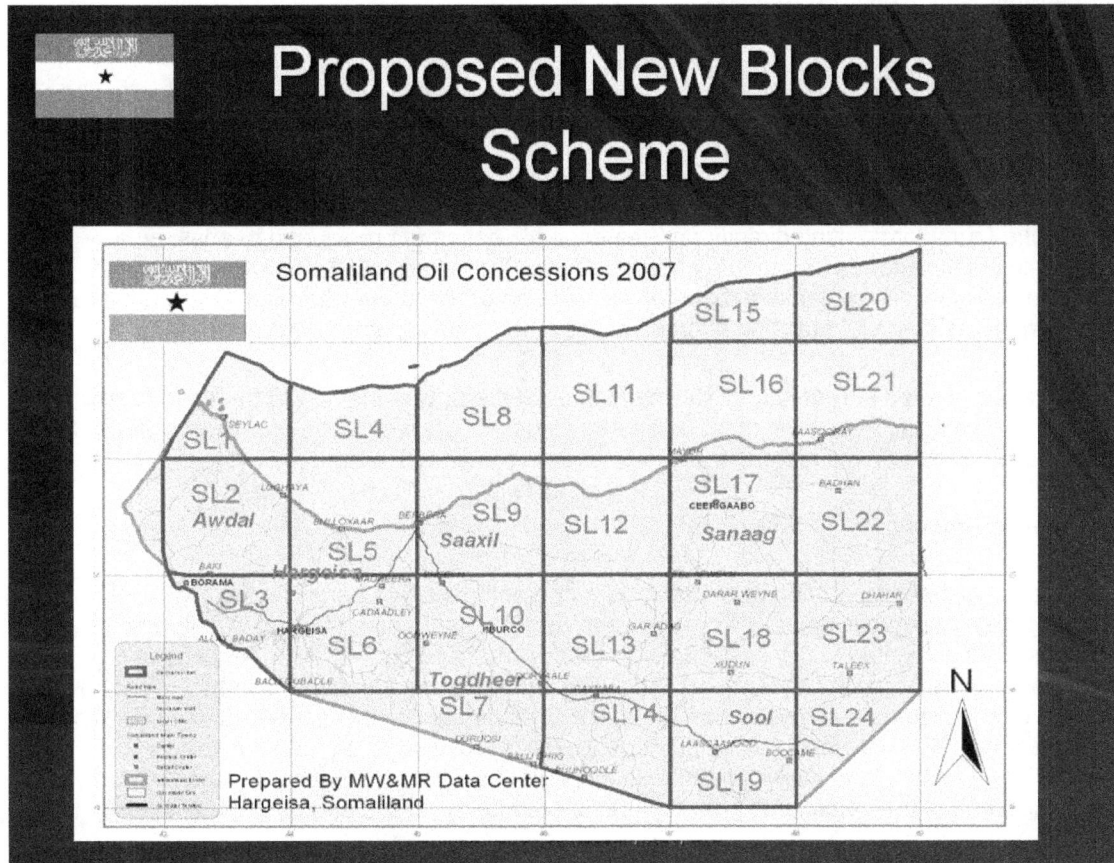

Somaliland (Northern Somalia) is situated on the northern side of the Horn of Africa with the Gulf of Aden to the north, Somalia to the east, Ethiopia to the south and west, and Djibouti to the north-west (Fig.1). The morphology of the country is typical of areas in extension, with basins and mountains of up to 2000 m. There is little folding, but much normal faulting, some of which has very great throws. These strong vertical movements have controlled the accommodation space available for sediment deposition since the Lower Jurassic.

To date there have only been 21 wells drilled in Somaliland (19 onshore and two offshore), many of which were only stratigraphic tests (Fig. 2). In fact few of the wells evaluated the hydrocarbon potential of the country and the type of prospects in the drilled basins. In addition, modern seismic reflection surveying has had very limited application in Somaliland. Therefore, many prospective petroleum systems in the onshore and offshore regions of the country remain relatively unexplored.

In this paper, seismic, well, and outcrop data have been used to determine the petroleum systems of Somaliland. These data demonstrate that the country has favourable stratigraphy, structure, oil shows, and hydrocarbon source rocks. In addition, the results show that the Upper Jurassic and Cretaceous units, and possibly Oligocene-Miocene units, show potential for hydrocarbon generation. Traps are provided by rollover anticlines associated with listric growth faults and rotated basement faults which are controlled by Upper Jurassic to Lower Cretaceous tensional stresses.

Stratigraphy and depositional setting

The sedimentary section of Somaliland can be divided into four parts (Fig. 2):

Jurassic rift sequences

The Jurassic deposits in Somaliland consist of a thick sequence of continental deposits (basal sandstone formation) resting directly on the peneplain basement rocks and overlain by a succession of limestones (Bihendula group) generally with some marl and shale intervals. Jurassic sediments were deposited in NW-SE trending grabens (e.g., Bihendula graben) that were formed as a result of tensional forces associated with the rifting of India from Africa.

The Jurassic outcrop at Bihendula, 35 km south of Berbera, was the first to be recognized in the country and has since been the most extensively studied. It is where the greatest thickness (more than 1200 m) of fossiliferous marine Jurassic beds are exposed in the country.

Cretaceous sequences

The Cretaceous sedimentation of Somaliland is characterized by lateral lithologic variability resulting from transgressing seas from the east. As a consequence, thick carbonate and shale sections were deposited in the eastern part of the country and equally thick sequences of sandstones were deposited in the west. The widely used term 'Nubian sandstone' has been applied by several workers to describe the entire Cretaceous clastic sequences seen in outcrop (MacFadyen, 1933). However, some authors (Bosellini, 1992) divided the Cretaceous into Yesomma sandstone and Tisje carbonates, although it is difficult to distinguish the different formations due to the transitional nature of the interfingering clastic and carbonate facies.

Eocene sequences

Eocene deposits of Somaliland consist of massive limestones of Auradu and Karkar formations separated by massive to banded gypsum and anhydrites. This is the result of Eocene seas transgressing from the east depositing Auradu limestones. Periodic regression in the Middle Eocene resulted in evaporatic conditions, which led to the deposition of the Anhydrite (Taleh) series. Further transgression in the Upper Eocene caused the deposition of marine cherty limestone of Karkar formation.

Oligocene-Miocene rift sequences

Oligocene and Miocene sediments are mostly restricted to narrow and isolated sub-basins along the coastal belt bordering the Gulf of Aden, occasionally extending inland in low lying regions.

They deposited in localized grabens caused by the rifting of the Gulf of Aden. They consist of a thick (up to 2500 m) syn-rift sequence of red-brown, green sand, silts, and gypsiferous sandstone. These sediments are almost entirely terrigenous deposited in lagoon, delta, and alluvial environments. The best outcrops of Oligocene-Miocene sediments occur in Daban basin (south-east of Berbera) which is a down-faulted rotated block bordering the Somaliland plateau (Fig. 2).

A summary of the stratigraphy of Somaliland is given in Fig. 3. This figure shows the major formations, general thicknesses, and known occurrences of oil shows in these rocks.

Exploration history

Petroleum exploration in the country began in 1912 when an oil seep at Dagah Shabel, 38 km south-east of Berbera, was reported. In 1959 Standard Vacuum (Mobil and Esso) drilled three dry wells (Dagah Shabel-1, -2, and -3) near the Dagah Shabel oil seep, without the aid of subsurface control. One of the wells recovered free oil from the Wanderer limestone (Upper Jurassic) and Nubian sandstone (Upper Cretaceous). However, no oil was recovered from the follow-up wells.

Interest in oil exploration recommenced in the late 1970s and, in 1980, GECO conducted an extensive offshore speculative seismic survey in the Gulf of Aden for the Somali government. In the same year a vast concession known as the Guban concession was awarded to a consortium consisting of two oil companies, the Quintana Oil Company and Hunt Oil Company. They conducted a detail exploration programme which included an aeromagnetic survey and a seismic programme over onshore blocks 32 and 35. However, after two years they relinquished the concession.

Exploration interest in the country intensified in the mid 1980s during which most of the concessions were awarded to different oil companies (Fig. 2). The Hunt and Quintana concession was divided into two with one part awarded to Chevron and the other to a partnership of Amoco and International Petroleum Corporation. Phillips and Agip also held concessions in the country. Shell was awarded an offshore concession which encompassed most of the Gulf of Aden coastline. However, it relinquished that in 1984 after the failure of two wells (Bandar Harshau-1 and Dab Qua1), although oil shows were encountered in pre-rift Eocene carbonates and post-rift clastics. The two wells were drilled in block M-10 in water depths of around 300 m.

All of the oil companies operating in the country at the time including Amoco, Chevron, Agip, and Conoco declared *force majeure* on 11 July, 1989 due to continued civil unrest.

Hydrocarbon plays

The most compelling evidence that oil and gas accumulations may exist in Somaliland, as illustrated in Figs. 4-7, include: N Occurrence of oil seeps at Dagah Shabel. N Very good oil shows from several zones in most of the wells drilled including Dagah Shabel wells, Biyo Darer-1, Bandar Harshau-1, and Dab Qua-1.

N Occurrence of mature oil-prone source beds with sufficient levels of organic carbon, together with potential reservoir rocks and structures in a variety of geological settings.

N A number of Jurassic rift basins as well as Oligocene-Miocene sedimentary basins. These include Berbera/Guban (conjugate of Balhaf basin, Yemen), Daban, Las Dureh, Raguda, Al Mado (conjugate of the Masilah basin in Yemen), and Nogal basins.

N Widespread and appreciable thickness of porous and permeable reservoir rocks together with sealing rocks of Jurassic, Cretaceous, and Tertiary in age.

N Evidence of structural growth during Jurassic, Cretaceous, and Tertiary times, which resulted in the formation of structural and stratigraphic traps.

The lack of success in the early exploration wells drilled in Somaliland is primarily due to the complexity of the subsurface geology, and the lack of subsurface control by seismic data. Somaliland is a region of relatively abrupt lateral changes of stratigraphy that is related to the rifting and differential vertical movement during Mesozoic and Tertiary times (Ali, 2005). From post-drill analysis of the failed wells, the majority were as a result of poorly defined trap, thin, or absent reservoir, or due to the seal being either thin or absent. In addition, several of the wells were almost certainly stratigraphic tests. These include Zaila-1, Zaila-2, Las Dureh-1, and Dagah Shabel-3.

Source rock potential

The country contains several good quality source rocks which have potential for hydrocarbon generation (Table 1).

Jurassic

Numerous excellent quality source rocks of Jurassic age are known in outcrops along the coastal margin, including Bihendula area. Gahodleh and Daghani shales are the most important source rocks in the area (Fig. 4). Field investigations in Bihendula area (during July 2005) demonstrated that the Jurassic formations extend approximately 10 km along an east-west striking sequence of limestone ridges and shale valleys that dip generally south at about 17° (Fig. 5). The shales are dark to medium gray kerogen-rich fossiliferous claystones that have fine texture (Fig. 4). It is likely, therefore, that these shales have played an important part in the generation of hydrocarbon in the area. The 28 barrels

Good oil source; Type = Amorphous algal; Hydrogen Index = 537 mg/g; Genetic Potential = 11.47 kg/ton; Vitrinite Reflectance = 0.5-1.0. Fair oil source; Hydrogen Index = 434 mg/g; Genetic Potential = 6.76 kg/ton; Vitrinite Reflectance = 0.4-0.9.

Good oil source; Type = Amorphous algal; HC/ Non HC = 0.57; Vitrinite Reflectance = 0.6. Fair to good source for condensate and gas; Type = Amorphous; HC/Non HC = 0.44.

Jurassic (Upper Daghani shale)

Jurassic (Gahodleh shale)

Dagah Shabel

Jurassic (Calcareous shale) Jurassic (Daghani shale)

Daban Basin			
Eocene/Oligocene (Lignite from lower Daban Series)	Outcrop	11.3	Potential gas; immature; Hydrogen Index = 104 mg/g; Genetic Potential = 12.17 kg/ton; Vitrinite Reflectance = 0.4.

For additional analytical, business and investment opportunities information, please contact Global Investment & Business Center, USA at (202) 546-2103. Fax: (202) 546-3275. E-mail: rusric@erols.com

Bandar Harshau-1			
Upper Miocene (syn-rift shale) Upper Cretaceous (Yesomma shale) Cretaceous (shale) Lower Cretaceous (shale)	Bandar Harshau-1 cuttings (650 m) Bandar Harshau-1 cuttings (2271 m) Bandar Harshau-1 cuttings (2268 m) Bandar Harshau-1 cuttings (2376 m)	1.92 3.26 1.1 1.26	Potential gas and oil; immature, Hydrogen Index = 268 mg/g; Genetic Potential = 5.41 kg/ton; No Vitrinite Reflectance. Overmature; Hydrogen Index = 17 mg/g; Genetic Potential = 0.84 kg/ton; Vitrinite Reflectance = 1.0; Type II/III organic matter. Hydrogen Index = 35 mg/g; Genetic Potential = 0.48 kg/ton. Hydrogen Index = 21 mg/g; Genetic Potential = 0.35 kg/ton; Type III organic matter.

Dab Qua-1

Outcrop	2.01
Outcrop	1.43
Dagah Shabel cuttings	0.75
Dagah Shabel cuttings	0.46

Middle Eocene	Dab Qua-1 cuttings
(15 m thick shale)	
Upper Cretaceous,	Dab Qua-1 cuttings
Yesomma shale	
Jurassic (Daghani shale)	Dab Qua-1 cuttings

of 32.2° API oil recovered from the Wanderer limestone in the Dagah Shabel-1 well supports this suggestion. Offshore wells have also indicated good source rocks of Jurassic age. For example, Dab Qua-1 well intersected shales of Daghani formation that had TOCs in the range of 0.53-1.18%.

The results of the hydrocarbon source potential evaluation are summarized in Table 1. As indicated in the table, the composition of the kerogen in samples of Gahodleh and Daghani shales is primarily amorphous (Type I), which are algal remains that have greatest oil source potential.

Cretaceous

The Upper Cretaceous shales of Yesomma formation contain fair to good source potential. In both the Bandar Harshau-1 and Dab Qua-1 wells, shales in the Yesomma formation had shown good source potential with TOC up to 5%.

3	Very good oil source; Type I organic matter.
5 0.531.18	Good oil and gas source; Type II; Genetic Potential = 8 kg/ton. Fair oil and gas source; Type II/III organic matter; thin shale (6 m); Type I/II organic matter.

For additional analytical, business and investment opportunities information,
please contact Global Investment & Business Center, USA
at (202) 546-2103. Fax: (202) 546-3275. E-mail: rusric@erols.com

Eocene-Oligocene

The offshore well of Dab Qua-1 encountered a very good potential source rock of 15 m thick and TOC of 3%. In addition, good potential source rocks which had TOC of 11.3% outcrop in the Daban basin, although the succession is immature.

Thermal maturation and migration

Maturity levels of the source rocks vary from early to post-mature (Table 1). The Jurassic units (Gahodleh and Daghani shales), and possibly the Eocene units in the offshore areas, which may contain multiple source sequences, are situated within the oil window and are highly prospective for oil and gas. In addition, thermal modelling of the Gulf of Aden has identified a number of offshore kitchen areas that have excellent source potential (Bott et al., 1992). Furthermore, seismic and well data suggest both structural migration and stratigraphic migration are operative in these locations (Fig. 6). However, in general the potential Oligocene-Miocene source rocks are likely to be immature to early-mature for the majority of the onshore areas.

Reservoir rocks

The sedimentary strata of Somaliland contain numerous reservoirs within the pre-syn- and post-rift rocks of the Gulf of Aden. Reservoir rocks for the pre-rift sequence include both carbonates (Eocene and Cretaceous-Jurassic) and sandstones (Cretaceous and basal Jurassic). Reservoir rocks in syn- and post-rift sequences are principally sandstones with secondary carbonate reservoirs.

Jurassic

Two onshore wells, Dagah Shabel-2 and Biyo Dader-1, intersected 191 m and 160 m of sandstones in the Adigrat respectively. Porosity of the sandstones was variable, but as high as 15%. At Dagah Shabel-2 they produced fresh water. The reservoir potential of the Middle-Upper Jurassic deposits of Bihen, Wandere, and Gawan limestones is also good.

Cretaceous

In the Upper Cretaceous, good clastic reservoirs have been recognized. Dagah Shabel-1 well intersected very thick (790 m) fine to coarse-graded fluvial sands of the Nubian (Yesomma) formation. The well encountered two highly porous sand units where small quantities (four barrels) of good quality (33.6° API) oil were recovered. In the offshore, the Bandar Harshau-1 well penetrated 536 m of Upper Cretaceous sediments of restricted shallow marine environment that had porosities of up to 14%.

Tertiary (Eocene-Oligocene)

Clastics and carbonates of Eocene-Oligocene age also offer reservoir possibilities in syn- and post-rift traps. In the offshore, the Dab Qua-1 well penetrated a total of 183 m of Auradu limestone that have oil shows. Bandar Harshau-1 well also had minor oil and gas shows.

Traps

In Somaliland, there is no evidence of large-scale compressive folding like that of north-eastern Arabia. However, at many localities in the country, minor folds are known to occur which are believed to have been caused either by rejuvenation of old fault blocks or drag along major faults parallel to the Gulf of Aden. Such folds are mainly confined to the Guban region where the intensity of the faulting has been very much greater than in the plateau. One such example is the minor folds recorded in the Dagah Shabel district, close to the Dagah Shabel fault.

As a result the primary structural traps in the country are rollover anticlines associated with major growth faults that become listric above the pre-rift section. Stratigraphic traps are also important, particularly in the offshore areas where thick successions of Jurassic and Cretaceous sediments were eroded. The seismic profile across the Dagah Shabel and Daban basin, as seen in Fig. 7, provides a sample of the type and density of structures present in the area. The figure illustrates the trapping styles in the area. In addition, the general magnitude of area of uplift of some of the structures might be a guide to possible structural size.

Seals

The country has ideal conditions for seal development. Seals are constituted principally by interbedded shales for the Jurassic and Cretaceous sequences, with Eocene anhydrites also forming a regional seal. For the syn-rift sequence of Gulf of Aden Oligocene, anhydrites and interbedded shales are the main seals.

Comparison with Yemen

The geology of Yemen shows many similarities with Somaliland. This can be supported by reconstructing the Arabian plate to the position before the opening of the Gulf of Aden when many basins in southern Yemen seem to extend to Somaliland. For example, the Balhaf graben appears to be a continuation of the Berbera basin, and Masila basin appears to be a continuation of Al Mado basin (Fig. 1). As in the case of the Jurassic basins in Somaliland, drilling within the Balhaf and Masila grabens have indicated the majority of basin infills are Jurassic and Cretaceous in age. Furthermore, significant accumulations of oil and gas have been found in Jurassic grabens in Yemen including the Masila basin. Therefore, exploration interest to date in Somaliland has centred on searching for Jurassic rifts similar to those in Yemen.

The available well, seismic, and outcrop data show that the potential for commercial accumulations of hydrocarbons in Somaliland is good. These data show that the hydrocarbons may have accumulated in numerous large tilted fault-blocks and isolated sub-basins. Jurassic rift basins form the main exploration plays. Secondary exploration targets include Oligocene-Miocene rift sequence of the Gulf of Aden together with underlying pre-rift Eocene carbonates. Hence, favourable hydrocarbon plays could exist over many thousands of untested square kilometres along the entire north coast and south-east of the country at various drilling depths. However, much more exploration work and exploratory drilling activities are needed especially in the basins adjacent to the Gulf of Aden to determine whether Oligocene-Miocene successions are mature.

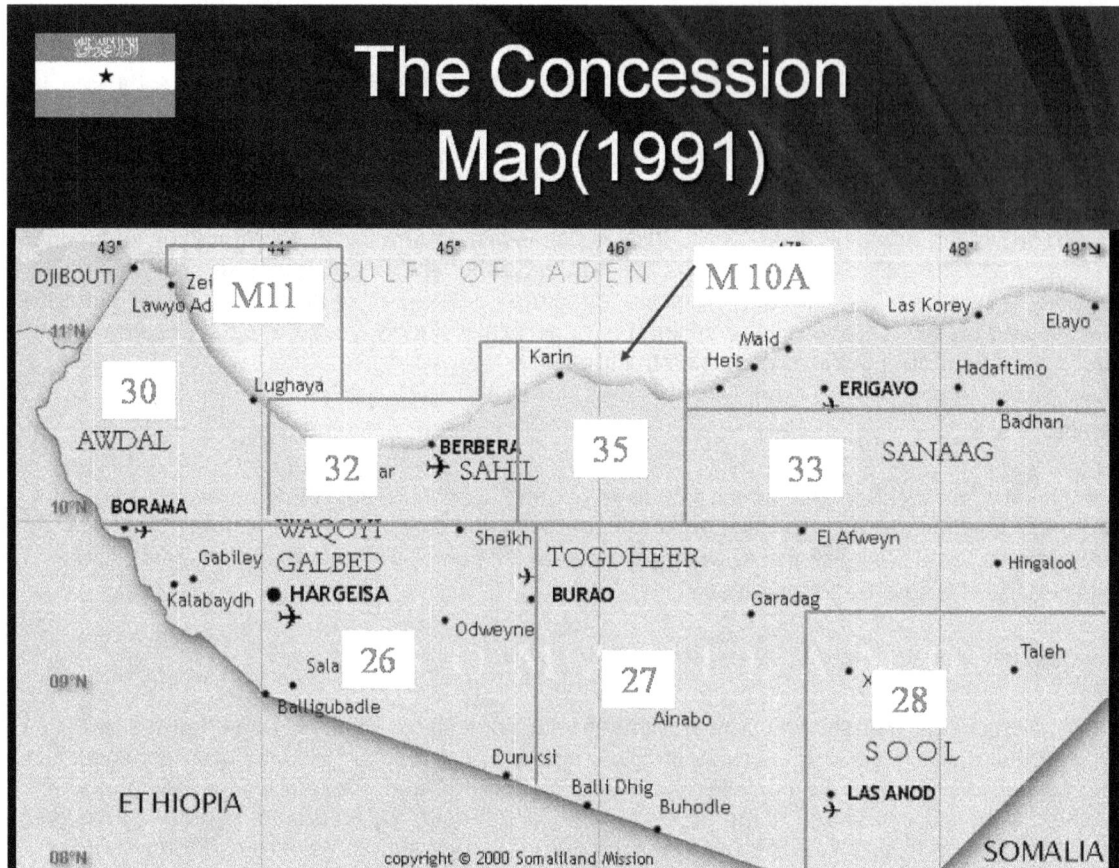

The Concession Map(1991)

copyright © 2000 Somaliland Mission

NATURAL RESOURCES AND ECONOMIC INFRASTRUCTURE

Somalia is not well-endowed with natural resources that can be profitably marketed internationally, and at independence the economic infrastructure was poorly developed. Throughout all three eras in post-independence Somalia, officials had sought, with mixed results, to develop the economic infrastructure.

LAND

Estimates vary, but from 46 to 56 percent of Somalia's land area can be considered permanent pasture. About 14 percent is classified as forest. Approximately 13 percent is suitable for cultivation, but most of that area would require additional investments in wells and roads for it to be usable. The remaining land is not economically exploitable. In the highlands around Hargeysa, relatively high rainfall has raised the organic content in the sandy calcareous soils characteristic of the northern plains, and this soil has supported some dry farming. South of Hargeysa begins the Haud, whose red calcareous soils continue into the Ethiopian Ogaden. This soil supports vegetation ideal for camel grazing. To the east of the Haud is the Mudug Plain, leading to the Indian Ocean coast; this region, too, supports a pastoral economy. The area between the Jubba and Shabeelle rivers has soils varying from reddish to dark clays, with some alluvial deposits and fine black soil. This is the area of plantation agriculture and subsistence agro-pastoralism.

Practices concerning land rights varied from rural to urban areas. In precolonial times, traditional claims and interclan bargaining were used to establish land rights. A small market for land, especially in the plantation areas of the south, developed in the colonial period and into the first decade of independence. The socialist regime sought to block land sales and tried to lease all privately owned land to cooperatives as concessions. Despite the government's efforts, a de facto land market developed in urban areas; in the bush, the traditional rights of clans were maintained.

The Siad Barre regime also took action regarding the water system. In northern Somalia from 1988 to 1991, the government destroyed almost all pumping systems in municipal areas controlled by the Somali National Movement (SNM) or failing that, stole the equipment. In rural areas, the government poisoned the wells by either inserting animal carcasses or engine blocks that leaked battery acid. As a result, northern Somalis had to rely on older gravity water systems, use poor quality water, or buy expensive water. Following the declaration of the independent Republic of Somaliland in the north in May 1991, the government of the republic began ongoing efforts to reconstruct the water system.

In the south, in the late 1980s onward, as a result of war damage and anarchy, the water situation in the towns tended to resemble that in the north. Few pumping systems were operational in early 1992. Conditions in rural areas varied. Many villages had at least one borehole from which poor quality water could be obtained in buckets; pumps generally were nonfunctioning. Somalis who lived near the Jubba or Shabeelle rivers could obtain their water directly from the river.

ENERGY

Somalia relied principally on domestic wood and charcoal and on imported petroleum to meet its energy needs. Attempts to harness the power of the Jubba River at the proposed Baardheere Dam had not come to fruition as of early 1992. Electrical utilities had been state owned since 1970, when foreign-owned enterprises were nationalized. Throughout the country, about eighty different oil-fired thermal and diesel power plants relied on imported petroleum. With aid from Finland, new plants were constructed in the Chisimayu and Baidoa areas in the mid-1980s.

Somalia relied on foreign donors (first the Soviet Union and then Saudi Arabia) to meet its petroleum needs. In the late 1970s, Iraq helped Somalia build a refinery at Jasiira, northeast of Baraawe, that had a capacity of 10,000 barrels a day. But when the Iran-Iraq War broke out in 1980, deliveries were suspended, and Somalia again required refined oil imports. As of mid-1989, Somalia's domestic requirements were again being met by this refinery, but deliveries of Iraqi crude oil were erratic. In May 1989, Somalia signed an agreement with the Industrial Export, Import, and Foreign Trade Company of Romania by which the company was to construct an oil refinery on the outskirts of Mogadishu. The project was to cost US$500 million and result in a refining capacity of 200,000 barrels per day. Because of events in Romania and Somalia, the refinery project had not materialized as of early 1992.

Throughout the 1980s, various international oil companies explored for oil and natural gas deposits in Somalia. In October 1991, the World Bank and the UN Development Programme announced the results of its hydrocarbon study in the countries bordering the Red Sea and the Gulf of Aden. The study indicated the potential for oil and gas in northern Somalia was good. In view of the civil war in Somalia following the fall of Siad Barre, however, various foreign oil exploration plans were canceled.

A successful innovation was the completion of a wind energy utilization project. Four wind turbines, each rated at 50 kilowatts, were embedded in the Mogadishu electrical grid. In 1988 these turbines produced 699,420 kilowatt hours of energy. Total electric energy produced in 1988, the latest year for which figures were available in early 1992, was 257 million kilowatt hours. Five self-contained wind energy conversion systems in rural centers also were planned, but as of May 1992 there was no information that these had been built.

TRANSPORTATION

For additional analytical, business and investment opportunities information, please contact Global Investment & Business Center, USA at (202) 546-2103. Fax: (202) 546-3275. E-mail: rusric@erols.com

In 1988 the total expenditure for transportation and communications was US$57.8 million. Nearly 55 percent of this amount was for new infrastructure; 28 percent was for rehabilitation and maintenance of existing infrastructure. This activity must be understood in the context of the ongoing civil war in Somalia; much of the infrastructure particularly bridges in the north, either had deteriorated or been destroyed, as a result of the fighting. As of early 1992, no systematic study existed of the infrastructural costs of the civil war.

At independence, Somalia inherited a poorly developed transportation system consisting of a few paved roads in the more populated areas in the south and northwest, four undeveloped ports equipped only with lighterage facilities, and a handful of usable airstrips. During the next three decades, some improvement was made with the help of substantial foreign aid. By 1990 all-weather roads connected most of the important towns and linked the northern and southern parts of the country. Three ports had been substantially improved, eight airports had paved runways, and regular domestic air service also was available. But in early 1992, the country still lacked the necessary highway infrastructure to open up undeveloped areas or to link isolated regions, and shipping had come to a virtual halt because of the security situation.

In 1990 Somalia had more than 21,000 kilometers of roads, of which about 2,600 kilometers were paved, 2,900 kilometers were gravel, and the remainder were improved earth. The country's principal highway was a 1,200-kilometer two-lane paved road that ran from Chisimayu in the south through Mogadishu to Hargeysa in the north. North of Mogadishu, this route ran inland, roughly paralleling the border with Ethiopia; a 100-kilometer spur ran to the Gulf of Aden at Berbera. By early 1992 much of this road, especially the northern part between Hargeysa and Berbera, was relatively unsafe because of land mines. Somalia's 1988 plan provided for another connection from this main route to Boosaaso on the Gulf of Aden. Somalia had only one paved road that extended from north of Mogadishu to Ethopia; all other links to neighboring countries were dirt trails impassable in rainy weather.

Four ports handled almost all of Somalia's foreign trade. Berbera, Mogadishu, and Chisimayu were deepwater ports protected by breakwaters. Merca, just south of Mogadishu, was a lighterage port that required ships to anchor offshore in open roadsteads while loading and unloading. Mogadishu was the principal port of entry for most general cargo. Berbera received general cargo for the northern part of the country and handled much of the nation's livestock exports. United States aid enabled the doubling of the berths at the port of Barkera and the deepening of the harbor, completed in 1985 at a cost of US$37.5 million. Maydh, northwest of Erigaro, was the only other and much smaller northern port. Chisimayu's main function was the export of bananas and meat; the meat was processed and packed at the port. The United States also financed the US$42 million development of Chisimayu port in the latter half of the 1980s. Merca was an export point for bananas. In 1986 the Somali Ports Authority launched a modernization project for all ports, with concentration on Mogadishu. The cost was estimated at US$24.4 million, of which the IDA provided US$22.6 million as a credit.

Mogadishu International Airport was the nation's principal airfield; in the 1980s, was a runway extended to 4,500 meters one of the runway was Africa's longest with United States financial aid. The airport was further expanded in 1989 by Italy's contribution from its emergency aid fund for Africa. Only Mogadishu offered international flights. Somali Airlines, the nation's flag carrier, was partially owned by Alitalia, the Italian national airline. Somali Airlines in 1989 replaced its fleet of five aging 707 airplanes with one Airbus 310, making it a one-plane international airline. In 1990 domestic service linked Mogadishu with Berbera and six other Somali cities; flights were scheduled at least once a week. As of April 1992, Somali Airlines had no scheduled flights, domestic or international, and no other regular flights existed.

THE "REAL" SOMALI ECONOMY IN THE 1980S

The Somali economy in the 1980s, when viewed in standard economic terms, was characterized by minimal economic reform and declining GDP per capita. But the macroeconomic perspectives, which were based on questionable data, presented an unreliable picture of the actual Somali economy. In fact, the macroeconomic figures used by the IMF and the World Bank would lead one to wonder how any Somalis could have physically survived the recent years of economic crisis. Yet visitors to Somalia, although distressed by the civil war and the wanton killing, observed a relatively well-fed population up until the 1991-92 drought. Clearly a Somali economy existed outside the realm of international data collection. Examination of what has been called Somalia's "unconventional" economy allows a better appreciation of how the Somali economy actually worked.

EXPORT OF LABOR

Somalia was an exporter of labor to other members of the League of Arab States (Arab League), and Somali citizens received remittances from these workers. These remittances constituted the largest source of foreign exchange in the economy. Based on an assumption of 165,000 Somali overseas workers, with an average annual wage of US$6,150, one-third of which was being remitted, one economist has calculated that more than US$330 million was being remitted annually. This figure represented fifteen times the sum of Somalia-based yearly wages and nearly 40 percent of total GNP, including remittances. The official remittance figure was US$30 million, the amount channeled through banks. Most unofficial remittances--in the form of foreign exchange and household goods and appliances sent home from abroad--went to urban traders. This fact explains the apparent abundance of supplies in Somali cities, which, based on the foreign exchange estimates from official sources, would not have been possible. A large portion of the remittances went to supply arms to the rural guerrillas who toppled the government in January 1991.

EXPORT OF LIVESTOCK

As the macroeconomic data made clear, Somalia was primarily an exporter of livestock to the Arab states. The macroeconomic data did not make clear the proportions in which the foreign exchange earnings from livestock exports went to the government, based on the official exchange rate of those recorded sales, and to the traders and herders themselves, based on the difference between the official and informal exchange rates plus all revenues from unofficially recorded sales. A system known as *franco valuta* enabled livestock middlemen to hoard a considerable foreign exchange surplus. In the livestock export sector, traders had to give the government only 40 percent of their foreign exchange earnings; the traders could import anything they wished with the remaining foreign exchange. Thus, imports were substantial amid data of collapse. One needed only to be connected to a trading family to enjoy massive increases in consumption during the 1980s. In the livestock export system, *franco valuta* was officially discontinued as a result of the IMF structural adjustment program, but in practice *franco valuta* continued to be observed.

In the 1970s, northern trading families used their profits to buy real estate, much of it in Mogadishu. In the 1980s, they helped subsidize the rebels fighting the government of Siad Barre.

RURAL SUBSISTENCE SECTOR

Somalia's rural subsistence sector produced sufficient grain and animal products (mostly milk) to sustain the country's growing population, including its massive refugee population. According to economist Vali Jamal, data on the subsistence sector underestimated the amount of milk and grain produced. The official 1978 estimate of milk production was 451.4 million liters; by using alternate data (for example, statistics on lactating animals from an anthropology study, consumption surveys, and interviews with nomads), Jamal estimated 2.92 billion liters of

For additional analytical, business and investment opportunities information, please contact Global Investment & Business Center, USA at (202) 546-2103. Fax: (202) 546-3275. E-mail: rusric@erols.com

production, 6.5 times the official estimate. Taking into account only this change in milk production would raise GDP by 68 percent, making Somalia the forty-first rather than the eighth poorest country in the world, with an average annual per capita income of US$406.

Jamal's data showed a 58 percent increase in grain production between 1972-74 and 1984. Production of sorghum and corn reached a high of an estimated 260,000 tons and 382,000 tons respectively in 1985, before declining in the period 1987-89. Grain imports increased sixfold, however, between the early 1970s and 1985; the increase was largely caused by the refugee influx and the added imports needed to fill the food gap. After 1980 food production increased but imports continued, primarily as a result of food aid. Governments did not cut off food aid although the need for it steadily receded. Despite donor objectives, most of the imports went to urban shops rather than rural refugee camps.

Often missed by macroeconomic analyses was the vibrant agropastoralist sector of the southern interriverine area. Families mixed pastoralism--the raising of goats and sheep, and sometimes camels--with grain production. The family unit was highly versatile, and the division of labor within it changed depending on the season and the amount of rainfall. During a drought when women were obliged to trek for days in search of water, men tended the household and crops. When water was abundant, women maintained the household, and enabling the men to concentrate on the livestock.

Trade between the pastoralist and agropastoralist sectors has been greater than standard models of the Somali GNP have assumed. Agropastoralists accumulated small grain surpluses in the 1980s, and bartered this grain to pastoralists in exchange for milk. The agropastoralists received more value from this trade than by selling their grain directly to the government because government prices for grain were lower than the growers' costs. IMF agreements with the government repealed price limits on the sale of grain; the consequences of this agreement for trade between pastoralists and agropastoralists had not been reported as of early 1992.

One of the great agricultural success stories of privatization caused great embarrassment to the IMF. Qat (also spelled "kat," *catha edulis*) is a mild stimulant narcotic; many Somalis chew the qat leaf during leisure time. Qat is grown in the Ethiopian highlands and in Kenya and is transported through Somalia. In the late 1960s, farmers near Hargeysa began growing it. During the drought of the 1970s, the qat plants survived and their cultivators made handsome profits. Investment in qat plants soared in the 1980s. Sales of qat enabled farmers to stay ahead of inflation during a time when prices for other crops fell. Many farmers used their profits to rent tractors and to hire day laborers; doing so enabled them to increase food production while continuing to grow qat. The large surplus income going to qat farmers created a free market in land, despite national laws prohibiting land sales. The IMF never mentioned this economic success as part of the positive results of its program. The government wrongly believed that the production of qat was cutting into grain production; the data of political scientist Abdi Ismail Samatar indicates that farmers producing qat grew more grain than those who did not produce qat. The government also believed that qat was harmful because it was making the general population drug-dependent. The Siad Barre regime hence banned qat production, and in 1984 qat fields were destroyed by government teams. Nevertheless, the qat story of the 1980s demonstrated the vibrancy of the Somali economy outside the regulatory regimes of the government and the IMF.

UNDEVELOPED SECTORS

PLANTATION ECONOMY

For additional analytical, business and investment opportunities information, please contact Global Investment & Business Center, USA at (202) 546-2103. Fax: (202) 546-3275. E-mail: rusric@erols.com

In the early 1990s, the plantation economy remained undeveloped, even for bananas, which remained Somalia's principal cash crop and second most important export, after livestock. Because of government taxation of exports, this sector had been in decline in the early 1980s. In 1983 the government National Banana Board formed a joint venture with an Italian company to create Somalfruit. The higher producer prices, increased input availability, and improved marketing and shipping facilities resulted in a 180-percent increase in banana production from 60,000 tons in 1980 to 108,000 tons in 1987. By 1986 banana exports accounted for 13 percent of total exports, up from just over 1 percent in 1982.

MINING

Somalia's mineral sector was of minuscule value in the overall Somali economy (in 1988 it represented only .3 percent of GDP;. There was some production of salt with solar evaporation methods, mining of meerschaum (sepiolite) in the Galguduud Region, mining of limestone for cement in the Berbera and Baardheere areas, and some exploitation of some of the world's largest deposits of gypsum-anhydrite near Berbera, and of quartz and piezoquartz (useful for electronics). Somalia also has some large uranium deposits in the Galguduud and Bay regions, and in 1984 work began to develop them. In the Bay Region, there are also large iron ore deposits. The development plan in 1986 reported that results of natural gas exploration in Afgooye near Mogadishu were negative, but indications of favorable oil and gas resources in the country persisted. Results of testing for gold in the Ceelbuur area in Galguduud Region and Arabsiyo area near Hargeysa had not been published as of early 1992.

FORESTRY

Nearly 14 percent of Somalia's land area was covered by forest in 1991. Frankincense and myrrh, both forest products, generated some foreign exchange; for example, in 1988 myrrh exports were valued at almost 253 million shillings. A government parastatal in 1991 no longer had monopoly rights on the sale of frankincense and myrrh, but data on sales since privatization were not available. Savanna trees had been Somalia's principal source of fuel, but desertification had rapidly eroded this fuel source, especially because refugees from the Ogaden War had foraged the bush in the vicinity of refugee camps for fuel. The government's 1988 development report stated that its sand dune stabilization project on the southern coast remained active: 265 hectares of a planned 336 hectares had been treated. Furthermore, thirty-nine range reserve sites and thirty-six forestry plantation sites had been established. Forestry amounted to about 6 percent of the GDP.

FISHING

In part because Somalia has 3,025 kilometers of coastline, fishing was a sector with excellent economic potential. Considerable attention had been paid to this sector, especially since the 1974 drought, when 15,000 nomads were resettled in fishing cooperatives. Data in the latter half of the 1980s showed improvement in the fishing industry. Food and Agriculture Organization estimates of total tons of fish caught and processed rose from 16,900 in 1986 to 18,200 in 1988, an increase that resulted from the development of a national fishing fleet. Yet fishing remained a largely unexploited sector, contributing less than 1 percent of GDP in 1990.

For additional analytical, business and investment opportunities information, please contact Global Investment & Business Center, USA at (202) 546-2103. Fax: (202) 546-3275. E-mail: rusric@erols.com

IMPORTANT LAWS AND REGULATIONS

THE MINING CODE AND REGULATIONS OF THE REPUBLIC OF SOMALILAND

(All Previous Mining Laws Pertaining to Somali Democratic .... are repealed and replaced wholly by *(this)* Mining Law No. _____ of 2000)

PART I GENERAL

Article 1- Summary of the Mining Code and Regulation

Article 2 – Definition

Adit: Means a tunnel of indication of less than Fifteen-(15) degrees in the horizontal which is or might be used for access, travelling, drainage or ventilation in connection with prospecting or mining operations.

Agreement: Means a contract between the Government and a person relating to Hydrocarbon or Minerals.

Commercial Discovery: Means a discovery of Minerals or Hydrocarbons, which can be produced commercially.

Alluvial: Includes all those mineral deposits which occur as detrital grains within the near surface

Court: Means a territorially competent court of Somaliland

Director: Shall Mean the Director of Geology and Mining

To Explore: To carry out surveys, studies and Appraisal of Minerals and Hydrocarbon

Government: Means the Government of Republic of Somaliland

Holder: Means a person to whom a permit, License or lease has been granted pursuant to this code, and includes his representatives, transferees or assignees.

Hydrocarbons: Means all natural organic substances Composed of carbon and hydrogen, including crude oil and natural gas and all other Mineral substance, products and by products and derivatives found in conjunction with the same excluding coal which is considered on Mineral

Licence/Lease Area: Means a portion of the geographic Area of the Republic which is subject to a lease/license granted pursuant to this code.

Lessee: Means the holder of a lease issued under the provision of this code and includes all persons having a right or interest relevant to the lease

Licensed Mineral Dealer: Means a person to whom a mineral Dealer's license granted under the provision or article 80 of this code.

Reef/Lode: Includes all minerals occurring in Solid form

Mine/to Mine: Means any place, excavation or Working where any operation in connection with mining is carried on.

Minerals: Means any natural occurring substances of economic value that are formed within the earth's crust and includes slats, water, and geothermal deposits, metals, precious areas & industrial Minerals, excluding Hydrocarbon.

Mining Rights: Means the rights to mine as defined in this code and regulations.

Minister/Ministry: Means the Minister/Ministry of Mineral & Water resources.

Passageway: Means any required facilities for Mining operations

Person: Includes a corporation, company, Syndicate or other association or body of persons corporate or unincorporated.

Permit Area: Means a portion of the geographic Area of the Republic, which is subject to a permit granted pursuant to this code.

Pit/Shaft: Means any vertical or inclined tunnel or excavation other than Adit which is or may be used for access travelling, drainage, or ventilation in connection with prospecting or mining operations.

Petroleum: Means all natural hydrocarbons gas, Liquid or solid form produced from the ground.

Controller: Means an authorised of by licensed Authority.

To Prospect: Means to search for minerals through testing the Mineral bearing qualities of land.

Prospecting Rights: Means rights to prospect as defined in this code and the regulations.

Regulations: Means the regulations made under this code.

Rented Surface Area: Means the area of land within mining Lease area which is occupied by mining work, installation etc., for which a separate rent is prescribed in article 49.

Republic: Means the Republic of Somaliland

State: Means the Somaliland Government

Tailings: Means all stones, gravel, sand, slime or other substance derived from mining operations.

Water Course: Means any water channel which confines the flow of water, whether continuously or periodically.

Article 3 Property in and Control of Minerals

The entire property in and control of all Minerals in any land/sea territory of the Republic and on or under the sea bed, to a distance of two hundred (200) nautical miles from the low water mark may be determined by agreement or otherwise between the Republic and other states is vested in the state.

Article 4 Delegation of Power

The Minister may, by degree, delegate any of his powers conferred by this code or regulation except his powers to grant or revoke a permit license or lease.

Article 5 Powers to close areas to prospecting or mining

The Minister may, with the approval of the council of Ministers, by decree, declare any area to be closed to prospecting or mining, for minerals or for environmental reasons for limited time, unless the Minister offers special permit.

Article 6 Land/minerals required for public purpose

Whenever any land or mineral being the whole or part of the surfaces of any permit, license or lease area is required for any public purpose. The Minister with the approval of the Council of Ministries, give notice or shall pay reasonable compensation to the holder if agreed, if not agreed between the parties be determined by a court.

Article 7 Revocation of Permits, License or Leases in Cases of fraud and breaches

Where any permit, license or lease has been granted in pursuance of this code and found that such grant has been obtained as a result of any false or fraudulent representation or in the case of a breach, the Minister may give notice to the holder later on if the holder fails to comply with the case in specified time the Minister revokes such permit, License or leases with the approval of the Council of the Ministers.

Article 8 Certain persons prohibited from acquiring Rights

1. No member of the Government or civil service, nor any other person associated with the administration of this code or regulations shall directly or indirectly, by himself or by any other person, acquire or hold any right or interest under any prospecting or mining right. Any permit, license, lease, document, or other transaction purporting to confer such right or interest on any such person shall be null and void.

2. No person shall acquire by transfer or through an agent any prospecting or mining right, which he is otherwise barred from obtaining in his own behalf under provisions of this code or regulations.

PART II RIGHTS AND OBLIGATIONS OF HOLDERS OF PROSPECTING AND MINING RIGHTS

Section I – General Rights

Article 9- Rights of Entry, Access, etc.

Subject to the provisions of this code and regulations and except as may otherwise be expressly provided in the terms & conditions of any permit, license or lease and subject also to any other law which may prohibit, regulate or restrict the entry into any areas of the Republic, the holder of prospecting or mining rights within the permit, license or lease area may:

a) Enter upon and prospect in any land or under any Water (not excluded from prospecting or mining under Article 6) for such minerals as may be authorised in his permit, license or lease.

b) Whilst engaged in bona fide prospecting or mining operations within such area.

i)   Erect on unoccupied land a temporary camp and such temporary structures & works as may be necessary for his operations, & enter into temporary occupation thereof.

ii)   Take foreword, other than standing timber, for his domestic use & for his employees, agents or servants.

iii)   Graze such animals as may be necessary for the carrying out of his operations.

c) Dig pits and trenches and bore or drill holes provided that he shall not divert any water from any river stream or water course or abstract water from any lake, pool, or other source of water without the written consent of the competent authority controlling or the owner of such water.

d) Employ for such operations any number of people as he may require and such methods of transport as may be necessary.

Article 10 Amalgamations of Permits, etc.

1. The holder of any permits, license or lease, which are contiguous and form a single block, may apply in the prescribed manner to the director to have such permits, licenses or leases amalgamated.

Provided that Amalgamation shall not extend to difference classes of permits, licenses or leases or to different holders.

2. The total obligations imposed by this code & regulations in respect of all the permits, licenses or leases thus Amalgamated may then be performed in respect of any one of the holder.

3. Any prescribed returns, reports, & plans may be submitted in respect of the amalgamated block.

Article 11- Holder May Remove Plant, etc., on Termination of Permit, License or Lease

1. Any plant, machinery, engines or tools on the areas of any permit, license or lease which has terminated or which are on any passageways used in connection therewith may, within 90 days from the date of such termination, be removed by the holder or within such further time as the Minister may allow, but he shall not remove any timber from any mine, Adit or shaft except as may be approved by the Director in order to comply with the provisions Item (B) of Article 20.

For additional analytical, business and investment opportunities information,
please contact Global Investment & Business Center, USA
at (202) 546-2103. Fax: (202) 546-3275. E-mail: rusric@erols.com

2. If such plant, engines, engineers or tools aren't so removed, they may be sold by negotiation or auction by order of the Minister, and the net proceeds of such sale, after deducting the costs thereof and any sum which the holder is required by law to pay to the Government, shall be retained by the Minister, and held until applied for by the holder within a period of twelve months, after which any such sum shall be fortified to the Government:

Provided that where plant, machinery, engines or tools can not be sold negotiation or auction they shall become the property of the state, and may be dealt with in such manner as the Minister may direct.

Article – 12 Right of Passageway

1. If on any permit, license or lease area or on lands outside the boundaries thereof, the holder of the prospecting or mining rights is desirous of obtaining a right of passageway, he/she may apply to the Minister in the prescribed manner for a grant of such right of passage way.

2. If on any application made under the preceding paragraph the Minister is satisfied:

a) That it is necessary for the prospecting or mining operation or for the transportation, treatment, processing or storage of any minerals that the applicant should have the passageway: and

b) That it is reasonable for such right to be granted over the particular land, which is the subject of the application, or as may be amended by the Minister with the agreement of the applicant, he may make a grant of right of passageway in the prescribed manner.

Article – 13 Duration of Right of Passageway

1. Any passageway acquired under the preceding article shall expire when the permit, license or lease, which it serves, is terminated, and thereupon the holder shall comply with the provisions of articles 11 and 20.

Section 2- General Obligations

Article – 14 Surveys

1. Before granting any permit, license or lease or any passageway, and subsequent to such grant should the necessity arise, the Minister may require the area of land to be included or occupied or the boundaries thereof to be surveyed by a Surveyor approved by the Minister; the cost of such Survey shall be borne by the applicant or holder, as the case may be.

2. The Minister may require the boundary of any permit, license or lease or any part thereof to be demarcated in a manner approved by him including the clearing or any vegetation along such boundary, so that it shall be clearly visible, and the holder keep such boundary or part thereof permanently demarcated in such manner.

Article – 15 – Holder to Produce Permit, License, etc.

The Holder of any permit license or lease shall produce his permit license or lease whenever demanded by any person having lawful interest in the land on which he is carrying out prospecting or mining operations, or when demanded by a controller Regional Co-ordinators or the Director or any Officer Authorised by him.

Article – 16 – Notice and Security for Compensation

Any holder of prospecting or Mining Rights intending to prospect or mine on any land shall, whenever practicable, give notice to the person having lawful interest in such land before commencing operations thereon, and shall, if so require by such person or the Minister, deposit with the Minister such sum, or give security therefore, as the Minister may direct, for the payment of compensation which may be payable under article (17). Such sum or balance thereof (if any) may be refunded or released in accordance with the provision 5 of article 17.

Article –17 - Payment of Compensation

1. The holder of prospecting or mining rights shall, on demand being made by any person having lawful, interest in land where such prospecting or Mining operations are carried on by him, pay such person fair any reasonable compensation for any disturbance of his surface rights, and for any damage done to the surface of the land, or to any livestock, crops, trees, buildings or works, as a result of such operations.

2. The amount of compensation payable under the preceding paragraph shall be determined by agreement between the parties or, if the parties are unable to reach agreement, or if the agreed compensation is not paid, the party having lawful interest in the land may take proceedings before a court.

3. The holder shall pay the sum awarded by such court to the person entitled thereto within fourteen days of the date of communication of the decision.

4. If the sum awarded is not paid within the time specified in the preceding paragraph such sum may, where the party concerned has made a deposit under article 18, on application to the Minister, be paid out of such deposit under the order of the Minister, where no such deposit has been made, the award may be executed pursuant to the law.

5. The Minister, by notice to the holder of prospecting or mining rights who has failed to pay the sum awarded, suspend his mining or prospecting rights, until the sum awarded has been paid, and until the holder has lodged with the Minister such further sum as he may demand as security for any future compensation payable.

6. If such payment or deposit is not made within such time as the Minister may consider reasonable he may revoke the prospecting or mining rights of the holder in default, without prejudice to any further legal proceedings which may be instituted by reason of such default.

Article – 18 – Deposits

1. As a guarantee for the due performance of the obligations imposed by this code or the regulations, any person who has applied for, or is holding prospecting or mining rights, may be required by the Minister to deposit. In addition to any sum lodged under Articles 16 & 17, such sum, or security for like amount in lieu thereof, as may prescribe or the Minister may deny otherwise as   .

2. If such person fails to make deposit within the time specified, the Minister may refuse the application, or the prospecting or mining rights revoked.

3. The Minister may, in any case where the depositor has failed, after due notice to meet any obligations imposed upon him by this code or the regulations, take such steps, as may consider necessary to fulfil the obligation, and may expend from any deposit such sum as may consider reasonable to defray any expense incurred by him in so doing.

4. Where any depositor portion thereof is so expended, the Minister may require the deposit or to make good such deposit or portion. Failure to do so may render any prospecting or mining rights, in respect of which the any deposit was made, liable to revocation by the Minister.

5. Where upon the termination of all interest in any prospecting or mining rights, in respect of which a deposit has been made, the permit, license or lease is produced to the Minister and the termination of such interests is duly recorded, then the person by whom such deposit was made may make written application to the Minister for the refund or release of such deposit or balance thereof and, upon production of satisfactory evidence by the applicant, the Minister shall authorise such refund or release to be made:

Provided that such refund or release is made without prejudice to any claim or proceeding existing, or which may arise through the breach by the holder or his agents or servants of any of the provisions of this code or regulations, or existing or arising from any other cause.

6. Subject to the provision of Article 26, where the interest of a depositor in any permit, license or lease is terminated by transfer, no refund or release shall be made until the transferee has made a like deposit of such sum as the Minister may demand.

Article – 19 - Records of Prospecting and Mining Operations

1. The holder of prospecting or mining shall keep on the permit, license, or lease area or such other place in the Republic as the director approve, full and accurate records, plans and maps of his prospecting and mining operations, and shall render to the director such returns, reports and plans as may be prescribed, or as, may be required under the terms or conditions of his permit, license or lease.

2. One half of the cores of any drill-holes shall be preserved by the holder, together with proper geological logs and records, Thereof, during the currency of such permit, license or lease and on the termination thereof such core portions, logs and records shall be made available to the Ministry.

3. If the holder fails to comply with the requirements of this Article, the Minister may, without prejudice to any other penalty for which the holder may be liable, refuse to entertain any application by such holder for any permits, license or lease.

Article – 20 - Obligations on Termination of a Permit, License or Lease

The holder, of a permit, license or lease, which has terminated shall, not later than 30 days from the termination date:

a) Submit the permit, license or lease to the Minister for cancellation;

b) Fill in and remove all shafts, pits or other excavations and all beacons for marking respectively to the satisfaction of the Director.

c) Forward to the Director all plans both of surface and underground working, topographical, geological or assay plans, borehole core logs and other records of the area over which rights are terminated.

d) Restore all disturbed to original landscape

Article – 21 – Liability Incurred Before Termination of Permits, etc.

Termination of any permit, license or lease for whatsoever reason, including transfer and surrender shall not affect in any way any liability incurred by the holder before such termination takes effects.

Article – 22 – Appointment of Agents

1. When the holder is not personally residing on or sufficiently near his permit, license or lease area so as to maintain continuous supervision of any prospecting or mining operations in progress, he shall appoint an agent, who shall be approved/rejected by the Director on the basis of conditions pursuant to the code and regulations.

2. Any change in the appointment of an agent shall be notified to the Director forthwith.

3. Such appointment and approval shall in no way absolve the holder from any of his obligations and responsibilities under the provisions of this code or the regulations.

4. Every holder of an exclusive prospecting license, mining permit or lease, and every holder, of an oil, exploration, prospecting permit or mining lease when not resident in the Republic, or when such holder is a syndicate or company with it's head office elsewhere than in the Republic, shall appoint an agent resident in the Republic at all times to represent the holder in all matters relating to any prospecting and mining operations, including the obligations imposed by this code or regulations, and the terms and conditions of such permit, license or lease.

5. A copy of the power of attorney duly signed by the agent in acceptance of his appointment shall be sent immediately to the Minister for record, and any subsequent documents by which such power of attorney is altered shall similarly be signed and submitted to the Minister.

PART III PROSPECTING AND MINING FOR MINERALS OTHER THAN HYDROCARBON

Section 1 – Prospecting Permit

Article 23 No Prospecting Without Permit

No person shall prospect for minerals other than Hydrocarbon without a prospecting permit issue under the provisions of this part.

Article 24 "Grant of Prospecting Permit"

1. The Minister may on application in the prescribed manner grant a prospecting permit in the prescribed form to any individual who:

a) Has attained the age of 21 years;

b) Is able to prove to the satisfaction of the Minister, or other Authorised Officer, that he can understand the provisions of this code and regulations to such an extent as to unable him to carry out the obligation imposed by them

2. The Minister may issue a prospecting permit for all minerals, which are open to prospecting or for such minerals or class of Minerals, as he deems fit. He may restrict the rights under any prospecting permit by endorsement thereon, either in respect of certain minerals, or, class of minerals, or in respect of any specified area or areas in the Republic.

3. When prospecting is to be carried out by corporation company syndicate, partnership, society, or other body, such body shall employ an individual or individuals, as its prospecting agent. The prospecting permit shall be in the name of such individual as agent for such body.

4. When application is made for prospecting permit to be issued to an individual to act as an agent for another person:

a) Such person shall complete and undertaking in the prescribed form to be responsible for the acts and omissions of the individual who shall also be responsible for his own acts and omissions:

b) The individual shall surrender for cancellation any valid prospecting permit he may hold in his own behalf.

5. The Minister may refuse to issue a prospecting permit to an individual who, or whose employer has previously:

a) Held any prospecting or mining right, which has been revoked.

b) Being convicted of an offence against this code or regulations or of an offence against laws relating to the employment of labour.

Article 25 "Duration and Renewal"

A prospecting permit shall remain enforce for one year from the date of issuing, and may be renewed on application in the prescribed manner for further periods of one year each.

Article 26 "Prospecting Permit Not Transferable"

A prospecting permit shall not be transferable.

Article 27 "Rights and Obligations under a Prospecting Permit"

1. Subject to the provision of this code and regulations and to any conditions on his prospecting permit, the holder of the prospecting permit may prospect on any land, not otherwise closed to prospecting, for such minerals as are endorsed on his permit.

2. The holder shall be present at site of any prospecting or other operations being carried out under the authority of this prospecting permit, but may employ at such site such persons working under his direct supervision as may be necessary for such operations, such persons shall not require prospecting permits.

3. The holder may, in the prescribed manner demarcate and apply for an exclusive prospecting license, mining permit or mining lease.

Section 2 "grant of an exclusive prospecting license exclusive"

Article 28 "Grant of an Exclusive Prospecting License"

1.The Minister may, on application in the prescribed manner by the holder of the prospecting permit, and on being satisfied that applicant has sufficient capital to ensure proper prospecting of the area applied for, grant an exclusive prospecting license in the prescribed form.

2.The Minister may, after approving the grant of the license, authorise where to begin on the license area, bending the issue of the license.

Article 29 "License Area, Duration and Renewal"

The area of an exclusive prospecting license shall not exceed eight square miles which will be valid for one year, and may, on application prescribed manner renewed by the Minister at his discretion, by endorsement thereon, for further terms of one year each up to a maximum of five years duration.

Article 30 "Rights on obligations under an exclusive prospecting license"

1. Subject to the provisions of this code and regulations and to the terms and conditions contained in the exclusive prospecting license, the holder shall have the sole right of prospecting within a license area for such minerals as may be authorised in the license.

Provided that such right shall not extend to the area of any other license, permit or lease lying within the boundaries of the license during the currency of such other license, permit or lease.

2. The holder may apply in the prescribed manner for the grant of a mining permit or mining lease within the license area.

3. Throughout the currency of the license the holder shall continuously carryout prospecting operations within the license area to the satisfaction of the director, unless suspension of such operations has been authorised by the Minister in the prescribed manner.

Article 31 "Transfer of license"

The holder of an exclusive prospecting license or any interested therein shall not transfer his license or any such interest without the prior written approval of the Minister

Article 32 "Surrender of license"

An exclusive prospecting license may be surrendering in the prescribed manner at any time on giving thirty (30) days notice to the Minister:

Provided that where the holder desires to surrender a part of the license area, he shall apply in the prescribed manner for approval of the Minister.

Section 3 – Mining Permit

Article 33 "No Mining without Mining Permit or Lease"

Same as provided by Article 8, no person shall mine minerals other than hydrocarbons without the Ministry Permit or Mining Lease issued under the provision of this part.

Article 34 "Grant of Mining Permit"

1. The holder of a valid prospecting permit or exclusive prospecting license may apply to the Minister on the prescribed manner for a grant of mining permit: if the Minister is satisfied that application is prima facie in order, he shall grant the mining permit in the prescribed form to the applicant as authorised in the prospecting permit or exclusive prospecting license.

Article 35 "Duration and Renewal"

A mining permit shall be valid for one year from the date of the demarcation, and may be renewed in the prescribed manner for further periods of one year each, subject to the Minister being satisfied the other requirements of this code and regulations have being met, and that mining operations are being carried on in a safe and satisfactory manner.

Article 36 "Conversion to Lease"

Where, in the opinion of the Minister, the scale of the operations on a mining permit or permits is of such a scale to warrant the grant of a mining lease, he may require the holder to apply for a lease, and such lease shall be granted, but subject to such terms and conditions that the Minister may think fit.

Article 37 "Rights and Obligations of the Holder of Mining Permit"

1. Subject to the provisions of Articles 16 and 19, the holder of a mining permit, shall, within the permit area, have the right;

a) To prospect for and to mine such minerals as may be specified in the permit

b) Subject to the provisions of part five (part V), to dispose of such minerals.

c) To make all necessary excavations.

d) To stack and subject to the provisions of Article 96 to dump any of the product of mining.

e) To erect permanent houses, buildings, engines, machinery, and other works and to make such passageways as may be necessary for the mining operations.

2. The holder shall throughout the currency of the permit carry on mining operations continuously within the permit area to the satisfaction of the Minister:

 Provided that the Minister may, on application in the prescribed manner authorise the holder to suspend work within the permit area for periods not exceeding ninety days (90) where he is satisfied that circumstance make it desirable to do so.

Article 38 "Transfer of Permit or Shares"

1. Subject to the approval of the Minister, which shall not be unreasonably with held, and to the provisions of Article 11, the holder may transfer his mining permit or permits in the prescribed manner.

2. Subject to the approval of the Minister which shall not be unreasonably with held, the holder may by instrument in writing divide his interest in any mining permit into such shares as he shall think proper, but not exceeding 12 in number, and may transfer such shares, and the rights and interests in the permit in the prescribing manner.

3. When the transfer of shares in a permit is effected, all or any of the shareholders may be held responsible for the obligations imposed by this code or regulations, unless otherwise provided in the instrument creating the shares.

Article 39 "Surrender of Permit"

A mining permit may be surrendered at any time by notice to the Minister and submission of the permit for cancellation, together with the confirmation required by Article 20.

Article 40 "Revocation of Permit"

Without prejudice to the generality of Articles 6 and 7, a mining permit shall be liable to revocation:

a) If subsequent to its grant it's found that the area was not properly demarcated prior to application.

b) If the holder ceases work for a period exceeding (14) days in any month without the authority of the Minister, or if failure to submit of any prescribed return or report.

c) If after due warning in writing the holder fails to maintain the beacons demarcating the area;

d) If the holder fails to keep proper records and accounts of his operations as required by Articles 19 and 71.

Section 4 - Mining Lease

Article 41 "Grant of Mining Lease"

1. Where the holder of a prospecting permit, exclusive prospecting license or mining permit in the course of his exploration and operations discoveries deposits of minerals of sufficient size and has carried out development work or preparations for mining, or such other prospecting work as in his opinion indicates a reasonable probability of steady and continuous production for a period of at least five years, such holder may, in the prescribed manner, apply for the grant of a mining lease.

2. If the Minister is satisfied with the evidence submitted and is further satisfied:

a) That the applicant has or can command sufficient capital for the proper development of a mine;

b) That a market exists or can be found for the products, the Minister may, with the approval of the Council of the Ministers, grant a mining lease in the prescribed manner, subject to such conditions as he may think fit.

Article 42 "Duration and Renewal"

1. The initial term for mining lease shall not be less than (5) years and not more than (21) years.

2. Not less than (6) months before the end of the term granted the lessee may apply in the prescribed maner for the renewal of the lease for further terms, and if the Minister satisfied that the lessee is carrying out work in a normal and businesslike manner, and that, the lease is not otherwise liable to revocation under the provisions of this code or regulations, the Minister shall renew the lease by endorsement thereon for a further term, not exceeding (21) years, as may seen to him reasonable, if in view of probable life of the operations.

3. Each such renewal shall be subject to such conditions as may apply to the grant of new leases.

Article 43 "Rented Surface Area"

The lessee shall define within the lease area the rented surface area or areas which he requires to occupy with surface installations, dumps, excavations, etc, but not passageways, and shall pay a special rents herein after called the surface rent, in respect of such rented surface area at the prescribed rate. Such surface rent may be revised at intervals of (7) years, and the rented surface area occupied may be varied by the lessee, upon giving notice in the prescribed manner, as required by the progress of his mining operations.

Article 44 "Rights of Lessee"

1. Subject to the provision of Article 16 & 17 lessee shall, within the lease area have the right;

a) To prospect & mine for such minerals as may be specified in the lessee.

b) Subject to the provisions of part V, to process for sale, transports & disposes of such minerals or mineral products.

c) To stack and, subject to the provision of Art 91, to dump any of the products of mining.

d) To make all necessary excavations

e) To erect permanent houses, buildings, engines machinery, plant & other works, and to make such passageways as may be necessary for the mining operating.

2. Pending issue of a mining lease the grant of which has being approved, the applicant may apply to the Minister for permission to begin mining within lease area or parts thereof. The Minister may grant permission subject to such conditions or restriction, as he may think fit. Such permission may be withdrawn at any time by the Minister.

Article 45 Working Obligations on a Lease

The lease shall throughout the currency of the lease carry out continuously bonafide mining operations within the lease area to the satisfaction of the Minister:

Provided that the Minister may on application in the prescribed manner authorise the lease to suspend work within the lease area for such period not exceeding six months as he may think fit.

Article 46 "Transfer of a lease or interest therein"

The lease shall not transfer his lease or credit or transfer any right or interest therein, except as may be specifically authorised in the terms and conditions of the lease, until such transfer or interest has being approved by the Minister

Article 47 "Surrender of Lease"

A mining lease may surrender either in whole or in part in the prescribed manner, after given six months notice to the Minister.

PART 1 – IV - "HYDROCARBONS"

Section 1 – General Provisions

Article 48 Scope of this Part

The provisions of this part relating to exploration, prospecting and mining apply only to hydrocarbons.

Article 49 No Prospecting or Mining without permit or lease

No person shall explore, prospect or mine any hydrocarbons except in accordance with a permit or lease granted under the provision of this part

Article 50 Grant of Permits, etc.

1. Subject to the provisions of this code & regulations the Minister, may, with the approval of the Council of Ministers, in the prescribed manner grant:

a) An oil exploration permit to explore for hydrocarbons in any land and under any water in or adjacent to the Republic as may be specified in the permit.

b) An oil prospecting permit to prospect for drill for, extract, and remove for purpose of test and research, hydrocarbons from any lands and water is in or adjacent to the Republic as may be specified in the Permit.

c) An oil mining lease to explore & prospect for, mine, remove, process for sale and dispose of hydrocarbons from any lands or water in or adjacent to the republic as may be specified in the lease,

2. Such a grant may be subject to such terms and conditions as the Minister may, with the approval of the Council of the Ministers determine

Provided that such terms and conditions shall not be contrary to or inconsistent with the provision of this code or regulations.

Section 2 – Oil Exploration Permit

Article 51 Duration and Renewal

1. The initial term for an oil exploration permit shall be two years.

2. Not later than three months before the expiry of the term the holder may apply in the prescribed manner to the Minister for a renewal of the permit. The minister may, with the approval of the Council of Ministers, renew the permit for not more than three further terms of one year each, either in respect of the whole permit area, or part thereof.

Article 52 Size of Permit Area

An oil prospecting permit shall not be granted over an area or areas exceeding 500 square miles in extent.

Article 53 "Working Obligations in Permit Area"

1. Subject to any conditions of the permit the holder of an oil exploration permit shall, with all reasonable despatch, and in any case not later than four months from the grant of the permit, commence to explore by geological and/or geophysical methods the permit area, and shall, during the currency of the permit, continue with due diligence to carry out such work as may be necessary to determine the geological structure of the area.

2. In the event that a formation is identified and is shown to be potentially productive of Hydrocarbons, the holder shall carry out an adequate program of appraisal drilling and such other activities that may be necessary to determine whether the deposit of Hydrocarbons so identified is a commercial discovery

Section 3 – Oil Prospecting Permit

Article 54 "Grant of Permit"

An oil-prospecting permit shall only be granted:

a) To the holder of an oil exploration permit within such permit area; or

b) To the holder of an oil prospecting permit, adjacent to such permit area.

Article 55 "Size of Permit Area"

An oil-prospecting permit shall not be granted over an area or areas exceeding 500 square miles in extent.

Article 56 "Duration and Renewal"

1. The initial term of an oil-prospecting permit shall be two years.

2. Not later than three months before the expire of the term the holder may apply in the prescribed manner to the Minister for a renewal of the permit

3. The Minister may, with the approval of the council of the Ministries renew the permit for not more than three further terms of one year each, either in respect of the hold permit area, or part thereof.

Article 57 "Working Obligations in Permit Area"

1. Subject to any conditions of the permit, the holder of an oil prospecting permit shall, in addition to geological and geophysical work as may be necessary, carry out a program of test drilling determining whether a deposit of mineral oil exists within the permit area.

2. The scheme of operations shall be conducted in accordance with a program submitted to and approved by the Minister, where more than one oil-prospecting permit is granted to one holder, the program of drilling on the various permits shall be agreed between the holder and the Minister.

Section 4 – Oil Mining Lease

Article 58 "Grant of Lease"

An oil-mining lease shall only be granted to:

a) The holder of an oil prospecting permit within such permit area; or

b) The holder of another oil mining leases adjacent to such leases area.

Article 59 "Comprehensive Oil Mining Lease"

The Minister may with the approval of the Council of Ministers, grant a comprehensive oil-mining lease covering two or more areas, provided the areas are on the same geological structure, or cover of a group of similar or related structures.

Article 60 "Size of Lease Area"

The size of oil mining lease and the sum of the areas of a comprehensive oil mining lease shall not exceed 160 square miles;

Provided that where the Minister is satisfied that there is a

reasonable prospect of commercial production over a greater area, he may, with the approval of the Council of Ministries, grant an oil mining lease over a large area, but not exceeding 500 square miles.

Article 61 "Duration and Renewal"

1. The initial term of an oil mining lease shall not exceed twenty-five years but renewal shall be granted at the end of such term for such further period or periods as, in the opinion of the

For additional analytical, business and investment opportunities information,
please contact Global Investment & Business Center, USA
at (202) 546-2103. Fax: (202) 546-3275. E-mail: rusric@erols.com

Minister, represents the remaining productive live of the deposit, not to exceed in any case a total fifteen (15) years for any lease.

2. Every renewal of an oil-mining lease shall be subject to a review of the conditions of such lease in the light of prevailing conditions at the time of such renewal.

Article 62 "Working Obligation on a lease"

Subject to the general provisions for this code and regulations and to any conditions of the lease, the leasee shall at all times develop and exploit every discovery of mineral oil at the maximum rate which is deemed economically suitable and possible according to good technological practice.

Article 63 "Rights of Leasee"

1. Subject to the provisions of this code and regulations and to any conditions of the lease, the leasee shall have the right:

a) To prospect and mine for mineral oil within the lands and under the waters subject lease area.

b) Subject to the provisions of part V; to process for sale, transport, and dispose of all solid, liquid & gaseous products of mineral oil, and subject to the provisions of Article 92, to dispose of any waste products of the mining or treatment process.

c) Within the lease area to erect permanent houses, buildings, engines, machinery, plant and other works, and to make such passageway as may be necessary for the proper execution of operations under the lease;

d) Subject to the requirements of any land legislation in force to operate and maintain at any place in the Republic approved by the Minister, such facilities and works as may be necessary for carrying out in developing the mineral oil industry.

Sections 5 – Miscellaneous Provision

Article 64 "Transfer of Permit and Lease"

1. An oil exploration permit, oil-prospecting permit, and oil-mining lease shall not be transferred without the prior written approval of the Minister.

2. Such approval may be granted subject to any conditions as the Minister may think fit, and he may require as a condition to such approval that the transferee at his own expense execute a bond to perform the obligations imposed under the permit or lease.

Article 65 "Surrender of Permit or Lease"

An oil exploration permit, oil-prospecting permit or oil-mining lease may be surrendered either as a whole or in part, in the prescribed manner, after giving six months notices to the Minister.

Article 66 "Rights of Entry into Areas Excluded from Prospecting"

Notwithstanding the provisions of Article 6, the holder of a permit or lease issued under the provisions of this part may, upon giving notice of at lease two weeks to the Minister, and subject to any conditions of his permit or lease, enter such areas as are described in items (c), (d), (e), (f), (g), (h), (i), (j), (k), (l), (m), and (n), of Article 6 for the purpose of making geological, geophysical, topographical or hydrological examination thereof:

a) Not excavate or otherwise disturb the surface of such areas;

b) Not engage in any form drilling activities.

c) So conduct his operations as to cause as little damage in such areas as possible; and

d) On completion of such examination, forthwith make good any damage caused in such areas.

PART V – ROYALTY ON, EXPORT AND LOCAL SALE OF MINERAL

Article 67 "Liability to Royalty"

1. All Minerals obtained in the course of prospecting or mining operations and any substance or matter extracted there from shall be liable to such royalty as may be prescribed by regulations.

2. Notwithstanding any other provisions of this code or regulations, liability for the payment of royalty shall be deemed to have arisen immediately the minerals that have been extracted.

3. Where it is not possible to calculate the exact amount of royalty payable before export or local sale, provisional royalty shall be payable to the Minister in such sum as he may assess. Thereafter, a final assessment shall be made after receipt of account sales, assays, valuations or other documents as may be necessary to establish the proper amount of royalty due.

4. The secretary may exempt from the payment of royalty such quantities of Minerals as he may deem to be necessary for the purposes of experiment or assay, or for commercial or scientific specimens, such exemption shall be endorsed on the export permit.

Article 68 "Minerals Obtained In Prospecting"

1. Save as may be provided in the terms of any permit or license to prospect, minerals obtained in the course of prospecting shall be property of the state, and shall not be removed from the permit or license area or disposed of by the holder or by any other person except with the prior written approval of the Minister who may authorise their removal for safe custody, or for any other reason which he may deem fit and subject to such conditions as he may impose.

2. If the Minister is satisfied that the applicant has been conducting only such work as is reasonably necessary to enable him to test the Mineral bearing quality of the permit or license area, he may authorise the applicant to retain or dispose of the minerals on payment of the prescribed royalty.

Article 69 "Export and Local Sale of Minerals"

1. No person shall export any mineral or any product or substance refined or derived from any mineral unless he is in possession of a permit to export issued under the provisions of this code

For additional analytical, business and investment opportunities information,
please contact Global Investment & Business Center, USA
at (202) 546-2103. Fax: (202) 546-3275. E-mail: rusric@erols.com

or regulations, which shall contain a certificate to effect that royalty has been paid or secured to the satisfaction of the Minister.

2. The director or any authorised Officer may inspect any consignment of Mineral before export and may take free of cost samples there from, for the purpose of ascertaining the mineral content and its worth

Provided that any sample materials remaining after examination shall be returned to the exporter if requested at the time of sampling.

3. When minerals or mineral products or substances are sold to persons within the Republic for any purpose whatsoever, the holder of the prospecting or mining rights shall be liable to pay such royalty as may be prescribed for such minerals or minerals products within one month of such sale unless such royalty is otherwise secured to the satisfaction of the Minister.

Article 70 "Records of Buying and Selling"

The holder of a mining permit, mining lease, or oil mining and any other persons buying or selling minerals or mineral products, shall keep adequate records to the satisfaction of the Minister, to show the quantity of mineral or mineral products produced, bought or sold, and accounts of such purchases, sales or exports, such records may be inspected by the Director or other authorised Officer at any reasonable.

Article 71 "Permit for Small Quantity of Mineral"

The Minister may grant to any person a permit to possess or by small quantities of minerals subject to such conditions as may be specified in the permit.

PART VI – RESTRICTED MINERALS

Article 72 "Possession of Restricted Minerals"

1. Under the provisions of this part the Minister may, with the approval of the Council or Ministries, by decree published in the official bulletin, restrict the possession of dealing in any minerals. Such decree may specify the state of processing at which such restriction shall apply or cease to apply.

2. No person shall possess any such restricted minerals unless;

a) He is a mineral dealer licensed under the provisions of this part

b) He is the holder of prospecting or mining rights which specifically authorise the prospecting or mining of such minerals;

c) He is a person to whom a permit to possess small quantities of such minerals has been granted by the Minister under Article 75, and such possession is in accordance with the conditions of the permit; or

d) He is the duly authorised employee of any person specified in sub paragraphs (a) to (c) of this paragraph, and his official employment necessitates possession of such minerals.

Article 73 "Sale and Purchase of Restricted Minerals"

1. No person shall sell restricted minerals to or buy restricted minerals from any person in the Republic, other than a licensed mineral dealer, or a person to whom a permit has been granted under the provision of Article 75.

2. In this article "Buy" and "sell" includes barter, exchange, give or receive as a gift or pledge, and all other forms of acquisition or disposal.

Article 74 "Mineral Dealer's License"

The Minister may grant a mineral dealer's license in the prescribed manner subject to such conditions as he may think fit. This license shall be in addition to any other authorisation prescribed by any other law.

Article 75 "Obligations of Licensed Mineral Dealer"

1. Every licensed mineral dealer shall pay to the state royalties due on any restricted minerals bought or received by him under the provisions of this part and, if so required by the Minister, shall give security for such payments.

2. Every licensed mineral dealer shall:

a) Keep a register showing:

i)   All purchases and sales of minerals made by him;

ii)   The nature and weight of such minerals;

iii) The date of each transaction;

iv)   The name and address of the vendor and his title to such minerals;

v)   The name and address of the purchaser or consignee to whom such minerals are sold or consigned.

b) Cause every transaction to be entered in such register within twenty four hours of being made;

c) Produce such register to the Minister, to any officer authorised in writing by him or to any police officer whenever so required; and

d) Render to the Director such returns as he may require.

PART VII – SAFETY, INSPECTION AND ACCIDENTS

Article 76 "General Safety"

1. The holder of any permit, license or lease shall take all due and proper precautions for the safety of all persons employed by him in any prospecting or mining operations, to the satisfaction of the directors.

2. The holder shall, during the currency of any permit, license or lease keep all edits, shafts, pits and other excavations, whether made prior to the grant of such permit, license or lease or during its currency, secured to the satisfaction of the director in such a manner as to prevent inadvertent entry of persons or livestock.

3. The holder shall also take proper precautions to prevent any persons being injured by any blasting operations or the operations of any plant, machinery, conveyors, moving belts, camel ways, train way, electricity supply or other works or apparatus, and shall provide suitable fencing, guards and warning notices where such dangerous exists or is likely to arise.

4. In any quarry, gravel or sand pit, or other open cast working or open excavation the holder shall ensure that working faces of such excavation are stepped or sloped, and restricted in height so as to avoid collapse, and shall take proper precaution when men are working near faces to prevent injure due to fallen materials.

Article 77 "Power to Remedy Dangerous Practice, etc"

1. If the director or the medical officer finds anything conducted with prospecting or mining operations or any passageway to be dangerous or effective so as to be detrimental to welfare or health of any person, or livestock, he shall give notice in writing thereof to the holder of the prospecting or mining right or right of passageway, or his agent in charge of the operations or mine.

2. Such notice shall contain such particularises of the matter considered to be dangerous or defective, which shall be remedy either forthwith or within such time as may be specified.

3. The Director or the Medical Officer may order work to be suspended until the danger is removed to his satisfaction.

4. On receipt of such notice the holder of the prospecting or mining right or right of passageway, or his agent, shall comply reweigh, or, if he objects thereto, he shall immediately state his objection in writing to the Minister who shall make a decision on the objection.

5. Where the holder of the prospecting or mining right or right of passageway, or his agent states his objections to the Minister under the proceeding paragraphs he shall cease to use the mine, or part thereof, machine, plant, matter or practice as to which such notice has been given, and shall withdraw all men from the danger indicated by such officer until such time as the matter is desired by the Minister.

Provided that if, in the opinion of the officer giving such notice, there is no immediate danger, such officer may allow work to proceed during the time the matter is being determined, under such restriction and upon such conditions to issue safety as he may consider necessary and may specify in writing.

Article 78 "Proceedings in Case of Accident"

1. Whenever an accident occurs in connection with prospecting and or mining operations causing or resulting in loss of live or serious injury to any person, the person in-charge of the operations shall, as soon as possible, report in writing the facts of the matter so far as they are known to him, to the Director who shall hold and enquire in the cause there of and record a finding.

2. As copy of the report and finding shall be submitted to the competent labour authority.

3. The Director shall, for the purpose of an inquiry under this Article have the powers of a court to summon witnesses, to call for the production of books and documents and to exam witnesses and parties concerned on oath.

4. Any witness required to attend by the Director for an inquiry may be paid reasonable expenses as are applicable to court witnesses.

5. The work "Director" in this article includes an Officer appointed by him for the purpose for of this Article.

PART VIII- REGISTRATION

Article 79 "Prospecting and Mining Rights shall be registered"

All permits, license or leases and rights of passageway shall be registered in the office of the Director in the prescribed manner.

Article 80 "Transfers of Interests to be registered"

1. When any permit, license, or lease or right of passageway is transferred to, vests in or devolves upon any person; such person shall within 30 days thereafter, or of the date of approval where approval is required apply in the prescribed manner to the director to register such transfer, vesting or devolution.

2. Where any interest in any permit and license, lease or right of passageway has been created, renewed or terminated, the person concerned shall apply in the prescribed manner to the Director to register the instrument creating, renewing or terminating such interest within 30 days of the date of the execution thereof.

Provided that the director may, for good cause showed, extend the period for the making of such application.

Article 81"Registration Not to Cure Defect"

Registration shall not cure any defect in any document registered or confer upon it any effect or any validity which it wouldn't otherwise have had.

Article 82 "Inspection of Register"

The Director shall on application, and on payment of the prescribed fee:

For additional analytical, business and investment opportunities information,
please contact Global Investment & Business Center, USA
at (202) 546-2103. Fax: (202) 546-3275. E-mail: rusric@erols.com

a) Allow inspection of the register at all reasonable times; and

b) Give copies of copies of or extracts from any entry in the register.

Article 83 "Copies of Prospecting or Mining Right, etc to District Commissioner"

The Director shall forward a copy of every permit, license or lease (other than a prospecting permit issued under part III) and every right of passageway, and of any instrument transferring, renewing, creating or terminating any of these or any interest therein, which is registered in his office to the district commissioner of the district or districts in which the area in question is situated.

PART IX – DISPUTES

Article – 84 "Application to Investigate Dispute"

Where any matter respecting the provisions of this code or regulations, or the terms or conditions of any permit, license or lease, or arising out of any prospecting or mining operations is in dispute between two or more holders of prospecting or mining rights, the parties may jointly apply to the Director to investigate such dispute.

Article 85 "Memoranda, Statements, etc"

1. The parties to the dispute shall submit to the Director written memoranda covering the matter in dispute.

2. The Director, or other officer dully authorised by him, may investigate such dispute, and for such purpose shall have the same powers of inspection and inquiry as are provided in Article 83 of this code.

Article 86 "Adjustment of Disputed Boundaries"

1. Where such dispute is in any respect of any area, boundary or beacon, the Director or other authorised officer shall make a survey of the disputed area, boundary or beacon, and shall have power to amend such area, boundary or beacon in whatever manner seems to him best in the circumstances.

2. Such amendment shall be binding upon all the parties to the dispute.

Article 87 "Director to Submit Report"

At the conclusion of every investigation, the Director or other Authorised Officer shall make a report to the secretary, together with his recommendations, and a plan showing any amendments made under the provisions of the proceeding Article.

PART X – MISCELLANEOUS, PENAL AND FINAL PROVISIONS

Section 1 – Miscellaneous

Article 88 "Discovery of Minerals"

1. When the holder of prospecting or mining rights discovers minerals which he believes may be of economic value or capable of development, and which have not been reported in the locality previously, he shall notify the secretary, giving details of such discovery, and shall supply a sample of the minerals.

2. In the event of any government officer discovering minerals which he believes may be of economic value or capable of development, he may demarcate an area not exceeding one square mile, or several, or several such areas, and shall report such demarcation with a plan thereof to the Minister, and shall supply a sample of the minerals Demarcation shall be by the same method as prescribed for a mining permit. Such shall be designated a "Government Mineral Area".

Article 89 "Pollution of Water"

No person shall in the course of prospecting or mining operations permit any anxious or poisonous matter to pollute water in use by the public, nor shall he discharge sand, slime or other tailings in a manner as to interfere with any such use

Article 90 "Priority of Applications"

If applications for a permit, license or lease are received for the same area or for overlapping areas from two or more persons that application which is first received by the Minister shall have the priority.

Provided that application has been made in the prescribed manner, and that the area applied for shall have been properly demarcated, as may be required by this code or regulations.

Article 91 "Lateral Limits"

1. The lateral limits of any permit, license or lease shall be Vertical planes passing through the sides by which such permit; license or lease area is bounded.

2.This lateral limits of the occupied or rented surface area required for prospecting or mining operations on the surface may be less than permit, license or lease area, and may vary from time to time depending upon the requirements of the operations.

Article 92 "Use of Mining Road, etc"

1. On any permit, license or lease area, or on any passageway the holder who has constructed any road shall permitstructed, and any officer of the Government duly authorised by the Minister to have access to and the use of such road:

Provided that:

a) Where any such person uses such road in a manner as, in the opinion of the holder, to do appreciable damage thereto, or to enhance substantially the cost of upkeep thereof, the holder shall be entitled to call upon such user to contribute to the cost of upkeep;

b) Where any such person uses such road in a manner to interfere materially with the free use and enjoyment of such road by the holder, the holder may give notice to the user to limit his use of the road so as to limit such interference.

2. Except as provided in the preceding paragraph a road constructed by the holder of any permit, license, lease or passageway shall be considered to be a private road, and members of the public may not use such road without the consent of the holder under such conditions as he may require.

3. Any landing ground for aircraft constructed by the holder of prospecting or mining rights shall be treated as a private landing ground and may not be used, but for emergency, by other aircraft without consent of the holder, and subject to the laws for the time being in force for the regulation of private landing grounds, and flying generally in the Republic.

Article 93 "State of War"

In the event of a state of war dully declared, the Minister shall have the right of pre-emption of all minerals mined under any permit, license or lease, and all products thereof, and shall have the right to take control of the mining operations from the holder for such time as the state of war exists.

Article 94 "Interference with Prospecting or Mining Rights, Passageway, Beacon, Mine timbers etc""

 No person shall at any time:

a) Interfere with or obstruct any prospecting or mining operations authorised under this code or regulation;

b) Interfere with any passageway;

c) Interfere with any machinery, plant, works or property on any area the subject of any permit, license, lease or passageway;

d) Without lawful authority wilfully break, deface or remove any boundary mark, beacon, pillar, post or notice erected for the purposes of this code or regulations.

e) Without lawful authority interfere with any timber, support, door or barrier in any mine, shaft or adit;

f) Without the consent of the lawful owner remove or otherwise interfere with tailings.

g) Obstruct any person in the exercise of his rights conferred by the code or regulations

Section 2 – Penalties

Article 95 " Illegal Prospecting or Mining"

Any person who prospects or mines on any are referred to in Article 2 otherwise than in accordance with provisions of this code and regulations shall be guilty of an offence, and shall be liable on conviction to a fine not exceeding us $ 5000 – or to imprisonment for a term not exceeding twelve months, or to both such fine and imprisonment.

Article 96 " Failure to Comply with Notice"

1. If the holder of any prospecting or mining rights or right of passageway or his agent, fails to comply with the requirements of any safety notice given under Article 82 or with any decision of the Minister when an objection has been determined, he shall be guilty of an offence and liable on conviction to a fine not exceeding us $ 3000 or to imprisonment for a term not exceeding twelve months or to both such fine and imprisonment.

2. Any person failing to comply with the requirement of any other notice lawfully given under the provisions of this code or regulations shall be guilty of an offence and liable on conviction to a fine not exceeding us $ 1,000 – or to imprisonment for a term not exceeding three months, or to both such fine and imprisonment.

Article 97 "Failure to Attend Inquiry, etc"

Any person summoned to attend or produce books or documents at any inquiry held under the provisions of Article 7 and refusing or neglecting to do so, or refusing to answer any question put to him by or with the concurrence of the Director, or other authorised officer holding such inquiry shall be guilty of an offence and liable on conviction to a fine not exceeding us $ 1000.

Article 98 " General Penalty"

Any person who violates any of provisions of this code or regulations for which no penalty is expressly provided shall be liable on conviction to a fine not exceeding us $5,000 or to a term of imprisonment not exceeding six months, or to both such fine and imprisonment.

Article 99 " Forfeiture of Mineral etc, by Court"

1. In addition to any other penalty, the court shall order the forfeiture of all minerals obtained in the course of illegal prospecting or mining, or obtained as the result of any violation of this code or regulations, or in default of such minerals, such a sum as the court may assess as the value of such minerals.

2. The court may further order to forfeiture of any implements or machinery used for any illegal prospecting or mining.

Section 3 – Final Provisions

Article 100 " Repeal and Saving"

1. Any other law or provision relating to prospecting or mining contrary to or inconsistent with the provision of this code is also repealed.

SOMALILAND MINING REGULATIONS

PART I – GENERAL PROVISIONS

SECTION 1 – INTERPRETATION

REGULATION 1 : DEFINITIONS

For additional analytical, business and investment opportunities information,
please contact Global Investment & Business Center, USA
at (202) 546-2103. Fax: (202) 546-3275. E-mail: rusric@erols.com

1. In these regulations, the code means, the Somaliland Mining Code (March-April 2000), and, unless the text otherwise specifies, the term:

a) **Art stone,** means any stone such as marble, extracted for its natural pretty for ornaments and polishing, etc.,

b) **Building Mineral**, includes all minerals used for the construction of buildings, roads, dams and similar works such as stones, gravel, sand clay literate, volcanic ash for the production of burned breaks and tails, and limestone for the production of lime, but does not include industrial Minerals

c) **Crude oil, natural gas** means hydrocarbons, which are produced which are produced at the well head in liquid state, while the natural gas is produced in gaseous face at atmospheric pressure.

d) **Explosives**, means all forms of blasting preparations used in connection with prospecting or mining operation including the micro explosives.

e) **Gemstones**, means any form of mineral, which is commonly cut and polished for jewellery use.

SECTION 2 – FEES, RENTS AND ROYALTY

REGULATIONS 2: FEES, RENTS AND ROYALTY

1. The fees and rents set forth in the first schedule shall be payable in respect of the matters specified therein, and shall be payable to the Ministry in advance, as prescribed by this regulations.

2. Application fees payable under the first schedule shall not be refundable.

3. Subject to any special terms and conditions in any lease, the royalty at rates not less than those prescribed the second schedule, shall be payable in respect the Mineral specified therein.

4. In respect of Royalty on Hydrocarbons, The Minister may at his option and subject to terms and conditions of any lease, ask for payment of all or part of Royalty to be made in liquid or gasous Hydrocarbons, to be delivered free of cost to the Government.

SECTION 3 – DEMARCATION

REGULATION 3: Demarcation by temporary beacons etc.,

1. Every applicant for an exclusive prospecting license, Mining Permit or Mining lease, before lodging the application in the prescribed, manner, shall demarcate the area required by temporary beacons; with which the boundary of the area to be demarcated shall be: location beacon, corner beacons and boundary beacons shall be erected at one corner, at the other corners and where highways or water courses cross the boundary. All these beacons are designed to make for the limitation, designation and duration wise.

For additional analytical, business and investment opportunities information, please contact Global Investment & Business Center, USA at (202) 546-2103. Fax: (202) 546-3275. E-mail: rusric@erols.com

2. After an area has been demarcated with temporary beacons, the holder of the prospecting permit, exclusive prospecting license, mining permit or mining lease shall submit the relevant application to the Minister in the prescribed manner within (30) day of such demarcation.

REGULATION 4: REMOVAL OF TEMPORARY BEACONS

The removal of Temporary beacon for an exclusive prospecting license, mining permit/or lease comes through replacement into permanent, when the internal beacons found necessary for mining operations, and or if revocation or refusal an application of renewal may arise as prescribed manner.

PART II PROSPECTING PERMIT

REGULATION 5: Form of Application

1. An application for a prospecting permit shall be in form one (1) of the third schedule and shall be submitted to the Minister in duplicate together with, the annual fee for issue as prescribed in the first schedule; if an application for a prospecting permit is applied as an agent for another person, an undertaken prescribed in form (2) two shall be completed by the agent.

2. A prospecting permit shall be in form (3) of the third schedule.

REGULATION 6: Renewal of Permit

Application for renewal of prospecting permit shall be made (30) days before the date of its expiry, together with the annual fee for renewal of a prospecting permit prescribed in the first schedule, and other required documents.

PART III- EXCLUSIVE PROPECTING LICENSE

REGULATION 7: Shape of License Area

The area demarcated and applied for and exclusive prospecting license shall be rectangular shape.

REGULATIONS 8: Form of Application etc.,

1. An application for an exclusive prospecting license shall be in form (4) of the third schedule, and shall be submitted to the Minister in triplicate, together with:-

a) Application fee, annual rent a sketch plan and a deposit for work obligations for the first year.

REGULATION 9: Notice of Intention to Grant License.

Notice of intention to grant an exclusive prospective license shall be published by the Minister in an official newspaper and in any other manner as seems appropriate to him.

REGULATIONS 10: Form of License, etc.

For additional analytical, business and investment opportunities information, please contact Global Investment & Business Center, USA at (202) 546-2103. Fax: (202) 546-3275. E-mail: rusric@erols.com

1. An exclusive prospecting license shall be in form (5) of the third schedule and any terms or conditions associated with it shall be endorsed on the license; a copy of the sketch plan shall be annexed to the licensee.

REGULATION 11: Application for Renewal

An Application for renewal of an exclusive prospecting license shall be made to the Minister in writing, together with the original license, annual rent, detailed report, account of the incurred expenditure, work proposals and provision for deposit.

REGULATION 12: Minimum Work Obligations

1. The Minimum Work Obligation for every exclusive prospecting License shall be (US$10,000) PER SQURE KILO METER PER ANNUM; any over-expenditure in any one-year may be carried over to the following year.

2. Failure to perform the minimum obligation required in any one year shall render any deposit made under article 18 of the Code.

3. Direct expenditure on the following Technical Activities shall be acceptable in performance of work obligations (i.e. geological, Geophysical, Geo chemical cost of logistical/administrative factor (not more than 10% of the total).

PART 1V- MINING PERMIT

REGULATION 13

The classes of Mining Permits, which may be granted, and the maximum dimension of the permit area for each class shall be:

a) Building/alluvial Mineral – one hundred (100m) in length and (100m) in width for building, while for alluvial (100m) in length and (300m) in width.

b) For all Mineral (other than Hydrocarbon) previous or non precious/industrial (500m) length and (200m) in width

REGULATION 14: Shape of Mining Permit Area

The Mining Permit shall be rectangular

REGULATION 15: Form of Application, etc.,

1. The Application for a prospecting Permit shall be made in form (6) of the third schedule in triplicate and shall be accompanied by application fee and rent, sketch plan (i.e. Dimension, Area, Demarcation, etc.)

2. Mining Permit shall be in form (7) of the third schedule.

REGULATION 16

For additional analytical, business and investment opportunities information,
please contact Global Investment & Business Center, USA
at (202) 546-2103. Fax: (202) 546-3275. E-mail: rusric@erols.com

Adjustment of mining permit area:-

If subsequent to the grant of a Mining Permit, it is found that the Permit area exceeds the prescribed dimension, or come with inconsistencies, the Director or Authorised Public Officer will adjust the area.

REGULATION 17: Renewal of Mining Permit

A Mining Permit may be renewed by submission of the original Permit to the Minister before its expiry date; together with the annual rent for the ensuing year.

PART V- MINING LEASE

REGULATION 18: Form of A an Application etc.,

The holder of a valid Prospecting Permit or an exclusive Prospecting License shall apply for the grant of a mining lease in form (8) of the third schedule to the Minister in quadruplicate with application fee, annual rent , sketch plan (for demarcation, dimension, topographic and other data's), statement of finance, etc.,

REGTULATION 19: Notice of intention to grant lease

Notice of intention to grant Mining lease shall be published by the minister in an official newspaper and in any other manner as seems appropriate to him. Any person wishing to object the grant shall lodge written objection within (30) days of such notice.

REGULATION 20: Survey of Boundaries, etc

Upon notification of the grant of a Mining lease, the applicant shall forth with, at his own expenses make a precise survey of the boundaries of the lease area and shall compute the exact area thereof and submit or supply to the Minister in quadruplicate.

REGULATION 21: Form of Mining Lease

A Mining lease shall be in form (9) of the third schedule and one copy of the survey plan shall be annexed thereto; if there is any special terms and conditions related to it, shall be endorsed on the lease.

REGULATION 22: Renewal of Mining Lease

An application for renewal of a mining lease shall be in letterform together with the original lease, application fee and report showing calculated ore reserves, or other related information to indicate the expected working life of the mine beyond the current term of the lease.

PART VI MISCELLANOUS APPLICATION

REGULATION 23: Application for Amalgamation of Contiguous

1. An application for amalgamation of contiguous permits, licenses or leases, shall be in form (10) of the third schedule, and be submitted to the director, together with the fee.

2. The amalgamation certificate shall be in form (11) of third schedule.

REGULATION 24: Application for the suspension of obligations, etc.,

An application for the suspension of an obligation shall be in form (12) of the first schedule and shall be submitted to the Minister in triplicate together with the fee prescribed in the first schedule. Upon approval suspension certificate shall be issued by the Minister in form (13) of third schedule.

REGULATION 25: Application for the transfer of rights, shares, etc

1. An Application for the transfer of rights, shares of an exclusives prospecting license, mining permit or mining lease shall be in form (14) of the third schedule and shall be submitted to the Minister in triplicate, together with prescribed fee in the first schedule.

2. An Application for the transfer of shares in an exclusives prospecting license, mining permit or mining lease shall be in form (15) of the third schedule and be submitted to the Minister in triplicate with the fee prescribed in the first schedule; upon approval, the transferee shall, within (30) days amend the name of the holder on all beacons marketing the area concerned.

REGULATION 26: Surrender of License or Lease

1. When the holder of an exclusive prospecting License or Mining Lease desires to surrender his rights, shall give notice of his intention in form (16) of the third schedule, which shall be submitted to the Minister in triplicate, together with the surrender fee.

2. When a portion of the license or lease area is to be surrendered, the holder shall submit a plan showing the area to be surrendered and that to be returned; together with demarcation and work with the obligations required.

REGULATION 27: Right of Passageway

1. When the holder of a permit, license or lease requires a right of passageway outside his boundary, shall apply in form (17) of the third schedule, this application shall be submitted to the Minister in triplicate, together with the fee prescribed in the first schedule.

2. If there are persons having rights (prospecting/Mining) or alleging lawful interest in such land, their names shall be declared in the application.

3. The grant of a right of passageway shall be in form (18) of the third schedule.

REGULATION 28: Notice to Show Cause

When the Minister gives notice to the holder of a prospecting or mining rights, such notice shall be in form (19) of the third schedule and shall be sent to the holder through all means, together with specification on the complaint, time and the place.

PART VII – PRMITS AND LEASES FOR HYDROCARBONS

For additional analytical, business and investment opportunities information,
please contact Global Investment & Business Center, USA
at (202) 546-2103. Fax: (202) 546-3275. E-mail: rusric@erols.com

REGULATION 29: Scope and Applications

The regulations contained in this part shall apply solely to the exploration and exportations of Hydrocarbons; while regulations contained in part I up to part VI (excluding regulations 21, 22, 25 and 26), shall not apply to hydrocarbon exploration and Mining operations.

REGULATION 30: Graticulation and Constitution of Blocks

For the purpose of establishing the blocks, the surface area of the Republic shall be deemed to be divided into graticules by reference to meridians of longitude, which are 5 minutes apart, measured from Greenwich and by reference to parallels of latitude, which are 5 minutes apart measured from the equator.

REGULATION 31: Reservation of Blocks, etc.,

The Minister may, declare that a block or blocks shall not be subject to any permit or lease such block or blocks shall be shown on the Republic block map.

REGUALTION 32: Application for Oil Exploration Permit

An application for an oil exploration permit shall be in form (20) of the third schedule, such application shall give the name and the nationality of the applicant, and in case of a corporate, the place of its incorporation and principle place of business it may also be necessary that the applicant furnish evidence of previous experience and technical and economical capabilities and shall be in respect of not more than one block at a time.

REGULATION 33: Application for an Oil Mining Lease

1. The holder of an oil exploration permit make an application for an oil mining lease with respect to any area contained within his permit area provided that the holder satisfied that such area contains a commercial discovery of Hydrocarbons.

2. An application for oil Mining Lease shall be in form (20) of the third schedule. Such application shall give the name and nationality of applicant, shall be submitted in triplicate and must be accompanied by a detailed report for the development, extraction, production, storage, transportation, sale or other disposition of Hydrocarbons.

3. No oil mining lease shall be granted if, the applicant is not able to comply obligations, commitments, terms and conditions of the oil mining lease.

REGUALTION 34: Grant of Permits or Leases Relating to Hydrocarbons

An oil exploration permit or lease shall be granted, together with, at least statement of the date of the grant, description of the permit or lease area and under agreement contained the terms and conditions, additional to those of the code and regulations.

REGULATION 35: Application for Renewal of Oil Exploration Permit

1. An application for Renewal of an Oil Exploration Permit shall be made in any area within the permit area, not later than (90) days before the permit expiration.

For additional analytical, business and investment opportunities information,
please contact Global Investment & Business Center, USA
at (202) 546-2103. Fax: (202) 546-3275. E-mail: rusric@erols.com

2.   The application for renewal of the oil exploration permit shall be accompanied with the original permits, the application fee, annual service rentals, detailed work report and work plan. There upon the Minister shall grant the renewal of the oil exploration permit to the applicant as prescribed by the regulation.

REGULATION 36: Application for Renewal of An Oil Mining Lease

1.   The holder of an oil mining lease may apply for renewal of his oil mining lease, in respect of all or any of the area comprising the lease area, such application for renewal shall be made not later than (6) six months prior to the expiration of the lease.

2.   The application for renewal of an oil-mining lease shall be accompanied by the original lease, prescribed application fee, annual fee, and detailed report and annual service rentals.

REGULATION 37: Surrender and transfer of Permit or Lease

1.   An application for the approval of the transfer of an oil exploration permit or oil mining lease shall be made in letter form to the Minister together with the prescribed application and transfer fees, the permit or lease, name and nationality of the proposed transfer.

2.   If the holder of an oil prospecting permit or oil mining lease wishes to surrender all or part of the permit or lease area, he/she must shall give notice to the Minister in letter form not less than (90) days before the date he wish to surrender.

REGULATION 38: General Work Practices and Directions

The holder of an oil exploration permit or oil mining lease shall, in carrying out direction of exploration and mining operations, always act in accordance with generally accepted practices in the international petroleum industry (well design drilling operations, holders casing, cementing well spacing and plugging operations).

REGULATION 39: Authorisation of Pipelines, etc

The holder of an oil mining lease shall prior to commence the construction alteration or operation of a pipeline, pumping station apply to the Minister for authorisation; together with proposed design, proposed size and capacity, proposed work programme. There upon after the result the Minister may authorise the pipeline as prescribed in the code and the regulations.

PART VIII – RETURNS, RECORDS,ANNUAL PLANS, ETC

REGULATION 40: Monthly returns

On or before the 20th day of each month, the holder of exclusive prospecting license, oil exploration permit, mining permit, mining lease or oil mining lease shall submit to the Director a return of the average number of persons employed, amount dispersed and the total operating and the capital expenditure incurred.

REGULATION 41: Quarterly Progress Report

The holder of an exclusive prospecting license, oil exploration permit and oil mining lease shall submit to the Minister, on or before the 30th day of January, April, July and October, a report on progressive of work carried out during the preceding quarter.

REGULATION 42: Annual Program of Work and Report

The holder of an exclusive prospecting license, oil exploration permit or oil mining lease shall submit to the Minister for approval, a programme of work to be carried out during the issuing (12) twelve months, together with expenditure details.

REGULATION 43: Annual Plans, Records, etc

The holder of an exclusive prospecting license, oil exploration permit, mining permit or oil mining lease shall submit to the Minister a survey plan of the permit, licences or lease area at a scale not less than 1:2500 with detailed parameters.

REGULATION 44: Final Report on Termination of Permit, etc

After the date of termination or expiration of any prospecting permit, exclusive prospecting license, mining permit or mining lease, the holder shall submit a summarised final report of the work carried out and conclusions reached (60) sixty days before the date of termination.

REGULATION 45: Periodic Information Relating to Oil Exploration and Mining Operations

The holder of an oil exploration permit or oil mining lease shall within (6) six months submit to the Director all geological and geophysical data's records and maps associated with the operations

REGULATION 46: Confidentiality

All returns, reports and other information's submitted under the code and this regulations shall be treated as confidential by the Government and will not be disclosed to third parties

PART IX – REGISTRATION, ETC

REGULATION 47: Director to Keep Register, etc.,

The Director shall keep a register of an exclusive prospecting licenses, Mining Permits, Mining Leases of passageways and all other documents.

REGULATION 48: Stamp Duty

All applications under the code and these regulations shall, before presentation to the competent authority by duly stamped in accordance with the law on stamp tax, and so does all other documents associated.

REGULATION 49: Inspection of Register, etc.,

The Director shall upon request, upon payment of the fee prescribed in the first schedule, allow a search of the register and filed copies of any permits, licenses/leases, or any other registered documents, and shall give certified true copies or extracts there from on payment of the fee prescribed in the first schedule.

REGULATION 50: Notice the General Public

The Minister shall publish notices from time to time for the information of the general public, giving details of the grant and termination of every permit, licenses or lease, other than a prospecting permit.

PART X – USE OF EXPLOSIVES FOR PROSPECTING & MINING

REGULATION 51: Use of Explosives

The holder of prospecting or mining rights who requires using explosives for his operations shall comply with the provisions of this part and to any other law on explosives in force. The application for and the grant of authority to use explosives shall be in form (21) of the third schedule and be submitted to the Director.

REGULATION 52: General Responsibilities of Reasons Concerned with Explosives, etc.,

Every person storing issuing for use, transporting or handling any explosive or carrying out blasting operations in connection with prospecting or mining shall take all reasonable precautions to prevent accidents.

REGULATION 53: Application for a blasting permits and issue thereof

1. Application for a blasting permit shall be in form (22) of the third schedule, which shall be submitted to the Director in duplicate together with the fee prescribed in the first schedule.

1. A blasting permit shall be issued in form (23) of the third schedule, and shall be valid for (5) years. It shall not be renewable.

REGULATION 54: Storage of Explosives

1. No person shall store explosives for prospecting or mining proposes unless he has a storage place of approved design.

2. Approval of explosive storage arrangements shall be in form (24) of the third schedule, together with relevant documents.

PART XI – MISCELLANEOUS AND FINAL PROVISIONS

REGULATION 55: Mineral Export and Dealer's License

An export license for minerals shall be in form (25) of the third schedule and shall be issued on payment of the fee prescribed in the first schedule. A license to deal in minerals shall be in form (26) of the third schedule and shall be issued on payment of the fee prescribed.

REGULATION 56: Employment of Somaliland Citizens

In carrying our prospecting or mining operations under the code, and these regulations, the holder shall employ, train and undertake programme of schooling for Somaliland Citizens. On the other hand, the holder shall give preference to goods produced or available in the Republic and services rendered by Somaliland Citizens and the reasonable price and qualities better than goods and services imported.

REGULATION 57

Any Regulation inconsistent with these Regulations is hereby repealed.

PETROLEUM LAW

LAW NO. • DATED •2007 PETROLEUM LAW OF SOMALIA

Pursuant to Articles 28 and 67 of the Transitional Federal Charter of the Somali Republic, the Transitional Federal Parliament enacts the following that shall have the force of law throughout the Somali Republic:

CHAPTER I - GENERAL PROVISIONS

ARTICLE 1 DEFINITIONS

In this Law: "**Authorisation**" means a Reconnaissance Authorisation, a Production Sharing Agreement, a

Surface Access Authorisation, or any agreement made by the Government in respect of such an authorisation or agreement; "**Authorised Area**" means the area from time to time the subject of an Authorisation; "**Authorised Person**" means:

(a) in respect of a Production Sharing Agreement, a Contractor; and

(b) in respect of any other Authorisation, the Person to whom the Authorisation has

been granted;

"**Calendar Year**" means a period of twelve months commencing on January 1 and ending on the following December 31, according to the Gregorian calendar;

"**Contract Area**" means the Authorised Area under a Production Sharing Agreement; "**Contractor**" means a Person with whom the Somalia Petroleum Authority has made a Production Sharing Agreement;

"**Control**" means, in relation to a Person, the power of another Person to secure:

(i) by means of the holding of shares or the possession of voting power, in or in relation to the first Person or any other Person; or

(ii) by virtue of any power conferred by the articles of association of, or any other document regulating, the first Person or any other Person, that the affairs of the first Person are conducted in accordance with the wishes or directions of that other Person; "**Crude Oil**" means crude mineral oil and all liquid hydrocarbons in their natural state or obtained from Natural Gas by condensation or extraction;

"**Decommission**" means, in respect of the Authorised Area or a part of it, as the case may be, to abandon, decommission, transfer, remove and/or dispose of structures, facilities, installations, equipment and other property, and other works, used in Petroleum Operations in the Authorised Area, to clean up the Authorised Area and make it good and safe, and to protect the environment;

"**Good Oil Field Practice**" has the meaning given in Section 25.1;

"**Government**" means the Government of the Somali Republic, acting through its appropriate officials or ministry, as determined by the Council of Ministers;

"**Inspector**" has the meaning given in Section 28.1;

"**Law**" means this Petroleum Law, as amended or modified from time to time;

"**Ministry**" means the ministry from time to time responsible for the administration of this Law, as established by the Government, and which shall initially be the Ministry of Petroleum;

"**Minister**" means the minister of the Government from time to time responsible for the administration of this Law, as established by the Government, and which shall initially be the Ministry of Petroleum;

"**Natural Gas**" means all gaseous hydrocarbons and inerts, including wet mineral gas, dry mineral gas, casing head gas and residue gas remaining after the extraction of liquid hydrocarbons from wet gas, but not Crude Oil;

"**Operator**" means an Authorised Person or other Person named in an Authorisation or unitisation agreement to organise and supervise Petroleum Operations;

"**Parliament**" means the Transitional Federal Parliament of Somalia or any successor federal parliament that may be established pursuant to a constitution adopted by referendum of the people of Somalia;

"**Person**" includes a corporation or other legal entity;

"**Petroleum**" means:

(i)   any naturally occurring hydrocarbon, whether in a gaseous, liquid or solid state;

             or

(ii)   any mixture of naturally occurring hydrocarbons, whether in a gaseous, liquid or solid state. "**Petroleum Operations**" means activities for the purposes of:

(i) prospecting for Petroleum;

(ii) exploration for, development, production, sale or export of Petroleum; or

For additional analytical, business and investment opportunities information,
please contact Global Investment & Business Center, USA
at (202) 546-2103. Fax: (202) 546-3275. E-mail: rusric@erols.com

(iii) construction, installation or operation of any structures, facilities or installations for the development, production and export of Petroleum, or decommissioning or removal of any such structure, facility or installation;

"**Production Sharing Agreement**" means an agreement made or given pursuant to Article 13, pursuant to which the Contractor receives a share of the Petroleum resulting from the conduct of Petroleum Operations as compensation for its activities;

"**Public Officer**" means a civil servant or equivalent individual, members of Parliament or of Government, Judges or Public Prosecutors, or the Somalia Petroleum Authority;

"**Reconnaissance Authorisation**" means an authorisation granted pursuant to Article 12;

"**Regulations**" shall mean those rules and regulations issued from time to time by the Ministry with respect to the management of Petroleum Operations, as contemplated by this Law;

"**Reservoir**" means a porous and permeable underground formation containing an individual and separate natural accumulation of producible hydrocarbons (oil and/or gas) that is confined by impermeable rock and/or water barriers and is characterized by a single natural pressure system;

"**State-Owned Contractor**" means a Person incorporated under the laws of Somalia which is Controlled, directly or indirectly, by a government of a State of Somalia;

"**Somalia Petroleum Authority**" or "**SPA**" means the authority established pursuant to Article 8;

"**Somalia Petroleum Corporation**" or "**SPC**" means the corporation established pursuant to Article 9;

"**Surface Access Authorisation**" means an authorisation granted pursuant to Article 14;

"**Territory of Somalia**" consists of all lands and waters over which Somalia has sovereignty, including its territorial sea and its continental shelf, and further includes its exclusive economic zone where, pursuant to accepted norms of international law, Somalia has sole and exclusive rights for the purposes of exploring for, developing and producing its natural resources;

"**Somalia**" means the Somali Republic; and

"**Well**" means a perforation in the earth's surface dug or bored for the purpose of producing Petroleum.

Article 2 Purpose

This Law shall have as its purpose:

2.1 to confirm the sovereign rights of Somalia to explore, develop, produce, utilize and manage its Petroleum resources, located onshore and offshore;

2.2 to allow efforts to be undertaken to determine the extent of the Petroleum resources which may exist in Somalia, by creating a regulatory, contractual and financial regime that allows the reconnaissance and exploration of Petroleum, and development, production and marketing of any Petroleum which is discovered;

For additional analytical, business and investment opportunities information,
please contact Global Investment & Business Center, USA
at (202) 546-2103. Fax: (202) 546-3275. E-mail: rusric@erols.com

2.3 if Petroleum resources are discovered in Somalia, to provide maximum benefit to Somalia and its people from the development and production of Petroleum;

2.4 to ensure the protection, conservation and preservation of the environment in the conduct of Petroleum Operations;

2.5 to encourage and support foreign investment which occurs to attain the other purposes of this Law;

2.6 to establish the Somalia Petroleum Authority as the competent regulatory authority to regulate Petroleum Operations, applying regulatory principles of equality, openness, accountability, transparency and non-discrimination;

2.7 to establish Somalia Petroleum Corporation as an entity Controlled by the Government for the participation in Petroleum Operations in Somalia;

2.8 to comply with international initiatives to ensure transparency of extractive industries, by enhancing public financial management and accountability, recognizing that management of natural resource wealth for the benefit of Somali citizens is in the domain of the Government, to be exercised in the interests of national development; and

2.9 to ensure fair treatment of specified persons holding rights pursuant to Petroleum grants made by the Somali Democratic Republic on or before December 30, 1990.

ARTICLE 3 TERRITORIAL SCOPE OF LAW

This Law applies to the Territory of Somalia.

Article 4 Material Scope of Law

4.1 SCOPE. THIS LAW APPLIES TO PETROLEUM OPERATIONS.

4.2 **Other Minerals**. The existence of an Authorisation in force in a given area does not prevent authorisation of the exploration and production of mineral substances other than Petroleum, provided that such other activity does not hinder the proper performance of the Petroleum Operations.

Article 5 Title to Petroleum

5.1 **Title to Petroleum**. Title to, and control over, Petroleum in the Territory of Somalia are public property and are vested in Somalia, in trust for its people.

5.2 **Transfer of Title after Recovery**. A Person may acquire title to Petroleum only after it has been lawfully recovered under a Production Sharing Agreement issued pursuant to this Law.

Article 6 Exercise by the Ministry and SPA of its Powers and Functions

6.1 **Exercise of Power and Functions**. The Ministry and the Somalia Petroleum Authority shall exercise their powers and discharge their functions under this Law and the Regulations, including under Authorisations made hereunder, in such a manner as:

6.1.1 TO ENSURE SOUND RESOURCE MANAGEMENT;

6.1.2 to ensure that Petroleum is developed in a way that minimises damage to the natural environment, is economically sustainable and contributes to the long-term development of Somalia;

6.1.3 IS REASONABLE; AND

6.1.4 is consistent with Good Oil Field Practice.

6.2 **Opportunity for Representations**. Before exercising any such power or discharging any such function, the Ministry and the Somalia Petroleum Authority may give opportunity to Persons likely to be affected to make representations to it, and shall give consideration to the relevant representations received by it.

Article 7 Functions of Ministry

7.1 *FUNCTIONS OF MINISTRY*. THE MINISTRY SHALL PERFORM THE FOLLOWING FUNCTIONS:

7.1.1 make decision on strategies, plans and policies for the development of the Petroleum industry;

7.1.2 issue regulations with respect to the management of Petroleum Operations as recommended to the Ministry by the Somalia Petroleum Authority as contemplated by this Law;

7.1.3 make decision on policies and forms of cooperation with foreign entities, including the approval of the forms of Model Authorisations prepared by the Somalia Petroleum Authority;

7.1.4 manage the process of substituting Production Sharing Agreements for rights granted by the Somali Democratic Republic on or before December 30, 1990, as contemplated by Section 48.1;

7.1.5 establishing policies to promote or restrict Petroleum export to protect the interest of Somalia;

7.1.6 to monitor developments in Petroleum Operations in Somalia and in border regions close to Somalia; and

7.1.7 deal with regulators or government ministries and departments responsible for regulation in adjacent countries regarding Petroleum activities that may have cross-border impacts, such as cross-border Reservoirs or pipelines.

The Government may confer on the Ministry such additional functions in relation to the regulation and monitoring of Petroleum Operations and, where appropriate, associated matters connected with the functions for the time being of the Ministry as are appropriate.

7.2 **Ministry Confidentiality**. When staff of the Ministry perform their lawful functions, they shall be obligated to maintain the confidentiality of commercial secrets of persons and enterprises of which they become aware where the Ministry is satisfied that:

7.2.1 disclosure of the information could reasonably be expected to result in a material loss or gain to a person directly affected by the functions of the Ministry, or could reasonably be expected to prejudice the person's competitive position; or

7.2.2 the information is financial, commercial, scientific or technical information that is confidential information supplied to the Ministry and the information has been consistently treated as confidential information by a person directly affected by the functions of the Ministry, and the Ministry considers that the person's interest in confidentiality outweighs the public interest in disclosure.

Article 8 Establishment and Functions of Somalia Petroleum Authority

8.1 *Establishment of SPA*. The Somalia Petroleum Authority is established by this Law as the competent regulatory authority to regulate Petroleum Operations.

8.2 ***Time of Formation***. The SPA shall be formed and be entitled to exercise its powers on the date specified by the Government. Until that date, the functions and powers of the SPA shall be exercised by the Petroleum Regulatory Affairs department of the Ministry, and the other provisions of this Law shall be read accordingly. The Government shall cause the SPA to be formed once it is satisfied that the quantity of Petroleum Operations in Somalia are sufficient to justify the costs of establishing the SPA.

8.3 ***Membership of SPA***. The Government shall appoint members to the SPA. There shall be not less than three and not more than seven members. A quorum of the SPA shall be constituted by three members. Members shall hold office during good behavior for a period of at least four years, but may be removed for cause at any time by the Government. Cause for removal shall include any breach of Sections 8.8 or 8.9 or ceasing to be eligible to be a member under Section 8.5.

8.4 ***Staff of SPA***. The Secretary-General and the other staff necessary for the proper conduct of the business of the SPA shall be appointed by the members of the SPA.

8.5 ***Qualifications of Members***. A person is not eligible to be appointed or to continue as a member of the SPA if that person is not a Somali citizen or is, as owner, shareholder, director, officer, partner or otherwise, engaged in the business of producing, selling, buying, transmitting, exporting, importing or otherwise dealing in Petroleum in Somalia or holds any bond, debenture or other security of a corporation engaged in any such business.

8.6 ***Qualifications of Staff.*** A person is not eligible to be appointed or to continue as staff of the SPA if that person is, as owner, shareholder, director, officer, partner or otherwise, engaged in the business of producing, selling, buying, transmitting, exporting, importing or otherwise dealing in Petroleum in Somalia or holds any bond, debenture or other security of a corporation engaged in any such business.

8.7 ***SPA Chair***. The Government shall designate one of the members to be Chairperson of the SPA and another of the members to be Vice-Chairperson of the SPA. The Chairperson is the chief executive officer of the SPA, and has supervision over and direction of the work and staff of the SPA. If the Chairperson is absent or unable to act or if the office is vacant, the Vice-Chairperson has all the powers and functions of the Chairperson.

For additional analytical, business and investment opportunities information, please contact Global Investment & Business Center, USA at (202) 546-2103. Fax: (202) 546-3275. E-mail: rusric@erols.com

8.8 **Duty of Care**. Members and staff of the SPA shall perform their duties faithfully, do their work according to law and be impartial and honest. They may not take advantage of their positions to seek illegitimate gains.

8.9 **SPA Confidentiality**. When the SPA and its members and staff perform their lawful functions, they shall be obligated to maintain the confidentiality of commercial secrets of persons and enterprises of which they become aware where the SPA is satisfied that:

8.9.1 disclosure of the information could reasonably be expected to result in a material loss or gain to a person directly affected by the functions of the SPA, or could reasonably be expected to prejudice the person's competitive position; or

8.9.2 the information is financial, commercial, scientific or technical information that is confidential information supplied to the SPA and the information has been consistently treated as confidential information by a person directly affected by the functions of the SPA, and the SPA considers that the person's interest in confidentiality outweighs the public interest in disclosure.

8.10 **SPA Office**. The SPA's principal office shall be in the municipality designated by the Ministry.

8.11 **Regional Offices of SPA**. The SPA shall keep under review the volume of regulatory work that relates to persons whose Petroleum Operations fall wholly within the boundaries of a particular State of Somalia. Where the SPA finds that the volume of such work justifies the creation of a regional office of the SPA in that State, or that a regional office should be established for more than one State, it shall so advise the Ministry. The Ministry may then authorise the establishment of such a regional office and the Government shall appoint three members to the SPA, who shall reside in that State. Two of the SPA members from that region shall be selected from a list of at least five eligible and qualified candidates presented by the government of that State. The provisions of this Law regarding appointment, term, dismissal, eligibility, confidentiality and other matters shall apply equally to SPA members serving in such a regional office. Applications, Authorisations, decisions, directions or orders which the SPA is required or entitled to handle and that relate to Petroleum Operations that are wholly within the boundaries of a State which the regional office of the SPA has been established to serve shall be handled by that office and the regional SPA members, who shall do so in accordance with the rules of practice and procedure of the SPA. In performing its duties, the regional office of the SPA shall observe national principles, policies, objectives and standards and adhere to national guidelines specified by the SPA.

8.12 **Duty of SPA**. The SPA shall regulate Petroleum Operations according to this Law and other laws of Somalia.

8.13 FUNCTIONS OF SPA. THE SPA SHALL PERFORM THE FOLLOWING FUNCTIONS:

8.13.1 to regulate, through the issuance, monitoring, modification and enforcement of Authorisations and the issuance of decisions, orders and directions under this Law and the Regulations, the conduct of Petroleum Operations in accordance with and subject to the provisions of this Law;

8.13.2 to ensure proper qualification of Authorised Persons, including without limitation, ensuring that Authorised Persons are commercially viable, creditworthy persons with the technical capability to perform their obligations;

8.13.3 to implement and ensure compliance by the relevant persons with any Authorisation, rule, decision, order or direction issued by the SPA in accordance with this Law; and

8.13.4 study and keep under review matters relating to the Petroleum industry which the Ministry requests the SPA to monitor, and report from time to time on such matters and recommend such measures as it considers necessary or advisable in the public interest for the control and development of that industry.

The Government, on the recommendation of the Ministry, may confer on the SPA such additional functions in relation to the regulation, monitoring and control of Petroleum Operations and, where appropriate, associated matters connected with the functions for the time being of the SPA as are appropriate.

8.14 *Powers of SPA*. When performing its functions according to law, the SPA shall have the following powers:

8.14.1 to grant Reconnaissance Authorisations in accordance with Section 12.1;

8.14.2 to grant Production Sharing Agreements in accordance with Section 13.1;

8.14.3 to grant Surface Access Authorisations in accordance with Section 14.1;

8.14.4 to grant exemptions in accordance with Article 23;

8.14.5 to modify and revoke any Authorisation in accordance with this Law, the Regulations and the provisions of the Authorisation;

8.14.6 to make and enforce directions to ensure compliance with Authorisations;

8.14.7 inquire into, hear and determine any matter where it appears to the SPA that any person has failed to do any act, matter or thing required to be done by this Law, the Regulations or by any Authorisation, decision, order or direction made by the SPA, or that any person has done or is doing any act, matter or thing contrary to or in contravention of this Law, the Regulations or any such Authorisation, decision, order or direction;

8.14.8 order and require any person to do at any specified time and in any manner prescribed by the SPA, any act, matter or thing that such person is or may be required to do under this Law, the Regulations or any Authorisation or rule, or any decision, order or direction made or given under this Law or the Regulations; and forbid the doing or continuing of any act, matter or thing that is contrary to this Law, the Regulations or any such Authorisation, rule, decision, order or direction;

8.14.9 in connection with the foregoing, to gather information, including compelling the provision of information from any Authorised Person;

8.14.10 assess penalties for the breach of any Authorisation, decision, order or direction of the SPA, in accordance with Chapter VII;

8.14.11 work cooperatively with foreign regulators, ministries or departments responsible for regulation in adjacent countries regarding cross-border Petroleum Operations or pipelines;

8.14.12 to make rules in accordance with Sections 8.17 and 8.18; and

8.14.13 of its own motion inquire into, hear and determine any other matter or thing that under this Law or the Regulations it may inquire into, hear and determine.

8.15 **Investigation**. It shall be the duty of the SPA to investigate or cause to be investigated whether any relevant requirement or condition of an Authorisation has been or is being contravened.

8.16 **Cooperation with SPA**. When the SPA and its members and staff perform their lawful functions, persons and enterprises under inspection or investigation shall cooperate and provide truthful and relevant documents and materials. Such persons and enterprises may not refuse to cooperate, obstruct inspection or investigation or conceal relevant documents or materials.

8.17 **SPA Operational Rules**. The SPA may, following consultation with the Ministry, make such rules as appears to it requisite or expedient having regard to its duties and functions, including rules requiring or prohibiting certain commercial conduct of Authorised Persons so as to ensure the orderly functioning of the Petroleum industry in Somalia. The SPA may only make such rules after consulting with Authorised Persons and with persons or bodies appearing to it to be representative of persons likely to be affected by the rules. Rules made pursuant to this Section 8.17 may not have the effect of amending or materially altering the provisions or conditions of any Authorisation. Amendments and material alterations to Authorisations may only occur pursuant to Article 23.

8.18 **SPA Procedural Rules**. The SPA may make rules respecting the sittings of the SPA, the procedure for making applications, representations and complaints to the SPA and the conduct of hearings before the SPA, and the manner of conducting any business before the SPA, and generally, the carrying on of the work of the SPA, the management of its internal affairs and the duties of its staff. When making these rules, the SPA shall seek to incorporate principles of openness, transparency, accountability and independence.

8.19 **Annual Report**. As soon as may be after the end of year, but not later than six months thereafter, the SPA shall cause a report on the performance of its functions during that year to be provided to the Ministry.

8.20 PUBLIC DOCUMENTS. THE **SPA** SHALL MAKE AVAILABLE TO THE PUBLIC:

8.20.1 THE RULES ESTABLISHED BY THE **SPA** PURSUANT TO SECTIONS **8.17** AND **8.18**;

8.20.2 decisions, orders and directions of the SPA;

8.20.3 penalties imposed by the SPA;

8.20.4 annual reports of the SPA contemplated by Section 8.19;

8.20.5 the model forms of any Reconnaissance Authorisation, Surface Access Authorisation or Production Sharing Agreement; and

8.20.6 THE AUTHORISATIONS ISSUED BY THE **SPA.**

8.21 **Ministry Role re SPA**. The Ministry may provide general policy guidance to the SPA in connection with the performance of the SPA's functions under this Law and the Regulations. Policy guidance provided by the Ministry shall be published by the Ministry in the same manner

For additional analytical, business and investment opportunities information,
please contact Global Investment & Business Center, USA
at (202) 546-2103. Fax: (202) 546-3275. E-mail: rusric@erols.com

as other legislative and policy matters are published. When performing its duties under this Law or the Regulations, the SPA shall take into account the policy directives issued by the Ministry. The Ministry should not intervene in any specific issue or matter that may be brought before the SPA.

8.22 *Appeal*. Except as provided in this Section 8.22, every decision, order or direction of the SPA is final and conclusive. An appeal may be made to the SPA from a decision, order or direction of a regional office of the SPA on any question. An appeal may be made to Supreme Court from a decision, order or direction of the SPA on a question of law, or of jurisdiction, or bias on the part of a member of the SPA who participated in the decision, order or direction, or of compliance with the rules of procedural fairness described in Section 8.23. No appeal lies from a decision of the SPA on any other grounds. An application for appeal must be made within sixty days after the release of the decision, order or direction sought to be appealed.

8.23 *Procedural Fairness*. In performing its functions under this Law or the Regulations, the SPA shall:

8.23.1 give notice to interested persons of any application received or hearing that the SPA is to conduct in the manner provided in this Law or the Regulations;

8.23.2 conduct hearings with respect to the issuance, revocation or suspension of Authorisations in those circumstances provided for in this Law or the Regulations;

8.23.3 give written reasons for its decisions, orders and directions, which reasons shall be given at the time of the decision, order or direction; and

8.23.4 where a decision, order or direction is made after a hearing, render its decisions based on the evidence, argument and information presented at the hearing.

8.24 *Fees, Levies and Charges*. The Ministry may, based on a recommendation from the SPA, and for the purposes of recovering all or a portion of such costs as the SPA determines to be attributable to its responsibilities under this Law or the Regulations, impose reasonable fees, levies or charges on any enterprise that holds an Authorisation issued pursuant to this Law or the Regulations, and provide for the manner of calculating the fees, levies and charges in respect of the person or company and their payment to the Ministry of Treasury. The SPA may also specify the rate of interest or the manner of calculating the rate of interest payable by an enterprise on any fee, levy or charge not paid by the person or company on or before the date it is due.

Article 9 Establishment and Functions of Somalia Petroleum Corporation

9.1 *Formation of SPC*. Somalia Petroleum Corporation is established as a juridical person in the form of a corporation.

9.1.1 The head office of Somalia Petroleum Corporation shall be at a place in Somalia that the Ministry shall designate.

9.1.2 Somalia Petroleum Corporation has, in respect of its powers, all the rights, powers, privileges and capacity of a natural person.

9.1.3 This Law shall apply to the Somalia Petroleum Corporation in the same terms as is applicable to any other Authorised Person, with the required adaptations.

9.2 **Purpose of SPC**. The purpose of the Somalia Petroleum Corporation is to be a commercial enterprise Controlled by the Government to conduct Petroleum Operations in Somalia. Somalia Petroleum Corporation shall be entitled to exercise the right of participation referred to in Section 24.1. Somalia Petroleum Corporation may acquire an Authorisation by direct acquisition or pursuant to a bid process conducted by the SPA in the same manner as any other Person.

9.3 **SPC Board of Directors**. Somalia Petroleum Corporation shall have a Board of Directors comprised of the Chairperson, the Managing Director and not fewer than three, but no more than seven, other directors.

9.3.1 The Chairperson is to be appointed by the Government to hold office during pleasure for a term that the Government considers appropriate.

9.3.2 The Managing Director is to be appointed by the Government to hold office during good behaviour for a term that the Government considers appropriate and may be removed for cause. The Managing Director is eligible for reappointment on the expiration of his or her term of office.

9.3.3 The other directors are to be appointed by the Government based on recommendations of the Ministry, for a term of no more than three years so as to ensure, as far as possible, the expiration in any one year of the terms of office of not more than half of the directors. Any other director is eligible for reappointment on the expiration of his or her term.

9.3.4 Subject to Section 9.3.5, no individual is eligible to be appointed or to continue as Chairperson, Managing Director or a director unless the individual is a Somali citizen.

9.3.5 WHEN APPOINTING THE CERTAIN DIRECTORS, THE MINISTRY NEED NOT APPLY SECTION

9.3.4 where the Ministry is satisfied that an individual who is non-Somali citizen can assist Somalia Petroleum Corporation owing to his or her experience in the Petroleum industry; provided that the majority of directors (including the Chairperson and the Managing Director) shall be Somali citizens.

9.4 **Role of SPC Board**. The Board shall direct and manage the business and affairs of Somalia Petroleum Corporation.

9.4.1 The Board may, by resolution, make by-laws to regulate the business and affairs of Somalia Petroleum Corporation.

9.4.2 The Board may establish an Executive Committee, or any other committee or advisory group that the Board considers advisable, and determine its composition and duties and the tenure of its members.

9.4.3 The Board may delegate power to, and specify duties and authority of, the Executive Committee to act in all matters that are not by this Act or any bylaw or resolution specifically reserved to be done by the Board.

9.4.4 THE CHAIRPERSON SHALL CARRY OUT THE DUTIES DETERMINED BY BY-LAW.

9.4.5 The Managing Director is the chief executive officer of Somalia Petroleum Corporation and has, on behalf of the Board, the direction and management of the business and affairs of Somalia Petroleum Corporation with authority to act in all matters that are not by this Law or any by-law or

For additional analytical, business and investment opportunities information,
please contact Global Investment & Business Center, USA
at (202) 546-2103. Fax: (202) 546-3275. E-mail: rusric@erols.com

resolution specifically reserved to be done by the Board or the Executive Committee. The Government may change the title of the Managing Director to such other title as it determines appropriate, so long as the functions of the holder of that office remain as chief executive officer.

9.4.6 If the Managing Director is absent or unable to act, or if the office of Managing Director is vacant, the Board may authorise an officer or employee of Somalia Petroleum Corporation to act as Managing Director, but that person may not act as Managing Director for a period of more than ninety days without the approval of the Government.

9.5 *SPC Officers and Employees*. Somalia Petroleum Corporation may employ such officers and employees, and may engage such agents, advisers and consultants, as it considers necessary to carry out the purpose of this Law and for the proper conduct of its business and Somalia Petroleum Corporation may fix the terms and conditions of their employment or engagement.

9.6 *Remuneration of SPC Board*. The Chairperson and each director, except the Managing Director and any director employed in the public service of Somalia, are entitled to be paid by Somalia Petroleum Corporation the remuneration fixed by the Ministry for their time to attend meetings of the Board or any committee of the Board and to perform their duties under this Law.

9.7 *SPC Directors Expenses*. Directors are entitled to be paid by Somalia Petroleum Corporation reasonable travel and living expenses incurred in connection with the performance of their duties under this Act while absent from their ordinary places of residence.

9.8 *Remuneration of SPC Officers and Employees*. Officers, employees, agents, advisers and consultants are entitled to be paid by Somalia Petroleum Corporation the remuneration, expenses and benefits that Somalia Petroleum Corporation may determine.

Article 10 Restrictions to Rights of Public Officers

10.1 *Conflict of Interest Restrictions*. A Public Officer shall not acquire, attempt to acquire or hold:

10.1.1 an Authorisation or an interest, whether direct or indirect, in an Authorisation; or

10.1.2 A SHARE IN A CORPORATION (OR AN AFFILIATE OF IT) THAT HOLDS AN AUTHORISATION.

10.2 *Consequence of Contravention*. Any instrument that grants or purports to grant, to a Public Officer, an interest, whether direct or indirect, in an Authorisation shall, to the extent of the grant, be void.

10.3 *Relations*. The acquisition or holding of an Authorisation, interest or share by the minor children or spouse of a Public Officer shall be deemed to be an acquisition or holding by the Public Officer.

10.4 *Exception*. This Article 10 does not apply to Public Officers who are directors, officers or employees of or consultants to Somalia Petroleum Corporation to the extent that their interest in an Authorisation is held by Somalia Petroleum Corporation.

Article 11 Graticulation

For the purposes of this Law, the Territory of Somalia, or parts thereof, shall be divided into blocks according to a grid system which conforms to accepted international standards and norms of graticulation.

CHAPTER II -AUTHORISATION OF PETROLEUM OPERATIONS

ARTICLE 12 RECONNAISSANCE AUTHORISATIONS

12.1 *Power to Grant*. The Somalia Petroleum Authority may grant a Reconnaissance Authorisation, in respect of a specified area, to a Person or a group of Persons.

12.2 RIGHTS UNDER RECONNAISSANCE AUTHORISATION.

12.2.1 A Reconnaissance Authorisation grants a right to perform geological, geophysical, geochemical and geotechnical surveys in the Authorised Area.

12.2.2 The Reconnaissance Authorisation shall require the Authorised Person to report on the progress and results of such prospecting, and to maintain confidentiality with respect thereto.

12.2.3 Nothing in a Reconnaissance Authorisation authorises the holder to drill a Well or to have any preference or right to enter into a Production Sharing Agreement.

12.3 *Overlapping Authorisations*. Prior to granting a Reconnaissance Authorisation in respect of an area that is the subject of an existing Authorisation, the SPA shall give written notice to the holder of the existing Authorisation.

12.4 SURRENDER AND TERMINATION.

12.4.1 The holder of a Reconnaissance Authorisation may surrender it at any time by written notice to the SPA, provided that the Authorised Person has fulfilled all its obligations thereunder.

12.4.2 If the holder has not complied with a condition to which the Reconnaissance Authorisation is subject, the SPA may terminate it by written notice to the holder after giving the holder a reasonable opportunity to cure the condition.

Article 13 Production Sharing Agreements

13.1 *Power to Grant*. The Somalia Petroleum Authority may conclude a Production Sharing Agreement, in respect of a specified area, with a Person or a group of Persons provided that if a group, such group has entered into a joint operating agreement approved by the SPA under Section 20.1. Each Production Sharing Agreement shall be signed by the Minister, based on a recommendation from the SPA.

13.2 *Qualification of Contractors*. In order to be eligible to enter into a Production Sharing Agreement, a Person must:

13.2.1 have, or have access to, the financial capability, and the technical knowledge and technical ability, to carry out the Petroleum Operations in the Contract Area;

13.2.2 not have a record of non-compliance with principles of good corporate citizenship; and

For additional analytical, business and investment opportunities information, please contact Global Investment & Business Center, USA at (202) 546-2103. Fax: (202) 546-3275. E-mail: rusric@erols.com

13.2.3 BE A LIMITED LIABILITY CORPORATION OR ENTITY WITH LIMITED LIABILITY.

13.3 EXCLUSIVITY.

13.3.1 Without prejudice to Article 14, or the right of the SPA to grant a Reconnaissance Permit, a Production Sharing Agreement grants to the Contractor the exclusive right to conduct Petroleum Operations in the Contract Area.

13.3.2 The Production Sharing Agreement may be limited to Crude Oil, Natural Gas or other constituents of Petroleum.

13.3.3 The initial contract area under a Production Sharing Agreement may not exceed 15,000 km².

13.4 NOTICE OF DISCOVERY.

13.4.1 A Contractor shall give written notice to the SPA within twenty four (24) hours whenever any Petroleum is discovered in its Authorised Area.

13.4.2 The Contractor shall provide such information relating to the discovery requested by the SPA.

13.5 **Work Programmes, Plans & Budgets**. A Production Sharing Agreement shall oblige the Contractor to carry on Petroleum Operations only in accordance with work programmes, plans and budgets approved by the SPA.

13.6 **Required Provisions of PSA**. A Production Sharing Agreement shall include provisions addressing the following matters:

13.6.1 a minimum work obligation to be performed during an exploratory phase of the term of the Production Sharing Agreement;

13.6.2 RELINQUISHMENT OF PORTIONS OF THE CONTRACT AREA DURING THE EXPLORATORY PHASE;

13.6.3 financial terms respecting royalties (if any), and the sharing of Petroleum between the Contractor and the Government;

13.6.4 if appropriate, financial features other than royalties and sharing of Petroleum, including signature and production bonuses;

13.6.5 environmental provisions directed at protecting and preserving the environment;

13.6.6 if appropriate, obligations respecting the supply of Petroleum to the Somali domestic market, especially in emergency situations;

13.6.7 TRAINING AND HIRING OF SOMALI CITIZENS;

13.6.8 preference for the supply of Somali-sourced goods and services;

13.6.9 if appropriate, assurances of financial and contractual stability; and

13.6.10 international arbitration.

13.7 TAXATION UNDER PSA.

13.7.1 A Production Sharing Agreement may provide that the Contractor is subject to corporate income tax in Somalia, or that it is exempt from corporate income tax in relation to the conduct of Petroleum Operations under that Production Sharing Agreement.

13.7.2 Corporations who are Contractors under a tax-exempt Production Sharing Agreement shall not be liable to pay corporate income tax in respect of the Petroleum Operations conducted under that Production Sharing Contract.

13.7.3 If a Production Sharing Agreement provides that the Contractor is exempt from corporate income tax, the financial provisions shall be adjusted appropriately to reflect the value to the Contractor of this exemption.

13.8 SURRENDER AND TERMINATION.

13.8.1 The holder of a Production Sharing Agreement may surrender it at any time by written notice to the SPA, provided that the Contractor has fulfilled all its obligations thereunder.

13.8.2 If the Contractor has not complied with a condition to which the Production Sharing Agreement is subject, the SPA may terminate it by written notice to the Contractor after giving the Contractor a reasonable opportunity to cure the condition.

Article 14 Surface Access Authorisations

14.1 POWER TO GRANT.

14.1.1 The Somalia Petroleum Authority may grant a Surface Access Authorisation, in respect of a specified area, to a Person or a group of Persons.

14.1.2 The SPA may not grant a Surface Access Authorisation in respect of an area that is the subject of a Production Sharing Agreement or a Reconnaissance Authorisation until it has taken into account any submissions made by the holders of such Authorisations in such a way that there is no undue interference with the rights of that other Authorised Person.

14.2 RIGHTS GRANTED.

14.2.1 A Surface Access Authorisation, while it remains in force, authorises the holder to do one or more of the following:

14.2.1.1 construct, install and operate structures, facilities and installations; and

14.2.1.2 CARRY OUT OTHER WORKS;

as specified in the Authorisation in the Authorised Area.

14.2.2 Nothing in a Surface Access Authorisation authorises the holder to drill a Well.

14.3 *SURRENDER AND TERMINATION.*

14.3.1 A SURFACE ACCESS AUTHORISATION:

14.3.1.1 may be surrendered by the holder by written notice to the SPA, provided that the Authorised Person has fulfilled all its obligations thereunder; and

14.3.1.2 may be terminated by the SPA at any time by written notice to the holder, if the holder has not complied with a condition to which the Authorisation is subject after giving the holder a reasonable opportunity to cure the condition.

14.3.2 The SPA shall provide written notice of the surrender or termination to any Authorised Person in whose Authorised Area operations were authorised to be carried on by the Surface Access Authorisation concerned.

14.4 *Coordination of Operations*. The SPA may give a direction to the holders of Surface Access Authorisations and to other Authorised Persons regarding the coordination of their respective Petroleum Operations.

Article 15 Invitation to Apply

15.1 *APPLICATION FOR AUTHORISATIONS.*

15.1.1 The Somalia Petroleum Authority shall invite, wherever possible by public notice, applications for Authorisations, which shall be the preferred method of granting such Authorisations.

15.1.2 Notwithstanding Section 15.1.1, the SPA may elect to award Authorisations through direct negotiation without issuing such invitations:

15.1.2.1 IN THE CASE OF SURFACE ACCESS AUTHORISATIONS; OR

15.1.2.2 in the case of all other Authorisations, where it is in the public interest to do so, based on a direction from the Ministry or the Government.

15.1.3 If the SPA grants an Authorisation without inviting applications, it shall provide reasons for its so doing to the Ministry and the Government.

15.1.4 The application shall be submitted in one of the official or second languages of Somalia or, in the event that they are written in any other language, be accompanied by an official translation into one of the official or second languages of Somalia, and shall be submitted in a closed envelope.

15.2 *CONTENTS OF INVITATION.*

15.2.1 An invitation shall specify the area concerned, the proposed activities, the criteria upon which applications will be assessed, the applicable fees (if any) to be paid with the application, and the time by which, and the manner in which, applications may be made and considered, through the public opening of bids.

15.2.2 Unless the invitation otherwise states, the SPA may choose not to award an Authorisation to any of the applicants.

15.3 CONTENTS OF APPLICATION.

15.3.1 AN APPLICATION FOR AN AUTHORISATION SHALL INCLUDE PROPOSALS FOR:

15.3.1.1 securing the health, safety and welfare of persons involved in or affected by the Petroleum Operations;

15.3.1.2 protecting the environment, preventing, minimising and remedying pollution, and other environmental harm from the Petroleum Operations;

15.3.1.3 training of, and giving preference in employment in the Petroleum Operations to, nationals of Somalia;

15.3.1.4 commitments to benefit the local community in the Authorised Area and to minimise and mitigate any adverse effects of Petroleum Operations in the Authorised Area; and

15.3.1.5 the acquisition of goods and services from Persons based in Somalia.

15.3.2 An Authorisation awarded to an applicant obliges it to comply with its proposals as mentioned in Section 15.3.1.

15.4 **Due Consideration of Applications**. The SPA shall not grant an Authorisation in respect of an area until it has given due consideration to all applications made in response to, and in compliance with, an invitation.

Article 16 Petroleum Operations Generally

16.1 Third Party Access. Every Production Sharing Agreement and Surface Access Authorisation shall require that third party access be granted on reasonable terms and conditions.

16.2 JOINT AND SEVERAL.

16.2.1 If there is more than one Authorised Person in respect of a particular Authorisation, the obligations and liabilities of the Authorised Person under an Authorisation are the obligations and liabilities of them all, jointly and severally.

16.2.2 With respect to a Production Sharing Agreement, the Somalia Petroleum Corporation and any State-Owned Contractor may be exempted by the SPA of the requirement set out in Section 16.2.1.

16.3 **Effect of Violation of Laws**. An Authorisation is void *ab initio*, if obtained in violation of the laws of Somalia, including laws concerning corruption.

Article 17 Environmental Protection

17.1 Environmental Duties. Authorised Persons conducting Petroleum Operations are required to:

17.1.1 MINIMIZE ECOLOGICAL DAMAGE;

17.1.2 avoid waste of Petroleum;

17.1.3 prevent damage or waste of Petroleum-bearing strata;

17.1.4 prevent pollution and waste to land and structures, fresh water resources/aquifers, crops, marine and animal life;

17.1.5 prevent the escape of Petroleum into the environment through uncontrolled flows or discharges;

17.1.6 PROVIDE FOR EMERGENCY CLEAN-UP OPERATIONS AND PROCEDURES;

17.1.7 in appropriate circumstances, conduct an environmental base line study before commencing Petroleum Operations, and an environmental impact assessment of any major proposed Petroleum Operations; and

17.1.8 utilize Good Oil Field Practice in the restoration of the environment at the conclusion of Petroleum Operations.

17.2 **Environmental Regulations**. The Minister shall enact Regulations which more clearly define the obligations of an Authorised Person under Section 17.1.

Article 18 Restitution and Reparation

18.1 **Requirement for Authorisation**. No person shall conduct Petroleum Operations in the Territory of Somalia except pursuant to an Authorisation issued pursuant to this Law or the Regulations.

18.2 **Restitution**. Without prejudice to any criminal liability of that Person, a Person who engages in Petroleum Operations other than pursuant to an Authorisation shall:

18.2.1 make restitution to Somalia of an amount equal to the market value of Petroleum developed, produced or exported, together with late payment interest thereon at a rate not to exceed the legal rate of interest to be determined by the Ministry;

18.2.2 either forfeit all infrastructure and equipment used in engaging in those Petroleum Operations, or remove such infrastructure and equipment or be liable for the payment of the costs of such removal; and

18.2.3 clean-up pollution resulting from those Petroleum Operations, or reimburse the costs of clean-up to Somalia.

18.3 **Quantum**. The liabilities under Section 18.1 shall apply cumulatively, or not, as is determined to be appropriate by the SPA, with a view to place Somalia in the position in which it would have been were it not for the Petroleum Operations engaged in other than pursuant to an Authorisation.

For additional analytical, business and investment opportunities information,
please contact Global Investment & Business Center, USA
at (202) 546-2103. Fax: (202) 546-3275. E-mail: rusric@erols.com

18.4 *Joint and Several Liability*. The liabilities under Section 18.1 of Persons who, together, are engaged in, or have engaged in, Petroleum Operations are the liabilities of them all, jointly and severally.

Article 19 Restrictions on Exercise of Rights

19.1 FAIR COMPENSATION TO SURFACE OWNERS.

19.1.1 An Authorised Person shall not exercise any of the rights granted under an Authorisation or under this Law:

19.1.1.1 ON ANY PUBLIC IMMOVABLE PROPERTY WITHOUT THE CONSENT OF THE **SPA;**

19.1.1.2 on any private immovable property of the State without the consent of the SPA; or

19.1.1.3 ON ANY PRIVATE IMMOVABLE PROPERTY

without payment of fair and reasonable compensation to the owner, as may be determined by the SPA.

19.1.2 The owner of any immovable property in an Authorised Area retains rights to the use of its land except in so far as the use interferes with Petroleum Operations.

19.1.3 An Authorisation may limit or otherwise control the use by an Authorised Person of public infrastructure, and the consumption of other natural resources, including trees, sand, gravel, rock and water.

19.1.4 An Authorisation does not constitute a waiver of the obligation to seek the written consent of responsible authorities, except as may be specifically described in the Authorisation.

19.2 *No Interference with Lawful Offshore Activities*. An Authorised Person shall not exercise any of the rights under an Authorisation or under this Law or the Regulations in a way that interferes with fishing, navigation or any other lawful offshore operation without the written consent of the responsible authority.

19.3 COMPENSATION FOR DISTURBANCE.

19.3.1 The Authorised Person is liable to pay fair and reasonable compensation as determined by the SPA if, in the course of Petroleum Operations, it:

19.3.1.1 disturbs the rights of the owner of any immovable property, or causes any damage thereon; or

19.3.1.2 demonstrably interferes with fishing, navigation or any other lawful offshore activities.

19.3.2 Where the value of any rights have been enhanced by the Petroleum Operations, compensation payable in respect of such rights shall not exceed any amount which would be payable if the value had not been so enhanced.

**For additional analytical, business and investment opportunities information,
please contact Global Investment & Business Center, USA
at (202) 546-2103. Fax: (202) 546-3275. E-mail: rusric@erols.com**

19.4 *Fair and Reasonable Compensation*. What constitutes fair and reasonable compensation under this Article 19 shall be decided by the SPA, after having considered representations by interested parties.

Article 20 Approvals by SPA

20.1 *Approval of Agreements.* A joint operating agreement, a lifting arrangement and any agreement related to the Petroleum Operations, as well as any changes to such agreements, shall be subject to prior approval by the SPA. The SPA shall approve any such agreements or amendments where they are consistent with the Authorisations, the Law and the Regulations.

20.2 APPROVAL OF CHANGE IN CONTROL.

20.2.1 All changes in Control of an Authorised Person shall be subject to prior approval by the SPA.

20.2.2 Where a change in Control occurs without the prior approval of the SPA, the SPA may terminate the applicable Authorisation.

20.2.3 For the purposes of Section 20.2.1, change in Control includes a Person ceasing to be in Control (whether or not another Person becomes in Control), and a Person obtaining Control (whether or not another Person was in Control).

20.3 *Approval of Transfers*. Except with the prior written consent of the SPA (which consent may not be unreasonably withheld or delayed), or as explicitly provided in the terms of the Authorisation, no assignment, transfer, conveyance, novation, merger, encumbrance or other similar dealing in respect of an Authorisation shall be of any force or effect. The Regulations shall describe the criteria by which the SPA shall assess the suitability of its consent.

Article 21 Unitisation Contract

21.1 UNITISATION.

21.1.1 If and when a Reservoir is discovered to lie partly within a Contract Area, and partly in another Contract Area:

21.1.1.1 the SPA may require by written notice the Contractors to enter into a unitisation agreement with each other for the purpose of securing the more effective and optimised production of Petroleum from the Reservoir; and

21.1.1.2 if no agreement has been reached within a period of eighteen (18) months from receipt of written notice as required in Section 21.1.1.1, the SPA shall decide on the unitisation agreement.

21.1.2 If and when a Reservoir is discovered to lie partly within a Contract Area and partly in an area that is not the subject of a Production Sharing Agreement:

21.1.2.1 the SPA may require by written notice the Contractor to enter into a unitisation agreement with the SPA for the purpose of securing the more effective and optimised production of Petroleum from the Reservoir; and

21.1.2.2 if no agreement has been reached within a period of eighteen (18) months from receipt of written notice as required in Section 21.1.2.1, the SPA shall decide on the unitisation agreement, unless otherwise provided in the Production Sharing Agreement.

21.2 **Unitisation Agreement.** Without limiting the matters to be dealt with, the unitisation agreement shall define the amount of Petroleum in each area covered by the unitisation agreement, and shall appoint the Operator responsible for production of the Petroleum covered by the unitisation agreement.

21.3 **Requirement of Approval.** The SPA may approve the continued development or production of a Reservoir partly within a Contract Area under Section 21.2 only after it has approved or decided the unitisation agreement.

21.4 **Approval of Changes**. Any changes to the unitisation agreement shall be subject to prior approval by the SPA.

Article 22 Resolution of Disputes

22.1 SPA ROLE IN DISPUTES.

22.1.1 The SPA may inquire into and decide all disputes involving Persons engaged in Petroleum Operations, either:

22.1.1.1 among themselves, where agreements between them do not specify a dispute resolution mechanism; or

22.1.1.2 in relation to third parties (other than the Government) not so engaged, as long as these third parties accept the jurisdiction of the SPA for the resolution of the dispute.

22.1.2 The SPA may refuse to decide any dispute referred to it and, if it does so, it shall notify the parties to the dispute in writing.

22.1.3 The SPA may, taking into account all relevant circumstances, give any direction which may be necessary for the purpose of giving effect to its decision in proceedings pursuant to this Article 20, including ordering the payment, by any party to a dispute, to any other party to the dispute of such compensation as may be fair and reasonable.

22.2 DISPUTES RE AUTHORISATIONS.

22.2.1 If a dispute arises relating to the interpretation and/or application of the terms of an Authorisation between an Authorised Person and the SPA, the parties shall attempt to resolve that dispute by means of negotiation.

22.2.2 If the dispute cannot be resolved amicably by negotiation, either Party may submit the dispute to international arbitration under recognized rules, in a neutral venue, or to the Supreme Court, at the election of the submitting Party.

ARTICLE 23 EXEMPTION FROM OR VARIATION OF CONDITIONS

The SPA may exempt an Authorised Person from complying with the conditions of its Authorisation, and may also agree to vary or suspend those conditions, either with or

without conditions and either temporarily or permanently, provided that the SPA shall provide written reasons for its doing so to the Ministry. This Article 23 does not include the power to waive or suspend an obligation to pay any amount due under an Authorisation.

CHAPTER III - SOMALIA PARTICIPATION

ARTICLE 24 SOMALIA PETROLEUM CORPORATION AND STATE PARTICIPATION IN PETROLEUM OPERATIONS

24.1 *SPC AND STATE PARTICIPATION.* EACH PRODUCTION SHARING AGREEMENT SHALL STIPULATE:

24.1.1 the right of Somalia Petroleum Corporation to participate in Petroleum Operations, up to a maximum participation right of 30%; and

24.1.2 the right of a State-Owned Contractor which is Controlled by the State of the Somalia Republic in which the Authorized Area is located to participate in Petroleum Operations, up to a maximum participation right of 10%.

24.2 **Decision to Participate**. The decision by Somalia Petroleum Corporation to participate in Petroleum Operations under a particular Production Sharing Agreement shall be made by the Minister, if a recommendation to participate has been made by Somalia Petroleum Corporation. The decision by a State-Owned Contractor which is Controlled by the State of the Somalia Republic in which the Authorized Area is located to participate in Petroleum Operations shall be made by the government of the State in which the Authorized Area is located.

24.3 **Timing of Decision**. The participation rights under Section 24.1 may occur during any phase of Petroleum Operations in accordance with the terms and conditions established in the Production Sharing Agreement.

CHAPTER IV - CONDUCT OF PETROLEUM ACTIVITIES

Article 25 Work Practices

25.1 **Good Oil Field Practice**. Petroleum Operations shall be conducted in accordance with Good Oil Field Practice, that is, in accordance with such practices and procedures employed in the petroleum industry worldwide by prudent and diligent operators under conditions and circumstances similar to those experienced in connection with the relevant aspect or aspects of the Petroleum Operations, principally aimed at guaranteeing:

25.1.1 conservation of Petroleum resources, which implies the utilization of adequate methods and processes to maximize the recovery of hydrocarbons in a technically and economically sustainable manner, with a corresponding control of reserves decline, using principles of maximum efficient production rates and other conservation principles, and to minimize losses at the surface;

25.1.2 operational safety, which entails the use of methods and processes that promote occupational security and the prevention of accidents;

25.1.3 environmental protection, that calls for the adoption of methods and processes which minimize the impact of Petroleum Operations on the environment;

25.2 *CONSERVATION.* PRODUCTION OF PETROLEUM SHALL TAKE PLACE:

25.2.1 in such a manner that as much as possible of the Petroleum in place in each individual Petroleum deposit, or in several deposits in combination, will be produced;

25.2.2 in accordance with Good Oil Field Practice and sound economic principles; and

25.2.3 IN SUCH A MANNER THAT WASTE OF PETROLEUM OR RESERVOIR ENERGY IS AVOIDED.

25.3 *Continuous Evaluation.* Contractors shall carry out continuous evaluation of production strategy and technical solutions, shall take the necessary measures in order to achieve this, and shall inform the SPA of any relevant changes, in accordance with Good Oil Field Practice.

Article 26 Decommissioning

26.1 *Timing of Decommissioning.* An Authorised Person shall Decommission on the earlier of:

26.1.1 TERMINATION OF THE AUTHORISATION; AND

26.1.2 when no longer required for Petroleum Operations;

and, in either case:

26.1.3 except with the consent in writing of the SPA and in accordance with the conditions of the consent; or

26.1.4 UNLESS THE AUTHORISATION OTHERWISE PROVIDES.

26.2 *Detail in Authorisations and Regulations.* Authorisations shall contain provisions addressing the Decommissioning of Petroleum Operations. The Ministry, based on advice and recommendations from the SPA, may make Regulations under this Law relating to Decommissioning of Petroleum Operations.

CHAPTER V - INFORMATION AND INVESTIGATION

ARTICLE 27 DATA AND INFORMATION

27.1 *Title to Data and Information.* Somalia shall have title to all data and information, whether raw, derived, processed, interpreted or analysed, obtained pursuant to any Authorisation. Appropriate obligations of confidentiality shall apply, as contemplated by Sections 7.2 and 8.9.

27.2 *Export of Data.* Data and information acquired during the course of Petroleum Operations may be freely exported by Authorised Persons provided that the SPA may require that an original, or in the case of a core, rock, fluid or other physical sample, a usable portion of the original, of all data and information, both physical and electronic, be kept in Somalia.

Article 28 Audit and Inspection

28.1 *INSPECTOR.*

28.1.1 The SPA may appoint a person to be an inspector for the purposes of this Law (an "Inspector").

28.1.2 The Inspector will have the powers and rights provided to it in the Regulations.

28.2 **Access to Books and Accounts**. On request, an Authorised Person shall make its books and accounts available to the SPA for auditing.

Article 29 Termination of Authorisations

29.1 *TERMINATION.*

29.1.1 Termination of an Authorisation for any reason is without prejudice to rights and obligations expressed in this Law, the Regulations or the Authorisation to survive termination, or to rights and obligations accrued thereunder prior to termination, and all provisions of an Authorisation reasonably necessary for the full enjoyment and enforcement of those rights and obligations survive termination for the period so necessary.

29.1.2 The SPA shall have the power to terminate an Authorisation as set out in the Authorisation.

29.2 *MULTIPLE AUTHORISED PERSONS.*

29.2.1 If there is more than one Authorised Person in respect of a particular Authorisation and circumstances arise in which the SPA may terminate an Authorisation, the SPA may elect to terminate an Authorisation only in respect of those Authorised Persons whose acts or omissions (or in relation to whom acts, omissions or events have occurred which) have led to such circumstances, and shall so notify the remaining Authorised Persons.

29.2.2 Should the SPA terminate an authorisation under Section 29.2.1, it shall give the remaining Authorised Persons right of preference in the acquisition of the terminated share, in proportion to their respective shares. Any share not acquired by the remaining Authorised Persons shall revert to Somalia.

Article 30 Indemnification of the Government and Ministry and SPA

30.1 *INDEMNIFICATION.* AN AUTHORISED PERSON SHALL:

30.1.1 defend, indemnify and hold harmless the Government, Ministry and the SPA from all claims by third parties resulting, directly or indirectly, from Petroleum Operations, and pay all compensations relating to any civil liability claims, pretensions or demands; and

30.1.2 unless the Ministry is satisfied, after consultation with the Authorised Person, that the potential liability under Section 30.1.1 can be covered by other means, including the posting of corporate or bank guarantees or standby letters of credit, maintain insurance in respect thereof on a strict liability basis for such amount as the Ministry requires from time to time.

CHAPTER VI - PUBLIC INFORMATION

Article 31 Publication by SPA

For additional analytical, business and investment opportunities information,
please contact Global Investment & Business Center, USA
at (202) 546-2103. Fax: (202) 546-3275. E-mail: rusric@erols.com

31.1 *PUBLICATION.* THE SPA SHALL PUBLISH, IN THE *GAZETTE*:

31.1.1 notice of the grant of Authorisations, and a summary of the terms of such Authorisations;

31.1.2 INVITATIONS FOR APPLICATIONS FOR AUTHORISATIONS UNDER SECTION **15.1.1;** AND

31.1.3 notice of the termination of Authorisations.

31.2 *Publishing Invitations.* The SPA shall publish invitations for applications for Authorisations under Section 15.1.1 in the media, in such manner as is required by the Regulations.

ARTICLE 32 PUBLIC INFORMATION

32.1 *Public Access.*

32.1.1 THE SPA SHALL MAKE AVAILABLE TO THE PUBLIC:

32.1.1.1 summaries of key terms of all Authorisations and amendments thereto, whether or not terminated;

32.1.1.2 details of exemptions from, or variations or suspensions of, the conditions of an Authorisation under Article 23; and

32.1.1.3 COPIES OF ALL UNITISATION AGREEMENTS.

32.1.2 The SPA shall make available to the public, within a reasonable period of time of a request having been made therefor, summary details of:

32.1.2.1 AN APPROVED DEVELOPMENT PLAN; AND

32.1.2.2 all assignments and other dealings consented to in respect of Authorisations, subject to commercial confidence as to the commercial terms.

32.2 *Publication of Reasons.* Within ten (10) business days of a request having been made, the SPA shall publish brief reasons for:

32.2.1 granting an Authorisation subsequent to an invitation, as contemplated at Section 15.1.1;

32.2.2 granting an Authorisation without inviting applications, as contemplated at Section 15.1.2;

32.2.3 APPROVING A DEVELOPMENT PLAN UNDER A PRODUCTION SHARING AGREEMENT;

32.2.4 granting an exemption from, or agreeing to a variation or suspension of, the conditions of an Authorisation under Article 23; and

32.2.5 making any decision or granting any approval that, under an Authorisation, requires publication.

32.3 *COMPLIANCE REPORTS.*

32.3.1 Companies shall report on their compliance with requirements under the Law and Authorisations in such manner and detail as required by their Authorisation and as provided by the Regulations.

32.3.2 The SPA shall make available such reports to the public, except for any portions of such reports which the Authorised Person requests be maintained confidential, and which the SPA reasonably considers to be commercially confidential.

32.4 **Public Access to Payment Information**. The SPA shall make available to the public such reports by Authorised Persons on payments relating to Petroleum Operations made to the Government of Somalia.

32.5 **Fees for Access.** The information contemplated in this Article 32 shall be available to any Person on payment of the fee therefor, to be provided by regulation.

32.6 **Language**. The information contemplated in Section 32.1.2 shall be available in at least one official or second language of Somalia.

Article 33 Transparency

33.1 **Transparency Principles**. The following principles shall apply in respect of Petroleum Operations, and shall be implemented in this Law, and in Regulations enacted pursuant to this Law, and in the rules, directions, decisions and orders made pursuant to this Law:

33.1.1 There shall be regular publication of all material Petroleum-related payments by Authorised Persons to the Government and all material revenues received by the Government from Authorised Persons to a wide audience in a publicly accessible, comprehensive and comprehensible manner.

33.1.2 All material payments and revenues are the subject of a credible, independent audit, applying international auditing standards.

33.1.3 All material payments and revenues are to be reconciled by a credible, independent administrator appointed by the Government, applying international auditing standards and with publication of the administrator's opinion regarding that reconciliation including discrepancies, should any be identified.

33.1.4 Persons representing the Somali business community who are not involved in Petroleum activities shall be actively engaged as a participant in the design, monitoring and evaluation of the processes contemplated by this Section 33.1.

33.1.5 These principles shall apply to Somalia Petroleum Corporation and any other State-Owned Contractor.

CHAPTER VII - REGULATIONS AND DIRECTIONS

Article 34 Regulations

34.1 **Power to Make Regulations**. The Ministry, based on advice and recommendations from the SPA, may make Regulations under this Law relating to the following:

34.1.1 graticulation of the Territory of Somalia;

34.1.2 the exploration for and the development and production of Petroleum;

34.1.3 the use and disclosure of data, information, records and reports;

34.1.4 the measurement and sale or disposal of Petroleum;

34.1.5 health and safety;

34.1.6 protection and restoration of the environment;

34.1.7 resource management;

34.1.8 structures, facilities and installations;

34.1.9 the clean-up or other remedying of the effects of the escape of Petroleum;

34.1.10 abandonment and Decommissioning;

34.1.11 the control of movement into, within and out of Somalia of persons, vessels, aircraft, vehicles and any other man-made platforms and structures;

34.1.12 work programmes and budgets;

34.1.13 the control of tariffs charged for third party access;

34.1.14 the auditing of an Authorised Person and of its accounts and records;

34.1.15 reporting by Authorised Persons on compliance with obligations set out in the Law and Authorisations, including in relation to:

34.1.15.1 the training and employment of Somalia nationals,

34.1.15.2 procurement of Somalia goods and services,

34.1.15.3 occupational health and safety, and

34.1.15.4 environmental protection.

34.1.16 fees to be paid, including by applicants for Authorisations, Authorised Persons, and Persons wishing to inspect the public register; and

34.1.17 ANY OTHER MATTERS RELATING TO THIS LAW.

34.2 *Regulatory Principles*. When making regulations, the Government shall seek to minimize prescriptive provisions in favour of results-based or performance-based provisions, and utilize accepted international standards to the greatest extent possible.

34.3 *PUBLICATION OF REGULATIONS.* THE MINISTRY SHALL PUBLISH REGULATIONS IN THE *GAZETTE.*

Article 35 Directions

In addition to its power to give directions under Section 14.4 and Section 22.1.3, the SPA may give a direction to an Authorised Person:

35.1 RELATING TO ANY MATTER SET OUT IN SECTION 34.1; OR

35.2 otherwise requiring compliance with this Law, the Regulations or its Authorisation.

CHAPTER VIII - PENALTY PROVISIONS

Article 36 Territorial and Material Scope of this Chapter

The provisions of this Chapter are without prejudice to criminal and civil liability under the general law.

Article 37 Unauthorised Activities

37.1 *Lack of Authorisation Offence.* Whoever engages in Petroleum Operations other than pursuant to an Authorisation shall be punished by imprisonment from three (3) months up to five (5) years or fine between one thousand and fifty thousand United States Dollars.

37.2 *Serious Offence*. If the damaged caused to Somalia is of an amount of fifty thousand United States Dollars or greater, the penalty shall be imprisonment from one (1) up to eight (8) years or fine between ten thousand and two hundred thousand United States Dollars.

Article 38 Danger to People, Property and Environment

38.1 *Endangerment Offence*. Whoever, by conduct that contravenes the provisions of this Law or the Regulations, endangers the life or physical integrity of a person, endangers property of high value, or gravely endangers the environment, shall be punished by:

38.1.1 Imprisonment from one (1) up to eight (8) years or fine between one thousand and fifty thousand United States Dollars, if the conduct and the creation of the danger are malicious;

38.1.2 Imprisonment up to five (5) years or fine between five thousand and one hundred thousand United States Dollars, if the conduct is malicious and the creation of the danger is negligent.

Article 39 Hindering the Exercise of Powers by the Inspector

39.1 *Offence of Hindrance.* Whoever, directly or indirectly, in any measure or by any means, hinders, or leads someone else to hinder, the exercise of powers and rights by the Inspector, shall be punished by imprisonment from three (3) months up to four (4) years or fine between one thousand and fifty thousand United States Dollars.

39.2 *Offence of Attempt*. An attempt leading to a valid prosecution with verifiable proof is also punishable.

For additional analytical, business and investment opportunities information, please contact Global Investment & Business Center, USA at (202) 546-2103. Fax: (202) 546-3275. E-mail: rusric@erols.com

Article 40 Misleading Information

40.1 *Offence of Misrepresentation*. Whoever,

40.1.1 in, or in connection with, any application under this Law or the Regulations, knowingly or recklessly gives information that is materially false or misleading; or

40.1.2 in any report, return or affidavit submitted under any provision of this Law or the Regulations or an Authorisation thereunder, knowingly or recklessly includes or permits to be included, any information which is materially false or misleading;

shall be punished by imprisonment up to three (3) years or fine between one thousand and fifty thousand United States Dollars.

40.2 *Offence of Attempt*. An attempt leading to a valid prosecution with verifiable proof is also punishable.

Article 41 Non-compliance with Regulations or Directions

41.1 *Offence of Non-Compliance*. Where a Person fails or neglects to comply with a regulation to which Article 34 refers, and/or with a direction to which Article 35 refers, or fails to comply with fundamental term of an Authorisation, the SPA may cause to be done all or any of the things required by the regulation or direction to be done at the cost and expense of that Person.

41.2 *Determination of Costs*. Costs and expenses incurred by the SPA under Section 41.1, together with interest thereon at a rate to be determined by the SPA, shall be a debt due to the Government.

41.3 *Restitution*. Without prejudice to any other liability of that Person, a Person who fails or neglects to comply with a regulation to which Article 34 refers, and/or with a direction to which Article 35 refers, or fails to comply with fundamental term of an Authorisation, shall make restitution to Somalia of an amount equal to the costs of any consequences suffered as a consequence of the failure, neglect or non-compliance.

Article 42 Accessory Penalties

42.1 *Additional Penalties*. In relation to the crimes provided for in the Law, the following accessory penalties may be applied:

42.1.1 Temporary deprivation of the right to participate in public tenders concerning Petroleum Operations, in particular those regarding Authorisations and the procurement of goods and services;

42.1.2 Embargo of any construction works, in such cases as they may result in irreversible damage to relevant public interests;

42.1.3 Disability, up to a maximum of two (2) years, of the exercise of activities, if the Person has, within the period of one (1) year starting from the date of the first contravention, contravened this Law, or Regulations or directions issued thereunder;

42.1.4 Termination of Authorisations;

42.1.5 Good conduct bond;

42.1.6 Disability of rights to subsidies awarded by public entities or services;

42.1.7 Publication of the sentence; and/or

42.1.8 Other writs of prevention which are adequate taking into account the circumstances of the case in question.

Article 43 Liability of Legal Persons, Corporations and Other Legal Entities

43.1 *Liability of Entities and Representatives*. Legal persons, corporations or any other legal entities, including those without juridical personality, are liable for contraventions provided for in this Chapter when committed by its organs or representatives in its name and in the collective interest.

43.2 *Due Diligence Defence*. The liability is excluded where the agent has acted against express orders or instructions properly issued.

43.3 *Agent Liability*. The liability of the entities mentioned in Section 43.1 does not exclude the individual liability of the respective agents.

43.4 *Joint and Several Liability*. The entities mentioned in Section 43.1 are jointly and severally liable, as provided for in civil law, for the payment of any fines or compensations, or for the fulfillment of any obligations, derived from the facts or with incidence on matters covered by the scope of this Law.

Article 44 Fines to Legal Persons, Corporations and Other Legal Entities

44.1 *Fines*. In the case of legal persons, corporations or any other legal entities, including those without juridical personality, the amount of the fines shall be as determined by the court, taking into account the economic and financial situation of the legal person, corporation or other legal entity and the severity and consequences of the offence.

44.2 *Access to Assets.* If the fine is applied to an entity without juridical personality, its payment will be guaranteed by the entity's assets and, in the event of non-existence of such assets or under-capitalisation, jointly and severally, the assets of each of the associates.

Article 45 Inspection

The SPA and the Inspector, as well as any other organs of the public administration to whom inspection duties may be delegated in accordance with law and regulations, are responsible to ensure the inspection of compliance with the provisions of this Law or the Regulations.

Article 46 Extrajudicial Writ of Execution

For purposes of coercive collection under general law, a certification issued by the SPA in relation to a debt constituted, or amount due, as a result of the application of the provisions of this Law or the Regulations, which is not paid within a reasonable period to

be determined by the SPA, and which shall be notified in writing to the debtor, constitutes an extrajudicial writ of execution.

Article 47 Subsidiary Legislation

47.1 *Criminal and Other Legislation*. The general criminal law, as well as relevant administrative and civil legislation, of Somalia are applicable in a subsidiary manner, with the required adaptations, to give effect to the provisions of this Chapter.

47.2 **No Conflict**. To the extent that the provisions of any other laws of Somalia conflict with the provisions of this Law or the Regulations, they shall be null and vold as regards their application to Petroleum Operations.

CHAPTER IX - OTHER AND FINAL PROVISIONS

Article 48 Transitional Provision

48.1 *Prior Grants*. With the approval of the Government, the Ministry shall issue Regulations setting out the administrative procedure to be followed, as well as obligations to be undertaken, by Persons who have engaged in or are engaging in Petroleum Operations ("Prior Contractors") pursuant to rights granted by the Somali Democratic Republic on or before December 30, 1990 ("Prior Grants"). Such Regulations shall include the following provisions:

48.1.1 a Prior Contractor shall have the right to convert its Prior Grant into the form of Authorisation that is most similar to the Prior Grant. A Prior Grant in the form of a concession entitling the Prior Contractor to conduct exclusive Petroleum Operations shall be convertible into a Production Sharing Agreement. A Prior Contractor wishing to convert its Prior Grant shall:

48.1.1.1 provide to the Ministry:

48.1.1.1.1 a true copy of a fully executed Prior Grant;

48.1.1.1.2 evidence satisfactory to the Ministry that it was on December 30, 1990 in full compliance with its obligations under the Prior Grant;

48.1.1.1.3 a copy of a record of its performance under the Prior Grant, including the relinquishment of any part of the contract area under the Prior Grant;

48.1.1.1.4 a copy of all data and information required by the Prior Grant to be delivered to the Government;

48.1.1.1.5 identification of the current parties to the Prior Grant, and how the current parties acquired their interest in the Prior Grant from the original parties;

48.1.1.2 agree that its Decommissioning obligations under the new Authorisation shall include Decommissioning of its activities conducted pursuant to the Prior Grant;

48.1.1.3 agree to the terms of a new Authorisation between the Prior Contractor and the Ministry on or before a date specified by the

Ministry, which shall not be later than the date described in Section

For additional analytical, business and investment opportunities information, please contact Global Investment & Business Center, USA at (202) 546-2103. Fax: (202) 546-3275. E-mail: rusric@erols.com

48.2.

48.1.2 an Authorisation under Section 48.1.1.3 shall be consistent with the principles of this Law, the Regulations and the model contract published by the SPA pursuant to Section 8.20.5.

48.2 **Effort to Contact**. The Ministry shall make reasonable efforts to contact each Prior Contractor, so far as it is able to determine who they may be, to advise them of their rights under Section 48.1. Where a Prior Grant appears to be held by more than one Person, the Ministry need only make a reasonable effort to contact the Person who appears to the Ministry to be the operator. No Prior Contractor shall have any right against the Ministry or the Government for a failure by the Ministry to fulfil this Section

48.2.

48.3 **Deadline for Conversion**. If any Prior Grant that has not been converted into a Production Sharing Agreement under this Law pursuant to the provisions of Section 48.1 on the first anniversary of the coming into force of this Law, then:

48.3.1 the Prior Grant shall terminate and cease to be a binding obligation on the Government on the first anniversary of the coming into force of this Law;

48.3.2 the Government shall not be liable for any loss, costs, claim or damage resulting from such termination of the Prior Grant; and

48.3.3 as a sovereign entity, the Government declares itself immune from any claim made by a Prior Contractor for termination of its Prior Grant.

48.4 **Post-1990 Grants**. Effective on the date of the coming into force of this Law:

48.4.1 any right to conduct Petroleum Operations in Somalia granted after December 30, 1990 shall terminate and cease to be a binding obligation on the Government;

48.4.2 the Government shall not be liable for any loss, costs, claim or damage resulting from such termination; and

48.4.3 as a sovereign entity, the Government declares itself immune from any claim made by any Person for termination of any such right.

Article 49 Entry into Force

This Law shall enter into force on the day after its publication in the *Gazette*.

Approved on • by the Transitional Federal Parliament of the Somali Republic

Assented to on • The President of the Somali Republic Abdillahi Yusuf Ahmed

PRACTICAL INFORMATION FOR CONDUCTING BUSINESS

Intermittent civil war has been a fact of life in Somalia since 1977. In 1991, the northern portion of the country declared its independence as Somali land; although de facto independent and relatively stable compared to the tumultuous south, it has not been recognised by any foreign government. Beginning in 1993, a two-year UN humanitarian effort (primarily in the south) was able to alleviate famine conditions, but when the UN withdrew in 1995, having suffered significant casualties, order still had not been restored.

Sources on the Somali economy remain scarce. There has been no government for almost 10 years in Somali. It ranks near or at the bottom in terms of life expectancy, per capita income and child mortality rate and one of the world's poorest countries, with few natural resources. Moreover, much of the economy has been devastated by the civil war.

Agriculture is the most important sector, with livestock accounting for about 50% of GDP and about 65% of export earnings. Nomads and semi-nomads, who are dependent upon livestock for their livelihood, make up a large portion of the population. Crop production generates only 10% of GDP and employs about 20% of the work force. Due to fragile environment, vagaries of the weather (both drought and flooding), famine frequently occurs resulting to persistent food insecurity among its population. After livestock, bananas are the principal exports followed by fish myrrh, hides and skins. Sugar, sorghum, corn, and fish are produced mainly for the internal market and for subsistance consumption.

The small industrial sector based on the processing of agricultural products, accounts for less than 10% of GDP; most facilities have been shut down because of the civil strife. Mining contribution to GDP negligible (0.3 percent of GDP in 1988) despite substantial deposits of gypsumanhydrite , quartz and piezoquartz, uranium, and iron ore, Meerschaum sepiolite mined; gold deposits suspected but not confirmed . Moreover, ongoing civil disturbances in Mogadishu and outlying areas are interfering with any substantial economic development.

Main destinations of exports are Saudi Arabia, United Arab Emirates and Yemen, while Kenya, United States of America, Djibouti and Italy are the main origins of imports. Domestic wood, charcoal, and imported petroleum provide basic sources of energy. Prior to civil war, eighty state-owned oil-fired and diesel power plants provided electricity to cities and towns.

POLITICAL SITUATION

In May 1991 the north west area region of Somalia declared independence, unrecognised, as the 'Republic of Somali land'. It claims the borders of the former British Protectorate. A 'government' was elected for an initial 2-year period at a conference in Boroma in May 1993. Here, an agreement was reached on the formation of a new, inter-clan government of 'Somali land'. Clan representatives elected former Somali Prime Minister Mohamed Ibrahim Egal as 'President'. He was re-elected for a five-year term by the National Communities Conference in Hargeisa in February 1997. Following Parliamentary 'elections' (for which members were nominated by the clans participating in the Congress), a new 'government' was formed and Constitution approved.

Immediately after attaining independence in July 1960, the former British Somali land Protectorate and the Italian-administered UN Trust Territory of Somalia merged to form the Somali Republic. Despite an initial period of political stability inter clan tensions threatened the coalition government. Following an unsuccessful war with Ethiopia in 1963-64 and two

For additional analytical, business and investment opportunities information, please contact Global Investment & Business Center, USA at (202) 546-2103. Fax: (202) 546-3275. E-mail: rusric@erols.com

presidential assassinations, the army under General Mohamed Siad Barre seized power in October 1969. He established a regime of 'scientific socialism'.

By the 1980s, opposition groups began to form. One such group in north-west Somalia, the Somali National Movement (SNM), launched an unsuccessful offensive in 1988 against the forces of Siad Barre based in the north-west. Barre countered with great violence, resulting in thousands of deaths and the destruction of Hargeisa. By October 1990, other opposition groups had come out against Siad Barre, including the United Somali Congress (USC) whose military wing was led by General Aideed. In January 1991, the USC gained control of Mogadishu. Barre fled to his south-western homeland (he took refuge in Nigeria in 1992). The ensuing power vacuum triggered an intense battle between the self-appointed interim president, Ali Mahdi and General Aideed. This later escalated into full-blown civil war, which lasted throughout the 1990s.

POLITICAL STRUCTURE

In July 2000 a charter for an interim government was agreed - a 225-member National Assembly, selected on a clan basis (25 seats reserved for women members), would be nominated by the peace conference delegates. The Assembly would nominate members of an interim three-year government and elect an interim president, who would appoint a prime minister.

NATIONAL LEGISLATURE

The interim National Assembly inaugurated on 13 August 2000 was Somalia's first legislature since the ousting of President Siad Barre in 1991.

POLITICAL PARTIES

There are no formal political parties.
Warlords and their supporters wield most of the power; political organisation largely reflects membership of clans and sub-clans. There are 28 main factions; the main groups include the United Somali Congress/Somali National Alliance and the Somali Salvation Alliance.

Total UK Exports	£ 000's	Total UK Imports	£ 000's
Tobacco & tobacco manufactures	2,011	Oil seeds & oleaginous fruit	32
Beverages	273	Miscellaneous Manufactured Articles	22
Organic chemicals	144	Textile yarn, fabrics, made-up articles nes and related products	21
Electrical machinery, apparatus and appliances nes	143	Professional, scientific and controlling instruments nes	11
Professional, scientific and controlling instruments nes	93	Road vehicles (including air-cushion vehicles)	2

ECONOMIC SITUATION

Somalia's economy has been almost completely dislocated by years of fighting and political strife as well as a severe long-term drought which has affected the whole of East Africa. Somalia now ranks amongst the poorest countries in the world. Subsistence agriculture and livestock rearing

For additional analytical, business and investment opportunities information, please contact Global Investment & Business Center, USA at (202) 546-2103. Fax: (202) 546-3275. E-mail: rusric@erols.com

occupy most of the working population, although any improvements have been hampered by primitive techniques, poor soil and climatic conditions, and a chronic shortage of skilled labour.

Bananas are the main cash crop and provide nearly half the country's export earnings; cotton, maize, sorghum and other crops are produced for domestic consumption. Animal products, particularly hides and skins, are another key source of revenue, mainly from Saudi Arabia. Plans to develop the fishing industry have been formulated but political conditions have prevented their implementation. Exploitation of probable oil and gas reserves has been in abeyance since the 1980s for the same reason. There is little industry other than to meet domestic needs, mainly food processing and oil refining.

Northern Somalia is the world's largest source of incense and myrrh, which are forestry products.

Serious flooding in southern Somalia in 1997 led to severe crop and cattle losses, and halved the country's banana exports. The economy remains in the unstable hands of clan-based militias, with rival clans even competing for control of the banana harvest in order to fund their war efforts. By 1995, inflation had reached 400% in some parts of Somalia, and in the next two years bad drought conditions made things even worse.

Somalia relies on large injections of foreign aid, especially from the various United Nations relief organisations (the UN is the country's largest employer) and is burdened by a huge foreign debt. The main suppliers of goods to Somalia are Italy, the USA, Germany, Saudi Arabia and the UK.

Until the early sixteenth century, Somalia was part of the Arab-controlled Indian Ocean trading network.

The importance and prosperity of the Somali ports of Mogadishu and Brava were reduced once the Portuguese discovered a sea route to India via the Cape of Good Hope.

In the nineteenth century much of the Ogaden Desert - ethnically part of Somalia - was annexed by the Ethiopian empire of Menelik I; the area has remained part of Ethiopia ever since.

1900 Somalia was divided between Britain which controlled the northern region (the British Somaliland Protectorate) and Italy which controlled the southern region (Italian Somaliland - a UN Trust Territory under Italian administration between 1950-60).

1960 The northern and southern regions were united upon independence from Britain and Italy.

1969 Following the assassination of President Abdirashid Ali Shermarke, the army seized control and Mohammed Siad Barre became President. The country was renamed the Somali Democratic Republic, political parties were banned and the National Assembly dissolved.

1981 The Somali Salvation Front (which had staged an unsuccessful coup in 1978) joined forces with two other opposition groups to establish the Democratic Front for the Salvation of Somalia (DFSS).
1982 The DFSS linked up with the Somali National Movement (SNM) and with Ethiopian military support, invaded Somalia in July.
Although the government repulsed the rebels, clashes continued throughout the 1980s.

1989 As the security situation worsened, President Barre offered to resign and hold free elections in 1990.

For additional analytical, business and investment opportunities information, please contact Global Investment & Business Center, USA at (202) 546-2103. Fax: (202) 546-3275. E-mail: rusric@erols.com

1991 On 28 January President Siad Barre fled the country after rebels entered Mogadishu. Ali Mahdi Mohammed, leader of the Somali Salvation Council (SSA) was appointed interim President, but the three-way coalition soon broke down and Mahdi was overthrown in November.

In May, Somaliland (in the north) broke away from war-torn Somalia. The self-styled Somaliland Republic is headed by Mohammed Ibrahim Egal but does not have international recognition.

1992 After a period of intense conflict between the numerous clans, the US sent a peacekeeping force to Somalia to protect the international humanitarian aid effort and restore order.

1993 A partial peace pact was signed in January. On 1 May, the UN began peacekeeping operations, taking over from the US Marines. From June through to October, the US launched a military offensive against General Aideed and the Somali National Alliance (SNA) in Mogadishu after UN peacekeepers were killed in an ambush.

1994 After an unsuccessful campaign, the US withdrew all of its forces out of Somalia.

1995 Remainder of the UN peacekeeping force withdrew.
1996 General Aideed, leader of the USC and SNA (one of the largest clans), died from gunshot wounds in August. His son, Hussein Aideed, replaced him as head of the clan-based gang.

1997 On 22 December, 26 of Somalia's 28 factions signed the Cairo Declaration peace accord.

2002 The north-eastern region followed the example set by Somaliland and declared independence as Puntland under the leadership of Colonel Abdullahi Yussef Ahmed.

1999 Inter-clan violence continued in central and southern Somalia. In September, President Omar Guelleh of Djibouti announced an international peace plan based on the participation of Islamic and civil groups rather than warlords.

2000 In August, the four-month reconciliation conference in Djibouti ended when the transitional national government (TNG) elected the country's first civilian president since war broke out in 1990 - Abd Al-Qasim Salad Hasan, the interim president, appointed Ali Khalifa Galad as prime minister in October. SNA chairman, Hussein Aideed, forms an opposition group to the TNG, the Somali Restoration and Reconciliation Council (SRRC).

2001 Fighting continues in the south of the country. In a referendum in May, a huge majority in Somaliland voted in favour of independence from the rest of Somalia.

POPULATION

Annual population growth rate: 2.2 per cent (1990-98). Life expectancy: 48 years (2002). Approximately 47 per cent of the total population is under 14 years; 50 per cent 15-64; 3 per cent over 65. Population density: 14 inhabitants per square km. Urban population: 26.4 per cent (2002).

PRESS

Dailies: Daily publications from Mogadishu include *Mogadishu Times*, *Quran* and *Xog-Ogaal*. *Jamhuurriya* is published from Hargeisa. There are internet daily news services from *Somali Press Online* (http://home.ica.net/~somalipress/), *Somali News Online* (http://www.etek.chalmers.se) and *Dhambaal* (http://www.dhambaal.com) has links to other weekly news services.
Weeklies: Weeklies include *Dadka*, *Panorama*, *Republican* (Hargeisa), *Sanca* and *Xurmo*.

For additional analytical, business and investment opportunities information, please contact Global Investment & Business Center, USA at (202) 546-2103. Fax: (202) 546-3275. E-mail: rusric@erols.com

Periodicals: Periodicals are mainly monthly publications including *Ayaamaha* and *Himilo*.

RISK ASSESSMENT

Economic Poor
Political Poor
Regional stability Poor
Exports are dominated by livestock rearing, which is the country's principal foreign exchange earner. Since 70 per cent of the country lives on subsistence agriculture, with some working as nomadic herders, much of the economy is reliant on the weather. However, with periodic floods and droughts, harvests frequently produce fewer crops than the amount needed to sustain the population.

This means that Somalia is dependent on foreign food aid.
The permanent economic gloom has been heightened by civil war and famine, which have destroyed Somalia's economy. Since hostilities began, the economy has been broken down under the jurisdiction of several regional strongmen or clan leaders. The situation is complicated by the break-away Republic of Somaliland, which has become an autonomous zone with its own currency and government. Within the self-declared territory of Somaliland, there is also an autonomous region known as Puntland State, which also has its own chaotic economic policy.

However, Somaliland represents the strongest local economy and has undergone something of a boom since it declared independence in 1991. In a situation of relative peace and without the tyranny of the central Somalian state, the autonomous region has undergone a modest transformation with infrastructural improvements and an emergent business elite. However, without international recognition, Somaliland cannot access funds from the IMF or World Bank or develop trade relations. The May 2001 referendum, which voted in favour of full independence from Somalia, could pave the way towards full statehood and therefore greater economic prosperity. However, the Puntland State, where many Somalis wish to remain part of Somalia, faces many of the problems faced by Somalia proper - the widespread existence of regional strongmen and almost complete economic collapse.

EXTERNAL TRADE

The poor balance of trade reflects the continuing need for the large-scale import of fuels and food.

EXPORTS

Principal exports are livestock and bananas. Saudi Arabia imposed a ban on the import of Somali sheep and goats in February 2002 after an outbreak of Rift Valley fever.

The backbone of the economy is livestock. The total livestock in the country is estimated at 24 million. In 1996, 3 million heads of livestock were exported to the Middle Eastern countries. The country also exports Hides, Skins, Myrrh and Frankincense in smaller scale.

LIVESTOCK EXPORTS

	1994	1995	1996	1997	2002
TOTAL	1,779,109	2,780,637	2,484,601	2,926,735	1,071,100
SHEEP	1,685,265	2,683,597	2,376,646	2,808,764	967,224
CATTLE	55,729	75,047	65,127	66,939	92,213

For additional analytical, business and investment opportunities information, please contact Global Investment & Business Center, USA at (202) 546-2103. Fax: (202) 546-3275. E-mail: rusric@erols.com

| CAMEL | 38,025 | 21,993 | 42,828 | 51,032 | 11,663 |

IMPORTS

Annual imports exceed US$200 million. Principal imports include food commodities, apparel and footwear, fuel, building material, Machinery, vehicles, and chemicals.

AGRICULTURE

Agriculture is less significant. There is, however, a considerable potential for both cereal production and horticulture.

MINING

Mining is limited to quarrying at the moment. There are, however, confirmed deposits of:

Oil, Gas, Gypsum, Lime, Mica, Quartz, Lignite Coal, Lead, Gold, Sulphur.

FISHERY

The fishing industry is still underdeveloped, but the country has 600 mile long coast with rich fishing grounds. Somaliland is strategically located at cross roads between Africa, Europe, The Middle East and South East Asia. In 1996 up to 846 vessels called on Berbera port on the Red Sea which has the potential to develop into a major commercial centre.

HEALTH

In1999 , the number of Health centres was 44 and these can be found in most districts. Several private clinics (some catering for inpatients) are also functioning.

Currently a new hospital is under construction in Hargeisa specialising exclusively in the treatment of for women & children. This hospital is expected to open in July 2000 and will be run by a Trust Charity. This hospital is initiated and funded by a Somali Nurse with other contributions.

EDUCATION

There are 163 primary schools with student population of 33,000 as per the no of teachers in primary education in the same educational year 1996/97 was 954. Several private schools catering for primary, secondary and vocational trainings exist. TWO universities have been opened in Somaliland during the last few years.

MAIN DESTINATIONS

Saudi Arabia (typically 49 per cent of total), United Arab Emirates (25 per cent), Yemen (18 per cent)

IMPORTS

Principal imports are manufactures, non-fuel primary products, fuels, food, machinery and transport equipment, construction materials.

Main sources: US (typically 17 per cent of total), Djibouti (16 per cent), Italy (14 per cent)

AGRICULTURE

The agricultural sector is the most important in the economy. It contributes about 65 per cent to GDP and employs 65 per cent of the working population.
It is mostly a pastoral form of production. Before the civil war, land was owned by the state and leased by farmers.

Much of the land is desert or semi-desert and only 13 per cent is cultivated, making food security a constant concern. Some crops are grown on the fertile land in the Juba and Scebali valleys.

The grasslands are suitable for grazing livestock.

Subsistence farmers grow maize and sorghum; wheat and rice are imported.
The most important cash crops are livestock, bananas, cotton and frankincense (of which Somalia was the world's largest producer).

In 1999 there were poor rains in the south where most of the food is grown and pest infestation devastated crops. Less than half of Somalia's minimum requirement of 300,000 tonnes of grain was produced. Although better rains increased production to 212,000 tonnes of cereal in 2000, a drought in 2001 threatened to lead to famine in much of Somalia. The UN's World Food Programme claimed that famine was almost certain, since much of the population is increasingly reliant on food bought on local markets, which have seen prices rise beyond the reach of most Somalis' incomes.

INDUSTRY AND MANUFACTURING

The industrial sector as a whole contributes about 9 per cent to GNP and employs 8 per cent of the working population.
Main industries are meat and fish processing, sugar refining, fruit and vegetable canning, textiles and leather goods.

Many factories are idle because foreign exchange shortages have cut off foreign inputs.

MINING

There are significant mineral resources, but they have not yet been commercially exploited. The most important regions include an area extending from the Ethiopian border to beyond Berbera in Somaliland and west of the River Scebali near Mogadishu. The former contains reserves of copper, gold, molybdenum and bismuth while the latter contains iron, gold and apatite.
The country also contains reserves of uranium, marble, manganese, tin, beryl and columbite. Salt and gypsum were extracted commercially before the civil war began.

HYDROCARBONS

Potential oil and gas reserves have been found near Mogadishu and in the north, but the country still relies on imports for most of its fuel needs. Somalia has one natural gas field with reserves of around 6 billion cubic metres, although political and economic chaos have prevented exploitation. Downstream, Somalia has a single oil refinery with a capacity of 10,000 barrels per day (bpd), although it has not been in use for some years and is probably in a state of disrepair.
The Republic of Somaliland has invited international companies with exploration rights within its self-declared territories to return - including Agip, BP Amoco, Chevron and Conoco. It has also

For additional analytical, business and investment opportunities information,
please contact Global Investment & Business Center, USA
at (202) 546-2103. Fax: (202) 546-3275. E-mail: rusric@erols.com

invited companies to take over the Berbera fuel distribution centre which contains the Republic's main port. This has attracted attention from TotalFinaElf and Royal/Dutch Shell. However, international investors appear to be waiting until Somaliland achieves full international recognition before resuming operations in this area.

ENERGY

Electricity generation (all thermal) amounts to under 100MW and is fuelled by diesel which has to be imported. A monopoly of electricity generation and supply is owned by the Ente Nazionale Energia Elettrica (ENEE).

IMPORTANT FACTS

Local time
GMT + 3.
Population
Population: 7,253,137

Note: this estimate was derived from an official census taken in 1975 by the Somali Government; population counting in Somalia is complicated by the large number of nomads and by refugee movements in response to famine and clan warfare (July 2000 est.)

Capital City
Mogadishu.

Language

Somali and Arabic are the official languages. Swahili is spoken, particularly in the south. English and Italian are also widely spoken.

Principal Religions

The state religion is Islam and the majority of Somalis are Sunni Muslims.

International dialling code from UK

00 (252)
Somali shilling (So. Sh.).

Currency exchange: US Dollar bills are the easiest currency to exchange; hotels are the easiest and safest places. Avoid money changers in crowded areas.

Credit cards: Credit cards are generally not accepted although some larger establishment do accept Diners Club. It is very difficult to change any form of currency that is not US Dollars.

Travellers cheques: US travellers cheques are preferred but generally not recommended.

GDP

GDP: purchasing power parity - $4.3 billion (1999 est.)
GDP - real growth rate: NA%

For additional analytical, business and investment opportunities information,
please contact Global Investment & Business Center, USA
at (202) 546-2103. Fax: (202) 546-3275. E-mail: rusric@erols.com

GDP - per capita: purchasing power parity - $600
GDP - composition by sector:
agriculture: 59%
industry: 10%
services: 31%

Weights and measures

Metric system.

Telephone

Telephone system: the public telecommunications system was completely destroyed or dismantled by the civil war factions; all relief organisations depend on their own private systems

Domestic: recently, local cellular telephone systems have been established in Mogadishu and in several other population centres.

International: International connections are available from Mogadishu by satellite.

IDD is available. Country code: 252. Outgoing international calls must be made via the operator.

Post

Post: Airmail to Europe takes up to two weeks.

BUSINESS CONTACTS AND INFORMATION SOURCES

TELEPHONE AREA CODES

Dialling code for Somalia: IDD access code +252 followed by area code (52 for Bosasso, 21 for Hargeisa), followed by subscriber's number.

BANKING

Commercial and Savings Banks of Somalia, PO Box 203, Mogadishu.
Somali Development Bank, PO Box 79, Mogadishu (tel: 21-800).

OTHER USEFUL ADDRESSES

Agricultural Development Corporation, PO Box 930, Mogadishu.
Livestock Development Agency of Somalia, PO Box 1759, Mogadishu.
National Petroleum Agency of Somalia, PO Box 573, Mogadishu.
Somali Broadcasting Service, Ministry of Information and National Guidance, Private Bag, Mogadishu (tel: 2455).
Statistical Department, PO Box 1742, Mogadishu (tel: 80-385).

INTERNET SITES

Africa Business Network: http://www.ifc.org/abn
Africa.com: http://africa.com
African Development Bank: http://www.afdb.org

For additional analytical, business and investment opportunities information, please contact Global Investment & Business Center, USA at (202) 546-2103. Fax: (202) 546-3275. E-mail: rusric@erols.com

Africa News Online: http://www.africanews.org
Africa Online: http://www.africaonline.com
Africa Trade and Business Bulletin: http://www.bizafrica.com/index.html
Harambee Afrika (UK business club for traders with east, central and southern Africa; includes annotated web resource list): http://www.harambee.co.uk

IMPORTANT LAWS AND REGULATIONS FOR CONDUCTING BUSINESS

THE FOREIGN INVESTMENTS LAW

PROMOTION PROTECTION AND GUARANTEE OF INVESTMENTS REPUBLIC OF SOMALILAND

The Government of the Republic of Somaliland:

§   *Endeavouring to avail itself of the economic resources and potentialities available in its country and to mobilize and utilize them in the best possible manner.*

§   *Anxious to provide a favourable climate for foreign investments so that optimum utilization could be made of its economic resources.*

§   *In keeping with the objectives of the Agreement of the Promotion, Protection and Guarantee of Investments among Member States of the Organization of the Islamic Conference...*

Has enacted the following law on the Promotion, Protection and Guarantee of the Foreign Investments in its country.

ARTICLE 1 DEFINITIONS

The following terms which are used in this law shall have the meanings assigned to each one of them for the purpose of this law unless the context indicates a different meaning:

1. THE AGREEMENT

The agreement signed by the Foreign Investment Board of the Government of the Republic of Somaliland and the contracting Foreign Investor.

2. CONTRACTING PARTIES

The Foreign Investment Board of the Republic of Somaliland and the Foreign Investors signatories to agreements with the Board and in respect of which these agreements have become effective.

3. HOST STATE

The Republic of Somaliland in which the invested capital is present lawfully and permits the investor to employ his capital therein.

4. CAPITAL

All assets (including everything that can be evaluated in monetary terms) owned by a foreign contracting party to the agreement with the Board whether a natural person or a corporate body and is present in the territories of the Republic of Somaliland whether these were transferred to or earned in it, and whether these be movable, immovable, in cash, in kind, tangible as well as everything pertaining to these capitals and investments by way of rights or claims and include the net profits occurring from such assets and the undivided shares and intangible rights

5. INVESTMENT

The capital employed in the permissible fields in the Republic of Somaliland by the foreign contracting party with the board with a view to achieving a profitable return in accordance with this law.

6.   Investor

Any foreign contracting party with the Board whether a natural person or a legal personality in his own country who owns. the capital and invests it in the Republic of Somaliland. The nationality of the investor shall be determined as follows:-

a. Natural person

Any individual enjoying the nationality of his own foreign country in accordance with the provisions of the nationality law in force therein.

b. Legal Personality

Any entity established in accordance with the law in the country of the contracting party and is recognized there by the law under which its legal personality is established.

INVESTMENT RETURNS

The sums yielded by the investment or derived therefrom for a specified period which shall include, without limitation, the profits, dividends, licences, fees, royalties, leases, services and all the increases achieved on the capital assets and the utilization of the intangible property rights.

8.   The Board:
"The Board" is the Foreign Investment Board established at the Ministry of Commerce and Industry. It is the supreme decision-making authority over all matters concerning foreign investment in the Republic of Somaliland.

9.   The Office
The "Office" is the Foreign, Investment Promotion Office established at the Ministry of Commerce and Industry to assist the "Board" in the performance of its administrative and promotional functions.

ARTICLE 2 FOREIGN INVESTOR

Under this law a foreign investor is any foreign juridical or physical person.

ARTICLE 3 FOREIGN INVESTMENT FORMS

Foreign investment can be made in any of the following forms:

1. Convertible currency specified by the Central Bank of Somaliland

2. Machinery; equipment ; spare parts installations; and current production inputs; whose importation is permitted under the prevailing import legislation.

3. Patent rights, trade marks, and licenses duly registered in Somaliland, provided they are necessary for the activities to be passed under the approved investment.

4. The amount of foreign currency spent on studies and technical documentation, prepared in connection with the approved investment.

5. Profit reinvested, originating from foreign investment approved in accordance with this law.

The said investment shall be made for the purpose of the establishment or the expansion of an enterprise incorporated and registered in Somaliland

ARTICLE 4 INVESTMENT PRIORITIES AND SECTORS

Priority shall be given to foreign investment in those areas where it.

1. Puts to productive use Somaliland's human and natural resources

2. introduces innovative technology suited to the country's conditions.

3. Generates new earnings or savings of foreign exchange, through exports, resource-based import substitution or service activities.

4. Contributes to regionally balanced socio-economic development, this refers especially to foreign investment in, or closely related to:

    a)   Agriculture

    b)   Livestock

    c)   Fishing

    d)   Mineral resources

    e)   Industrial activities using significant amounts of inputs produced, by afore-mentioned sectors.

    f)   Tourism, provided the investment harmonizes with the prevailing social, economic and infrastructural condition.

    g)-   Any other investment, in production and service activities, suited to support and stimulate, in a significant degree, the development of the afore-mentioned sectors.

ARTICLE 5 THE FOREIGN INVESTMENT BOARD

1. The foreign investment Board, here after referred as " The Board", has the supreme, decision making authority over all matters concerning foreign investment in Somaliland. It is established at the Ministry of Commerce & Industry where it shall convene at least twice a month.

2. The BOARD SHALL CONSIST OF:

   2.1. The Director General of the Ministry of National Planning.

   2.2. The Director General of the Ministry of Foreign Affairs.

   2.3. The Director General of Ministry of Finance

   2.4. The Director General of Ministry of Commerce and Industry

   2.5 The Director General of Ministry of Health and Labour

   2.6 The Director General of Central Bank of Somaliland

   2.7. The Chairman of the Chamber of Commerce, Industry and Agriculture

Chairman of the Board is the Director General of the Ministry of Commerce and Industry.

ARTICLE 6 FUNCTIONS OF THE BOARD

The functions of the Board shall be the following:

1. To approve proposed foreign investment in accordance with the policy guidelines laid down in Article 4 and the provisions concerning quorum and vote, as per Article 7.

2. To approve the registration of foreign investment and to sign an agreement with the foreign investor in accordance with the provisions of this law

3. To review the registration of foreign investment made under previous foreign investment laws from the more favourable provisions, as per Article 25 of this law.

4. To determine the value of foreign investment made as per Article 3, paragraph 2,3 and 4 of this law.

5. To ensure compliance with the provisions of Article 14 concerning the contracting of debt from domestic sources.

6.   To facilitate the granting of visas to foreign personnel to be employed by enterprises registered under this law.

7.   To perform any other function concerning foreign investment in conformity with this law.

ARTICLE 7 THE BOARD, QUORUM AND VOTE

Six members of the Board, including the Chairman, shall constitute a quorum, decisions will be taken by simple majority vote.

ARTICLE 8 THE FOREIGN INVESTMENT PROMOTION OFFICE

The Foreign Investment Promotion Office, here after referred to as "The Office", is the administrative and promotional offices to assist the Board in performing its functions. The duties of the office shall be the following:

1.   To implement the decisions taken by the Board.

2.   To propose the administrative and regulatory procedures required for the implementation of the law.

3.   To provide information and advice to the foreign investor on matters such as application and registration procedures under this law, taxation, foreign exchange terms, economic legislation, foreign trade terms, investment opportunities. Institutional frame work, local sources of debt financing partner search.

4.   To assist the foreign investor in meeting the application requirements related to foreign investment.

5.   To assist approved foreign investment at the setting up stages, with guidance and advice concerning official institutions and channels, and related administrative procedures,

6.   To formulated proposals concerning foreign investment policy and improvement of investment conditions.

7.   To promote and attract new foreign investment, in collaboration with other institutions evolved in this field.

8.   To perform any ether duty related to foreign investment, arranged to it by the Board.

ARTICLE 9 PROCEDURES FOR APPLICATION

The application by the foreign investor shall be made by completing the form" Application form for Approval and Registration" available at the office located in the Ministry of Commerce and Industry, and mailing it, by a registered letter, to the Foreign Investment Board.

ARTICLE 10 CONDITIONS AND PROCEDURES OF APPROVAL

1.   Within Sixty days from the date of the receipt of duly completed investment application, the Board shall notify the applicant, by registered mail, of its decision. At the applicant's option,

For additional analytical, business and investment opportunities information,
please contact Global Investment & Business Center, USA
at (202) 546-2103. Fax: (202) 546-3275. E-mail: rusric@erols.com

this notification may be collected by his representative directly from the Office, against issue of a delivery receipt.

2.   In case a modification of an application is required the Board shall notify the applicant, to this effect, by registered letter, At the applicant's option, this notification may be collected by this representative directly from the office, against issue of a delivery receipt.

3.   The Board shall notify, through the office, the approval of a foreign investment by issuing a " Certificate of Foreign Investment in an approved enterprise". Such approval shall be construed by the foreign investor as being eligible for registration under this law.

4.   The " Certificate of Foreign Investment in an approved enterprise" shall be valid for the period of 18 months as of date of issue. During said period, the applicant shall have effected the transfer of assets to Somaliland listed in article 3, paragraph 1,2,3 and 4. In case this period is extended. The Board may grant, at the applicant's request, an additional period, or ask for a new application.

5.   Additional investment to be made as per article 3, paragraph 1,2,3 and 4, in an enterprise object of a foreign investment already duly registered, shall require application and approval as per Article 9, and paragraphs 1,2,3 and 4 of this article.

ARTICLE 11 PROCEDURE FOR REGISTRATION

1.   The Board shall proceed with the registration of an approved investment as soon as the foreign investor has effected the transfer of assets, to Somaliland, listed in Article 3 paragraph 1,2,3 and 4, in accordance with the terms and conditions contained in the "Certificate of Foreign Investment in an approved Enterprise". To this effect, the Board shall issue to the foreign investor, a "Certificate of Foreign Investment Registered".

2.   In the case of a transfer , to Somaliland, of assets listed under paragraph 2,3 and 4, of article 3, the Board shall proceed with said registration as soon as it is satisfied that the value assigned, by the Foreign investor, to the assets transferred, represents fair market value. The Board may ask the foreign investor to produce sufficient documentary evidence to demonstrate the fair market value of the assets a per paragraph 2, of Article 3. This value shall be determined in accordance with the prevailing import legislation.

3.   The foreign investment shall be registered in convertible currency as specified by the Central Bank of Somaliland.

ARTICLE 12 GUARANTEES FOR FOREIGN INVESTMENT

1.   All enterprise object of foreign investment shall receive as favourable treatment as domestic enterprise.

2.   The property of foreign investment duly registered under this law shall not be subject to expropriation measures, except in the only case where public interest cannot be satisfied by measures other than expropriation.

3.   In the case of such expropriation, prompt compensation shall be paid. Said compensation shall reflect the fair market value of the assets as freely transferable.

ARTICLE 13 INVESTMENT INCENTIVES

Foreign investment shall be eligible for incentives and facilities, in accordance with the legislation in fore ruling on such incentives and facilities.

For additional analytical, business and investment opportunities information, please contact Global Investment & Business Center, USA at (202) 546-2103. Fax: (202) 546-3275. E-mail: rusric@erols.com

1. Foreign Investment is exempted from payment of tax on profit for a period of three years from commencing operations. In addition, after the expiry of the initial tax holiday period, foreign investors shall be entitled to a 50% reduction of the tax due for the profit reinvested.

2. Imported machinery, equipment, installations and any other outfits as well as raw materials, supplies and components imported for production purposes are exempted from import custom duties.

ARTICLE 14 LIMITS TO CONTRACTING DEPT FROM DOMESTIC SOURCES

1. Any enterprise subject to a duly registered foreign investment may contract dept from Institutional domestic financial sources up to the limit established by the Central Bank of Somaliland, in consultation with Boar. Sources shall be used strictly for the carrying out of the activities specified in the "Certificate of Foreign Investment Registered" The Board shall be authorized to verify the due application of proceeds.

ARTICLE 15 FACILITIES FOR FOREIGN PERSONNEL

1. The Board shall ensure that the immigration authorities facilitate the granting of the entry permits and residence visas to foreign personnel employed by an enterprise registered under this law, and to their families.

2. The Board shall also ensure that said personnel and their families be granted access, for reasons of work, to any part of Somaliland.

3. Said personnel may freely transfer abroad up to fifty percent of their salaries, wages, gratuities and allowances paid in Somaliland by the enterprise employing them.

4. Any enterprise registered under this law shall employ qualified Somaliland national whenever they are available. Foreign investment shall seek to make a significant contribution towards the transfer of technology and managerial know how, and the upgrading of professional skills available in Somaliland.

ARTICLE 16 REINVESTMENT OF PROFIT

1. "Profit" shall be understood as the "net income" less income taxes payable, as applicable, in accordance with the prevailing legislation.

2. Profit organisation from duly registered foreign investment may be invested in the same enterprise, object of the investment, or in another enterprise in accordance with the provisions of this law.

3. When such profit is to be reinvested , the Board, shall be notified to this effect by registered mail or directly against issue of delivery receipt.

4. The Board shall proceed to register profit reinvested in the convertible currency specified in the "Certificate of foreign investment registered" The amount shall be determined in accordance with the prevailing laws and regulations governing foreign exchange.

5. To this effect, The Board shall issue a " Certificate of Reinvestment".

6. Subsequent rights to transfer profit and repatriate investment, as well as other benefits under this law, shall be determined on the basis of the original investment registered plus profit reinvested.

7.   In case of reinvesting profit in an enterprise other than the enterprise object of a duly registered foreign investment, the provisions of article 9 and 10 of this law shall apply.

ARTICLE 17 TRANSFER OF PROFIT

1.   profit organising form a duly registered foreign investment, as per paragraph 1 of Article 11, may be freely transferred abroad.

2.   In case that only part of such profit is transferred abroad in one year, the foreign investor may transfer the remaining portion in any one of the following years.

ARTICLE 18 TRANSFER OF CAPITAL AND PROFIT

1.   Duly registered foreign investment, defined as the original investment, plus profit reinvested, shall be freely transferable abroad after three years from the date of the registration of the original investment, as specified in the "Certificate of Foreign Investment Registered.

2.   The Board may reduce the said period, taking into consideration the priorities under the policy guidelines as per Article 4, of this law.

3.   The transfer abroad shall be effected in the original currency specified in the "Certificate of Foreign Investment Registered. "The funds destined for transfer shall originate from the liquidation of assets or the transfer or capital stock of the enterprise, object of the foreign investment, to other juridical or physical persons. The foreign investor is free to transfer abroad the physical assets, that were the object of the investment, in the event this alternative is opted for.

4.   In case were the amount realised from the liquidation or sale of capital stock exceeds the amount of the original investment plus reinvested profit registered, the foreign investor shall be free to transfer abroad, in the freely convertible currency exchange conducted and warranted by the Bank of Somaliland, the difference, in accordance with the prevailing tax legislation and foreign exchange regulations.

ARTICLE 19 SETTLEMENT OF DISPUTES

1.   Disputes in respect of the implantation of this laws shall be settled.
a)   in a manner to be agreed upon with the investor, or in the absence of such agreement.
b)   within the frame work of the agreements in force between the Somaliland Republic and the investor's home country.

In the absence of agreements, disputes shall be settled through arbitration, An arbitration board shall be established, comprising one member on behalf of each disputing party and a third member acting as a chairman, to be jointly named by the said two members. Failing agreement of the monition of the third member, the chairman shall be appointed, at the request of either party, by the president of the supreme court of Somaliland.

The Arbitration Board shall lay down its rules of procedures unrestricted by the rules contained in the civil and commercial code of procedures, save for the rules which relate to the basic guarantees and principles of litigation.

The Board shall see to it that the disputes be expediently resolved.
Awards shall be rendered by majority vote, and shall be final and binding on both parties and enforceable as any other final judgement. The Arbitration board shall decide who shall bear the arbitration costs.

For additional analytical, business and investment opportunities information, please contact Global Investment & Business Center, USA at (202) 546-2103. Fax: (202) 546-3275. E-mail: rusric@erols.com

ARTICLE 20 ALIENATION OF FOREIGN INVESTMENT AND NOTIFICATION REQUIREMENTS

1.   Alienation of foreign investment shall be effected either through liquidation of assets or through the transfer of capital stock of the enterprise, object of such investment, to juridical or physical person.

2.   In the event of alienation of a foreign investment to a resident Somaliland juridical or physical person, the transfer shall case enjoy the benefit derived from the status of a foreign investor.

3.   Any alienation is subject to prior notification, to the Board by both the transfer or and the transferred, such notification shall be accompanied by appropriate supporting documentation.

4.   The alienation of foreign investment to the other foreign investors shall not require approval, as per paragraph 3 of the Article.

ARTICLE 21 BENEFITS TO EXISTING FOREIGN INVESTMENT

1.   Existing foreign investment in Somaliland, duly registered under current or previous laws concerning foreign investment, shall continue to enjoy the rights and obligations conferred to it by said laws.

2.   Such foreign investment shall be benefited, at foreign investor's option, by the provisions of this law, provided the registration requirements and other provisions of the previous laws have been complied with, and satisfactory documentary evidence is produced, to this effect, by the foreign investor. In such case, the foreign investor may apply to the Board for registration under this law within 180 days as of date of its promulgation.

ARTICLE 22 OBLIGATIONS TO REPORT TRANSACTIONS CONCERNING FOREIGN INVESTMENT

Bank notaries public and public entities involved with foreign investment shall notify the Board of the particulars of any important pertinent acts and transactions within thirty days from the date of completing such acts or transactions. This refers, among others, to acts or transactions concerning incorporation, contracting of dept from institutional domestic financial sources, transfer of profit and repatriation of investment.

ARTICLE 23 FOREIGN INVESTMENT NOT SUBJECT TO THIS LAW

The provisions of this law shall not apply to foreign investment in mineral research and mining activities, including those related to the petroleum Industry and nuclear power. Such investment shall be subject to the mining code and the mining regulations, and of agreements reached, hereunder, between the Government of Somaliland and the interested party.

ARTICLE 24 NON-COMPLIANCE WITH THE PROVISIONS OF THIS LAW

Failure to comply with the provisions of this law, on the part of the foreign investor, shall result in the for feature of benefits provided hereunder.

ARTICLE 25 ENJOYMENT OF BENEFITS UNDER SUBSEQUENT MORE FAVOURABLE PROVISIONS

No provisions of this law shall preclude the enjoyment, by the foreign investor, of benefits under more favourable provisions which might be subsequently promulgated.

ARTICLE 26 REGULAT IONS

The president of the Somaliland Republic, on the proposal of the Board, and having heard the Minister of Commerce and Industry and the council of Ministers, may issue regulations for the proper implementation of this law.

ARTICLE 27 ENTRY INTO FORCE

This law shall come into force following its signature by H.E. President of the Republic of Somaliland.
Mohamed Ibrahim Egal
President.

THE LAW OF THE REFERENDUM ON THE CONSTITUTION OF THE REPUBLIC OF SOMALILAND

THE PARLIAMENT OF THE REPUBLIC OF SOMALILAND

HAVING SEEN Article 125 of the Constitution, which relates to the preparation of the law of the Referendum on the Constitution;

HAVING SEEN Clauses 1 and 2 of Article 130 of the Constitution, which relate to the holding of the Referendum on the Constitution;

HAVING DEBATED AND PERUSED the Government's proposals on this law of the Referendum on the Constitution;

CONSIDERING that the end of the period of the implementation of the Constitution, which was increased by Parliament is fast approaching;

PASSED THE FOLLOWING LAW

CHAPTER I GENERAL PRINCIPLES

Article 1: The Purpose of the Referendum

Every citizen shall cast his vote for or against the Constitution in the Referendum to which this law refers.

Article 2: The Right to Vote and its Exercise

1. Every citizen who fulfils the conditions set out in Article 6 shall be entitled to one vote, which he can cast at the district where he is .
2. Voting is personal, free, and direct; and all persons are equal.

Article 3: The Polling Station

To make the conduct of the Referendum possible, it shall be based on the boundaries of the legally formed districts , which currently exist in the country, and each district shall be sub-divided into polling stations.

Article 4: The Administration of the Referendum

The Referendum shall be administered at:
1. The polling stations;
2. The District Referendum Office;
3. The Central Referendum Office.
The District Referendum Office shall be at the seat of the District, and the Central Referendum Office shall be at the capital city, Hargeisa.

Article 5: The Date of the Referendum

The voting at the Referendum shall be conducted in one day only, the date of which will be set in a Presidential Decree to be issued in an official publication within a maximum period of up to sixty days before the date of the Referendum.

CHAPTER II CONDITIONS FOR PARTICIPATION IN THE REFERENDUM

Article 6: The Right to Vote

Any one (male or female) who meets the following conditions shall have the right to vote in the Referendum:
1. He must be a citizen who is a patrial descending from the persons who were resident in the Republic of Somaliland on 26 June 1960 or before.
2. He must not be aged less than 18 years.
3. He must not be certified as insane.
4. He must not be a prisoner serving a sentence passed by a court.

Article 7: The Identification of Persons who have the Right to Vote

The Polling Station officers shall reach decisions about the eligibility of individuals to vote expeditiously and in line with the provisions of this Law.

CHAPTER III POLLING STATIONS

Article 8: The Number and Location of Polling Stations

The National Referendum Committee shall, after receiving the advice of the Chairmen of the Regions , designate twenty days before the date of the Referendum:
1. The location of the polling stations in each district, which shall be based on its size and the estimated number of its residents.
2. The estimated number of persons casting their votes at each polling station shall be planned to be 1500 or more.
3. Polling stations outside towns shall be situated in accessible locations which (potential) voters can reach and return from in no more than a half day's walking.

Article 9: The Structure of the Polling Stations

A. The Polling Station Committee shall consist of:
1. A Chairman
2. An Assistant who may be designated as deputy Chairman
3. A Secretary.
The above members shall be appointed by the Chairman of the Region after consulting the Mayor or Chairman of the District .

B. If it becomes necessary to replace the Assistant or the Secretary whilst the voting is in progress, the Chairman shall replace him with someone selected from the persons present at the polling station and meeting the criteria for eligibility for voting set out in Article 6. If, however, it is the Chairman of the polling station that has to be replaced, the Chairman of the Region shall do so in accordance with the procedure set out above.

Article 10: Structure of the District Referendum Office

A. The District Referendum Office Committee shall consist of:
1. A Chairman.
2. Three Assistants, the oldest of whom shall act as deputy Chairman.
3. A Secretary.
4. Three Counting Officers.
B. The National Referendum Committee shall, after consulting the Chairman of the Region, appoint the members of the District Referendum Office. If there are urgent circumstances which necessitate the replacement of any of the above members, the Chairman of the Region shall have the power to do so.

Article 11: The Structure of the Central Referendum Office

The Central Referendum Office Committee shall consist of :
1. A Chairman.
2. A Deputy Chairman.
3. Three Assistants.
4. A Secretary.
The members of the Central Referendum Office shall be appointed by a Presidential Decree .

Article 12: Notice of Appointment and Oath

A. No one may be excused from an appointment to serve as a member of the Referendum administration (committees), if he does not proffer a satisfactory reason. The appointing authority of the member shall have the power to accept such a reason.
B. Appointments shall be communicated to the persons concerned, at the latest, 20 days before the date of the Referendum.
C. The following oath shall be administered to all members of the Referendum administration mentioned in Article 4 of this Law before they assume their offices: "I swear in the name of Allah that I shall fulfil the duties relating to the Referendum that I have been entrusted with, in a conscientious and honest manner and shall observe this Law and the other laws of the Republic of Somaliland".

Article 13: The Preparation of Polling Stations, the District and Central Referendum Offices

1. The Mayors or Chairmen of the Districts shall be responsible for the preparation of polling stations and the district offices.
2. The National Referendum Committee shall be responsible for the preparation of the Central Office.
3. The above-mentioned authorities shall inform the public 20 days before the date of the Referendum:
A. the number and location of the polling stations;
B. the printed materials to be used in public places, notice boards, meetings, assemblies and the media.

For additional analytical, business and investment opportunities information,
please contact Global Investment & Business Center, USA
at (202) 546-2103. Fax: (202) 546-3275. E-mail: rusric@erols.com

CHAPTER IV THE VOTING EQUIPMENT

Article 14: The Polling Station Equipment

A. The National Referendum Committee shall send to each polling station the following equipment:
1. A copy of the Constitution.
2. A copy of this Law.
3. A sealed envelope containing the stamp of the polling station, ink and inkpad.
4. A sealed envelope containing the ballot papers.
5. Ballot boxes.
6. A container for carrying the voting and office equipment.
7. A number of registers for recording any incidents relating to the conduct of the voting.
8. A bottle of indelible ink.
9. A number of printed large boards explaining the voting procedure to the public.
10. Office equipment and any other necessary materials.
B. The Referendum Committee shall also prepare for the District and Central Referendum Offices sealed envelopes containing:
1. Stamps, ink and inkpads.
2. Counting Sheets.
3. Registers.
4. Office equipment.
5. The printed materials needed for the above-mentioned Referendum equipment shall be in a closed and sealed container, accompanied by the ballot boxes.
C. The National Referendum Committee shall also prepare for the Mayors or the Chairmen of the Districts spare sets of the materials needed for the voting, which can be used when a signed and stamped request containing the reasons for the expressed need are received from a Chairmen of a polling station.

Article 15: The Standardisation of Voting Equipment

1. The voting equipment, the stamps of the polling stations and the Referendum office(s), the ballot papers, the registers, the ballot boxes, (and) the counting sheets shall be of the same type throughout the country.
2. The stamps shall have different serial numbers, and each polling station shall have its own number.
3. The Referendum ballot papers shall be made of white perforated paper with detachable counterfoil and each set shall contain one hundred sheets. The counterfoil of each sheet shall have a serial number of its own.

Article 16: Envelopes and Ballot Boxes

1. At each polling station, the Mayor or Chairman of each District shall prepare a room with a curtain in the middle to enable secret balloting.
2. A ballot box shall be placed in each of the partitions. One of the ballots boxes shall be white and is for ballot papers accepting the Constitution, and the other shall be black and is for ballot papers rejecting the Constitution.
3. The top part of the white ballot box shall be marked (YES), and that of the black ballot box (NO).

Article 17: The Explanation of the Voting Procedure

A copy of the board mentioned in Article 14(9) shall be displayed at a place inside and outside of the polling station, where the public can see. The board shall be displayed, in the same way, inside each partition (of the polling station).

CHAPTER V THE VOTING

Article 18: The Delivery of Voting Equipment

The Mayor or Chairman of the District shall:
1. cause to deliver the containers and ballot boxes at each polling station at 6.00 o'clock in the morning before the date of the Referendum;
2. cause to deliver the containers for the District Referendum Office at 4.00 o'clock the day before;
3. ensure that notice of the appointments of the members of each polling station office or the District Referendum Office are received at their respective locations.

Article 19: The Setting up of the Polling Station

On receipt of the equipment set out in Article 18 of this Law, the Chairman of the polling station shall:
1. start preparing the layout of the polling station, and assembling the Assistant and the Secretary;
2. confirm, in the presence of the other members, that the seals of the containers holding the voting equipment are intact, and ensure that all the contents are there;
3. after waiting for the presence of the other members who shall confirm with him that all the seals are intact, open the envelope containing the stamp of the polling station and place it in the above mentioned container; and shall record in the register the numbers of the stamp and of the ballot papers;
4. confirm, in the presence of the other members, that the ballot boxes are empty and then proceed to close them and seal them whilst leaving clear the slots for insertion of the ballot papers; and then place them in their appropriate places;
5. display a copy of the Constitution of the Republic of Somaliland Republic;
6. hand over the rest of the equipment to the Secretary;
7. ensure that all the voting equipment has been provided in a way which makes possible the proper conduct of the Referendum.
As soon as the above activities are carried out in the shortest time possible, the Chairman shall announce the opening of the voting.

Article 20: The Power to Keep the Peace

The Chair of the Polling Station shall:
1. be responsible for the preservation of the security of the polling station to which the public are congregating, and its surroundings;
2. call for the assistance of the security forces which will remove or arrest anyone who causes acts which are detrimental to the proper conduct of the Referendum or commits offences;
3. have his orders only fulfilled by the officials of the agencies of the state and the commanders of the security forces so as to enable all voters to have access to the polling station.
4. The above powers can also be exercised by the Chairmen of the District Referendum Office and the Central Referendum Office.

Article 21: Access to the Referendum Polling Station

1. Other than the polling station committee members, only persons who have the right to vote may enter the polling station.
2. Voters shall enter the polling station one at a time whilst observing the order in which they arrived.
3. Voters shall not enter the polling station if they are in possession of weapons or other objects which may cause harm.

Article 22: Steps Before the Voting

Every citizen may cast his vote at the (polling) station where he is and shall
prove:
1. his name and age;
2. place of residence;
3. that he can be accepted at the (polling) station that he is eligible to vote. Taking note of any evidence in writing or by witnesses or any other matters that may convince them, the Polling Station Committee shall reach a decision about his eligibility in a quick and brisk manner.
4. Before a ballot is issued to a voter, he shall have indelible ink marked on his left hand, or if he does not have one, his right hand. If the voter has no hands, the mark shall be placed on another visible part of his body.

Article 23: Voters who are Unable to Cast their Votes

1. Votes may be cast by persons who are eligible to vote and who attend the polling station in person.
2. The Chairman shall allow any person, who is unable to vote because of a clear physical infirmity, and is accepted at the polling station as someone who cannot vote, to choose a person who can help him and in whom he has confidence.
The Secretary shall record any such event in the register and shall note the names of the person and his helper and the reasons for the decision.

Article 24: The Voting Procedure

On completion of the steps set out in Article 22 of this Law:
1. The Chairman shall hand, one at a time, to each voter a stamped ballot paper which is detached from the sequentially numbered counterfoil.
2. The voter shall proceed with the ballot paper to one of the partitions in the polling room.
3. Votes accepting the Constitution shall be cast in the White ballot box, and those rejecting it shall be cast in the Black ballot box.
4. If a voter is handed a ballot paper, which is deficient, he may hand it back to the Chairman and ask for a replacement.
5. Any voter who deliberately loiters whilst voting may be ejected by the Chairman and have his ballot paper confiscated.
6. Any such ejected voter shall be allowed to vote after all the other waiting persons have cast their votes.
7. Any voter who is found to have:
A. more than one ballot paper;
B. a (ballot) paper different from the standard paper in use;
C. cast his vote before;
shall have his ballot paper(s) removed by the Chairman, who shall hand him over to the security forces so that appropriate legal steps, including court proceedings, can be taken against him.
8. If any of the above incidents take place, they shall be recorded in the register accompanied by the following: the name of the relevant voter, and the ballot paper(s) removed from the person,

For additional analytical, business and investment opportunities information,
please contact Global Investment & Business Center, USA
at (202) 546-2103. Fax: (202) 546-3275. E-mail: rusric@erols.com

which shall be signed by the Chairman and, at least one of the other members of the polling station committe and placed in the envelope provided for this purpose.

Article 25: The Hours of Voting
The voting shall start at 6.00 o'clock in the morning and shall carry on continuously until 6.00 o'clock in the evening. If necessary, the voting may continue until 10.00 o'clock in the evening. Nonetheless, so long as (potential) voters are waiting in front of the polling station, the vote shall not be closed.

Article 26: The End of the Voting

On conclusion of the activities mentioned in the preceding Article, the Chairman shall proceed promptly to undertake the following activities:
1. Announce that the vote is closed.
2. Seal the ballot boxes, and impress the polling station stamp and the signatures of the Chairman and the other members of the polling station committee on the seals.
3. Confirm and note in the register the (total) number of ballot papers used by checking the remaining counterfoil.
4. Confirm and note in the register the (total) number of ballot papers taken from voters:
a. because of the papers being imperfect or incomplete ;
b. who deliberately loiters whilst voting;
c. who have been found to be in possession of ballot papers which do not conform to the legal ones;
d. who have been found to have cast their votes previously.
5. Confirm and note in the register the (total) number of ballot papers which remain unused.
6. On the basis of the above matters, confirm and note in the register the (total) number of persons who actually cast their votes.
7. Close the registers of the polling station.
8. Place all the printed materials mentioned above in their respective envelopes, and close and seal the envelopes in the manner set out in Clause 2 of this Article.
9. Place the polling stations stamps in the envelope provided, seal the envelope and add the signatures on top of the seal in the manner set out in Clause 2 of this Article.
10. Place all the envelopes in the container, and close and seal the container and add the signatures on top of the seal in the manner set out in Clause 2 of this Article.
11. The container(s) shall be dispatched with the ballot boxes.

Article 27: The Presence of the Polling Station Committee Members

All the polling station committee members must be present whilst the vote is in progress. The short absence of one member, at a time, is permissible subject to the approval of the Chairman of the polling station.

Article 28: The Polling Station Register

The recording in the register of the incidents that take place at the Referendum polling station shall be made triplicate which shall be signed by all the members of polling station committee. One copy shall be for the District Referendum Office to use it for fulfilling its responsibilities, and the other two copies are for the Mayor or Chairman of the district.

Article 29: The Return and Handing Over of Polling Equipment

1. On conclusion of the activities set out in the above Articles, the Chairman, accompanied by, at least, one other member of the polling station committee and protected by the security forces, shall transport promptly the container carrying the materials set out in Article 26 of this Law and the ballot boxes, and shall deliver them at the District Referendum Office.

2. On receiving the container(s) and the ballot boxes, the District Referendum Office shall check that that they are properly sealed and shall record that in a register with two copies, one of which shall be handed to the Chairman of the polling station and the other to be retained by the District Referendum Office.

3. The Chairman of the polling station shall then hand over to the Mayor or the Chairman of the District the two copies of the polling station register, which are referred to in Article 28.

CHAPTER VI THE FUNCTIONS OF THE DISTRICT REFERENDUM OFFICE

Article 30: The Setting up of the District Referendum Office

On receipt of the materials set out in Article 18 of this Law, the Chairman of the District Referendum Committee shall:

1. start setting up the district office and shall assemble the Assistant, the Secretary and the Counting Officers;

2. after confirmation by him and other the members that all the seals are intact, open the container and take out and check the materials therein;

3. after confirmation by him and the other members that all the materials, are there, open the envelope containing the stamp, and note its number in the register;

4. hand over the rest of the materials to the Secretary of the District Referendum Office. The District Referendum Office shall then wait for the arrival of the materials set out in Article 26 of this Law.

Article 31: Receipt of the Materials from the Polling Station

The District Referendum Office shall, in accordance with Clause 2 of Article 29 of this Law, receive the containers and the ballot boxes of the polling stations in the order of their arrival.

Article 32: The Closing of the District Referendum Office

1. The District Referendum Office shall not be closed until all the materials from the polling stations in the district have reached it or have been handed over to it formally.

2. When the Office is closed, no one shall remain inside it, and, whilst fulfilling the orders of the Chairman, the security forces shall secure it from the outside.

Article 33: The Start of the Counting Activities

Notwithstanding the setting up of the District Referendum Office, the counting activities shall start at 8.00 o'clock in the morning after the date of the Referendum, but the count of the polling station votes shall not start until the completion of the process of receipt of the Referendum materials from all the polling stations in the district.

1. Before the count of each polling station vote is started, the Chairman shall, having checked that the seal is intact, open the containers and shall also check the seals of the envelopes enclosed in the container and the seals of the ballot boxes.

2. The chairman shall announce in a loud voice:
- the unique number of the polling station and its location;
- the (total) number of the persons who actually cast their votes at the polling station as set out in the register of that polling station.

Article 34: The Sifting of Ballot Papers

1. On completion of the activities mentioned in the preceding Article, the Chairman, aided by one of Assistants, shall remove the seal from and open the White ballot box, which contains the votes accepting the Constitution.
2. The ballot papers in the White boxes shall be removed one at a time, and shall be checked, counted and then placed together in a particular place. At the same time, the running tally of such votes accepting the Constitution shall be announced in a loud voice.
3. When the sifting of the ballot papers accepting the Constitution is completed, the ballot papers shall returned to their boxes, which shall be sealed. Any improper ballot papers shall be placed in a special envelope, and the Secretary shall mark a running tally of the votes. After removing, in front of the Committee , the seal of the Black ballot boxes, which contain the votes rejecting the Constitution, the Chairman shall open them and follow the procedure laid down in the preceding Clause.
4. No one, other than the Committee members, can handle the ballot papers.

Article 35: Improper Ballot Papers

Improper ballot papers are:
1. those which do not carry the stamps of the polling stations;
2. those which have on them signatures, names or other markings written or made by the voters in their own hands;
3. those which have not be issued by the relevant polling station.

Article 36: The Presence of All the Members of the Office

All the members of the District Referendum Office shall be present during the period of the count of the ballot papers. The short absence of one member, at a time, is permissible subject to reasons being given for the absence and the approval of the Chairman.

Article 37: Decisions about Complaints

On completion of the sifting of the ballot papers, the District Referendum Office Committee shall reach decisions, by a simple majority, on all written complaints brought from the polling station during the voting or afterwards.

Article 38: The Confirmation of the Polling Station Result

On completion of the activities set out in the preceding Article of this Law, the Chairman of the District Referendum Office Committee shall:
1. confirm any differences between the total number reached by the District Referendum Office and that noted in the polling station register, whilst explaining any reasons for the differences;
2. declare loudly the total number of voters, the total number of ballot papers cast, the total number of ballot papers which were proper and that of the improper papers;
3. declare loudly the result of the Referendum whilst showing the number of votes accepting the Constitution and those which reject it;
4. note all the above matters in the Register of the District Referendum Office.

Article 39: The Postponement of the Sifting

1. When the sifting of the ballot papers of the polling station is started, it shall not be stopped until it is all completed.

2. If, however, it cannot be completed within the day, the Chairman may postpone it until 8.00 o'clock of the following day.

Article 40: The Tally of the Total Result of the District Referendum

On completion of the activities of the District Office set out in the preceding Article of this Law, the Chairman shall:
1. add up the totals of the votes cast in all the polling stations of the District as well as the totals of the proper ballot papers, the improper ballot papers, the votes accepting the Constitution, and those rejecting the Constitution;
2. declare loudly the tentative result of the District, whilst making clear the numbers of those who accepted and those who rejected the Constitution;
3. inform the Central Referendum Office the result, which shall be written in both numbers and words;
4. note in the register in triplicate and signed by all the members of the committee the activities of the District Referendum Committee and its declared result.
The three registers: one shall be handed to the Mayor or Chairman of the District; of the other two one shall go to the Supreme Court and the other to the Central Referendum Office, and shall be accompanied by various sealed separate envelopes containing all the complaints received by the District Referendum Office, with each envelope identifying on its cover the name of the relevant polling station to which the incident relates
5. The Chairman shall store the voting equipment and materials of the polling station and of the District Referendum Office in a special room and shall inform the Mayor or the Chairman of the District. The room shall be locked, sealed and kept secure for the Supreme Court to approve formally the Constitution.

CHAPTER VII THE FUNCTIONS OF THE CENTRAL REFERENDUM OFFICE

Article 41: The Structure of the Central Referendum Office

On receipt of the equipment and materials set out in Article 14 of this Law from the National (Referendum) Committee, the Chairman of the Central Referendum Office shall:
1. assemble the other members of the Committee who are:
a. the Deputy Chairman;
b. the Assistants;
c. the Secretary;
d. the Counting Officers;
2. open the containers, check and remove the enclosures after the seals have been confirmed by him and the other members;
3. open the envelope containing the stamp of the Office, after the seal have been confirmed to be intact by him and the other members;
4. hand over the rest of the materials to the Secretary.

Article 42: The Functions of the Central Referendum Office

1. On receipt of the telegrams referred to in Clause 3 of Article 40 of this Law, the Central Referendum Office shall declare the tentative overall result of the Referendum.
2. On receipt of the registers and the complaints referred to in Clause 4 of Article 40 of this Law, the Central Referendum Office shall add up and declare the tentative overall result of the Referendum by:
a) reaching tentative decisions about the complaints including those which have reached the Central Referendum Office at a later stage;

For additional analytical, business and investment opportunities information, please contact Global Investment & Business Center, USA at (202) 546-2103. Fax: (202) 546-3275. E-mail: rusric@erols.com

b) adding up the total number of votes cast in all the polling stations of the Republic, and the totals of the number of proper and improper ballot papers, as well as the total number of votes for and against the Constitution.

The Chairman shall then declare loudly the tentative result of the Referendum of the whole country of the Republic of Somaliland.

3. The above-mentioned activities shall be recorded in a register with two copies. One of the registers, together with other materials and the complaints which reached the Central Referendum Office, shall be sent to the Supreme Court for the fulfilment of its duties as laid down in this Law, and the other shall be sent to the National Referendum Committee.

CHAPTER VIII CRIMES

Article 43: Crimes

Anyone who commits the following criminal acts which may affect the proper conduct of the Referendum activities and the acceptance of the Referendum result, such as:
· the obstruction of the holding of the Referendum ;
· any acts which are detrimental to the right to vote ;
· the unlawful entry of a polling station or a Referendum office;
· falsification, forgery, or the fraudulent alteration of the Referendum accounts;
· unlawful voting;
· offences committed by the members of the Polling Station Committees and of the Referendum Offices;
· obstruction of the proper conduct of the Referendum ;
· refusal of the appointment to membership of the Polling Station Committee and that of the Referendum Offices.

Article 44: The Oversight of the Referendum Activities

1. The National Committee for arranging the Referendum shall have the overall responsibility for the conduct of the Referendum activities.
2. As representative of the above Committee, the Chairman of each region shall monitor and ensure that Referendum activities in the region are completed within the planned time limits.
3. The Mayor or the Chairman of the District shall be responsible, in the same way, at District level.

Article 45: Responsibility for Security

The security and peaceful conduct of the Referendum shall be the responsibility of the security forces, which shall always obey the instructions and directions of the Chairmen of the Regions, the Districts, the polling stations and the Referendum Offices.

Article 46: The Approval of the Referendum

The Supreme Court shall have the power to approve the Referendum activities, and shall declare its decision within 10 days of the announcement of the tentative results by the Central Referendum Office.

When the Court approves the Referendum, it shall issue the final outcome of the Referendum.

Article 47: The Outcome of the Referendum

1. If, in the Referendum, the Somaliland public accept the Constitution (YES), the Constitution shall be promulgated by the President.
2. If the outcome of the Referendum is (NO), the two Houses (the Representatives and the Elders) shall meet urgently within 7 days so as to reach a resolution about the period of the interim implementation of the Constitution , and the preparation of a new Constitution.

Article 48: Implementation

This Law shall be applicable to the Referendum on the Constitution only.
This Law shall come into force on the date it is signed by the President of the Republic of Somaliland, and shall published in the Official Bulletin.

THE CONSTITUTION OF THE REPUBLIC OF SOMALILAND
(As Amended)

The people of Somaliland in a Referendum, under Article 130 of the Constitution, formally adopted this Constitution on 31 May 2001
IN THE NAME OF ALLAH, THE COMPASSIONATE AND THE MERCIFUL

PREAMBLE

IN PURSUANCE of the resolutions of the Conference of the Somaliland Communities held in Burao on 27th April to 5th May 1991, which reaffirmed (our) independence with effect from 18th May 1991;

NOTING that the Conference of the Elders of the Somaliland Communities held in Borama from 24th January to 25th May 1993 adopted a National Charter which:

· laid down that a national constitution which will replace the national charter be prepared and consulted upon within a year; (*and*)
· set out clearly the constitutional principles and the governmental structures, confident in their communities' inalienable right to decide their destiny;

HAVING experienced the dire consequences of the application of a constitution not grounded on the nation's beliefs, culture and aspirations, as was the case for a period of thirty years;

HAVING experienced the devastation wrought by a regime based on dictatorship and a policy of divide and rule to which the country was subjected for over twenty years, and ever vigilant of the return of such a regime;

REMEMBERING the series of struggles waged by the people, such as that of the "Darawiish"[2], religious leaders and political parties;

MINDFUL of the vigorous campaign led by the patriotic organisation, the SNM[3], which culminated in the reassertion of (our) independence which was achieved through sacrifice of life and property so that the nation can enjoy a governmental system which meets its needs;

DESIROUS of a state which fulfils the aspirations of the nation, and is thereby appreciated by all, and which is founded on equality and justice;

For additional analytical, business and investment opportunities information, please contact Global Investment & Business Center, USA at (202) 546-2103. Fax: (202) 546-3275. E-mail: rusric@erols.com

RECOGNISING that lasting stability and peace can be achieved through a synergy between the economic system and the aspirations of the nation;

CONFIDENT that the Somaliland nation is a family that has everything in common, such as religion, culture, customs and language; and whose members are no different from each other and are ready to build together a state in which everyone has equal status;

AWARE that the preparation of the Constitution has gone through various stages and committees, such as the Constitution Working Party which was enjoined by the third General Conference on 26th November 1996[4] to sift through the two draft versions of the Constitution; and more recently, the corrections and amendments made by the two Houses of Parliament on 30th April 2000; and that the Constitution was based on the following issues:

a. The Islamic Sharia.
b. Conclusions from the various consultations.
c. The separation of powers of the state as between the legislative, the executive and the judiciary.
d. The decentralisation of the administration of the government.
e. Guarantees of private property rights and the protection of the free market.
f. Sanctity of human life through the entrenchment of fundamental rights and individual freedoms.
g. Peaceful and proper co-existence with the states in the region and world wide;

HAVING thoroughly considered the spirit and words of the preamble and the rest of the Constitution;

The people of Somaliland hereby approve and proclaim to the whole world on this ...... day of ...., that this constitution has been adopted as the nation's Constitution.

CHAPTER ONE DESCRIPTION OF THE STATE, GENERAL PRINCIPLES & FUNDAMENTAL RIGHTS

PART ONE GENERAL PROVISIONS

ARTICLE 1: THE STATE OF THE REPUBLIC OF SOMALILAND

1. The country which gained its independence from the United Kingdom of Great Britain and Northern Ireland on 26th June 1960 and was known as the Somaliland Protectorate and which joined Somalia on 1st July 1960 so as to form the Somali Republic and then regained its independence by the Declaration of the Conference of the Somaliland communities held in Burao between 27th April 1991 and 15th May 1991 shall hereby and in accordance with this Constitution become a sovereign and independent country known as "**The Republic of Somaliland**".
2. Sovereignty resides in the people who shall exercise it in accordance with the Constitution and other laws.

ARTICLE 2: THE TERRITORY OF THE REPUBLIC OF SOMALILAND

1. The territory of the Republic of Somaliland covers the same area as that of the former Somaliland Protectorate and is located between Latitude 8' to 11' 30' north of the equator and

For additional analytical, business and investment opportunities information, please contact Global Investment & Business Center, USA at (202) 546-2103. Fax: (202) 546-3275. E-mail: rusric@erols.com

Longitude 42' 45 to 49' East; and consists of the land, islands, and territorial waters, above and below the surface, the airspace and the continental shelf.

2.   The Republic of Somaliland is bordered by the Gulf of Aden to the north; Somalia to the east; the Federal Republic of Ethiopia to the south and the west; and the Republic of Djibouti to the north west.

3.   The territory of the nation is inviolable, and shall not be trespassed upon.

Article 3: The Capital

The capital of the Republic of Somaliland is Hargeisa.

Article 4: Citizenship

1.   Any person who is a patrial[5] of Somaliland, who is the descendant of a person residing in Somaliland on 26th June 1960 or earlier, shall be recognised as a citizen of Somaliland.

2.   The law shall determine the acquisition or loss of the citizenship of Somaliland.

Article 5: Religion

1.   Islam is the religion of the nation, and the promotion of any religion in the territory of Somaliland, other than Islam, is prohibited.

2.   The laws of the nation shall be grounded on, and shall not be valid if they are contrary to Islamic Sharia.

3.   The state shall promote religious tenets (religious affairs), and shall fulfil Sharia principles and discourage immoral acts and reprehensible behaviour.

4.   The calendar shall be the Islamic Calendar based on the hijra[6] and the Gregorian Calendar.

Article 6: Language

1.   The official language of the Republic of Somaliland is Somali, and the second language is Arabic.

2.   Other languages shall be used when necessary.

Article 7: The Flag, the Emblem and the National Anthem

The flag of the Republic of Somaliland shall consist of three horizontal, parallel and equal sections, the top section of which is coloured green and has inscribed in its midst in white in Arabic language (*the phrase*) La Ilaaho Ila-Allaah Muhammad Rasuulah-Allaah *(There is no God, but Allah and Mohammad was his Prophet)*; the middle section is white and has inscribed in its midst an equally sided five pointed black star; and the bottom section is coloured clear red.[7]

The emblem[8] of the nation shall consist of a coffee coloured falcon with (the words), in Arabic language, "ALLAHU AKBAR" (*God is great)* inscribed on its breast. Below the eagle are two hands shaking, and a set of scales hang above it and come down on both of its sides. The falcon and (and the scales and hands) are in turn surrounded on both sides and below by two

---

[5] This is not the same as someone born in Somaliland, and patriality is defined in the rest of the clause.

[6] The flight of Muhammed (Moxammad, in Somali script) for Mecca to Medina in 620 AD.

[7] The Flag of the Republic of Somaliland:

[8] The emblem of the Republic of Somaliland.

strands of green leaves intertwined at the base, and with the Arabic words *Bismillahi Rahmani Rahim*[9] inscribed at the top gap between the two leaves.

3.   The National Anthem shall be determined by law and shall reflect the principles of the Constitution, the national aspirations, and co-operative social order; and shall have its own unique music which is different from those of other countries.

4.   Any partial or total changes to the flag, the emblem and the national anthem shall be approved by a resolution of the House of Representatives.

PART TWO GENERAL PRINCIPLES

Article 8: Equality of Citizens

1.   All citizens of Somaliland shall enjoy equal rights and obligations before the law, and shall not be accorded precedence[10][6] on grounds of colour, clan, birth, language, gender, property, status, opinion etc.[11][7]

2.   Precedence and discrimination on grounds of ethnicity, clan affiliation, birth and residence is prohibited; and at the same time programmes aimed at eradicating long lasting bad practices shall be a national obligation.[12][8]

3.   Except for the political rights reserved for citizens, foreigners lawfully resident in Somaliland shall enjoy rights and obligations before the law equal to those enjoyed by citizens.

Article 9: Political System

1.   The political system of the Republic of Somaliland shall be based on peace, co-operation, democracy and plurality of political parties.

2.   The number of political parties in the Republic of Somaliland shall not exceed three (3).

3.   A special law shall determine the procedures for the formation of a political party, but it is unlawful for any political party to be based on regionalism or clanism .

Article 10: Foreign Relations

1.   The Republic of Somaliland shall observe all treaties and agreements entered into by the former state of Somalia with foreign countries or corporations provided that these do not conflict with the interests and concerns of the Republic of Somaliland.

2.   The Republic of Somaliland recognises and shall act in conformity with the United Nations Charter and with international law, and shall respect the Universal Declaration of Human Rights.

3.   The Republic of Somaliland accepts the principles of the self-determination of the nations of the world.

4.   It accepts that political disputes which arise shall be settled through dialogue and peaceful means, and shall respect the territorial integrity of other countries.

5.   It shall endeavour to replace the long-standing hostitlity between the countries in the Horn of Africa with better understanding and closer relations.

---

[9] In the name of Allah, the compassionate and the merciful.
[10][6] I have chosen the word "precedence" to "preference" to indicated more aptly the meaning of the Somali phrase "kala saarayn" which refers literally to someone claiming a higher position than another.
[11][7] The abbreviation "etc" is used to reflect the Somali abbreviation "iwm" which is in the Somali text and is short for "iyo waxyaalaha la mid ah", meaning, "and other similar matters".
[12][8] This last part of the clause relating to bad practices is a new addition. It is submitted that this relates traditional practices that lead to discrimination and or precedence on the prohibited grounds listed in the clause.

6. The state of the Republic of Somaliland is an independent republic which has its place among the Arab nations, and the peoples of Africa and the Islamic World, and shall accordingly endeavour to join the United Nations, the Organisation of African Unity, the Arab League and organisation of Islamic states.

7. The state of the Republic of Somaliland shall oppose terrorism etc.[13][9] (*and similar acts*), regardless of the motives for such acts.

Article 11: The National Economy

1. The state shall lay down the national economic policy based on the principles of free enterprise and the joint working of private property, public property, the national wealth and foreign investment so as to realise the growth of productivity, the raising of the standard of living, the creation of jobs, and, in general, the advancement of the economy of the nation.

2. In order to ensure that the economic system does not lead to the exclusive enrichment of a group or a small section of the public, and to avoid (*both*) the creation of economic classes consisting of those who are prosperous and those who are not, and the widening of the economic gulf between the urban and rural communities, the state shall ensure that social benefits and economic opportunities are provided in a just and equitable manner.

3. The state shall ensure the security[14][10] of foreign investment in the country; and such investment shall be regulated by law.

Article 12: Public Assets, Natural Resources and Indigenous Production

1. The land[15][11] is a public property commonly owned by the nation, and the state is responsible for it.

2. The care and safeguarding of property (*public),* endowments and public assets is the responsibility of the state and all citizens; and shall be determined by law.

3. The Government shall have the power to own and possess movable and immovable property; and to purchase, sell, rent, lease, exchange on equivalent value, or otherwise expend that property in any way which is in accordance with the law

4. The central state is responsible for the natural resources of the country, and shall take all possible steps to explore and exploit all these resources which are available in the nation's land or sea. The protection and the best means of the exploitation of these resources shall be determined by law.

5. Where it is necessary to transfer the ownership or the benefits of a public asset, the transfer shall be effected in accordance with the law.

6. The state shall encourage indigenous economic production such as agriculture, livestock, fisheries, minerals, production of frankincense and myrrh and gum etc., and manufacture based on indigenous products.

7. The payment of Zakat[16][12] is a cornerstone of Islam, and its administration shall be determined by law.

---

[13][9] See footnote 7 above.

[14][10] The Somali phrase describing the State's obligation in respect of foreign investment, *"dammaanad qaad"* literally means "standing surety for". But, in the light of this article's emphasis on private enterprise, it is respectfully submitted that ensuring the security of such investment, which may include underwriting in certain circumstances, is more likely to be the accurate reflection of this obligation. The proposed law on foreign investment should clarify this point.

[15][11] In view of the various guarantees of private property rights (see the preamble, for example), the phrase "land" here is likely to refer to "common" land.

[16][12] Zakat is the payment of alms by individual muslims according to formulas based on their income.

For additional analytical, business and investment opportunities information,
please contact Global Investment & Business Center, USA
at (202) 546-2103. Fax: (202) 546-3275. E-mail: rusric@erols.com

Article 13: Banks

The state shall establish a Central Bank which shall direct the monetary system and the currency of the nation. The opening of commercial and development banks shall be made possible and private banks shall be accorded preferential status.

Article 14: Taxes and Duties

1.   The imposition of taxes and other duties shall be based on the interests and well being of the society. Therefore, no taxes or duties which have not been determined by law shall be collected
2.   The levying, non-payment and changes in taxes and other duties shall be determined by law.
3.   Usury and commercial practices which are against the interests of the society and unlawful enrichment are prohibited.

Article 15: Education, Youth and Sports

The state shall pay particular attention to the advancement, extension and dissemination of knowledge and education as it recognises that education is the most appropriate investment that can play a major role in political, economic and social development.
Education is in the public interest, and is rooted in the experience and the special environment of the Somaliland society.
The learning of and training in the Islamic religion is a fundamental path and shall be compulsory at all levels of education. At the same time, the promotion of Koranic schools is the responsibility of the state.
Citizens and resident foreigners may open schools and educational or training projects of all levels in accordance with the Education law.
The state shall accord a first priority to primary education, and shall endeavour to spread primary education to the regions and the districts.
The eradication of illiteracy and the *(provision)* of adult education is a national obligation, and the efforts of the public and the state shall be combined to fulfil this obligation.
The national policy is that primary education shall be free[17][13].
In order to ensure a healthy physical and mental growth of the young, and to improve their well being and maturity, the state shall give special attention to the promotion and encouragement of physical education and sports which will be recognised as one of the basic subjects in the educational curriculum of both state and other schools.

Article 16: Promotion of Knowledge, Literature, Arts and Culture

The state shall promote knowledge and literature, and shall encourage creativity and research.
The law shall determine the rights to authoring, creating and inventing.
The state shall promote the Arts and the modest culture of the society whilst at the same time benefiting from the knowledge of other world societies. Literature, the arts, and indigenous sports shall be specially encouraged whilst Islamic behaviour is observed.
The state shall promote the Arts and the modest culture of the society,[18][14] and shall eradicate customs which damage religion, development, culture and the health of the society.

---

[17][13] This clear commitment to free primary education is a new amendment, but it replaces a general provision that it was the aim of the state that education should, as soon as practicable, be free.
[18][14] In this revised Constitution, the first line of this clause appears to be a repetition of the first line of the preceding clause.

For additional analytical, business and investment opportunities information,
please contact Global Investment & Business Center, USA
at (202) 546-2103. Fax: (202) 546-3275. E-mail: rusric@erols.com

The manufacture of alcohol and the cultivation or the sale or use of intoxicants (*drugs*) in the territory of Somaliland is prohibited.

Article 17: Health

1. In order to fulfil a policy of promoting public health, the state shall have the duty to meet the country's needs for equipment to combat communicable diseases, the provision of free medicine, and the care of the public welfare.
2. The state shall be responsible for the promotion and the extension of healthcare and private health centres

Article 18: The Environment and the Relief of Disaster

1. The state shall give a special priority to the protection and safeguarding of the environment which is essential for the well being of the society and the care of the natural resources. Therefore, the care of and the damage to the environment shall be determined by law.
2. The state shall undertake relief in disasters such as famine, storms, epidemics, earthquakes, and war.

Article 19: The Care of the Vulnerable of Society

The state shall be responsible for the health, care, development and education of the mother, the child, the disabled who have no one to care for them, and the mentally handicapped persons who are not able and have no one to care for them

Article 20: Work, Trade, and the Welfare of Employees

1. All able citizens have a right and a duty to work. The state shall, therefore, be responsible for the creation of work and the facilitating of the skills training of employees.
2. The conditions of work of the young and women, night working and working establishments shall be regulated by the Labour Law.
3. All employees have a right to payment appropriate to the work they undertake, and are free to enter into agreements with their employers on an individual or collective basis. Forced labour is prohibited.
4. The state shall endeavour to create understanding and clear rights between employees and employers and shall accordingly introduce a law (*in this respect*).
5. Sate employees and members of the armed forces shall be entitled remuneration for their duties and to payments for sickness, injury, or disability in accordance with the law.
6. The state shall promote the support systems, insurance and safety of employees and shall strengthen the relevant responsible bodies.

PART THREE THE RIGHTS OF THE INDIVIDUAL, FUNDAMENTAL FREEDOMS AND THE DUTIES OF THE CITIZEN

Article 21: Implementation and Interpretation

1. The legislative, executive and judicial branches of the state and the local government of the regions and the districts of the Republic of Somaliland, of all levels, shall be bound by the provisions of this Part.
2. The articles which relate to fundamental rights and freedoms shall be interpreted in a manner consistent with the international conventions on human rights and international laws referred to in this Constitution.

Article 22: Political, Economic, Social and Electoral Rights

1.   Every citizen shall have the right to participate in the political, economic, social and cultural affairs in accordance with the laws and the Constitution.
2.   Every citizen who fulfils the requirements of the law shall have the right to be elected (*to an office)* and to vote.

Article 23: Freedom of Movement and Association

1.   Every person who is a citizen or lawfully resident in the country shall be free to move to or settle at any place of his choice, or leave or return to the country at will.
2.   The matters (*rights)* set out in Clause 1 of this Article are subject to any law which forbids the movement to or settlement at specific places or during specific times.
3.   All citizens shall have the right to form, in accordance with the law, political, educational, cultural, social, occupational or employees' associations.
4.   Associations with objectives which are contrary to the public interest or are secret or are military in nature or armed or are otherwise against the law, whatever their outward appearance might be, are prohibited.

Article 24: The Right to Life, Security of the Person, Respect for Reputations and Crimes against Human Rights

1.   Human life is the gift of Allah and is beyond price. Every person has the right to life, and shall only be deprived of life if convicted in a court of an offence in which the sentence laid down by law is death.
2.   Every person shall have the right to security of his person. Physical punishment and any other injury to the person is prohibited.
3.   Every person shall have the right to have his dignity, reputation and private life respected.
4.   Crimes against human rights such as torture, extra-judicial killings, mutilation and other similar acts shall have no limitation periods.

Article 25: The Right to Liberty, Guarantees and the Conditions of Rights and Freedoms

1.   No person shall be deprived of his liberty except in accordance with the law.
2.   No person may be arrested, searched, or detained, except in the case of flagranto delicto, or on the issue of a reasoned arrest warrant by a competent judge.
3.   The state shall guarantee to all citizens the rights and freedoms and the punishment for any of their infringements shall be determined by law.
4.   The freedoms of the person shall not override the laws protecting the national interest, the security of the country or the rights of other individuals.

Article 26: Crime and Punishment

1.   Crimes and (*their)* punishment shall be laid down by the law, and no punishment shall be administered in a manner which is contrary to the law.
2.   The liability for the punishment of any crime shall be confined to the offender only.
3.   An accused person is innocent until proven guilty in a court.

Article 27: The Rights of Persons Deprived of their Liberty

For additional analytical, business and investment opportunities information,
please contact Global Investment & Business Center, USA
at (202) 546-2103. Fax: (202) 546-3275. E-mail: rusric@erols.com

1. Any person who is deprived of his liberty has a right to meet as soon as possible his legal representative, relatives or any other persons he asks for.

2. Any person who is deprived of his liberty because of alleged criminal offences shall have the right to be brought before a court within 48 (forty eight) hours of his arrest.

3. No person shall be compelled to proffer a confession, a witness statement or testimony under oath. Any such matters *(evidence)* obtained under duress shall be void.

4. No person shall be detained in a place which is not determined by law.

5. The law shall lay down the maximum period in which a person can be detained in custody pending investigations.

6. Any accused person who is convicted by a court shall have the right to appeal to a higher court.

7. When a person is detained in custody or his detention is extended, he shall have the right to have his status communicated to any person he so chooses.

8. Prisons are for reform and correction. The state is responsible for the rehabilitation and skills training of prisoners so that they can return to society with reformed characters.

9. The punishment for the infringement of Clauses 1 to 7 of this Article shall be determined by law.

Article 28: Right to Sue and Defend

1. Every person shall have the right to institute proceedings in a competent court in accordance with the law.

2. Every person shall have the right to defend himself in a court.

3. The state shall provide free legal defence in matters which are determined by the law, and court fees may be waived for the indigent.

Article 29: The Sanctity of the Home

The home and other dwellings shall be inviolable, and their surveillance, search and entry shall not be allowed without a reasoned order from a judge. Any such order must be read properly to the proprietor or occupier before entry is effected. It is prohibited for any person carrying out a search to contravene the order of the judge.

Article 30: Freedom of Communication

No person's private written communication, postal letters, or telecommunications shall be interfered with except in matters in which the law allows their investigation, tracing or listening in and a reasoned order from a judge has been obtained.

Article 31: The Right to Own Private Property

1. Every person shall have the right to own private property, provided that it is acquired lawfully.

2. Private property acquired lawfully shall not be expropriated except for reasons of public interest and provided that proper compensation is paid.

3. The law shall determine matters that are within the public interest, which may bring about the expropriation of private property.

Article 32: Freedom of Public Demonstration, Expression of Opinion, Press and other Media

1. Every citizen shall have the freedom, in accordance with the law, to express his opinions orally, visually, artistically or in writing or in any other way.

For additional analytical, business and investment opportunities information,
please contact Global Investment & Business Center, USA
at (202) 546-2103. Fax: (202) 546-3275. E-mail: rusric@erols.com

2. Every citizen shall have the freedom, in accordance with the law, to organise or participate in any peaceful assembly or demonstration.

3. The press and other media are part of the fundamental freedoms of expression and are independent. All acts to subjugate them are prohibited, and a law shall determine their regulation.

Article 33: Freedom of Belief

1. Every person shall have the right to freedom of belief, and shall not be compelled to adopt another belief. Islamic Sharia does not accept that a Muslim person can renounce his beliefs.

2. The Mosque is a blessed place and deserves veneration. It is the place for preaching religion and for providing the nation guidance in spiritual and temporal matters, and the preaching therein of matters which would divide the nation (*sedition*) is prohibited. The state shall be responsible for its general protection and any practicable support.

Article 34: The Duties of the Citizen

1. Every citizen shall have the duty, in accordance with the law, to strengthen the unity of the nation, the protection of the sovereignty of the state, and the defence of the country and the religion.

2. Every person has the duty to respect the Constitution and the laws of the country.

3. Every person has the duty to pay promptly his taxes and other duties as imposed under the law.

4. Every person shall have the duty to care for, protect and save the environment.

5. The law shall determine the punishment for failure to fulfil the duties imposed in Clauses 1 to 4 (*of this Article*).

Article 35: Extradition of Accused and Convicted Persons and Political Asylum

1. Any foreigner who enters the country lawfully or is lawfully resident in the country and who requests political asylum may be accorded asylum if he fulfils the conditions set out in the law governing asylum.

2. The extradition of a Somaliland citizen to another country is prohibited.

3. The Republic of Somaliland may extradite to their countries convicted or accused foreigners if there is a treaty between the Republic of Somaliland and the country requesting their extradition.

Article 36: The Rights of Women

1. The rights, freedoms and duties laid down in the Constitution are to be enjoyed equally by men and women save for matters which are specifically ordained in Islamic Sharia.

2. The Government shall encourage, and shall legislate for[19][15], the right of women to be free of practices which are contrary to Sharia and which are injurious to their person and dignity.

3. Women have the right to own, manage, oversee, trade in, or pass on property in accordance with the law.

4. In order to raise the level of education and income of women, and also the welfare of the family, women shall have the right to have extended to them education in home economics and to have opened for them vocational, special skills and adult education schools.

---

[19][15] This commitment to issue a law on the rights of women is a new addition.

For additional analytical, business and investment opportunities information, please contact Global Investment & Business Center, USA at (202) 546-2103. Fax: (202) 546-3275. E-mail: rusric@erols.com

CHAPTER 2 THE STRUCTURE OF THE STATE

Article 37: The Sovereignty and Powers of the State,

1. Allah who created the Somaliland nation in this land has endowed it with sovereign status and powers. The people of the Republic of Somaliland have vested their sovereign powers, as set out in this Constitution, in a state founded on, and acting in accordance with, the Constitution.

2. The structure of the state shall consist of three branches which are: the legislative, the executive and the judiciary. The separation of the powers of these branches shall be as set out in the Constitution. Each branch shall exercise independently the exclusive powers accorded to it under the Constitution.

PART ONE THE LEGISLATIVE BRANCH

Article 38: The Parliament and Joint Sittings

1. The legislative powers of the Republic of Somaliland are vested exclusively in the Parliament which shall consist of two Houses - the House of Representatives and the House of the Elders. The power to legislate cannot be transferred to anyone outside the Parliament.

2. All bills passed by the Parliament shall come into force when the President publishes[20][16] them in accordance with the Constitution.

3. The Parliament shall fulfil its duties in accordance with the Constitution and its Rules.

4. The most important objectives and duties of the Parliament are as follows:

a) The protection of the peace and security of the Republic and Republic's sovereign rule over its land, sea and air.

b) The adoption by the Republic of Somaliland of all the laws necessary in a Muslim state.

c) The implementation of the laws of the Republic and the genuine achievement of justice which is the foundation of the Republic's general stability and the confidence that the members of the Somaliland public have in each other and their reliance on each other.

5. The two Houses of the Parliament shall hold joint and separate sittings.

6. The two Houses of the Parliament shall sit jointly when considering matters such as the following:

a) the receipt of the Report of the President on the opening of the two Houses;

b) the debates on the Republic of Somaliland joining international or cross regional organisations, or the ratification of international or regional treaties;

c) the Resolution on and declaration of a state of war when the Republic of Somaliland is faced with war;

d) the debates on natural disasters;

e) the debates relating to emergency laws;

f) the confirmation of the appointment of the Chairman of the Supreme Court; *(and)*

g) any other matters considered by the two Houses as meriting joint sittings.

The House of Representatives

Article 39: General Provisions of the House

The House of Representatives consists of members who represent the public, and forms the first part of the country's legislative, passing laws and approving and overseeing the general political situation and the direction of the country.

---

[20][16] See Articles 77 and 78.

For additional analytical, business and investment opportunities information, please contact Global Investment & Business Center, USA at (202) 546-2103. Fax: (202) 546-3275. E-mail: rusric@erols.com

Article 40: Membership and Election of the House

The House of Representatives shall consist of 82 members who shall be directly elected by secret ballot in a free general election.

Article 41: Eligibility for Candidacy

Any person who is standing for election to the House of Representatives must fulfil the following conditions:
1. He must be a Muslim and must behave in accordance with the Islamic religion.
2. He must be a citizen who is not younger than 35 (thirty five) years.
3. He must be physically and mentally able to fulfil his duties.
4. He must be educated to, at least, secondary school level or equivalent.
5. He must not have been subject of a final sentence for a criminal offence by a court within the preceding five years.
6. He must be a responsible person with appropriate character and behaviour.
7. No employee of the state shall be eligible for candidacy unless he has tendered his resignation from office prior to a period determined by law. Such resignation shall be accepted.

Article 42: Period of Office and Election Term

1. The period of office of the House of Representatives is 5 (five) years beginning from the date when the Supreme Court declares the electoral results.
2. The President shall announce the election of the new House a month before the expiry of the period of office of the outgoing House.
3. If the election of the House of Representatives cannot be conducted because of dire circumstances, the outgoing House shall continue in office until the end of these circumstances and a new House is elected. Dire circumstances are: a wide war, internal instability, serious natural disasters, such as earthquakes, epidemic diseases, (and) serious famines; and shall be determined and resolved by the House of Elders on the proposal of the Council of Government[21][17].

Article 43: The Seat of the House of Representatives

The seat of the House of Representatives is the Capital City[22][18].

Article 44: The Convening of the New House

1. The new House shall hold its inaugural meeting within 30 (thirty) days from the date when the electoral results are declared, and shall be convened by the President of the Republic.
2. If the President fails to convene the inaugural meeting, the House shall meet on its own initiative on the 45th (forty fifth) day beginning from the date when the electoral declaration is made.
3. The new House shall be opened by the Chairman of the Supreme Court who shall administer the oath of office to the members. The meeting of the House shall then be chaired by the oldest member (in age), and the House shall then elect, from amongst its members, a Speaker and a Deputy Speaker.

---

[21][17] This is the first reference to the "Council of Government", or as I prefer, the Cabinet. There is no definition of the Council of Government in the Constitution, but Article 94 sets out the "Council of Ministers" whose meetings shall be chaired by the President (or the Vice-President). It is submitted that the reference to the "Council of Government" relates to this body.
[22][18] See also Article 3 for the Capital City.

Article 45: The Meetings of the House of Representatives

1. The meetings of the House shall be open, but can also be closed; and their procedures shall be set out in Rules.
2. The quorum of the meetings of the House is the presence of over half of its total membership, excluding the seats that have been declared vacant.
3. Except for constitutional issues or matters which the Rules of the House state otherwise, resolutions of the House shall be passed by a simple majority of the members present at a meeting,.
4. The (*motion for*) postponement of a meeting shall be approved by a simple majority of those present, and the meeting may then be postponed for a maximum of period of seven (7) days.
5. Ministers and Deputy Ministers have a duty to attend the meetings of the House of Representatives if requested, in writing, to do so; and they shall have the right to participate in the debate, but can not vote. In the same way, the President may ask the Vice-President or any Minister to attend, on his behalf, the meetings of the House.

Article 46: Sessions and the Procedures of the House of Representatives

1. The House shall hold every year 3 (three) ordinary sessions which shall last 28 (twenty eight) weeks in total. The sessions shall be separated by a period of no less than 4 (four) weeks and no more than 8 (eight) weeks.
2. An extra-ordinary session of the House of Representatives may be held:
a) on request of the President;
b) on convening by the Speaker of the House of Representatives; (*or*)
c) on request, in writing, of 1/3 (one third) of the members of the House.
3. The House shall adopt its Rules at its first session, and shall establish such committees, as it deems necessary.
4. The President shall deliver the State of the Nation speech at the start of the first session of each year. The speech shall cover the political situation, the Government's programme, the economy, and the financial and security situations.

Article 47: The Pay and Remuneration of the House of Representatives

The members of the House of Representatives shall be entitled to pay and remuneration as determined by law.

Article 48: Prohibition of Holding other Office and of Private Gain

A member of the House of Representatives shall not hold any other public office whilst serving as a Representative, and shall not use his office for private gain.

Article 49: The Privileges of the Members of the House of Representatives

1. No member of the House may be detained, and no action may be taken against him for any matter which he learnt or raised at the House or on which he expressed his opinion.
2. Clause 1 does not extend to insults or slander committed by a member.
3. No member of the House of Representatives shall be investigated, questioned, arrested, imprisoned or otherwise subjected to any other acts relating to punishment without the consent of the House of Representatives.
4. Action may be taken against the member if he is caught *in flagrante delicto*, in which case, the House shall be informed promptly.
5. The House shall consider whether the action taken against the member is proper.

6.   If the House is not in session, consent for the action taken against the member must be sought from the Standing Committee of the House of Representatives, and the House shall be informed at the following session.

7.   Civil suits against a member of the House of Representatives may be instituted, and no consent is required[23][19].

Article 50: Loss of Membership of the House of Representatives

The membership of the House of Representatives shall be lost on:

1.   the death of the member or incapacity which makes it impossible for him to fulfil his duties;

2.   the voluntary resignation by the member, which has been accepted by the House;

3.   one of the pre-requisite conditions[24][20] of his election being broken; or on the member's failure to fulfil his duties;

4.   the passing of a final sentence for a crime which has been proven in a court; (and)

5.   the absence, without a valid excuse, from 20 (twenty) consecutive sittings.

Article 51: Filling Vacant Seats in the House of Representatives

If a seat of the House of Representatives becomes vacant during any period prior to the final six months of the term of office of the House, it shall be filled as determined by law, and the new member shall serve for the remainder of the term of office.

Article 52: Staff of the House of Representatives

1.   The House of representatives shall have a Secretariat headed by a General Secretary who is not a member of the House.   He shall assist the Speaker of the House in administrative matters, and in all financial and management issues; and shall have a deputy.

2.   The House of Representatives shall have Advisers[25], such as a Legal Adviser, and advisers on the economy, politics etc., who shall all be chosen for their expertise and knowledge.

3.   The other employees of the Secretariat shall be appointed by the Secretary General after he receives the approval to do so from the Speaker. The appointment, dismissal, remuneration and rights of the Secretary General, his deputy, the Advisers and other employees of the House shall be determined by the Rules of the House.

Article 53: The Powers and Duties of the House of Representatives

1.   All appointments of Ministers, Deputy Ministers or Heads of the organs of the state shall be subject to confirmation by the House of Representatives in accordance with the Constitution.

2.   The House of Representatives shall also have power to debate, comment on, refer back with reasons or approve the programme of the Government.

3.   The House of Representatives shall ratify international agreements (treaties) such as political, economic and security agreements or those agreements which impose new financial burdens which have not been covered in the Budget, or which will involve the promulgation or amendment of legislation.

4.   The House of Representatives shall submit to the Council of Government (the Cabinet) advice and recommendations about the direction of the general political situation.

---

[23][19]   This is, presumably, subject to Clauses 1 and 2 of the same article.

[24][20]   These are set out in Article 41 above.

[25]   This is a new addition as the previous Constitution mentioned a Legal Adviser only.

For additional analytical, business and investment opportunities information,
please contact Global Investment & Business Center, USA
at (202) 546-2103. Fax: (202) 546-3275. E-mail: rusric@erols.com

5.   The Council of Government (*the Cabinet)* shall seek the approval of both Houses (the House of Representatives and the House of Elders) for the imposition of a state of emergency in either the whole of the country or parts of it.

6.   The House of Representatives shall have the power to summon the Government or its organs or agencies in order to question them about the fulfilment of their responsibilities.

7.   The Committees of the House of Representatives shall have the power to question Ministers, Heads of the state organs or agencies or other senior national officers, whose duties are relevant to them, about the fulfilment of their duties

Article 54: The Legislative Powers of the House of Representatives

The legislative powers of the House shall extend to the following financial matters:

1.   The imposition of taxes, duties and other schemes for raising revenue.

2.   The establishment of a Somaliland Income Fund or other Funds which are earmarked for specific issues. The management, collection and disbursement of these Funds shall be determined by law.

3.   The printing of currency, and the issue of bonds, other certificates and securities.

4.   The regulation of the economic and the financial systems.

Article 55: The Budget

1.   The House of Representatives may debate and amend the Budget, and approve it by a resolution of the House.

2.   If the new Budget is not approved before the start of the new financial year, the old Budget shall continue to be in force until such time the new one is approved.

3.   The House of Representatives shall approve any expenditure which was not included in the Budget.

4.   The procedures for the preparation of the general Budget and the financial year shall be determined by law.

5.   The budgets and the annual accounts of the state organs, agencies, companies and other partly owned entities of the state and their presentation to the House of Representatives shall be determined by law.

6.   The annual accounts shall be presented to the House of Representatives within six months of the end of the financial year to which they relate, and the House shall debate them and reach a resolution thereof.

7.   The Auditor General shall have responsibility for the presentation of the annual accounts.

Article 56: Dissolution of the House of Representatives

The House of Representatives may be dissolved:

1.   When the House does not sit for two consecutive ordinary sessions without the existence of any circumstances beyond their control.

2.   When dissolution is proposed by a 1/3 (one third) of the members[26] of the House; and is approved by 2/3s (two thirds) of the total members of the House.

3.   The Constitutional Court shall issue a ruling in respect of the matters referred to in Clauses 1 and 2 of this Article, and shall submit the ruling relating to Clause 1 to the President and that relating to Clause 2 to the House of Representatives.

---

[26] This must refer to a third of the total membership of the House, as this part of the Clause does not refer to the members present and voting at a sitting, and the following part of the Clause refers expressly to the approval of the Dissolution by two thirds of the total membership (tirada guud).

For additional analytical, business and investment opportunities information,
please contact Global Investment & Business Center, USA
at (202) 546-2103. Fax: (202) 546-3275. E-mail: rusric@erols.com

4. The House of Representatives may also be dissolved by the President after the public has agreed, in a national referendum organised by the Constitutional Court, to the reasons for the dissolution.

5. When the President considers the ruling of the Constitutional Court issued in respect of the matters referred to in Clauses 1 or 2 of this Article, or the result of the national referendum under Clause 4 of this Article, he shall promulgate a Presidential Decree dissolving the House of Representatives and at the same time setting out the date of the election of the new House, which shall take place within 60 (sixty) days.

6. If the national referendum does not approve of the dissolution of the House of Representatives or the new elections cannot be held, the term of office of the House shall continue.

7. The House of Representatives shall not be dissolved during the first year of its term of office, or during the last year of the President's term of office.

PART TWO THE HOUSE OF ELDERS

Article 57: General Provisions of the House

The House of Elders[27][23] of the Republic of Somaliland is the second part of the legislative, and shall review the legislation passed by the House of Representatives before it is forwarded to the President; and shall have special responsibility for passing laws relating to religion, traditions (*culture)* and security.

Article 58: The Election of the Members of the House and their Period of Office

1. The members of the House of Elders shall be elected in a manner to be determined by law.

2. The period of office of the House of Elders is six (6) years beginning from the date of its first meeting.

Article 59: Eligibility for Candidacy

Without prejudice to the requisite age and level of knowledge as set out below, any person who is standing for election to the House of Elders must fulfil the same conditions[28][24] which are needed for eligibility for election to the House of Representatives:

1. He must not be aged less than 45 (forty five years).

2. He must be a person who has a good knowledge of the religion or an elder who is versed in the traditions.

Article 60: The Membership of the House of Elders

1. The House of Elders shall have 82 (eighty two) members, and shall elect from amongst its members a Speaker, two deputy Speakers and such committees, as it deems necessary. The House shall have a Standing Committee of 25 (twenty five) members.

2. The following shall always become honorary members:

---

[27][23] This Article starts with the statement that the "Golaha Guurtida" (which I have translated as the House of Elders) is the House of "Odayaaasha", which literally also means "elders". The word "Guurti" is a term applied to traditional leaders, who were invariably elders, but not necessarily chosen simply because of their age. As you can see in Article 59, members of this House must not only be aged 45 years or over, but must also have a good knowledge of religion or be well-versed in tradition.

[28][24] These conditions are set out in Article 41.

a) five members to be selected by the President on the basis of their special significance to the nation, whose term of office shall coincide with that of the House;

b) any person who has served as a Speaker of the House of Elders or the House of Representatives; *(and)*

c) any person who has served as a President or Vice-President of the Republic of Somaliland.

d) Honorary members do not have the right to vote in the House and cannot serve in the Standing Committee.

Article 61: The Powers and Duties of the House of Elders

1. The passing of legislation relating to religion, traditions *(culture)* and security.

2. With the exception of financial legislation, the review of legislation approved by the House of Representatives. It may refer back, with written reasons of its views, any such legislation to the House of Representatives only once within 30 (thirty) days beginning from the date when the relevant legislation was forwarded to the office of the Speaker of the House of Elders.

3. Advice on the shortcomings of the administration of the Government and the presentation of such advice to the House of Representatives.

4. Assistance to the Government in matters relating to religion, security, defence, traditions *(culture)*, economy and society, whilst consulting the traditional heads of the communities.

5. The summoning of the members of the Government and putting questions to them about the fulfilment of their duties.

6. The House of Elders shall also have the power to put to the House of Representatives proposals for projects[29][25] so that the House of Representatives can debate and reach resolutions thereof.

Article 62: The Inaugural Meeting of the House of Elders

The inaugural meeting of the House of Elders shall take place within 30 (thirty) days of the date when their selection[30][26] is completed. The meeting shall be opened by the Chairman of the Supreme Court who shall administer the oath of office, and shall then be chaired by the oldest member of the House *(in age)* until the election of the official Speaker of the House and his two Deputies.

Article 63: The Secretary of the House and Advisers

The House of Elders shall have a secretary, who is not a member of the House. The House may also have advisers, including a legal adviser. The structure of the Secretariat of the House shall be the same as that of the House of Representatives.

Article 64: The Rules of the House

At its first session, the House of Elders shall pass the Rules of the House.

Article 65: The Pay and Remuneration of the House of Elders

The members of the House of Elders shall be entitled to pay and remuneration as determined by law.

---

[29][25] The word "mashruuc" which means a project is used in this Clause, but the Government's draft amendments to the Constitution on the identical Article referred to "Mashruuc- Sharci"(i.e Bill – draft legislation). As this word has survived the revision of the Constitution, it must be assumed that it relates to any project that the House wishes to propose.

[30][26] Note that Article 58 states that elections to the House shall be laid down by law.

Article 66: The Privileges of the Members of the House of Elders

The privileges of the members of the House of Elders shall be the same as those of the House of Representatives[31][27]. Such privileges may be removed by the House of Elders.

Article 67: Resignation of Members of the House of Elders

Any member of the House of Elders may forward his resignation to the House of Elders which shall accept it.

Article 68: Loss of the Membership of the House of Elders

A person may lose his membership of the House of Elders[32][28].
if one of the conditions[33][29] under which he was selected is no longer valid, or he can not fulfil his duties in accordance with the Rules of the House of Elders;
1. if a member received a final sentence for a crime which has been proved in a court; (and)
2. if the House accepts his resignation.

Article 69: The Dissolution of the House

The House of Elders may be dissolved in the same manner[34][30] as the House of Representatives.

Article 70: Prohibition of Holding other Office and of Private Gain

A member of the House of Elders shall not hold any other public office whilst serving as a member of the House, and shall not use his office for private gain.

Article 71: Meetings and Sessions

The meetings of the House of Elders shall be open, and may be closed as provided in the Constitution. The quorum for meetings, the majority by which resolutions can be passed and the convening of extra-ordinary sessions shall be the same as the procedures applicable to the House of Representatives[35].

Article 72: Vacant Seats in the House of Elders and Procedures for Filling them

A seat at the House of Elders may become vacant on the realisation of one of the conditions set out in Article 50[36].

---

[31][27] See Article 49.
[32][28] I have re-arranged the beginning of this Article so that the first line is set out separately and applies to all the three Clauses, instead of being part of Clause 1 as it is in the original Constitution in Somali.
[33][29] See Articles 59 and 41 for the conditions.
[34][30] See Article 56.
[35] See Articles 45 and 46.
[36] Article 50 refers to loss of membership of the House of Representatives, but Article 68 relates to the loss of membership of the House of Elders. The former is wider than the latter, and it is submitted that it applies to the loss of membership of the House of Elders by virtue of this Article, but without prejudice to the conditions set out in Article 68.

If a seat of the House of Elders becomes vacant during any period prior to the final six months of the term of office of the House, it shall be filled as determined by law, and the new member shall serve for the reminder of the term of office of the House.

Article 73: The Seat of the House of Elders

The seat of the House of Elders is the Capital City[37].

Article 74: Introduction of Draft Legislation

Bills[38][34] (*draft legislation)* may be introduced at the House of Representatives by:
1.   The Council of Government (*the Cabinet).*
2.   The requisite number of members of the House of Representatives as laid down in Rules passed by the House.
3.   Except for financial bills, at least 5000 (five thousand) citizens who are eligible to vote.

Article 75: The Promulgation, Publishing and Implementation of Legislation

All laws shall be promulgated and published in the Official Journal by the President within three weeks (21 days) beginning from the date when the two Houses have forwarded them, and shall come into force within thirty (30) days beginning from the date of their publication, but a longer or shorter period for coming into force may be set out in each law.

Article 76:

A bill shall become law on approval by the House of Representatives, and shall come into force after its signature by the President in accordance with Article 38[39].

Article 77: The Procedures for Legislation

1.   Each House of Parliament shall forward any bills that it passes to other House for review and advice.
2.   Each House may refer a bill back to the other only once.
3.   The Rules of the Parliament shall lay down the procedures for the progress of bills, and shall make clear the special status of bills relating to finance and those that the Government considers to be urgent, which shall (*both)* be given priority.
4.   Any bill passed or approved by both Houses of Parliament on a 2/3 (two-third) majority or more shall not be referred back (*to the Parliament)* by the President who shall thereby sign it. If the President considers that the bill is in conflict with an Article or Articles of the Constitution, he shall inform the Speakers and the Attorney General, who shall refer it to the Constitutional Court[40][36].
5.   The President shall sign any bill forwarded to him by Parliament within three weeks (21 days) beginning from the date when the bill was received at the Office of the President, providing that he has not referred it back to Parliament.
6.   If the President fails to sign a bill forwarded to him by Parliament within the requisite period, and has not referred it back to Parliament, then the bill shall henceforth become law, and shall be promulgated by the House which forwarded it (*to the President).*

---

[37] See Article 3.
[38][34] I have used the word "bill" for "Mashruuc sharci", which means more aptly draft legislation, as a generic term for all draft primary legislation.
[39] See also Articles 77 and 78 for the procedures for legislation.
[40][36] Presumably, the decision of the Constitutional Court in this matter will be final.

For additional analytical, business and investment opportunities information, please contact Global Investment & Business Center, USA at (202) 546-2103. Fax: (202) 546-3275. E-mail: rusric@erols.com

Article 78:

1.   All bills, other than those relating to finance, passed by the House of Representatives by a majority shall be forwarded to the House of Elders which shall:

a) Approve them or propose amendments.

b) If the House of Elders does not approve the bill, or its proposed amendments are not accepted by the House of Representatives, the latter has the right to return the bill to the House of Elders during its next session. If the House of Elders *(still)* does not approve the bill, nor submit a response within a month, the bill shall pass and shall accordingly be forwarded to the President.

2.   All bills passed by the House of Elders by a majority shall be forwarded to the House of Representatives, which shall:

a) Approve it or propose amendments.

b) If the House of Representatives does not approve the bill, it shall not be referred back[41].

3.   If the President accepts a bill passed by both Houses and forwarded to him, he shall issue it in the Official Journal within (21) days. If, however, the President does not accept the bill or proposes amendments, he shall inform the Speaker of the House of Representatives his reasons for such action within (21) days.

4.   If the House *(of Representatives)* is not satisfied with the reasons given by the President, and the bill is passed again on a 2/3s (two thirds) majority of the members of the House, the President shall accept the bill. If there is no such majority *(in the House)*, the bill shall lapse.

5.   Except for financial bills, if the House of Elders refuses to accept on a point of principle and by a 2/3s (two-thirds) majority of its membership any bill passed by the House of Representatives, and the House of Representatives is not satisfied with that rejection, but fails to pass the bill again by a majority of less than 2/3s (two-thirds) of its membership, then the bill shall lapse.

Article 79: Accusations against the Members of the Houses

1.   The members of the Houses (Representative or Elders) may be indicted for a criminal offence if they are caught *in flagrant delicto* for an offence which carries a punishment no less than (3) three years imprisonment.

They cannot, however, be brought before a court, nor imprisoned until they are stripped of their privileges for the responsibilities that they hold for the nation.

2.   The criminal prosecution brought against the accused members of the Houses, shall be conducted by the Attorney General after the appropriate House to which the members belong has stripped them of their privileges on a majority vote of two thirds of the total membership of the House. Such cases shall be heard by the High Court of Justice[42][38].

CHAPTER THREE THE EXECUTIVE

PART ONE

Article 80: The President and the Vice-President

The state shall have an executive branch, which is separate and independent of the legislative and the judicial branches.

---

[41] The bill will thereby lapse.

[42][38] The other reference to this special court is in Article 96(5) which sets out its composition and gives it the jurisdiction to try impeachment cases against Ministers and Deputy Ministers.

For additional analytical, business and investment opportunities information,
please contact Global Investment & Business Center, USA
at (202) 546-2103. Fax: (202) 546-3275. E-mail: rusric@erols.com

Article 81: The Executive Branch

The Executive Branch (sometimes referred to as "the Government"), shall be headed by the President and shall consist of:

- The President;
- The Vice-President;
- The Council of Ministers[43] appointed by the President.

Article 82: The Conditions for Eligibility for Election as President or Vice-President

To be elected as President or Vice-President, a person must fulfil the following conditions:

He must be a citizen of Somaliland by birth, and, notwithstanding residence as a refugee in another country, must not hold any other citizenship,
He must be a Muslim, and must behave in accordance with Islamic religion.
He must not be aged less than 40 years.
He must be physically and mentally fit to fulfil his duties.
He must possess knowledge of and experience in management (public and otherwise).
He must not have been convicted by a court for an offence against the Somaliland nation.
His spouse must be Muslim.
He must be fully apprised of the realities of the country, having been resident in the country for a period of at least two years before the date when the election is scheduled to take place.
He must register his private property.

Article 83: Election Procedures

The President and the Vice-President shall be elected jointly through a direct general election by means of a secret ballot.
The joint election of the President and the Vice-President shall be based on the list system and shall take place a month before the end of the term of office of the outgoing President.
The outgoing President and Vice-President shall continue in office until the new President and the Vice-President assume their offices within a month (*of the election*).
The two candidates in the list which obtains the highest number of votes cast in the Presidential and Vice-Presidential election shall be recognised as the successful candidates.
If on the expiry of the term of office of the President and the Vice-President, it is not possible, because of security considerations, to hold the election of the President and the Vice-President, the House of Elders shall extend their term of office whilst taking into consideration the period in which the problems can be overcome and the election can be held.

Article 84: Oath of Office of the President and the Vice-President[44]

Before the President and the Vice-President can assume office, they shall be sworn at a ceremony attended by the Speakers of the House of Representatives and the House of Elders and the Chairman of the Supreme Court.

Article 85: Matters in which the President and the Vice-President are not Allowed

The President and the Vice-President and their spouses[45] shall not engage in any business[46] activities during their term of office.

The President shall not be absent from the country for a period exceeding 45 (*forty five*)[47] consecutive days unless the absence is for reasons of health.

All presents given, as a mark of respect for their office, to the President, the Vice-President, their spouses and the senior officers of the nation, who have a national standing, shall be the property of the nation.

Article 86: Vacancy of Office and the Procedure for the President and the Vice-President to Vacate their Office

The office of President or Vice president may become vacant in the event of the one of the following:

Conviction of a criminal offence which leads to loss of office.
Inability to fulfil the duties of the office because of ill health.

Death.

The President or the Vice-President may forward his written resignation from office to the Speaker of the House of Representatives and the Speaker of the House of Elders, and the two Houses may, in a joint sitting, accept it or reject it by a (*simple*) majority of their total membership.

If the two Houses reject the resignation referred to in Clause 4 of this Article, the President or the Vice-President shall have the right to submit again his resignation within three months of the initial resignation request, whereupon the two Houses shall be obliged to accept it.

Article 87: Salary and Emoluments

The salary, emoluments and the public property to which the President and the Vice-President are entitled to shall be determined by law.

Article 88: Term of Office

The term of office of the President and the Vice-President is 5 years beginning from the date that they are sworn into office.

No person may hold the office of President for more than two terms.

Article 89: Procedure for Filling the Vacancy

In the event of the one of the circumstances set out in Article 86 happening to the President within the first three years of his 5-year term of office, the Vice-President shall act as a temporary President, and the election of the President shall be held within six months.[48][6]

In the event one of the circumstances set out in Article 86 happening to the President within the last two years of his 5 year term of office, the Vice-President shall assume the office of President for *the remainder of the term*[49][7], and shall then nominate a Vice-President from among the members of the House of Representatives subject to the approval of the two Houses. If the two Houses refuse to confirm the nomination, he shall nominate another member (*of the House of Representatives*) within 30 days beginning from the date of the refusal of confirmation[50][8].

For additional analytical, business and investment opportunities information, please contact Global Investment & Business Center, USA at (202) 546-2103. Fax: (202) 546-3275. E-mail: rusric@erols.com

The person so appointed shall serve (*as Vice-President*) for the remainder of the constitutional term of office and shall, at the same time, relinquish his membership of the House of Representatives.

Similarly, in the event of the one of the circumstances set out in Article 86 happening to the Vice-President, the President shall nominate a member of the House of Representatives as Vice-President, subject to the approval of the two Houses. The honourable appointee shall hold office for the remainder of the term of office, and his seat at the House of Representatives shall then become vacant. If the two Houses refuse to confirm the appointment, the President shall nominate another member within 30 days beginning from the date of refusal of confirmation by the two Houses.

In the event of the one of the circumstances set out in Article 86 happening to both the President and the Vice-President at the same time, the office of President shall be assumed temporarily by the Speaker of the House of Elders. The election of the President and the Vice-President shall then be held within 60 days beginning from the date of the occurrence of the circumstance.

PART TWO

Article 90: The Powers of the President

The President is the Head of the nation and the state, and is the symbol of the unity of the citizens of the Republic of Somaliland. He is responsible for the care of the nation's resources, the protection of the peace, and the advancement of the society and the proper conduct of the administration of the state. In order to fulfil these responsibilities, the President shall have following powers:

The leadership of the general policy of the Government.

The appointment and removal from office of the members of the Council of Ministers.

Having consulted the appropriate Ministers and in accordance with the Constitution and other relevant special laws, the appointment and removal from office of the senior officers of the state. Such senior officers of the sate are:

> the Auditor-General;
> the Chairman of the Central Bank;
> the Chairman and the Committee members of the Civil Service Agency;
> the Chief Accountant;
> the Director Generals of the Ministries and the state organs and agencies;
> the Commanders of the Armed Forces and their deputies;
> Ambassadors;
> the Attorney General; and

any other senior officers (*heads*) whose appointment or dismissal has been assigned to the President in accordance with any law passed by legislative bodies.

The leadership of the national Armed Forces as he is the Commander-in-Chief.

Without prejudice to the principles of just retaliation (Qisaas) and the limits under Islamic Sharia, the exercise of pardon and amnesty, and the grant of political asylum after consultation with the appropriate bodies.

The signing of international agreements (*and treaties*).

The participation in international conferences as representative of the Republic of Somaliland.

Holding audience for foreign diplomats and receiving their credentials.

The appointment of Ambassadors representing the Republic of Somaliland in foreign countries, international and regional organisations.

The granting of awards and honours such as medals.

Leadership in conditions of war, and at the same time, the proclamation of state of emergency.

The implementation of laws which do not fall within the jurisdiction of the Judicial branch.

Any other powers set out in the Constitution or any other laws.

The President shall fulfil his duties in accordance with the Constitution and other laws of the land.

Article 91: Powers of the Vice-President

The Vice-President of the nation shall have the power:

To act as President in the absence or illness of the President.

To undertake such duties as delegated to him by the President.

To act[51][9] as President in the event of the office of President becoming vacant because of the following reasons:

> The resignation of the President;
> the conviction of the President for a crime which resulted in his loss of office;
> inability of the President to undertake the duties to which he was elected because of ill health; and
> death.

Article 92: Other Powers of the President Relating to Emergency Laws

In the event of the emergence of special circumstances which endanger the security of the country, jeopardise law and order, create upsets in the general stability or in the confidence in the economy, the President shall issue emergency laws which are aimed at combating such special circumstances as set out above.[52][10] If the two Houses are in session when the emergency laws are issued by the President, he shall present the laws to them within seven (7) days so that they can make their own resolutions. If, on other hand, the two Houses are not in session, the Speakers shall call an extra-ordinary meeting within 14 days.[53][11] The Government shall implement the emergency laws until such time the two Houses have made their own resolutions.

Emergency laws shall have the same effect as legislation passed by the House of Representatives or the House of Elders, and shall come into force on their signature by the President.

Emergency laws shall be reviewed once every three (3) months[54][12] by the two Houses whose resolutions shall be passed by a simple majority vote.

Article 93: Protocol of Senior Leaders of the State

1. The President and the Vice-President shall hold first position in the protocol of the nation.
2. The Speaker of the House of Elders shall hold the next position.
3. The Speaker of the House of Representatives shall hold the third position in the protocol of the nation.

Part Three

Article 94: The Council of Ministers

1. The Council of Ministers shall assist the President in the fulfilment of his duties and shall resolve collectively the general policies, planning and programmes of the state.
2. Ministers and Deputy Ministers shall be appointed or dismissed by the President. Their appointments shall be presented to the House of Representatives whose quorum shall be half of their total membership plus one, and the House shall confirm or reject the appointment, on a show of hands, by a simple majority vote.
3. The Minister or Deputy Minister so appointed shall be sworn into office, within thirty (30) days of the appointment being confirmed by the House of Representatives, by the Chairman of the Supreme Court, in the presence of the President or, in the latter's absence from the country or illness, the Vice-President.
4. Ministers and Deputy Ministers shall not hold any occupation other than that accorded to them by the nation.
5. No person who cannot fulfil the conditions necessary for eligibility for election to the House of Representatives[55][13] shall be appointed as a Minister or a Deputy Minister.[56][14]
6. A Minister may be responsible for one or more Ministries.
7. The President shall preside over the ordinary and extra-ordinary meetings of the Council of Ministers.
8. No Minister or Deputy Minister may be detained unless caught *in flagranto delicto* in respect of an offence punishable by imprisonment for three years or more, or the President has removed his privileges after having been satisfied by proposals put to him by the Attorney General.

Article 95: Continuation of Responsibilities

1. Any Minister or Deputy Minister who resigns or is dismissed shall remain in office until such time his successor takes over the responsibilities of the office.
2. A Minister or Deputy Minister who is awaiting the handing over of the responsibilities of office to his successor shall neither make any appointments nor enter into any agreements on behalf of his Ministry.

Article 96: Accusation against and Impeachment of the President, the Vice-President and the Ministers

1. If the President and the Vice-President are accused of following crimes:
a) high treason, or
b) contravention of the Constitution, the charges against the President or the Vice-President in respect of the crimes in this Clause shall be laid by at least one third of the members of the House of Representatives, who shall forward their charges to the Speaker of the House of Representatives. The House may approve of the charges on a majority vote of half of its total membership, plus one (absolute majority).
2. The House of Representatives shall empanel a committee of ten members who shall prosecute the charges against the President or the Vice-President in front of the House of Elders, and may also engage independent counsel who can assist the House in the prosecution.
3. The House of Elders shall consider the charges at a sitting chaired by the Chairman of the Supreme Court, and shall hear the prosecution brought by the committee on behalf of the House of Representatives. The President and the Vice-President shall have their own

defence counsel. The House of Elders shall approve of the charges on a majority vote of two thirds of its total membership.[57][15]

4.   If the Attorney General charges a Minister or a Deputy Minister with an offence set out in Clause 1 of this Article, he shall forward the details of the charges to the President. If the President is satisfied with the details provided by the Attorney General, he shall remove the privileges of the Minister or Deputy Minister. But, if he is not so satisfied, he shall order the Attorney General to drop the charges.[58][16]

5.   The charges relating to the Ministers shall be tried by the High Court of Justice which shall consist of the Chairman of the Supreme Court, four judges of the Supreme Court and four members elected, two each, by the two House of Parliament from amongst their members.

CHAPTER FOUR

Part One
The Judicial Branch

Article 97:

1.   The state[59][17] shall have a judicial branch whose function is to adjudicate on proceedings between the Government and the public and between the various members of the public.
2.   The Judicial Branch shall fulfil it duties in accordance with the Constitution, and shall be independent of the other branches of the state.

Article 98:

1.   The Judiciary shall have the power to:
a)   interpret, in accordance with the Constitution, the laws passed by the Constitutional bodies and emergency laws;
b) adjudicate on disputes between the governmental bodies and the public and between the members of the public;
c) adjudicate on all disputes which relate to compliance with the provisions of the Constitution
2.   A judge shall not engage in any other occupation whilst in office.
3.   The proper status of judges shall be determined by the law.

Article 99: The Structure of the Judiciary

1.   The Judiciary consists of the courts and the Procuracy[60][18].
2.   The judges and the members of the Procuracy are independent when exercising their judicial functions and shall be guided only by the law.

Article 100: The Courts

The courts of the Republic of Somaliland shall consist of:
1.   the Supreme Court;
2.   the Appeal Courts of the Regions;
3.   the Regional Courts;
4.   the District Courts; and

5.   the Courts of the National Armed Forces.

Article 101: The Supreme Court

The Supreme Court is the highest organ of the Judiciary and is also at the same time the Constitutional Court. In addition to the Chairman, the number of judges in the court shall not be less than four. A special law shall govern the court.

Article 102: The Lower Courts

The appointment and the conduct of the work of the lower courts (the Appeal Courts of the regions, the Regional and the District Courts) shall be determined by a special law.

Article 103: The Procuracy

The Procuracy of the state shall consist of the Attorney General and his deputies.

Article 104: The Courts and Procuracy of the Armed Forces

1.   The courts of the Armed Forces shall have special jurisdiction in hearing criminal charges brought against the members of the armed forces in peace or war.
2.   The courts and procuracy of the Armed Forces shall be determined by a special law.

Article 105: The Appointment of the Chairman and Judges of the Supreme Court

1.   The President, in consultation with the Judicial Commission[61][19] and having considered the level of education, professional experience and good character of the appointees, shall appoint the Chairman and judges of the Supreme Court. The appointment of the Chairman of the Supreme Court is subject to confirmation by the Houses of Parliament at a joint sitting which shall be held within three months of the date of the appointment. The highest ranking judge in seniority among the Supreme Court judges shall act as the Deputy Chairman of the Court.
2.   No person who does not fulfil the following conditions shall be appointed as Chairman of the Supreme Court:
a)   He must be a citizen of the Republic of Somaliland.
b)   He must possess a university degree in a recognised law course.
c)   He must have professional experience of not less than ten years[62][20] in total; and must have worked as a judge and/or a prosecutor, and/or lawyer, and/or law lecturer.
3.   The President may relieve the Chairman of the Supreme Court of his duties but shall require the approval of the both the House of Representatives and the House of Elders[63].

Article 106: The Relationship of the Judicial Bodies and the Ministry of Justice

1.   The Ministry of Justice shall be responsible for fulfilling the administrative decisions of the Judicial Commission.
The working relationship of the Ministry of Justice and the judicial organs shall be set out in a law.

CHAPTER FIVE MISCELLANEOUS PROVISIONS

For additional analytical, business and investment opportunities information,
please contact Global Investment & Business Center, USA
at (202) 546-2103. Fax: (202) 546-3275. E-mail: rusric@erols.com

Article 107: The Judicial Commission

1.   The Judicial Commission is the body which directs the administration of the Judiciary, and shall consist of the following:

§   The Chairman of the Supreme Court   Chairman
§   The two Supreme Court judges who rank highest in seniority   Member
§   The Attorney General   Member
§   The Director General of the Ministry of Justice   Member
§   The Chairman of the Civil Service Agency   Member
§   Two members selected from the public once every two years by the House of Representatives, one of whom to be chosen from among the intellectuals and the other from the businessmen, and
Two members to be selected from the public once every two years by the House of Elders, one of whom to be chosen from among those who are well versed in the traditions and the other from the religious scholars.

The quorum for the meetings of the Commission is (7) members.
If the Chairman of the Supreme Court is unable to fulfil the duties of chairing the Commission because of reasons of health, holidays or on vacating his office, the member of the Commission who is the Supreme Court judge with the highest rank in seniority, shall act as the temporary chairman. The Secretary of the Judicial Commission shall be the Chief Registrar of the Supreme Court.

Article 108: the Functions of the Judicial Commission

> The Judicial Commission shall be responsible for the appointment, removal of office, promotion, demotion, transfer and discipline of the judges of the lower courts (the Appeal, Regional and District Courts), and the Deputy Attorney Generals. The other personnel who work in the judiciary shall come under the provisions of the Civil Service Law.
>
> No judge or Deputy Attorney Generals may be detained without the consent of the Judicial Commission, but such consent shall not be required if the judge or the Deputy Attorney General is caught *in flagrant delicto* in relation to an offence which carries a sentence of no less than three (3) years imprisonment.

The Attorney General shall submit to the Commission the charges for the removal of the privileges and the disciplining of judges and Deputy Attorney Generals.

PART TWO

Article 109: The Structure of the Country

> The territory of the Republic of Somaliland shall consist of regions, and each region shall be divided into districts.
> The structure of the regions and the districts, their boundaries and hierarchy shall be determined by law.
> Changes in the number of regions and districts and their boundaries and the reasons for the changes shall be proposed by the Council of Government (*Cabinet*) and approved by the House of Representatives and the House of Elders.

Article 110: The Administration of the Regions and the Districts

The administration of the regions and the districts is part of the administration of the Government of the Republic of Somaliland.

The relationship of the central government and the regions and districts shall be set out in a special law.

Article 111: The Regional and District Councils

The regions and the districts of the country shall have legislative councils, whose powers are limited to passing by-laws which do not conflict with the laws of the country, and executive councils.

The total membership of each regional or district council, the conditions of membership and their election procedures shall be determined by law.

The Chairman of the district, shall, in consultation with the prominent members of village communities, propose village administration committees whose appointments shall be subject to the approval of the legislative council of the district.

The regional and district councils shall have power to plan their economic and social affairs.

The Chairman of the region shall be appointed by the Government and shall act as the representative of the central government in the region and the districts that come under it.

The Chairman of the region is the link between the central government and the districts of the region and shall come under the Ministry of Interior.

The term of office of the regional and district councils shall be 5 (five) years.

8. a) A regional or district council may be dissolved before the end of its term of office.

b) The conditions which could lead to such dissolution and the procedures for dissolution shall be determined by law.

The secretary of the region or the district and the heads of the branches or sections of the Ministries shall continue to fulfil the council's responsibilities[64] in line with the existing laws (*and by-laws)* until the election of a new council.

The regional and district councils shall have their own proper regulations, and shall be assisted in this task by the Ministry of Interior.

Article 112: The De-centralisation of Administrative Powers

The administration of community[65][23] services, such health, education up to elementary/intermediate school level, livestock husbandry, internal security, water, electricity, communication etc. shall be the responsibility of the regions and districts in so far as they are able to do so.

The demarcation of the administrative and tax levying powers between the central government and the regions/districts shall be determined by the law setting out the relationship between the central government and the regions/districts.

The demarcation referred to in Clause 2 of this Article must be such as to make it possible for the regions and districts to become self-sufficient in their provision of community services.

PART THREE THE ORGANS OF STATE

Article 113: The Special Organs of the state

The national organs of state are:

The Procuracy.

The Central Bank
The Civil Service Agency
The Auditor General

Other organs may be created, if deemed necessary, in accordance with the law.

Article114: The Appointment of and Removal from Office of Heads of the Organs of the State

The appointment of the Attorney General, the Governor of the Central Bank, the Chairman and the members of the Civil Service Agency and the Auditor General shall be proposed by the Chairman of the Council of Government (*Cabinet*)[66][24] and shall be approved by the House of Representatives before the appointee is sworn for duty.
The Heads listed in this Article may be removed from office by the President only.
The office holders of the state whose appointments are, according to the Constitution, subject to confirmation shall not hold office in a temporary capacity for more than three months (*whilst awaiting confirmation*).[67][25]

Article 115: The Ulema[68][26] Council and their Responsibilities

The Ulema Council is independent and shall have the responsibility of:
Formulating formal declarations on:
> religious disagreements that may arise; *and*
> any matters in which there is a conflict as to whether they are contrary to the Sharia[69][27], or appear to the Council as being contrary to the Sharia.

The Council shall forward their declarations to the offices which have requested the declarations or to the Constitutional Court, as they deem fit.
Undertaking research of all kinds from a religious perspective and, particularly, in a way which advances scientific and religious knowledge. (*Also, they shall*) review, and validate translated religious Sharia works, and specially those (prior to their acceptance as law) which the courts rely on in their rulings and those which are included in the educational syllabus and relate to religious traditions and knowledge.

Article 116: The Total Membership of the Council and Term of Office

The membership of the Ulema Council shall consist of 11 (eleven) members who shall serve for a 5 year term of office. Any suitable member may be re-appointed.

Article 117: The Conditions of Membership

Each member of the Ulema Council must fulfil the following conditions:
He shall be a citizen and is mentally and physically able to fulfil his duties.
He shall not be aged less than 40 (forty) years.
He shall be someone who is known for his piety (*allegiance to Allah*) and good manners.
He shall not have been convicted of a criminal offence that was proven in a court during the preceding five years.
He shall have been educated in religious matters to a university level or equivalent.
On the assumption of his duties, a member shall observe neutrality in political matters and in religious views.

Article 118: Matters in which Members are not Allowed

The members of the Ulema Council shall not be:
Associated with a political party or a special religious group;
Hold any other national office whilst still carrying the responsibilities of the Council.

Article 119: The Appointment of the Members of the Ulema Council

The members of the Ulema Council shall be nominated by a committee consisting of an equal number of persons chosen respectively by the Council of Government (*Cabinet)* and the House of Elders, and the nominations shall be confirmed by the House of Elders.
The Ulema Council shall elect from among its members a Chairman and a Deputy Chairman.

Article 120: Vacancies in the Membership of the Ulema Council

The membership of the Ulema Council may become vacant:
on resignation by a member or death;
on one of the conditions[70][28] of membership being no longer valid;.*(and)*
on a member being subject to a final sentence for a criminal offence.

Article 121: Salaries and Remuneration

The salaries and remuneration of the members of the Ulema Council shall be determined by law.

Article 122: The Law of the Organs of State

Each special organ of state shall have a law setting out its structure, responsibilities and the status of its head.

PART FOUR

Article 123: The Principles of the National Armed Forces

The national Armed Forces shall be responsible for protecting and defending the independence of the country. In addition, they shall, when needed, undertake duties in periods of state of emergency, in accordance with the Constitution.
The national armed forces shall always obey and act in accordance with the Constitution and the laws of the country.
The structure (*and composition*) of the Armed Forces shall reflect all the various Somaliland communities[71][29].
The person who is appointed as Minister of Defence shall be a civilian citizen.
The command structure of the national Armed Forces shall be determined by law.

Article 124: The Police and the Corrections Forces

. The Police Force shall be responsible for protecting the peace and for enforcing the law, and its structure and duties shall be set out by law.
The Corrections Force shall be responsible for guarding and reforming prisoners, and its structure and duties shall be set out by law.

Article 125: The Preparation of the Referendum Law and the Appointment of the Referendum Committee

Whilst taking note of the provisions of the Constitution, a referendum law shall be issued so as to make possible the holding of the referendum. A Committee to organise the referendum shall be appointed in accordance with the Constitution.

Article 126: Amendments or Corrections of the Constitution

Proposals for the amendments and/or corrections of the Constitution shall be made by:
a) The President, after consulting the Council of Government (*Cabinet*).
b) 1/3 (one-third) of the total membership of the House of Representatives.
c) 1/3 (one-third) of the total membership of the House of Elders.
Any proposal to amend and/or correct the Constitution must be reasoned and signed.
Amendments and/or corrections of the Constitution shall be debated by the House of Representatives and the House of Elders within two months after the House of Representatives resolves by a *(simple)* majority of their total number that the amendments and/or the corrections are necessary.
Any amendment and/or correction of an Article or Articles of the Constitution shall come into force after its approval by 2/3 (two-thirds) of the total membership of the House of Representatives and by 2/3 (two-thirds) of the total membership of the House of Elders in separate votes.
If the House of Representatives does not resolve by a *(simple)* majority of its total membership that the amendment or the addition or both is not necessary; or if one of the two Houses does not approve of the amendment and/or correction by a 2/3 (two-thirds) majority of its total membership, the proposal shall not be re-introduced during the following 12 (twelve) months.

Article 127: The Limits of Amendments or Corrections of the Constitution

No proposal to amend or correct the Constitution shall be made if it includes a provision which is in conflict with the:
> Principles of Islamic Sharia.
> Unity of the country (territorial integrity).
> Democratic principles and the multi-party system.
> Fundamental rights and personal freedoms.

Article 128: The Basis and the Supremacy of the Constitution

1. The Constitution shall be based on Islamic principles.
2. The Constitution shall be the supreme law of the land, and any law which does not conform to it shall be null and void.

Article 129: The Constitutional Oath

The Chairman of the Supreme Court, who is, at the same time, the Chairman of the Constitutional Court, shall administer this constitutional oath to any person who is obliged to take an oath under the Constitution before that person can assume his office. In the same way, he shall also take an oath to be administered by the President.

"I SWEAR BY ALLAH THAT I SHALL BE TRUE TO THE ISLAMIC RELIGION AND MY SOMALILAND COUNTRY, AND SHALL MANAGE MY PEOPLE IN EQUITY AND JUSTICE SO LONG AS I HOLD OFFICE."

Article 130: The Implementation of the Constitution

This Constitution shall come into force when a referendum has been held and the outcome of the referendum is known. It shall, however, be implemented, in the interim, for a period of three years (3) beginning from the date when it is approved by the 3rd Conference of the Somaliland Communities.

If the referendum cannot be held within the set period, the interim period in which the Constitution is implemented may be increased by the Parliament (the Representatives and the Elders).

In the event of one of the circumstances listed in Article 50[72][30] happening to a member of the House of Elders or the House of Representatives, the community which he represented shall fill that vacancy until such time the system of elections through parties is adopted.

In the event of the circumstances listed in Article 86 happening to the President or the Vice-President or both until such time a party system with direct elections is adopted, the two Houses (Representatives and Elders) shall elect jointly, within 45 days, the President or the Vice-President or both. The Speaker of the House of Elders shall fill the vacant office during the period preceding such election.

All the laws which were current and which did not conflict with the Islamic Sharia, individual rights and fundamental freedoms shall remain in force in the country of the Republic of Somaliland until the promulgation of laws which are in accord with the Constitution of the Republic of Somaliland.[73] At the same time, laws which conform to the Constitution shall be prepared, and each such law shall be presented within minimum time scales set by the House.

If the regions and districts fail to set up their councils within 3 (three) months, the Government, in consultation with the relevant members of the Houses of Representatives and Elders who represent these regions or districts and also with the elders in these communities, shall appoint, on a temporary basis, regional and district administrators.

The names of the Constitution Preparation Committee:
This is the Committee which prepared the Constitution at the 1997 Hargeisa Conference
(*Note: All the spellings of the names are in Somali Script*)

1.   Sh. Cabdilaahi Sh. Call Jawhar   **Chairman**
2.   Maxamed Axmed Cabdulle   **Deputy Chairman**
3. Clqaadir X. Ismaaciil Jirde   **Secretary**
Sh. Maxamuud Suufi Muxumed
Maxamed Siclid Maxamed (Gees)
Sh. Call Sh. Cabdi Guuleed
Faysal Xaajl Jaamac (Counsel)
Cismaan Xusseen Khayre (Judge)
Prof. Faarax Cabdllaahi Farlid
Prof. Maxamuud Nuur Caalin
Xasan Cabdi Xabad
Axmed Macaim Jaamac
Yuusuf Aadan Xuseen
Cismaan Cali Blue
Maxamed Jaamac Faarax

The Constitution Revision Committee

For additional analytical, business and investment opportunities information,
please contact Global Investment & Business Center, USA
at (202) 546-2103. Fax: (202) 546-3275. E-mail: rusric@erols.com

The House of Elders:
(Mud is short for Mudane "the honorable" – a title used by members of Parliament)

1) Mud. Siclid Jaamac Cali, Chairman
2) Mud. Axmed Nuur Aw Cali, Secretary
3) Mud. ClLaahi Sh. Xasan
4) Mud. Siclid ClLaahi Yaasir
5) Mud. Call X. Cabdi Ducaale
6) Mud. Clraxmaan Axmed Areye
7) Mud. Maxamed Clise Faarax
8) Mud. Yuusuf C/Laahi Cawaale
9) Mud. Muxumed Aw Axmed
10) Mud. Maxamed Gaaxnuug Jaamac
11) Mud. Maxamed Cismaan Guuleed

THE HOUSE OF REPRESENTATIVES

Mud. Xasan Axmed Ducaale, ChairmanMud. Cali Maxamed Cumar, SecretaryMud. C/raxmaan Xuseen CabdiMud. Maxamed Xuseen DhamacMud. Cabdi Daahir CamuudMud. C/Laahi Ibraahim KaarsheMud. Axmed C/Laahi CalMud. Faysal X. JaamacMud. Maxamed Aadan GabaloosMud. Cumar NuurAareMud. Yaasiin Faarax IsmaaciilMud. Yaasiin Maxamuud XiirMud. Cali Obsiiye Diiriye

The Committee for Corrections, Authentication and Production of Copies of the Constitution who also appended their signatures:Mud. Axmed Maxamed Aadan, Speaker of the House of Representatives   Mud Axmed Nuur Aw Cali, Secretary of the House of EldersMud C/ILaahi Sh. Xasan, member of the House of EldersMaxamed Xuseen Cismaan, Secretary of the House of Representative. SIGNED BY: Sh. Ibraahim Sh. Yuusuf Sh. Madar, Speaker of the House of Representatives.Axmed Maxamed Aadan, Speaker of the House of Representatives The Secretariat of the Constitution Committee:

> **Faisa Maxamed Axmed**
> **C/risaaq Siciid Ayaanle**

30 April 2000

LETTER TO THE SECURITY COUNCIL

To: HE. The President of the Security
       Council
       United Nations
       New York

From: His Excellency Mohamed Ibrahim Egal
       President of the Republic of Somaliland
       Hargeisa
       Fax#: 252 213 8324
       Fax#: 00 873 76128 1641

Excellency,

This memorandum of rebuttal to the UN Secretary-General's Report to the Security Council of December 19, 2000, does not in anyway impinge upon the person of the Secretary-General himself whom I hold in the very highest esteem. The Report, however, contains statements and accusations about Somaliland which cannot go unchallenged.

We have never opposed the Djibouti initiative as such. Indeed I arrived in New York two days after the President of Djibouti announced his intention to launch the initiative. A few days later I met with senior officials of the UN Secretariat and inadvertently and unofficially with the Secretary-General. I assured them of my support for the initiative and promised that Somaliland would do everything possible for the success of the initiative.

It is in fact of vital and of uppermost interest to Somaliland that a successful reconciliation in Somalia be secured. Our differences with the President of Djibouti and with the Representative of the Secretary-General, Mr David Stephen, arose out to their attempt to force us to participate in the Arta conference. Surprisingly, this attempt degenerated into bitter feud with Somaliland.

I personally went to Djibouti in January 2000 in an attempt to explain to the President the reason why we could not participate at Arta just as we had not participated in the twelve previous conferences on Somalia. Although the President feigned to have been convinced, it turned out that he had decided to go over our heads and ride roughshod over all our institutions, inviting dubious groups to Djibouti whom he then claimed to be representative of Somaliland. Mr David Stephen put the weight and prestige of his office behind this cavalier and perhaps even culpable interference in the affairs of a neighbouring country.

In his famous book The Rise and the Fall of the Third Reich, William Shirer said of the British Ambassador in Berlin that, during the last two fateful years before World War II, fate had conspired against world peace by placing in a critical diplomatic post a foolish mediocrity who misled and even lied to his principals and with blissful naivety encouraged Hitler and his Nazis to believe that they could get away with their piecemeal aggression in Europe.

Mr Stephen is a kindred spirit of that Ambassador and I respectfully but earnestly appeal to the Secretary-General to remove him before he does more irreversible damage to Somalia, Somaliland and to the whole region of the Horn of Africa.

As an example of his diplomatic artlessness, he telephoned me one day from Djibouti while the Arta conference was in progress and asked me to receive a telephone call from the President of Djibouti whom he said had something important to say to me. I, of course, welcomed that call but when the President telephoned all he said was that Mr Stephen had given him a full report and that he was ready to welcome me to Djibouti. When I telephoned Mr Stephen to ask what report he had given to the President of Djibouti, he avoided the question with a non sequitur. He replied that as the President of Djibouti and I were speaking in Somali he did not understand what we said to each other. Apparently, as we found out later, his only objective was to report to the UN Secretariat that he had been successful in establishing contact between the President of Djibouti and myself. He had no appreciation of the damage which that unnecessary telephone call had done in eroding all confidence between the leadership of Djibouti and Somaliland.

Now allow me to list the sequence of events in this unfortunate saga, together with errors in the Secretary-General's Report to the UN Security Council.

1. Somaliland's Consistent Policy towards Negotiations with the 'Somali National Peace Conference'
As the UN Report correctly states (para 6), I expressed a year ago to the Representative of the

For additional analytical, business and investment opportunities information,
please contact Global Investment & Business Center, USA
at (202) 546-2103. Fax: (202) 546-3275. E-mail: rusric@erols.com

UN Secretary-General the hope that the Djibouti initiative would provide Somalia with a leadership with which the Republic of Somaliland could negotiate a peaceful separation based on mutual respect and solidarity.

Seven months later, on August 26, Mr Abdikassim Salad Hassan was selected 'President of Somalia' at Arta and, consistent with my earlier comment, I stated that my Government would enter into negotiations with anyone who has legitimacy in Somalia (para 22).

In the following month, I declined a request by the UN Secretary-General's Representative to talk to Mr Abdikassim Salad Hassan. I did so on the grounds that he claimed to be 'President of Somalia' which, in his view but not in our view, included the Republic of Somaliland (para 31).

2. False Accusation: Officer Killed for Supporting Arta Conference
In paragraph 32 of the Report a reference is made to an invented, independent expert on human rights and his alleged accusation that an army officer in the Republic of Somaliland had been killed for opposing the forcible deportation of Majertein leaders who had wished to travel to the Arta conference. This reference and the accusation therein contain not an iota of truth. They are deliberate fabrications designed to depict Somaliland in adverse colours to the UN Secretariat and to the Security Council.

3. Principle of 'Arta Conference' - Peace and Reconciliation - Relegated to History
The underlying principle of the 'Arta conference', namely peace and reconciliation, appear to have been relegated to history, as evidenced by Abdikassim's bellicose outburst in the Egyptian newspaper Al Ahram on September 2, 2000. He declared that he would compel Somaliland to stay within the union (sic), if necessary by force of arms.

4. Somaliland's Terms for Holding Future Discussions with the 'TNG'
With due respect to the Secretary-General, I wish to state once and for all that any discussions between the Republic of Somaliland and the 'Transitional National Government' on future relations can only proceed with prior, unconditional acceptance by the 'Transitional National Government' of the Republic of Somaliland. We shall not surrender our sovereignty. We shall not tolerate the cult of political superiority towards Somaliland which is prevalent in Mogadishu, nor the preposterous claim, evidently shared by United Nations, that Somaliland and all its assets are by some mythical right legitimately vested in an authority in Mogadishu.

5. Somaliland Subscribes to OAU Resolution on Respect for Borders Existing on National Independence
The Organisation of African Unity, in its resolution AHG/Res. 16 (1), provided for a pledge by all member states 'to respect the borders existing on their achievement of national independence'. The Republic of Somaliland achieved its independence and sovereignty from Great Britain on June 26, 1960, and became the State of Somaliland with internationally recognised de jure borders with the then Trusteeship Territory of Italian Somaliland, Ethiopia and French Somaliland. These same borders comprise the territorial parameters of the Republic of Somaliland within which it restored its sovereign rights and its territorial integrity as an independent, sovereign nation on May 18, 1991.

6. Some of Somaliland's Reasons for Restoring its Sovereignty and Territorial Integrity
Somaliland's principal reasons for restoring its sovereignty, and the inviolability of the borders that existed on its achievement of national independence, are clear and straightforward. They involve the political and human rights of its people, and, in particular, their inalienable right of self-determination. Somaliland's voluntary experiment of merger with the UN Trusteeship territory in 1960, for which there was no Act of Union, turned out to be an unmitigated disaster. Like other groups of countries that have found unexpected incompatibilities with their merger partners, for example Singapore and the Malayan peninsula, Senegal and Mali, Egypt and Syria, Cape Verde

and Guinea-Bissau, among others, a voluntary separation was found to be normal, politically humanitarian alternative to hostilities.

Somaliland had even deeper reasons for separation. These included atrocities committed by Somalia's military forces against the people of Somaliland. These can be compared to the crimes committed by the Nazis against the population of Europe during World War II. Mass graves containing corpses tied together in groups of ten and then shot through the head as they fell into collective graves continue to be discovered in many urban centres. Hundreds of thousands of Somaliland's population were forced to flee the country for safety. Internally, the social and economic infrastructure was virtually destroyed and towns and villages were razed to the ground.

Somalia's campaign of terror compelled the Somaliland military personnel to revolt against the brutality to which their people were being subjected. They left en masse and took refuge in neighbouring Ethiopia where they formed and trained an army of liberation in the name of The Somaliland National Movement (SNM). The movement began fighting in earnest from 1982 for a separation from Somalia. The military dictatorship of Siyad Barre was overthrown in January 1991. The SNM, at a meeting of all the clans of Somaliland, decided in May 1991 to withdraw from the hasty and ill-considered merger with Somalia and restore its sovereignty and its separate national identity.

7. Somaliland has No Economic Ties with Somalia - Virtually all Trade is with Ethiopia
For the last ten years the Republic of Somaliland has not been 'orphaned' in any sense of the word, economically, socially or politically, by its separation from Somalia. Among the reasons for this are two overriding factors. First, Somaliland abides by the rule of law and its government is solidly in control. Secondly, Somaliland's economic relations, and virtually all its cross-border trade, are with Ethiopia and not with Somalia. Unlike Somalia, judging by its lack-lustre fiscal and economic track record, Somaliland's higher level of prosperity is largely due to Somaliland's balance of payments surplus; a controlled annual budget with a development appropriation, and no external debts.

8. An Invitation to UN Security Council Members to See for Themselves that which is Invisible In the UN Secretary-General's Report
If any members of the UN Security Council should wish to see for themselves the political, social and economic realities of the Republic of Somaliland and witness the reasons for its irrevocable policy on the question of sovereignty, they are cordially invited to visit the Republic of Somaliland and draw their own conclusions.

Hitherto, reports by the UN Secretary-General's Representative in Nairobi to the UN Secretariat have been the fountainhead of UN enlightenment about Somalia and Somaliland. Independent visits to Somaliland by members of the UN Security Council would, however, invoke astonishment at the inadequacy and often inaccuracy of these reports on Somaliland from the UN Political Office in Nairobi.

My last observation is that as the UN has not authority to recognise the sovereignty of a nation, it similarly has no right to campaign for the denial of recognition to any people seeking recognition of the international community. The previous Secretary-General launched this campaign, and the hostilities of the old days have now returned. They continue with and increasing momentum despite our persistent efforts to put our relations with the United Nations on an even keel. Our efforts appear to have been in vain.

I appeal most earnestly for the termination of this illegal campaign against Somaliland.

Please accept, Mr President, the assurances of my high consideration.

For additional analytical, business and investment opportunities information, please contact Global Investment & Business Center, USA at (202) 546-2103. Fax: (202) 546-3275. E-mail: rusric@erols.com

TRAVEL TO SOMALIA

US STATE DEPARTMENT SUGGESTION

TRAVEL WARNING (issued December 21, 1999): The Department of State warns U.S. citizens against all travel to Somalia. Interclan and interfactional fighting can flare up with little warning, and kidnapping, murder, and other threats to U.S. citizens and other foreigners can occur unpredictably in many regions. There is no national government in Somalia to offer general security or police protection for travelers. While parts of the north are relatively peaceful, including much of the self-declared "Republic of Somaliland," there is no U.S. diplomatic presence in Somalia to provide up-to-date security assessments or consular assistance to U.S. citizens.

U.S. citizens are urged to use caution when sailing near the coast of Somalia. Merchant vessels, fishing boats and pleasure craft alike risk seizure and their crew being held for ransom, especially in the waters near the Horn of Africa and near the Kenyan border.

Embassy Locations/Registration: U.S. citizens who plan to enter Somalia despite the Travel Warning are urged to register and obtain updated information on travel and security from either the U.S. Embassy in Nairobi, Kenya (for the northeastern and southern regions of Somalia), or with the U.S. Embassy in Djibouti (for the northwest.) However, neither mission has regular access to all parts of the country.

The U.S. Embassy in Nairobi is located on Mombasa Road, Nairobi, Kenya; telephone (254)(2) 537-800; after hours emergencies (254)(2) 537-809. The mailing address is P.O. Box 30137 or Unit 64100, APO AE 09831, USA.

The U.S. Embassy in Djibouti is located at Plateau du Serpent, Blvd. Marechal Joffre in the capital city of Djibouti; telephone (253) 35-39-95, Sunday - Thursday 7a.m. - 3:30 p.m.; fax (253) 35-39-40; after hours emergencies: (253) 35-13-43.

SUPPLEMENT

SOMALIA CONTACTS

UNITED KINGDOM

Osman Ahmed Hassan
SOMALILAND MISSION
Wickham House
10 Cleveland Way
London E1 4TR
UNITED KINGDOM
Tel: +44 (0) 20 7790 2424 Ext. 297
Fax: +44 (0) 20 7790 2616
Email: slrmission@btinternet.com

FEDERAL REPUBLIC OF ETHIOPIA

MR. ABDILLAHI ASKAR BARKHAD
SOMALILAND LIAISON OFFICER
ADDIS ABABA
ETHIOPIA
TEL: 251 1 611661
FAX: 251 1 518788, 251 1 534688

UNITED STATES OF AMERICA

DR. SA'AD SH. O. NOOR
THE REPRESENTATIVE OF THE REPUBLIC OF SOMALILAND
WASHINGTON
USA
FAX: 301 231 5990

ITALY

MR. MUHIYADIN AHMED ABDI GABOSE
CORSO UNIONE SOVIETICA 475
TORIN
ITALY

For additional analytical, business and investment opportunities information,
please contact Global Investment & Business Center, USA
at (202) 546-2103. Fax: (202) 546-3275. E-mail: rusric@erols.com

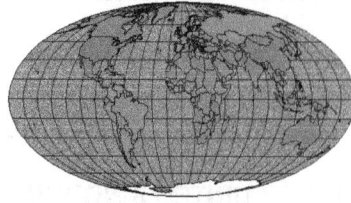

WORLD INVESTMENT AND TRADE LAWS AND REGULATIONS HANDBOOK LIBRARY

Web Address http://www.ibpus.com
Price: $149.95 each

1.	Afghanistan Investment and Trade Laws and Regulations Handbook
2.	Aland Investment and Trade Laws and Regulations Handbook
3.	Albania Investment and Trade Laws and Regulations Handbook
4.	Algeria Investment and Trade Laws and Regulations Handbook
5.	Andorra Investment and Trade Laws and Regulations Handbook
6.	Angola Investment and Trade Laws and Regulations Handbook
7.	Anguilla Investment and Trade Laws and Regulations Handbook
8.	Antigua and Barbuda Investment and Trade Laws and Regulations Handbook
9.	Antilles (Netherlands) Investment and Trade Laws and Regulations Handbook
10.	Argentina Investment and Trade Laws and Regulations Handbook
11.	Armenia Investment and Trade Laws and Regulations Handbook
12.	Aruba Investment and Trade Laws and Regulations Handbook
13.	Australia Investment and Trade Laws and Regulations Handbook
14.	Austria Investment and Trade Laws and Regulations Handbook
15.	Azerbaijan Investment and Trade Laws and Regulations Handbook
16.	Bahamas Investment and Trade Laws and Regulations Handbook
17.	Bahrain Investment and Trade Laws and Regulations Handbook
18.	Bangladesh Investment and Trade Laws and Regulations Handbook
19.	Barbados Investment and Trade Laws and Regulations Handbook
20.	Belarus Investment and Trade Laws and Regulations Handbook
21.	Belgium Investment and Trade Laws and Regulations Handbook
22.	Belize Investment and Trade Laws and Regulations Handbook
23.	Benin Investment and Trade Laws and Regulations Handbook
24.	Bermuda Investment and Trade Laws and Regulations Handbook
25.	Bhutan Investment and Trade Laws and Regulations Handbook
26.	Bolivia Investment and Trade Laws and Regulations Handbook
27.	Bosnia and Herzegovina Investment and Trade Laws and Regulations Handbook
28.	Botswana Investment and Trade Laws and Regulations Handbook
29.	Brazil Investment and Trade Laws and Regulations Handbook
30.	Brunei Investment and Trade Laws and Regulations Handbook
31.	Bulgaria Investment and Trade Laws and Regulations Handbook
32.	Burkina Faso Investment and Trade Laws and Regulations Handbook
33.	Burundi Investment and Trade Laws and Regulations Handbook
34.	Cambodia Investment and Trade Laws and Regulations Handbook
35.	Cameroon Investment and Trade Laws and Regulations Handbook

For additional analytical, business and investment opportunities information,
please contact Global Investment & Business Center, USA
at (202) 546-2103. Fax: (202) 546-3275. E-mail: rusric@erols.com
World Business Information Catalog http://www.ibpus.com

36. Canada Investment and Trade Laws and Regulations Handbook
37. Cape Verde Investment and Trade Laws and Regulations Handbook
38. Cayman Islands Investment and Trade Laws and Regulations Handbook
39. Central African Republic Investment and Trade Laws and Regulations Handbook
40. Chad Investment and Trade Laws and Regulations Handbook
41. Chile Investment and Trade Laws and Regulations Handbook
42. China Investment and Trade Laws and Regulations Handbook
43. Colombia Investment and Trade Laws and Regulations Handbook
44. Comoros Investment and Trade Laws and Regulations Handbook
45. Congo Investment and Trade Laws and Regulations Handbook
46. Congo, Democratic Republic Investment and Trade Laws and Regulations Handbook
47. Cook Islands Investment and Trade Laws and Regulations Handbook
48. Costa Rica Investment and Trade Laws and Regulations Handbook
49. Cote d'Ivoire Investment and Trade Laws and Regulations Handbook
50. Croatia Investment and Trade Laws and Regulations Handbook
51. Cuba Investment and Trade Laws and Regulations Handbook
52. Cyprus Investment and Trade Laws and Regulations Handbook
53. Czech Republic Investment and Trade Laws and Regulations Handbook
54. Denmark Investment and Trade Laws and Regulations Handbook
55. Djibouti Investment and Trade Laws and Regulations Handbook
56. Dominica Investment and Trade Laws and Regulations Handbook
57. Dominican Republic Investment and Trade Laws and Regulations Handbook
58. Ecuador Investment and Trade Laws and Regulations Handbook
59. Egypt Investment and Trade Laws and Regulations Handbook
60. El Salvador Investment and Trade Laws and Regulations Handbook
61. Equatorial Guinea Investment and Trade Laws and Regulations Handbook
62. Eritrea Investment and Trade Laws and Regulations Handbook
63. Estonia Investment and Trade Laws and Regulations Handbook
64. Ethiopia Investment and Trade Laws and Regulations Handbook
65. Falkland Islands Investment and Trade Laws and Regulations Handbook
66. Faroes Investment and Trade Laws and Regulations Handbook
67. Fiji Investment and Trade Laws and Regulations Handbook
68. Finland Investment and Trade Laws and Regulations Handbook
69. France Investment and Trade Laws and Regulations Handbook
70. Gabon Investment and Trade Laws and Regulations Handbook
71. Gambia Investment and Trade Laws and Regulations Handbook
72. Georgia Investment and Trade Laws and Regulations Handbook
73. Germany Investment and Trade Laws and Regulations Handbook
74. Ghana Investment and Trade Laws and Regulations Handbook
75. Gibraltar Investment and Trade Laws and Regulations Handbook
76. Greece Investment and Trade Laws and Regulations Handbook
77. Greenland Investment and Trade Laws and Regulations Handbook
78. Grenada Investment and Trade Laws and Regulations Handbook
79. Guam Investment and Trade Laws and Regulations Handbook
80. Guatemala Investment and Trade Laws and Regulations Handbook
81. Guernsey Investment and Trade Laws and Regulations Handbook
82. Guinea Investment and Trade Laws and Regulations Handbook
83. Guinea-Bissau Investment and Trade Laws and Regulations Handbook
84. Guyana Investment and Trade Laws and Regulations Handbook
85. Haiti Investment and Trade Laws and Regulations Handbook

86. Honduras Investment and Trade Laws and Regulations Handbook
87. Hungary Investment and Trade Laws and Regulations Handbook
88. Iceland Investment and Trade Laws and Regulations Handbook
89. India Investment and Trade Laws and Regulations Handbook
90. Indonesia Investment and Trade Laws and Regulations Handbook
91. InternationalInvestment and Trade Laws and Regulations Handbook
92. Iran Investment and Trade Laws and Regulations Handbook
93. Iraq Investment and Trade Laws and Regulations Handbook
94. Ireland Investment and Trade Laws and Regulations Handbook
95. Israel Investment and Trade Laws and Regulations Handbook
96. Italy Investment and Trade Laws and Regulations Handbook
97. Jamaica Investment and Trade Laws and Regulations Handbook
98. Japan Investment and Trade Laws and Regulations Handbook
99. Jersey Investment and Trade Laws and Regulations Handbook
100. Jordan Investment and Trade Laws and Regulations Handbook
101. Kazakhstan Investment and Trade Laws and Regulations Handbook
102. Kenya Investment and Trade Laws and Regulations Handbook
103. Kiribati Investment and Trade Laws and Regulations Handbook
104. Korea, North Investment and Trade Laws and Regulations Handbook
105. Korea, South Investment and Trade Laws and Regulations Handbook
106. Kosovo Investment and Trade Laws and Regulations Handbook
107. Kuwait Investment and Trade Laws and Regulations Handbook
108. Kyrgyzstan Investment and Trade Laws and Regulations Handbook
109. Laos Investment and Trade Laws and Regulations Handbook
110. Latvia Investment and Trade Laws and Regulations Handbook
111. Lebanon Investment and Trade Laws and Regulations Handbook
112. Lesotho Investment and Trade Laws and Regulations Handbook
113. Liberia Investment and Trade Laws and Regulations Handbook
114. Libya Investment and Trade Laws and Regulations Handbook
115. Liechtenstein Investment and Trade Laws and Regulations Handbook
116. Lithuania Investment and Trade Laws and Regulations Handbook
117. Luxembourg Investment and Trade Laws and Regulations Handbook
118. Macao Investment and Trade Laws and Regulations Handbook
119. Macedonia,Investment and Trade Laws and Regulations Handbook
120. Madagascar Investment and Trade Laws and Regulations Handbook
121. MadeiraInvestment and Trade Laws and Regulations Handbook
122. Malawi Investment and Trade Laws and Regulations Handbook
123. Malaysia Investment and Trade Laws and Regulations Handbook
124. Maldives Investment and Trade Laws and Regulations Handbook
125. Mali Investment and Trade Laws and Regulations Handbook
126. Malta Investment and Trade Laws and Regulations Handbook
127. Man Investment and Trade Laws and Regulations Handbook
128. Marshall Islands Investment and Trade Laws and Regulations Handbook
129. Mauritania Investment and Trade Laws and Regulations Handbook
130. Mauritius Investment and Trade Laws and Regulations Handbook
131. Mayotte Investment and Trade Laws and Regulations Handbook
132. Mexico Investment and Trade Laws and Regulations Handbook
133. Micronesia Investment and Trade Laws and Regulations Handbook
134. Moldova Investment and Trade Laws and Regulations Handbook
135. Monaco Investment and Trade Laws and Regulations Handbook

136. Mongolia Investment and Trade Laws and Regulations Handbook
137. Monserrat Investment and Trade Laws and Regulations Handbook
138. Morocco Investment and Trade Laws and Regulations Handbook
139. Mozambique Investment and Trade Laws and Regulations Handbook
140. Myanmar Investment and Trade Laws and Regulations Handbook
141. Namibia Investment and Trade Laws and Regulations Handbook
142. Nauru Investment and Trade Laws and Regulations Handbook
143. Nepal Investment and Trade Laws and Regulations Handbook
144. Netherlands Investment and Trade Laws and Regulations Handbook
145. New Caledonia Investment and Trade Laws and Regulations Handbook
146. New Zealand Investment and Trade Laws and Regulations Handbook
147. Nicaragua Investment and Trade Laws and Regulations Handbook
148. Niger Investment and Trade Laws and Regulations Handbook
149. Nigeria Investment and Trade Laws and Regulations Handbook
150. Niue Investment and Trade Laws and Regulations Handbook
151. Northern Mariana Islands Investment and Trade Laws and Regulations Handbook
152. Norway Investment and Trade Laws and Regulations Handbook
153. Oman Investment and Trade Laws and Regulations Handbook
154. Pakistan Investment and Trade Laws and Regulations Handbook
155. Palau Investment and Trade Laws and Regulations Handbook
156. Palestine Investment and Trade Laws and Regulations Handbook
157. Panama Investment and Trade Laws and Regulations Handbook
158. Papua New Guinea Investment and Trade Laws and Regulations Handbook
159. Paraguay Investment and Trade Laws and Regulations Handbook
160. Peru Investment and Trade Laws and Regulations Handbook
161. Philippines Investment and Trade Laws and Regulations Handbook
162. Pitcairn Islands Investment and Trade Laws and Regulations Handbook
163. Poland Investment and Trade Laws and Regulations Handbook
164. Polynesia French Investment and Trade Laws and Regulations Handbook
165. Portugal Investment and Trade Laws and Regulations Handbook
166. Qatar Investment and Trade Laws and Regulations Handbook
167. Romania Investment and Trade Laws and Regulations Handbook
168. Russia Investment and Trade Laws and Regulations Handbook
169. Rwanda Investment and Trade Laws and Regulations Handbook
170. Saint Kitts and Nevis Investment and Trade Laws and Regulations Handbook
171. Saint Lucia Investment and Trade Laws and Regulations Handbook
172. Saint Vincent and The Grenadines Investment and Trade Laws and Regulations Handbook
173. Samoa (American) Investment and Trade Laws and Regulations Handbook
174. Samoa (Western) Investment and Trade Laws and Regulations Handbook
175. San Marino Investment and Trade Laws and Regulations Handbook
176. Sao Tome and Principe Investment and Trade Laws and Regulations Handbook
177. Saudi Arabia Investment and Trade Laws and Regulations Handbook
178. Scotland Investment and Trade Laws and Regulations Handbook
179. Senegal Investment and Trade Laws and Regulations Handbook
180. Seychelles Investment and Trade Laws and Regulations Handbook
181. Sierra Leone Investment and Trade Laws and Regulations Handbook
182. Singapore Investment and Trade Laws and Regulations Handbook
183. Slovakia Investment and Trade Laws and Regulations Handbook
184. Slovenia Investment and Trade Laws and Regulations Handbook
185. Solomon Islands Investment and Trade Laws and Regulations Handbook

186. Somalia Investment and Trade Laws and Regulations Handbook
187. South Africa Investment and Trade Laws and Regulations Handbook
188. Spain Investment and Trade Laws and Regulations Handbook
189. Sri Lanka Investment and Trade Laws and Regulations Handbook
190. St. Helena Investment and Trade Laws and Regulations Handbook
191. St. Pierre & Miquelon Investment and Trade Laws and Regulations Handbook
192. Sudan Investment and Trade Laws and Regulations Handbook
193. Suriname Investment and Trade Laws and Regulations Handbook
194. Swaziland Investment and Trade Laws and Regulations Handbook
195. Sweden Investment and Trade Laws and Regulations Handbook
196. Switzerland Investment and Trade Laws and Regulations Handbook
197. Syria Investment and Trade Laws and Regulations Handbook
198. Taiwan Investment and Trade Laws and Regulations Handbook
199. Tajikistan Investment and Trade Laws and Regulations Handbook
200. Tanzania Investment and Trade Laws and Regulations Handbook
201. Thailand Investment and Trade Laws and Regulations Handbook
202. Togo Investment and Trade Laws and Regulations Handbook
203. Tonga Investment and Trade Laws and Regulations Handbook
204. Trinidad and Tobago Investment and Trade Laws and Regulations Handbook
205. Tunisia Investment and Trade Laws and Regulations Handbook
206. Turkey Investment and Trade Laws and Regulations Handbook
207. Turkmenistan Investment and Trade Laws and Regulations Handbook
208. Turks & Caicos Investment and Trade Laws and Regulations Handbook
209. Tuvalu Investment and Trade Laws and Regulations Handbook
210. Uganda Investment and Trade Laws and Regulations Handbook
211. Ukraine Investment and Trade Laws and Regulations Handbook
212. United Arab Emirates Investment and Trade Laws and Regulations Handbook
213. United Kingdom Investment and Trade Laws and Regulations Handbook
214. United States Investment and Trade Laws and Regulations Handbook
215. Uruguay Investment and Trade Laws and Regulations Handbook
216. Uzbekistan Investment and Trade Laws and Regulations Handbook
217. Vanuatu Investment and Trade Laws and Regulations Handbook
218. Vatican City Investment and Trade Laws and Regulations Handbook
219. Venezuela Investment and Trade Laws and Regulations Handbook
220. Vietnam Investment and Trade Laws and Regulations Handbook
221. Virgin Islands, British Investment and Trade Laws and Regulations Handbook
222. Wake Atoll Investment and Trade Laws and Regulations Handbook
223. Wallis & Futuna Investment and Trade Laws and Regulations Handbook
224. Yemen Investment and Trade Laws and Regulations Handbook
225. Yugoslavia Investment and Trade Laws and Regulations Handbook
226. Zambia Investment and Trade Laws and Regulations Handbook
227. Zimbabwe Investment and Trade Laws and Regulations Handbook

For additional analytical, business and investment opportunities information, please contact Global Investment & Business Center, USA at (202) 546-2103. Fax: (202) 546-3275. E-mail: rusric@erols.com World Business Information Catalog http://www.ibpus.com

www.ingramcontent.com/pod-product-compliance
Lightning Source LLC
Chambersburg PA
CBHW081500200326
41518CB00015B/2325